HOW TO READ CHINESE POETRY IN CONTEXT

HOW TO READ CHINESE LITERATURE

HOW TO READ CHINESE LITERATURE

ZONG-QI CAI, GENERAL EDITOR

YUAN XINGPEI, EDITORIAL BOARD DIRECTOR

How to Read Chinese Poetry: A Guided Anthology (2008)

How to Read Chinese Poetry Workbook (2012)

How to Read Chinese Poetry in Context: Poetic Culture from Antiquity Through the Tang (2018)

HOW TO READ CHINESE POETRY IN CONTEXT

Poetic Culture from Antiquity Through the Tang

EDITED BY ZONG-QI CAI

Columbia University Press / *New York*

Confucius Institute Headquarters (Hanban)
Columbia University Press wishes to express its appreciation for assistance given by the Confucius China Studies Program in the publication of this series.

Columbia University Press
Publishers Since 1893
New York   Chichester, West Sussex
cup.columbia.edu

Copyright © 2018 Columbia University Press
All rights reserved

Library of Congress Cataloging-in-Publication Data
Names: Cai, Zong-qi, 1955– editor.
Title: How to read Chinese poetry in context : poetic culture from antiquity through the Tang / edited by Zong-qi Cai.
Description: New York : Columbia University Press, 2018. | Series: How to read Chinese literature | Includes bibliographical references.
Identifiers: LCCN 2017019392 (print) | LCCN 2017033861 (ebook) | ISBN 9780231546126 (electronic) | ISBN 9780231185363 (cloth) | ISBN 9780231185370 (pbk.).
Subjects: LCSH: Chinese poetry—221 B.C.–960 A.D.—History and criticism. | Literature and society—China—History—To 1500.
Classification: LCC PL2313 (ebook) | LCC PL2313 .H69 2018 (print) | DDC 895.11/209—dc23
LC record available at https://lccn.loc.gov/2017019392

Cover design: Lisa Hamm
Cover image: Werner Forman Archive/Bridgeman Images

CONTENTS

Thematic Contents vii
Preface to the How to Read Chinese Literature Series xix
Preface to the Volume xxi
Chronology of Historical Events xxiii
Symbols and Abbreviations xxvii

Introduction: The Cultural Role of Chinese Poetry 1
ZONG-QI CAI

PART I: PRE-HAN TIMES 11

1. Poetry and Diplomacy in *Zuo Tradition* (*Zuozhuan*) 13
   WAI-YEE LI

2. Poetry and Authorship: The *Songs of Chu* (*Chuci*) 30
   STEPHEN OWEN

PART II: THE HAN DYNASTY 49

3. Empire in Text: Sima Xiangru's "Sir Vacuous/Imperial Park Rhapsody" ("Zixu/Shanglin fu") 51
   YU-YU CHENG AND GREGORY PATTERSON

4. Poetry and Ideology: The Canonization of the *Book of Poetry* (*Shijing*) During the Han 65
   ZONG-QI CAI

5. Love Beyond the Grave: A Tragic Tale of Love and Marriage in Han China 78
   OLGA LOMOVÁ

PART III: THE SIX DYNASTIES 97

6. Heroes from Chaotic Times: The Three Caos 99
   XINDA LIAN

7. The Worthies of the Bamboo Grove   116
   NANXIU QIAN

8. The Poetry of Reclusion: Tao Qian   130
   ALAN BERKOWITZ

9. The Struggling Buddhist Mind: Shen Yue   146
   MEOW HUI GOH

PART IV: THE TANG DYNASTY   157

10. Knight-Errantry: Tang Frontier Poems   159
    TSUNG-CHENG LIN

11. Tang Civil Service Examinations   173
    MANLING LUO

12. Tang Women at the Public/Private Divide   185
    MAIJA BELL SAMEI

13. Poetry and Buddhist Enlightenment: Wang Wei and Han Shan   205
    CHEN YINCHI AND JING CHEN

14. Drinking Alone Beneath the Moon: Li Bai and the Poetics of Wine   223
    PAULA VARSANO

15. Du Fu: The Poet as Historian   236
    JACK W. CHEN

16. Poetry and Literati Friendship: Bai Juyi and Yuan Zhen   248
    AO WANG

17. Li He: Poetry as Obsession   261
    ROBERT ASHMORE

Acknowledgments 275
Contributors 277
Glossary-Index 281

THEMATIC CONTENTS

1. POETRY AND THE STATE

1.1 DIPLOMACY AND GOVERNANCE

"Presenting a *Shijing* poem" (*fushi*) for diplomatic purposes, as recorded in *Zuo Tradition* (*Zuozhuan*), 1–3, 13–29, 65, 70

The formula of *fushi* (presenting a *Shijing* poem) in *Zuo Tradition* (*Zuozhuan*), 14

Airs or folk songs (*feng*) in the *Book of Poetry* (*Shijing*) facilitating communication between rulers and commoners, 67

Confucius's remarks on the political functions of the *Book of Poetry* (*Shijing*), 13

Poetry/literature as an enterprise comparable to state affairs (Cao Pi's thesis on literature), 107

Representations of state failure and social disorder in Du Fu's poems, 236–247

☞ *HTRCP* chap. 1 ("Tetrasyllabic *Shi* Poetry: *The Book of Poetry* [*Shijing*]") and *WKB* P01; *WKB* Unit 18 ("Meditation on History: Rise and Fall of Dynasties"). See also Du Fu's poems, *HTRCP* C8.1, C8.2, C10.14 and *WKB* P52

1.2 EMPIRE BUILDING IN TEXT

The unified empire as "all under heaven" (*tianxia*) in a Han rhapsody, 2, 51–64

The regulation of the ruler's desire in Han rhapsodies, 59

The rhapsody and Han imperial authority, 58–59

Pleasure parks as symbols of power in Han rhapsodies, 58–59

Competition between central and regional powers reflected in Han rhapsodies, 56–59

Sima Xiangru's great rhapsodies and the political identity of Emperor Wu of the Han, 2, 46, 52–63

Cao Cao's poetry as "poetic chronicle," 101–102

☞ *HTRCP* chap. 3 ("*Fu* Poetry: An Ancient-Style Rhapsody [*Gufu*]")

1.3 POETRY AND IDEOLOGY

The adoption of Confucianism as the state ideology in the Han dynasty, 68

The rhapsody and Han dynasty Confucianism, 59

Criticism of Confucian orthodoxy in "Old Poem Composed for the Wife of Jiao Zhongqing," 79, 88–93

Filial piety and Confucian morality during and after the Eastern Han, 89–93

Cao Cao's iconoclastic gesture to separate poetry from Confucian ideology, 103

The quest for alternatives to Confucian orthodoxy in the Six Dynasties, 224
Tao Qian as a model for Confucian conduct and values, 141
The Confucian ideal of an official career and the early and high Tang poet-knights, 166

☞ *HTRCP* "Thematic Contents," 1.1 Confucianism; *HTRCP* C3.1 and C4.8. See also Tao Qian's poems, *HTRCP* C6.1, C6.2, C6.3, and C6.4

2. POETRY AND LEARNING

2.1 CANONICAL AND ENCYCLOPEDIC TEXTS

The canonization of the *Book of Poetry* (*Shijing*) during the Han, 2–3, 65–77, 103
The rise to prominence of the Mao, Qi, Lu, and Han texts of the *Book of Poetry* (*Shijing*) in the Han dynasty, 66, 68
The compilation and annotation of the *Songs of Chu* (*Chuci*) during the Han, 4, 30–47
Things and names in the Han rhapsody, 60–62

☞ *HTRCP* chap. 1 ("Tetrasyllabic *Shi* Poetry: *The Book of Poetry* [*Shijing*]"), chap. 3 ("*Fu* Poetry: An Ancient-Style Rhapsody [*Gufu*]"), and "Thematic Contents," 1.1 Confucianism

2.2 ABSTRUSE LEARNING (*XUANXUE*)

Wei-Jin Abstruse Learning (*Xuanxue*), 6, 116–129
Zhi Dun combines Mahāyāna Buddhism and Abstruse Learning (*Xuanxue*) in interpreting the *Zhuangzi*, 126–127

☞ *HTRCP* chap. 6 ("Pentasyllabic *Shi* Poetry: Landscape and Farmstead Poems") and "Thematic Contents," 1.2 Daoism and Abstruse Learning (*Xuanxue*); *WKB* Unit 3 ("Fields and Gardens"), Unit 4 ("Landscape: Excursions"), and Unit 5 ("Landscape: Grand Scenes")

2.3 CIVIL SERVICE EXAMINATIONS

Genesis of the Tang civil service examination system, 174
The civil service examination in the Tang dynasty, 166, 173–184, 189, 251–252
Empress Wu expands the civil service examination system, 189
The inclusion of poetic composition in the presented scholar examination, 3, 174–175, 189
Poetic excellence as an important criterion for selecting government officials, 173–174
The debates over poetic composition and the presented scholar examination, 175
The format and content of poetic composition in the presented scholar examination, 175
Scroll presentations by presented scholar examination candidates to (potential) patrons, 3, 176
The content, etiquette, and strategies of scroll presentation, 177
The poetic exchange between a candidate and a patron, 3, 178–179
The celebration of examination success with poetry, 3, 179–180
Failure in the presented scholar examination as a major poetic topos, 3, 181

Anonymous poems of failed candidates criticizing the examiner, 180
The poems of unsuccessful candidates on their own failure, 3, 180–181
Encouragement of unsuccessful candidates through poetry, 181
Neo-Confucianism and the elimination of poetry from examinations, 183
Impromptu poetic composition as an informal test of talent, 263
Li He and the presented scholar examination, 264
Proposal of posthumous presented scholar titles for men overlooked in their own age, 265

> *HTRCP* chap. 8 ("Recent-Style *Shi* Poetry: Pentasyllabic Regulated Verse [*Wuyan Lüshi*]") and "Thematic Contents," 3.0 Prosody; *WKB* "List of Literary Issues Discussed," 2.0 Prosody. See also Li He's poems, *HTRCP* C9.4 and *WKB* P95

3. POETIC IDENTITIES: INDIVIDUALS AND GROUPS

3.1 REVERED PERSONALITIES

Zhuangzi's ideal personalities, 6, 116–118, 227, 233n6
Qu Yuan the moralist and "patriot," 4, 30–47
Cao Cao's ego, personality, and poems, 5, 99–107
Character appraisal, 99, 127, 225–227
The Bamboo Grove aura (*Linxia fengqi*) and Wei-Jin character traits, 6, 127, 225–227
The Perfected Person ideal in Ji Kang's poetry, 118–123
The Great Person ideal in Ruan Ji's and Liu Ling's poetic works, 123–126
Tao Qian's personal idealism and willful individualism, 4, 141
The "free and unrestrained" as a character trait, 225–227

> *HTRCP* chap. 6 ("Pentasyllabic *Shi* Poetry: Landscape and Farmstead Poems"). See also Li Bai's poems, *HTRCP* C8.3, C10.8, C10.9, C10.10, C10.13, C11.3 and *WKB* P19, P29, P35, P41

3.2 THE IMAGE OF A POET

The carpe diem motif in Cao Cao's poetry, 103–104
Achieving immortality through literary achievement (Cao Pi's thesis on literature), 107
Cao Zhi's autobiographical projection in his poems, 5, 109–114
Performative self-fashioning in literary works, 225–227
Development of the lyric self, 223–228
Shen Yue as both a Buddhist and a Daoist, 7–8, 150
Wang Wei, the poet Buddha, 4, 8, 205–209, 212–218, 220
"Han Shan" as a Chan master, 205, 210–212, 218–220
Li Bai's persona as a Daoist adept, 4, 228
Du Fu as poet-historian, 4, 236–247
Poets and their alter egos (Bai Juyi and Yuan Zhen), 248–260
The figure of the child prodigy in poetry (Li He), 263–264

Poetry and alienation, death, 4–5, 261–273
Poet as cursed or outcast figure, the "star-crossed talent," 261–273
Poet as demiurge, 264

> Wang Wei's poems, *HTRCP* C8.4, C10.6, C10.7 and *WKB* P24, P26, P39, P55, P56; Li Bai's poems, *HTRCP* C8.3, C10.8, C10.9, C10.10, C10.13, C11.3 and *WKB* P19, P29, P35, P41; Du Fu's poems, *HTRCP* C8.1, C8.2, C9.1, C9.2, C9.3, C10.14 and *WKB* P20, P52, P80, P81, P92, P93, P94; Bai Juyi's poems, *HTRCP* C11.4 and *WKB* P07; Li He's poems, *HTRCP* C9.4 and *WKB* P95

3.3 POETRY AND LITERATI FRIENDSHIP

Cao Pi and the Seven Talents of the Jian'an era, 107, 114
The Seven Worthies of the Bamboo Grove: Ruan Ji and Ji Kang, 118–125
The Seven Worthies of the Bamboo Grove: Ji Kang and Xiang Xiu, 126
Wine as a vehicle for communion with friends (Tao Qian), 135
Tao Qian and Yan Yanzhi, 130, 136, 143–144
Shen Yue and Wang Yun, 146, 154
Brotherly appreciation and friendship valued by Tang knights-errant, 160
Poetic exchange between patron and protégé, 179
Poetry as a means of celebration and bonding in the post-presented scholar examination phase, 179–181
Bai Juyi and Yuan Zhen, 248–260
Courtesans and scholars, 3–4, 182, 187, 195–197
Li He and Han Yu, 263–264
Poetry as solitary substitute for friendship and social interaction, 270

> *WKB* Unit 9 ("Parting"). See also Tao Qian's poems, *HTRCP* C6.1, C6.2, C6.3, and C6.4; Li Bai's poems, *HTRCP* C10.13 and *WKB* P41; Bai Juyi's poems, *HTRCP* C11.4 and *WKB* P07; Li He's poems, *HTRCP* C9.4 and *WKB* P95

4. WAR HEROES AND KNIGHT-ERRANTRY

4.1 DEPICTION OF WARS

Suffering of the soldiers (Cao Cao), 5, 102–103
Cao Cao's commentary on Sunzi's *Art of War* (*Sunzi bingfa*), 100
Suffering as a theme in the American Western and Tang frontier poetry, 5, 159
War weariness and antiwar overtones in Tang frontier poems, 168–170
Poetic imagination and wartime experiences (Du Fu), 236–247

> *HTRCP* C4.4 (an anonymous *yuefu* poem) and Du Fu's poems, *HTRCP* C8.1, C8.2, C10.14 and *WKB* P52

4.2 WAR HEROES

Aging hero facing his lot with grace (Cao Cao), 106
A hero's wish to gather under his banner all the talents under heaven (Cao Cao), 104
Self-image of a young hero driven by spontaneity and intuition (Cao Zhi), 112
Pursuit of military heroism by early and high Tang literati, 5, 167

☞ Wang Changling's poems, *HTRCP* C10.11 and *WKB* P50

4.3 KNIGHT-ERRANTRY

Political frustration and knightly values, 167
"Young urban knights" and Tang frontier poetry, 160
Drinking and the knight's heroism in Tang frontier poetry, 162
Knights and assassins, criminals, fugitives, and swordsmanship, 160
Knights and the seeking of justice, 166
Poet-knights (Du Fu, Gao Shi, Li Bai, and Luo Binwang), 5, 159–172
Li Bai's persona as a swordsman, 166, 228
Knights and foreign tribes in Tang frontier poems, 159–170

☞ *WKB* Unit 11 ("Frontiers and Wars")

5. DAOIST LIFESTYLE AND TRANSCENDENCE

5.1 DISENCHANTMENT AND RECLUSION

Experiences of unjust suffering (Qu Yuan; Sima Qian), 4, 30–47
Desires to leave the public world and live in isolation in Jia Yi's "Lament for Qu Yuan," 31
Poets' banishment from the Tang court (Li Bai, Bai Juyi, and Yuan Zhen), 227, 252–255
Reclusion as a way to disengage from the bureaucracy (Tao Qian), 132
Tao Qian as "the patriarch of poets of reclusion," 131, 143
Daoist monasticism during the middle Tang period, 187
Lifestyle of Daoist nuns, 187–200

☞ *HTRCP* chap. 2 ("*Sao* Poetry: The *Lyrics of Chu* [*Chuci*]"), chap. 6 ("Pentasyllabic *Shi* Poetry: Landscape and Farmstead Poems"), and "Thematic Contents," 2.8 Farming and Reclusion

5.2 WINE AND FREEDOM

Wine drinking in the *Book of Poetry* (*Shijing*) and *A New Account of Tales of the World* (*Shishuo xinyu*), 223–227
Wine as a vehicle for communion with the universe (Tao Qian), 135
Wine drinking and Daoist-inspired freedom from social and moral constraints, 224

Transcendence and wine drinking in *A New Account of Tales of the World* (*Shishuo xinyu*), 225–226
Wine and drunkenness as a poetic sign, 7, 123–129, 223–227
The portrayal of wine in Tao Qian's poems, 130–144, 226–227
Wine drinking and friendship as themes in chivalric novels, 162–163

☞ Tao Qian's poems, *HTRCP* C6.2 and C6.3; Li Bai's poem, *HTRCP* C10.9

5.3 DAOIST TRANSCENDENCE

The perception of "genuineness" in Tao Qian's poems, 131, 136, 143
Tao Qian and Daoism, 130–144
The concept of "naturalness" (*ziran*) in Tao Qian's poems, 6, 138–140
Detachment as a matter of heart and mind (Tao Qian), 139
Essence and material circumstances (Tao Qian), 139
Poetry as fragment of a heavenly music and as vehicle for access to uncanny
    states/beings, 265–272
Poetry and cosmic or occult power, 263–271
Poetry on cultic sites, 263–271
"Summons" of poet to court of Emperor of Heaven to compose texts there, 271–272

☞ *HTRCP* chap. 6 ("Pentasyllabic *Shi* Poetry: Landscape and Farmstead Poems") and "Thematic Contents," 2.9 Imagined Journey to the Celestial World; *WKB* Unit 3 ("Fields and Gardens"), Unit 4 ("Landscape: Excursions"), and Unit 5 ("Landscape: Grand Scenes")

6. MEDITATION AND BUDDHIST ENLIGHTENMENT

6.1 CHAN BUDDHIST IDEALS

Divergence between the Northern School and Southern School of Chan Buddhism, 214–215
Chan Buddhist ideals in Tang poems, 205–222
Southern Chan Buddhist ideals as manifested in Wang Wei's life attitude, 205–209, 212–218, 220

☞ *HTRCP* "Thematic Contents," 1.3 Buddhism; *WKB* Unit 6 ("Landscape: Chan [Zen] Vision")

6.2 BUDDHIST RECLUSION

Wang Wei as a half-official, half-hermit, 207
Shen Yue and his retreat into the garden, 7, 146–156
Buddhist monasticism during the middle Tang period, 187
"Han Shan" as a hermit, 211
Depiction of reclusive lifestyle and its natural setting in Han Shan poems, 218–220

☞ Wang Wei's poems, *HTRCP* C8.4, C10.6, C10.7 and *WKB* P24, P26

6.3 NATURE AND MEDITATION

Tangibility and intangibility in Wang Wei's poems, 217
Description of natural tranquility in Wang Wei's poems, 217–218
Emptiness in Wang Wei's poems, 216–217
Exhortations to Buddhist doctrines and lifestyles in Han Shan poems, 8, 219–220
Buddhist-inspired expressions in Han Shan poems, 220

☞ *WKB* Unit 6 ("Landscape: Chan [Zen] Vision")

6.4 BUDDHIST ENLIGHTENMENT

Shen Yue's *fu* and his struggling Buddhist mind, 7–8, 146–156
Shen Yue's quest of Buddhist enlightenment, 7, 149–153
Meditation and the attainment of Buddhist enlightenment, 8, 214–215

☞ *HTRCP* "Thematic Contents," 2.7 Landscape

7. WOMEN AS POETIC SUBJECTS AND AS WRITERS

7.1 LOVE AND COURTSHIP

Courtship in "There Is a Dead Doe in the Wilds," the *Book of Poetry* (*Shijing*), 24–25, 72–73
Courtship in "Ospreys" ("Guan ju"), the *Book of Poetry* (*Shijing*), 65–68
Courtship of a goddess as analogous to the ruler–minister relationship in *Encountering Misery* (*Li Sao*), 33, 38
Suffering of a daughter-in-law in "Old Poem Composed for the Wife of Jiao Zhongqing," 78–95
Separation between lovers in "Old Poem Composed for the Wife of Jiao Zhongqing," 78–95
Double suicide of lovers in "Old Poem Composed for the Wife of Jiao Zhongqing," 78–95

☞ *HTRCP* chap. 1 ("Tetrasyllabic *Shi* Poetry: *The Book of Poetry* [*Shijing*]"), chap. 2 ("*Sao* Poetry: The *Lyrics of Chu* [*Chuci*]"), and "Thematic Contents," 2.1 Love and Courtship; *WKB* Unit 1 ("Love: The Voice of Men") and Unit 2 ("Love: The Voice of Women")

7.2 THE FEMALE PERSONA

The transformative cosmic power of the "feminine" image in the *Zhuangzi*, 117
The routinized interpretation of the Fair One (especially a beautiful woman) as the desired ruler or the spurned minister, 47
Cao Pi's female poetic persona, 108
Voices of presented scholar examination candidates' wives, 181–182
Female persona in an examination candidate's poem to his patron, 178

Female speaker in Du Fu's "Parting When Newly Wed" ("Xinhun bie"), 242
Landscape description and female/divine presence, 270–271

> *HTRCP* chap. 2 ("*Sao* Poetry: The *Lyrics of Chu* [*Chuci*]"); *WKB* Unit 13 ("Plaints of Young Women [I]") and Unit 14 ("Plaints of Young Women [II]")

7.3 WOMEN'S STATUS AND EDUCATION

Chinese women defined by their relationship to their fathers, husbands, and sons, 90, 187
Education and social position of women in reality as opposed to prescriptions in the Confucian canon, 90–91
Women in the later Han, their upbringing and family obligations, 90–92
Women and ritual propriety, 186
Nei/wai (inner/outer) distinction, 185–204
Morality texts for women: *Admonitions for Women* (*Nü jie*) (ca. 106), by Ban Zhao; *Classics for Women* (*Nü sishu*); *Analects for Women* (*Nü lunyu*); *Book of Filial Piety for Women* (*Nü xiaojing*), 186, 192

> *HTRCP* chap. 17 ("*Shi* Poetry of the Ming and Qing Dynasties"); *HTRCP* C4.8. See also Li Qingzhao's poems, *HTRCP* C13.4 and *WKB* P08

7.4 THE WRITING WOMAN

The poetic exchange between candidates and courtesans, 3–4, 182
Women poets in the Tang, 9, 185–204
Women's literary talent and morally questionable lifestyles, 188, 198
Literary women in Daoist monasteries in the Tang, 187–200
Tang frontier poems: Xue Tao's exile to the frontier, 196–197

> *HTRCP* chap. 17 ("*Shi* Poetry of the Ming and Qing Dynasties"). See also Li Qingzhao's poems, *HTRCP* C13.4 and *WKB* P08

7.5 WOMEN IN TANG COURT

Poetry and Tang court entertainment, 187–204
Palace women in the Tang, 9, 187–204
Shangguan Wan'er and her influence in Empress Wu's court, 9, 189–192
Beautiful women and the historic/poetic imagination: the kingdom-toppling beauty (*qing guo*), 191
Yang Yuhuan, the Prized Consort (*Guifei*), 228, 236, 256–258

> *HTRCP* "Thematic Contents," 2.2 The Beautiful Woman; *WKB* Unit 15 ("Plaints of Palace Ladies")

8. FAMILY AND COUNTRY

8.1 ASPECTS OF FAMILY LIFE

The celebration of brotherhood in "Plum Tree," the *Book of Poetry* (*Shijing*), 22, 25

Husband–wife relationship for ancient Confucians, 65–68

Lament on the separation between brothers (Cao Zhi), 113

Parents meddling in love affairs of their children in "Old Poem Composed for the Wife of Jiao Zhongqing," 78–95

Marriage and divorce in Han China, 91

The theme of filial piety (*xiao*) in late Han and early medieval periods, 89–92

Tao Qian's personal accounts of family life, 132

Shen Yue and his family history, 147

Examination candidates and their families as seen in poetry, 180–181

Disintegration of social and family structures in Du Fu's poems, 10, 236–247

Military conscription and family destruction in Du Fu's poems, 239–243

WKB Unit 12 ("Homesickness"). See also Du Fu's poems, *HTRCP* C8.1, C8.2, C10.14 and *WKB* P52

8.2 THE WANDERING MAN AND THE ABANDONED WOMAN

Pining wife thinking about her traveling husband (Cao Pi), 107–108

The topos of the "abandoned woman" waiting or lamenting, 9, 186

Homesickness of a traveler (Cao Pi), 108–109

Knights, loneliness, and homesickness in Tang frontier poetry, 196

☞ *HTRCP* "Thematic Contents," 2.2 The Abandoned Woman and 2.6 The Wandering Man; *WKB* Unit 10 ("Sojourns of the Wandering Man"), Unit 13 ("Plaints of Young Women [I]"), Unit 14 ("Plaints of Young Women [II]"), and Unit 15 ("Plaints of Palace Ladies")

9. POETIC ART

9.1 IMAGES: ANALOGY AND ASSOCIATION

Bi (analogues), *xing* (affective images), and *bixing* (analogical-evocative images) in classical Chinese poems, 75–76

The primacy of the "affective image" (*xing*) in the *Book of Poetry* (*Shijing*), 17, 69

Aromatic plants as symbols of virtue in *Encountering Misery* (*Li Sao*), 33–38, 47

Exotica and cornucopia in the Han rhapsody, 60–61

"Connecting kinds" (*lianlei*) in the Han rhapsody, 54–55, 93

The use of *xing* (affective image) in "Old Poem Composed for the Wife of Jiao Zhongqing," 78

The Three Caos' use of stock images to enliven new poetic experience, 101–114

Floating weeds as an image for life's transience and fortuity, 253

☞ *HTRCP* "Thematic Contents," 6.1 Spatiotemporal-Logical Structure and 6.2 Analogical-Associational Structures; *WKB* "List of Literary Issues Discussed," 7.0 Imagery

9.2 POETIC GENRES AND SUBGENRES

Oral performance of Han rhapsodies, 53–54

Storytelling in Han rhapsodies, 52–53

Consequences of orality and writing in the Han court, 54–56

Memory and the composition of Han rhapsodies, 52, 55

The oral transmission of "Old Poem Composed for the Wife of Jiao Zhongqing," 78

Yuefu (Music Bureau) poem of the Han dynasty, 78, 92–93, 108–109, 113, 167, 228–229, 265–266

Earliest existent complete poem in heptasyllabic lines (Cao Pi's "Song of Yan"), 107–108

Evolution of pentasyllabic line poetry, 101–103, 108–114

Evolution of heptasyllabic line poetry, 107–108

The Three Caos' establishment of personal voice in lyric poetry, 101–114

Cao Zhi and Cao Pi's contribution to the development of the lyrical mode in poetry, 108–114

"Poems Singing of My Innermost Thoughts" ("Yonghuai shi") as a poetic subgenre created by Ruan Ji, 124–125

Character appraisal contributing to the formation of landscape poetry in the Eastern Jin, 127

Tao Qian's mode of autofictography in his works, 130, 226–227

The farmstead poetry of Tao Qian, 130–145

Li He and "Music Bureau" (*yuefu*) poetry, 265–266

Development of the *ci* (song lyric) genre during the Tang, 200–202

☞ *HTRCP* Introduction ("Major Aspects of Chinese Poetry"); *WKB* "List of Literary Issues Discussed," 1.0 Genres

9.3 POETIC FORM

Customary omission of personal pronouns in classical Chinese poems, 74

"Incremental repetition" used in "I Beg of You, Zhong Zi," the *Book of Poetry* (*Shijing*), 71–72

One word repeated in every line of a poem with different connotations (Tao Qian), 136

Composition of/in couplets, 269–270

Linked verse (*lian ju*) poems of Han Yu and Meng Jiao, 269–270

The "brocade bag" of fragments of poems to flesh out later, 268–271

☞ *HTRCP* chap. 18 (A Synthesis: Rhythm, Syntax, and Vision of Chinese Poetry) and "Thematic Contents," 4.0 Diction and 5.0 Syntax; *WKB* "List of Literary Issues Discussed," 3.0 Syntax, 4.0 Stanza Organization, 5.0 Poem Structure, 6.0 Diction, and 8.0 Rhetorical Devices

9.4 INTERPRETATION

Mencius's remarks on the ideal interpretation of the *Book of Poetry* (*Shijing*), 13
Ethico-sociopolitical interpretation of the *Book of Poetry* (*Shijing*), 8, 67–77
Interpretative strategies used in "Mao Prefaces," "Mao Commentaries," and "Zheng Annotations," 3, 69–73
The Confucian didactic tradition, 103
Translating "myth" into "history" in the *Records of the Historian* (*Shiji*), 32–33
Connection between the Han exegetes and Tang poets, 74
Poetry as virtual reality and as obsession, 261–273

9.5 AESTHETIC RECEPTION

"Meaning beyond words" (*yan wai zhi yi*) in Daoism and in Confucian aesthetic theory, 76–77
The relationship between meaning and words (Tao Qian), 139
Indefinite referents of nature images in classical Chinese poems, 74
Cooking and "flavor" in poetry, 53–56, 59
Aural dimensions of poetry, 54–56
Shen Yue and "refined" sounds of poetry, 153–154
The poetic style of *fenggu* (air and bone), 114
Li (beautiful) as the most distinctive genre trait of poetry (Cao Pi), 108–109
Shi yan zhi (poetry gives voice to the intent) and the expressive ideal in *shi* poetry, 202n1
Lyric nonfictionality in Du Fu's poems, 242, 245
The "free and unrestrained" poetic persona, 227–228
Tao Qian's poetic style, 142–143
Shen Yue's *fu* and the garden aesthetic, 146–154
Compilation, loss, and transmission of physical texts, 261–272
Textual survival and personal survival, 262
The style of Li He's poetry, 265, 268

PREFACE TO THE **HOW TO READ CHINESE LITERATURE** SERIES

Welcome to the How to Read Chinese Literature series, a comprehensive collection of literary anthologies and language texts covering the entire field of Chinese literature. The series will consist of ten volumes: five guided literary anthologies, one book on literary culture, and four language texts. Together, they will try to promote the teaching and learning of premodern Chinese poetry, fiction, drama, prose, and literary criticism.

In particular, the five guided anthologies offer innovative ways of overcoming some barriers that have long hindered the teaching and learning of Chinese literature. While fine scholarly monographs on Chinese literature abound, they are usually too specialized for classroom use. To make that scholarship more accessible, each guided anthology presents the highlights of scholarship on major genres and writers through commentary on individual texts as well as broad surveys.

Every reader of Chinese literature is aware of the gap between English translations and Chinese originals. Since most existing anthologies offer only an English translation, however, students will find it hard to see how diverse linguistic elements work together in the original. To remedy this, each guided anthology presents the Chinese text alongside an English translation, with detailed remarks on the intricate interplay of word, image, and sound in Chinese.

So far, scant attention has been given to the relation between sound and sense in English-language studies of Chinese literature. As a corrective, the poetry anthology explains in detail the prosodic conventions of all major poetic genres and marks the tonal patterning in regulated verse and *ci* poetry. Samples of reconstructed ancient and medieval pronunciation are also given to show how the poems were probably pronounced when first composed. For the fiction, drama, and prose anthologies, we will offer a sound recording of selected texts, read in normal Mandarin or chanted in the traditional style. Video clips of traditional storytelling and dramatic performance will also be provided free of charge online.

For decades the study of Chinese literature in the West was a purely intellectual and aesthetic exercise, completely divorced from language learning. To accommodate demand from an ever increasing number of Chinese language learners, we provide tone-marked romanizations for all poetry texts, usually accompanied by sound recording. For any text also featured in the accompanying language text, cross-references allow the reader to quickly proceed to in-depth language study of the original.

Designed to work with the guided anthologies, the four language texts introduce classical Chinese to advanced beginners and above, teaching them how to appreciate Chinese literature in its original form. As stand-alone resources, these texts illustrate China's major literary genres and themes through a variety of examples.

Each language text presents a select number of works in three different forms—Chinese, English, and tone-marked romanization—while providing comprehensive vocabulary notes and prose translations in modern Chinese. Subsequent comprehension questions and comments focus on the artistic aspect of the works, while unit exercises test readers' grasp of both classical and modern Chinese words, phrases, and syntax. An extensive glossary cross-references classical and modern Chinese usage, characters and compounds, and multiple character meanings. Online sound recording is provided for each selected text and its prose translation. Along with other learning aids, a list of literary issues addressed throughout completes each volume.

To achieve a seamless integration of literary anthologies and language texts, we draw from the same corpus of canonical texts and employ an extensive network of cross-references. Moreover, by presenting the ten books as a coherent set, we aim to help readers cross the divide between literary genres and between literary and language learning, thereby achieving a kind of experience impossible with traditional approaches. Thanks to the innovative features described above, we hope the series will reinvigorate—if not revolutionize—the learning and teaching of Chinese literature, language, and culture throughout the English-speaking world for decades to come.

ZONG-QI CAI

PREFACE TO THE VOLUME

This book is the last of a three-book set that aims to break down barriers that have long stood in the way of both teaching and learning Chinese poetry.

The first two books, *How to Read Chinese Poetry: A Guided Anthology* (2008) and *How to Read Chinese Poetry Workbook* (2012), seek to integrate research and teaching, translations and originals, sense and sound, and poetry and language learning. Under one cover, the *Guided Anthology* introduces some of the finest current scholarship on all the major genres and eras of Chinese poetry. It presents 146 famous poems in English and Chinese, along with detailed commentaries on the intricate play of word, image, and sound in each poem. It allows for both aural and oral engagement with the Chinese texts by providing tone-marked romanizations as well as a sound recording. The *Workbook* follows the same approach, but its emphasis is on language learning rather than literary studies.

This book aims to bring down a barrier of a different kind: one that separates literature from the broader culture. To date, few poetry anthologies have undertaken to represent the complex interweaving of circumstances in which these poems were composed, disseminated, and critiqued. Here, we have tried to give a fuller sense of the unique and central role of poetry in the making of Chinese culture. In the public arena, we show the key role poetry plays in diplomacy, court politics, empire building, the formation of state ideology, institutionalized learning, and more. Within the more personal, private sphere, we show people of different social classes using poetry as a means of gaining entry into officialdom, creating self-identity, fostering friendship, and airing grievances over mistreatment or injustice.

Instead of a brief summary repeating the standard grand narrative of Chinese history behind its poetry, it seems much more useful to present a number of anecdotes or stories relevant to individual poems. A form of historical snapshots—candid photos taken at the moment a poem was written, or a moment described in a poem—they frequently offer very telling commentaries on what the poem is actually about. In various ways, these seemingly innocent or naive stories sometimes pose serious challenges to the grand narrative, providing alternative and radically different ways of understanding what might have happened.

So this book can also serve as a good complement to the main text in a history or civilization course. Its rich collection of historical vignettes will testify to or challenge the veracity of the grand narrative. These stories will provide welcome relief from dry facts and data, enabling students to witness history come alive through the colorful lives of famous poets as well as the world of fiction they created. This movement between grand narrative and historical vignettes is facilitated by a chronological list of historical events mentioned. Likewise, the book's thematic table maps out the thematic terrain and provides alternative points of linkage with a history text.

Whether read as a stand-alone work, as a companion to a history text, or in conjunction with the two poetry anthologies, we hope this book will yield a reading experience pleasurable and intellectually stimulating.

ZONG-QI CAI

CHRONOLOGY OF HISTORICAL EVENTS

ZHOU DYNASTY (ca. 1046–256 BCE)

ca. 1046 BCE	Battle in Muye between the alliance led by King Wu of the Zhou dynasty and King Zhou of the Shang dynasty, 101
ca. 1000–ca. 600 BCE	Compilation of the *Book of Poetry* (*Shijing*), 13, 223
757–701 BCE	Rebellion led by Shuduan of Gong (younger brother of Duke Zhuang of Zheng), 71
722–468 BCE	The period covered in *Zuo Tradition* (*Zuozhuan*), 13
637 BCE	*Fushi* (presenting a *Shijing* poem) in diplomatic context first mentioned in *Zuo Tradition* (*Zuozhuan*), 14
506 BCE	*Fushi* (presenting a *Shijing* poem) in diplomatic context last mentioned in *Zuo Tradition* (*Zuozhuan*), 14
278 BCE	The Chu capital is sacked by the Qin, 41

HAN DYNASTY (206 BCE–220 CE)

206 BCE–8 CE	Compilation of the Mao Text of the *Book of Poetry* (*Mao shi*), 66
206 BCE–220 CE	Forerunner of Tang civil service examination in the Han dynasty, 174
after 143 BCE	Sima Xiangru leads a pacification campaign in the southwest, 56
141–87 BCE	Adoption of Confucianism as the state ideology, 68
ca. 135–ca. 126 BCE	Zhang Qian's travels and detention in western lands, 56
136 BCE	Emperor Wu formalizes the Confucian canon with five classical texts (the *Book of Changes*, the *Book of Poetry*, the *Book of Documents*, the *Book of Rites*, and the *Spring and Autumn Annals*) and establishes "erudites" (*bo shi*) for each of them, 68
134 BCE	Dong Zhongshu submits responses to Emperor Wu's edict, proposing that Confucian teachings receive exclusive imperial patronage, 57
130s BCE	Emperor Wu orders his uncle Liu An to write a prose account of *Encountering Misery* (*Li Sao*), 31
ca. turn of the first century BCE	Sima Qian composes the *Record of the Historian* (*Shiji*), 30

184	Yellow Turban Rebellion, 100
190	Dong Zhuo attempts to usurp the Han throne, 100
196–220	Jian'an era; traditional dating of "Old Poem Composed for the Wife of Jiao Zhongqing" ("Gushi wei Jiao Zhongqing qi zuo"), 78
ca. turn of the second century BCE	Wang Yi compiles the final version of the *Songs of Chu* (*Chuci*), 30
207	Cao Cao becomes the virtual ruler of northern China, 101
208	Battle of Chibi or Red Cliff, 106
220	Cao Pi forces Emperor Xian of Han to abdicate and replaces the dynasty with the state of Wei; the fall of the Han dynasty, 106, 224

THREE KINGDOMS (SHU, WU, WEI) PERIOD (220–280) AND THE JIN DYNASTY (265–420)

220–226	Cao Pi (Emperor Wen of Wei) compiles China's first encyclopedia (*leishu*), *The Imperial Reader* (*Huang lan*), 62
220–440	Philosophical debates known as *qingtan* (pure conversation) are on the rise, 224
220–581	The use of wine as an evocative lyric trope becomes widespread from the Six Dynasties (a collective noun for six Chinese dynasties during the periods of the Three Kingdoms, the Jin dynasty, and the Southern and Northern dynasties), 223
237	Project by Emperor Ming of the Wei (Wei Mingdi [r. 226–239]) to remove old Western Han palace monuments (including bronze immortals) from Chang'an to his capital at Luoyang, 266
249–265	The Simas' attempts to usurp the Wei throne, 116
262	Ji Kang is executed in the Eastern Marketplace of Luoyang, 118
265	Establishment of the Western Jin, 119
317	The Jin royal house move to the south and the establishment of Eastern Jin, 126
405	Tao Yuanming leaves official service for the rural life of a gentleman-scholar in retirement, 131

SOUTHERN AND NORTHERN DYNASTIES (420–589)

422	Liu Yu's (Emperor Wu, r. 420–422) usurpation of the Jin throne and the establishment of Liu-Song, 131
ca. 430	Compilation of *A New Account of Tales of the World* (*Shishuo xinyu*) by the Liu-Song prince Liu Yiqing (403–444) and his staff, 116, 225
479–486	Shen Yue serves Crown Prince Wenhui (of Southern Qi) (458–493), 148
507	Shen Yue begins to spend most of his time at his garden estate, 147

CHRONOLOGY OF HISTORICAL EVENTS xxv

early sixth century	Compilation of *New Songs from a Jade Terrace* (*Yu tai xin yong*), a collection of poems mostly about women and love, in which "Old Poem Composed for the Wife of Jiao Zhongqing" ("Gushi wei Jiao Zhongqing qi zuo") was first recorded, 78

SUI DYNASTY (581–618)

581–618	Annual degree examination system established in the Sui dynasty, 174

TANG DYNASTY (618–907)

618–907	The expansion of the Sui examination system in the Tang dynasty, 174
627–649	The Zhenguan reign period, 210
640	Wu Zetian enters the court as a consort to Emperor Taizong of the Tang, 189
655	Wu Zetian becomes Emperor Gaozong's (r. 649–683) empress and performs imperial sacrifices, 189
681	Emperor Gaozong's edict to include belles lettres in the presented scholar examination, 174
690	Wu Zetian declares a new dynasty, the Zhou (690–705), with herself as its empress, 189
705 onward	Presented scholar examinations routinely included poetic composition, 175
710	Emperor Xuanzong enthroned; Shangguan Wan'er executed, 190
721	Wang Wei (701–761) becomes a holder of the presented scholar degree, 176, 207
725	A man of letters named Zu Yong passes the presented scholar examination, 173
735	Du Fu fails the civil service examination, 167
737	The dismissal of Zhang Jiuling (673–740) from his chancellor post, 207
740s	Wang Wei meets Shenhui (684–758), a Chan master of the Southern School, 208
755–763	An Shi Rebellion, 207, 236, 248
756	Defeat of Geshu Han at Tong Pass, 238
	Flight of Xuanzong to Sichuan, 236
	Deaths of Yang Yuhuan and Yang Guozhong, 236
757	An Lushan murdered by An Qingxu, 238
	Retaking of capitals by Tang armies, 238
759	Defeat of Guo Ziyi by Shi Siming, 238
	Execution of An Qingxu by Shi Siming, 238
763	Yang Wan submits a memorial to recommend abolishing the presented scholar examination, 175
766–779	Dali reign period, 211
783	Rebel Zhu Ci (743–784) arises and briefly takes control of the capital under Emperor Dezong of Tang, 193
796	The poet Meng Jiao (751–814) passes the presented scholar examination, 179

799–800	The famous poet Bai Juyi passes the local presented scholar examination, in 799, and the national competition, in 800, 175
802	Bai Juyi and Yuan Zhen first meet in Chang'an, 248
806–820	Yuanhe era, 261
ca. 808	Li He's likely first contacts with Han Yu at Luoyang, 272n5
809	Xue Tao meets Yuan Zhen, 195
810	Li He fails (or is prevented from taking) presented scholar examination, 264
815	Both Yuan Zhen and Bai Juyi are banished to the south by the court, 252–253
827–835	Taihe era, 261
828	The poet Du Mu (803–852) participates in the presented scholar examination and wins the support of nearly twenty officials, 177
831	Shen Shushi entreats Du Mu to compose preface for Li He's collected poetry, 261
900	Wei Zhuang's memorial requesting presented scholar titles for Li He and other neglected talents of the early ninth century, 265
901	Five elderly people pass the presented scholar examination, 175

SYMBOLS AND ABBREVIATIONS

❦ ❦ ❦

C8.4	Chapter eight, the fourth poem discussed in *How to Read Chinese Poetry: A Guided Anthology* (*HTRCP*)
P01	The first poem presented in *How to Read Chinese Poetry Workbook* (*WKB*)
	Cross-reference marker
	Example: ( *HTRCP* C8.4; *HTRCP* chap. 8; *WKB* P01)
HTRCP	Cai, Zong-qi, ed. *How to Read Chinese Poetry: A Guided Anthology.* New York: Columbia University Press, 2008.
WKB	Cui, Jie, and Zong-qi Cai. *How to Read Chinese Poetry Workbook.* New York: Columbia University Press, 2012.

HOW TO READ CHINESE POETRY IN CONTEXT

INTRODUCTION

The Cultural Role of Chinese Poetry

For several millennia, Chinese poetry has had a unique role to play. Ordinarily, we think of the relation between poetry and the world as a one-way street: social and cultural circumstances shape the composition of a poetic text that in one way or another represents or expresses these shaping forces. Rarely, though, do we see poetry as shaping those forces that shaped it. In this respect, Chinese poetry stands out as unique: its representation of the forces that shaped it has in turn had its own shaping or formative effect on those forces. Here, in effect, we have a two-way street: social and cultural forces help to form Chinese poetry, which in turn, by the specific way it represents those forces, has a counter effect of transforming those very forces. Through this genuine *interplay* between poetry and the world, Chinese poets and their readers have acquired an extraordinary capacity to intervene in state affairs and private life in decisive ways seldom seen anywhere else. In the chapters of this anthology, you'll get a glimpse of the social and cultural circumstances out of which Chinese poetry arose. Meanwhile, you'll see many of the different means by which Chinese poetry shaped and colored Chinese life during different historical periods. As you finish reading this book, you will understand how this complex interplay between poetical text and world has made possible the unique poetic culture that is China.

POETRY AND THE STATE

From the earliest times, Chinese poetry has been inseparably bound up with the politics of the state, in ways seldom seen elsewhere. It would be hard to find a better illustration of this point than the ancient *fushi* use of the *Book of Poetry* (*Shijing*; the *Poetry*), the oldest extant poetic collection, comprising 305 poems dating back to the early Zhou. *Fushi* (literally "presenting a poem") refers to the practice whereby high officials of different states would use *Shijing* poems to convey their states' political views and positions at a diplomatic encounter. Specifically, *fushi* practitioners attempted to steer the course of politics by translating one or more *Shijing* poems into an imaginative analogy for a political situation or position. And because this tradition called for all parties to communicate almost solely through a performative presentation of the *Poetry*, all the political maneuvering would then take place around the *Poetry*, and efforts were made by the rival parties to exploit it to their advantage.

Chapter 1 by Wai-yee Li recounts famous instances of *fushi* practice shortly before and during Confucius's time. Both the initiators of and respondents to a *fushi* exchange seek to perceive and imaginatively exploit an analogy between what's described in a *Shijing* poem and the present political situation. Typically, interpersonal encounters in a *Shijing* poem analogically represent the current political and diplomatic encounters between two or more states, while the poets' or speakers' feelings and thoughts convey their own states' attitudes and stances toward the encounters in question. Reliable historical texts show that many instances of *fushi* brought about dramatic gains or disastrous losses for the states concerned, thanks to the clever manipulation or bungled handling of a *fushi* exchange by their diplomatic envoys.

As the fortunes of a state were often determined by success in *fushi* exchanges, a court official not only must know by heart the entire corpus of 305 poems but also must know how to use them imaginatively. Thus, Confucius made these remarks on the learning and use of the *Poetry*:

If one does not study the *Poetry*, one will not know the way of proper speech. (*Analects* 16.13; my translation)

The Master said, "If a man capable of reciting the Three Hundred Poems cannot accomplish anything when charged with governance or cannot respond properly when sent as envoy to other states, what is the use of him knowing many of these poems?" (*Analects* 13.5; my translation)

In the story about Sima Xiangru's (179–127 BCE) "Sir Vacuous/Imperial Park Rhapsody," told in chapter 3 by Yu-yu Cheng and Gregory Patterson, we witness an innovative reenactment of the old *fushi* practice. Here the author is reading or reciting aloud his rhapsody to a rapt listener, Emperor Wu of the Han (r. 141–87 BCE). The purpose of Sima's presentation is largely that of a typical *fushi* initiator: to persuade by alternating the use of praise and censure. On the one hand, Sima seeks to dazzle Emperor Wu with his seemingly endless catalog of fruits and plants, fauna and flora, mountains and rivers, parks and palaces, real and fantastic scenes. By giving names to "ten thousand things" in this grandiose fashion, Sima aims to praise the emperor for establishing the grandest Chinese empire and for aspiring to extend his dominion over "all under heaven" (*tianxia*). Meanwhile, Sima doesn't forget his duty to remonstrate; hence his disapproving depiction of extravagant hunting excursions. Of course, as in *fushi* practice, all his praise and censure employ imaginative analogy making—"connecting kinds" (*lianlei*) between the text and things, between the text/things and the Han empire, and, above all, between fictitious parties in the rhapsody and the emperor, together with Sima himself.

After the Han there are few famous instances of poetry being used to directly influence a dynastic ruler the way Sima Xiangru did. Nonetheless, poetry continued to render service to the state. Another story about the *Poetry*, which I recount in chapter 4, revolves around the *Poetry*'s didactic role in the Han period, when it became canonized as a Confucian classic to be read, taught, and promulgated as moral guidance for the ruler and his subjects alike. In 136 BCE, Emperor Wu of the Han established the Confucian canon with five classical texts long used and praised by Confucius and his followers (the *Book of Changes*, the *Book of Poetry*, the *Book of Documents*, the *Record of Rituals*, and *Spring and Autumn Annals*), creating an official title for each of them. These titles, collectively known as "erudites" (*bo shi*), represented the highest scholarly degree or honor conferred by the imperial court. Incidentally, the term "*bo shi*" has now become the word in Chinese for the title "PhD" or "Dr."

Following its canonization as a Confucian classic, four prominent editions of the *Poetry* were produced during the Han, of which only the Mao Text survives. Significantly, the compiler of the Mao Text displays less interest in what the poems say than in how they can be made into a comprehensive guidebook for ethical and political conduct by rulers and commoners alike. Typically, Mao traces the provenance of a poem and ties it to a prominent political figure from one particular period of the Zhou dynasty. Those tied to laudable political figures are considered poems of praise, while those tied to despicable figures become poems of censure. In effect, Mao's prefaces are best regarded as the offspring of *fushi* creative reinterpretation. Like *fushi* practitioners, Mao shows little regard for a poem's original meaning and has no qualms about cannibalizing it in ways that fit his purpose. Just as *fushi* practitioners cut off a section to derive a desired meaning (*duanzhang quyi*), he often reduces a poem of emotional intensity to a colorless abstract moral statement.

For better or worse, this fast-and-loose interpretive style had a liberalizing effect on the study of the *Poetry* and on poetry in general, leading to easy moral allegory. As an approach, it would reign supreme from the Han through the Tang and would continue to undergird allegorical interpretation of both the *Poetry* and poetry in general for centuries after.

POETRY AND LEARNING

Thanks in part to the *Poetry*'s canonization, poetry writing itself would gain steadily in prestige after the Han, finally becoming institutionalized in 681 when Emperor Gaozong (r. 649–683) issued an edict making poetic composition a central part of the presented scholar examination. Chapter 11 by Manling Luo tells an intriguing story of the Tang obsession with poetry writing in and outside the examination hall. For the exam itself, candidates for the most prestigious presented scholar degree were asked to compose, impromptu, one long rhapsody and one regulated verse of shorter length (eight, twelve, or sixteen lines). To complete these tasks, examinees needed to have a thorough and nuanced mastery of the entire poetic tradition. Often, the real battle was won outside the examination hall. Candidates were allowed—and sometimes even asked—to submit sample compositions to a prospective examiner for the year, a practice called "scrolls presentation" (*xingjuan*). So competition began well ahead of the examination date, with candidates sparing no effort to cultivate a literary reputation that might sway examiners to assess them favorably.

Significantly, poetry is not just an examination subject but also a means of liaison between candidates and examiner. Typically, the correspondence between them would be conducted in verse. Nor did poetry writing end with the examination. A whole gamut of emotion, ranging from wild elation to shame to utter despair, found vent through poetry. After the examination, those who had been successful would be busy writing poems to thank their examiners, patrons, and families, trying to forge bonds among themselves, and expressing their shared eagerness for official appointment. Meanwhile, those who failed would compose poems to decry unfairness and to vent their anger in one way or another. Pleasure quarters were frequented by successful and failed candidates alike, where they would exchange poems—erotic or otherwise—with beautiful and cultured courtesans in the midst of their revelry. From stories told about these activities, we can tell that, during the Tang, poetry writing wasn't just a core learning subject for provincial and national examinations but also an all-important cultural activity involving people of all kinds, from emperors presiding over the top-level examinations, through the entire literati class, down to courtesans at the bottom of society.

POETIC IDENTITY AND ENDURING FAME

Besides the tangible benefits of officialdom, poetry promised a much greater reward: an opportunity for lasting fame. Forging a poetic identity that will be remembered forever is very much a creative activity. A poet might make use of his own unique experiences, possibly blending these with conventional poetic personae, or he might simply recast stock images, motifs, and tropes in ways that bear his signature. The reader, meanwhile, is not passive either, often examining a work against the poet's known life or conjuring up an authorial presence from a style. The works that have stood the test of time are simply those with the capacity to keep generating in readers this re-creative process. Indeed, it is out of this process that the greatest Chinese poetic identities have emerged: Qu Yuan the moralist and "patriot" (chapter 2), Tao Qian the hermit poet (chapter 8), Wang Wei the Buddha poet (*shifo*; chapter 13), Li Bai the immortal poet (*shixian*; chapter 14), Du Fu the sage poet (*shisheng*; chapter 15), Li He the ghost poet (*shigui*; chapter 17), and so on.

Qu Yuan (ca. 340–278 BCE) is the first great poetic identity produced by the Chinese literary tradition. In chapter 2, Stephen Owen probes the interesting and unique dynamic behind the formation of this identity. Since we can't verify the real existence of Qu Yuan as a loyal Chu minister and the author of *Li Sao* (*Encountering Misery*), Stephen Owen argues, this great poetic identity is largely the brainchild of three prominent Han readers: Jia Yi (200–168 BCE), Sima Qian (145–86? BCE), and Wang Yi (fl. 114–119). As Owen points out, the readerly creation of Qu Yuan was driven by many factors—Jia Yi's and Sima Qian's sorrow over falling into disfavor and their effort to inculcate Confucian moral values being the most noteworthy. To Wang Yi, the *Chuci* (*Songs of Chu*) compiler, Qu Yuan the author serves as an indispensable focal point on which disparate subjects and styles converge to form a meaningful whole. And just as Qu Yuan helped to transform a jumble of hard-to-interpret shamanistic songs into a literary masterwork, the canonization of the *Chuci*, in turn, led to the emergence of Qu Yuan as a great cultural icon, a reciprocal process that, driven by ever more imaginative readers, has continued unabated since the Han. So, while the *Chuci* has achieved parity with the *Book of Poetry* in many ways, Qu Yuan has become a cultural symbol of many virtues—unbending integrity, loyalty, and, more recently, patriotism. This continual lionization of Qu Yuan is ritually ensured by the annual Dragon Boat Festival, with its *zongzi* (sweet rice cake wrapped in leaves) and dragon-shaped boat race, believed to prevent the drowned Qu Yuan from being devoured by river monsters (feeding them *zongzi* instead) and to scare them away with the drumbeat of racing boats.

After Qu Yuan—perhaps because of a proliferation of biographical documentation of various sorts—poetic identity is less a purely readerly creation and more closely tied to verifiable biographical experience. Indeed, the poetic identities discussed here were more demonstrably shaped by actual experiences of real poets living in the real world. Unlike Qu Yuan, these poets no longer obsessed over allegorization of court politics in the way Qu Yuan had done. Moreover, instead of allegorically depicting gods, goddesses, and spirits, these poets ushered in the real world of wars, nature, farm life, frontiers, entertainment quarters, and families.

In a somewhat different vein, we also have the strange case of the ghost poet, Li He (790–816), examined by Robert Ashmore (chapter 17). And, somewhat later, we have two poets (Yuan Zhen and Bai Juyi) mutually helping each other to create a poetic identity through their literati friendship, as demonstrated by Ao Wang (chapter 16). By depicting themselves in the world as we know it, all these poets helped to broaden the thematic terrain, foster the rise of new poetic subgenres, and thereby fashion a different kind of poetic identity.

WARS, HEROES, AND KNIGHT-ERRANTRY

As in the West, the realm of war and knight-errantry in China made possible the creation of a unique world in verse. Unlike the classical or medieval epic, with its celebration of particular martial heroes, Chinese poetry took a different course. A shared antipathy to war, shared by the Confucian, Buddhist, and Daoist traditions, meant that poems about war would focus more on a complex range of sentiments associated with it: hero worship, yearning for the freedom and abandon of knight-errantry, but also war weariness and lamentation for the dead. And because it didn't focus on the celebration of particular heroes, Chinese poetry became not only more subjective, more expressive, but also more imaginative.

Although most war poetry appeared in the generalized, impersonal *yuefu* (Music Bureau poetry) or *gushi* (ancient-style poetry), as seen in chapters 6 and 10, the best-known poems on war-related topics were by poets who could overcome the constraints of an impersonal genre by introducing a subtle but genuinely personal voice. As shown in chapter 6 by Xinda Lian, Cao Cao (155–220) possessed a unique perspective as the most powerful warlord of his time. Composing poems during military campaigns, he surprisingly dwelled on the miseries of war rather than the glory of military conquest. For this reason, his poems managed to relyricize the old tetrasyllabic poetry. His son Cao Zhi (192–232) likewise cultivated a personal voice in *yuefu* poetry. But instead of pouring out his feelings, he often chose to convey them through fictional characters, most notably heroic warriors fighting on the frontiers and daring, uncouth youths. Not seen elsewhere in the *yuefu* corpus, these two character types appear to express symbolically Cao Zhi's thwarted aspiration for military accomplishment.

With the Tang dynasty, these two imagined character types of Cao Zhi would be reborn as knights-errant (*xia*). As shown in chapter 10 by Tsung-cheng Lin, Tang knights-errant combined the distinct attributes of the two character types, beginning as urban daredevils and later joining the frontier garrison for greater adventures. In early and high Tang poetry, depiction of their stoic, adventurous lives led to a fashionable new subgenre called "frontier poetry" (*biansai shi*). Many famous Tang poets actually served as officials on the frontier garrisons, exemplifying a neglected ideal of the Chinese literati: a superb mastery of martial/military arts combined with excellence in belles lettres. The *yuefu*-style frontier poems featured in chapter 10 show some of the multiple perspectives they present. Artistically, however, these poems can't compare with those composed in the newer quatrain form (*jueju*; ☞ *WKB* P48–P51). By exploiting the interfacing of space and time inherent in this new form, frontier poets like Wang Changling (698–757), Wang Han (fl. 710), and others admirably blend accounts of themselves in the present war with accounts of past wars, thereby creating a new, imaginative universe soaring above historical time.

NATURE, THE UNIVERSE, AND DAOIST TRANSCENDENCE

For officials disillusioned with court politics, poetry offered a unique opportunity. After withdrawing from the court, they could turn to nature as a means of escape. By writing about nature in verse, however, they managed to make of it an emotional refuge. Imaginatively transformed, the nature depicted in their poetry becomes a place of spiritual transcendence: no longer merely an actual place, it now becomes a site invested with religious or moral significance through the practices they associated with it.

Appointment to the imperial court was a dream after which most literati poets strove—not least through excellence in poetic composition. However, court politics ceased to inspire great poetry after *Li Sao*, even becoming anathema to poetic achievement. Over and over, we find poetic genius incapable of producing great work until after withdrawal from politics into a private sphere. The famous remark "Only when one is in dire straits does one's poetry becomes refined" (*Shi qiong er hou gong*) by Ouyang Xiu (1007–1072) aptly describes the phenomenon.

Nature is the favored locale of retirement for officials disillusioned by court politics, attracting Chinese literati by its remoteness from the political world or by its soothing and uplifting powers. The earliest example is perhaps that of Boyi and Shuqi, who declined the Shang throne and fled to Shouyang Mountain. Their choice of hunger rather than disrepute is praised by Confucius as a great act of defiance against unrighteousness. Many centuries later, the "Seven Worthies of the Bamboo Grove" furnish an example of nature being used as the staging ground for an even more radical form of defiance against the political establishment. Although it's impossible to verify that these seven eminent figures actually lived together as a close community in a certain bamboo grove, it's undoubtedly in the world of nature that they performed their outlandish acts—binge drinking, taking deadly mineral drugs, practicing nudism, and so on—all calculated to ridicule the hypercritical and repressive Sima regime. As shown in chapter 7 by Nanxiu Qian, these worthies had an even more ambitious goal: to turn the philosophical teaching of Laozi (ca. 571–ca. 471 BCE) and Zhuangzi (ca. 369–ca. 286 BCE) into a bona fide lifestyle of absolute freedom or transcendence. Their vision of transcendence is both physical and spiritual. In a famous essay, Ji Kang (223–262) wrote about attaining physical transcendence through longevity drugs, but in poetry, both he and Ruan Ji (210–263) portrayed Zhuangzi's "perfected man" more as a spiritual embodiment of the cosmic Dao.

With Tao Qian, nature takes on a much more profound significance. As shown in chapter 8 by Alan Berkowitz, Tao Qian developed a deep emotional and spiritual bond with nature. A moving expression of this may be found in his famous poem "Returning to Dwell on the Farm, No. 1," where all the details of farm life are imbued with his fondness for it and where his return to his farmstead is celebrated as a return to his better self. This return provided not only solace to a wearied soul but also, more importantly, a means of achieving spiritual transcendence. Tao embraced the idea of "self-transformation" (attributed to Tao's near contemporaries Xiang Xiu [ca. 221–ca. 300] and Guo Xiang [252–312]), made possible by a belief that the eternal Dao and the nature of every individual thing is ultimately one. This belief enables Tao Qian to discern a profound transcendental promise in his life as a simple farmer: living the life he was born to live leads to self-realization and hence a communion with the Dao. Indeed, Tao Qian experienced a sense of that communion when his farming life became perfectly attuned to the rhythm of nature. By vividly capturing that sense of communion in his poems, he earned the homage of future great poets like Su Dongpo (1037–1101), who imitated Tao's oeuvre piece by piece.

Li Bai (701–762), aptly called the "immortal poet," is the next great icon of transcendence. If Tao Qian found a way to transcend mundanity by committing himself to the humble life of a hermit farmer, Li Bai poetically performed the celestial dream of cavorting with immortals. In some of his most famous poems he cast himself as the "banished immortal" he had once been dubbed, flouting social conventions with abandon and flamboyantly indulging in the pleasures of the moment. As shown in chapter 14 by Paula Varsano, Li Bai's poems on wine are a prime example of his theatrical appropriation and (deceptively) simple transformation of poetic convention. So, while Cao Cao and Tao Qian fell to brooding in their cups over human transience, Li Bai hailed the dissolving of ten thousand years of sorrows in a cup of wine and depicted himself inviting the moon to drink and dance with him. Ultimately, it is up to the reader to determine whether these gestures succeeded in quelling the quotidian human experiences and feelings to which he most certainly was subject. But his show of transcendent mastery—of both his mortal humanity and his inherited poetic legacy—captured the imagination of his readers, earning him immortal fame as Du Fu's (712–770) sole rival for the title of China's greatest poet.

NATURE, MEDITATION, AND BUDDHIST ENLIGHTENMENT

"Enlightenment" is the word we typically use when speaking of the spiritual transcendence sought or achieved by Buddhists. This word choice is judicious, as it aptly emphasizes transcendence as a state of mind. Since enlightenment is to be achieved through mental concentration, the tranquil world of nature offers an ideal setting for a Buddhist's spiritual quest, providing not only the tranquility conducive to mental concentration but also a prime object of meditation. By recording his engagement with nature, a Buddhist poet produces a new kind of nature poetry, quite different from that of Daoist-minded poets like Tao Qian—as borne out by poems of three eminent Buddhist poets examined in this book: Shen Yue (441–513), Han Shan (fl. seventh, eighth, or ninth centuries), and Wang Wei (701–761).

These three poets engaged nature quite differently. In chapter 9, Meow Hui Goh tells how Shen Yue, a tenacious political survivor who served three dynasties and lived to a rare old age, grew weary of politics and spent his last years living in and writing about his luxurious garden estate called Eastern Field, constructed not far from the capital city. In his *"Fu on Living in the Suburbs,"* we see Shen involved in a distinctly philosophical contemplation of nature. To him, as to the early nature poet Xie Lingyun (☞ *HTRCP* chap. 6), nature is essentially a source of sensory stimuli, affording much pleasure and at the same time prompting melancholy reflection. In this rhapsody, Shen laments the woes of politics and the evanescence of human life. But instead of resorting to carpe diem or embracing a Daoist lifestyle, he goes on to dismiss the phenomenal world as illusory, yearning for Buddhist deliverance from the endless suffering of cycles of life and death.

In chapter 13 by Chen Yinchi and Jing Chen, we see two new approaches to nature and enlightenment adopted by Han Shan and Wang Wei, Buddhist poets living in the Tang dynasty. The historical existence of Han Shan is doubted by many scholars—as is his alleged authorship of a body of poems collected under his name. Largely ignored by Chinese literary tradition, Han Shan gained prominence only in the twentieth century, after Gary Snyder's translation of the Han Shan poems became a spiritual inspiration for the Beat generation. But compared to Shen Yue's rhapsody, even the most polished Han Shan poems clearly lack intellectual rigor and literary elegance. Shen's rhapsody exhibits the influence of Chengshi Buddhism, a form of Indian scholasticism known for its abstruse analysis of the human mind. It also bears the hallmark of a literary titan taking pleasure in nature's sights and sounds and seeking to capture these in his prosody. By contrast, the Han Shan poems bear the indelible imprint of Chan Buddhism, a popular doctrine drawing much on native Daoism and primarily catering to the uneducated masses. These poems reflect the perspectives of a poor hermit too caught up in daily toil to appreciate nature, seeing it mainly metaphorically.

Wang Wei's approach to nature and enlightenment combines the best of Shen Yue and Han Shan. Like Shen Yue, Wang retired from a political career to commune with nature. But the circumstances of his retirement were different. If Shen Yue sought peace after a long and eminent career in the imperial court, Wang Wei looked to nature as well as Buddhism for consolation after falling out of favor. Likewise, their country residences also differed: Wang Wei's Wangchuan homestead bore no comparison in either scale or comfort with Shen Yue's garden estate of Eastern Field.

All these differences notwithstanding, Wang Wei approached nature with a poetic sensibility inherited from Shen Yue and other Qi-Liang poets, a sensibility marked by keen appreciation of sound and sight. While Shen Yue and his followers focused on matters like parallel phrasing and tonal patterning, however, Wang Wei set his sights on something grander: evoking the Buddhist cosmic vision in his landscape poetry and painting. By Wang Wei's time, the poetic devices championed by Shen had already been perfected and codified in recent-style poetry (☞ *HTRCP* chap. 8). Like Han Shan, Wang Wei came under the sway of Chan Buddhism and approached nature as a prime object of meditation. However, he refused to see nature abstractly, as metaphors of Buddhist ideas, but instead focused on the elusive play of nature captured in a heightened moment of observation. In his finest poems, he enthralls us with a blissful mode of perception where the boundaries between sound and silence, existence and emptiness, self and world, evaporate and the Chan Buddhist vision emerges. This embodiment of Buddhist vision in a deceptively simple style is one of the greatest achievements of Chinese poetry, an achievement that earned Wang Wei the title of the "Buddha poet."

WOMEN AS POETIC SUBJECT AND AS WRITERS

So far, women have hardly figured in the writing of Chinese poetry, either as poetic subject or as an active force. To be sure, a significant number of love poems in the *Book of Poetry* show women expressing a full gamut of feelings—trust, devotion, estrangement, love and hate, erotic yearnings, and so on. But since Han exegetes interpreted these songs as ethico-political allegory, they practically hollowed out any genuine female sensibility and thus reduced women to mere poetic personae to be co-opted by male poets seeking to express feelings about lords or patrons.

This "degendering" of woman by Han exegetes has had a profound impact on poetic writing about women ever since. It practically circumscribed the mental horizons of all—man or woman, reader or writer—where literary texts about women were concerned. An invisible wall of allegorization had to be breached by a writer trying to convey anything about real women and, likewise, by a reader trying to discern the same. The dominance of this allegorical mode seems a likely cause for the dearth of bona fide poems by or about women during the Han and the Six Dynasties. Here, then, the capacity of poetry to create its own autonomous sphere in Chinese culture can be seen—thanks to its shaping by commentators—to have a negative rather than a positive effect.

Of course, there are exceptions. A particularly outstanding one is the long narrative poem entitled "Old Poem Composed for the Wife of Jiao Zhongqing," studied in chapter 5 by Olga Lomová. What distinguishes this work from conventional poems about women is its resistance to allegorization. While other poems typically feature an anonymous abandoned woman (the standard persona for a disfavored, plaintive male poet), this text is about a woman named Liu Lanzhi, married to someone named Jiao Zhongqing, holding a particular official position at a given time. All these specifics serve a definite function: that of dislodging the tendency to allegorize, creating instead a sense of meeting real people in real life. The fact that all this personal information appears in a preface attests to the effect being intentional.

Appealing as it might be to the modern reader, this poem failed to inspire any similar efforts. Possibly the trouble lay in the way it subtly problematized Confucian mores, or in the marginality of the long narrative form (versus the dominant lyric), or in a lack of literati interest in depicting real women's lives—or in a combination of these factors.

Besides the repressive effect of Han *Shijing* allegoresis, the Confucian moral injunction against women interacting with men outside their families meant that their poems (like their physical selves) would never enter the public sphere. The impact of this injunction is obvious: in the huge corpus of the Han and Six Dynasties poetry, few poems are verifiably authored by women. A handful purportedly by Ban Jieyu (48 BCE–2 CE), a talented consort of Emperor Cheng, were probably composed and meant for the emperor's private perusal rather than public circulation. That they eventually spread beyond the palace walls and were preserved for posterity is largely due to Ban's eminence as a high-ranking consort.

With the Tang dynasty, women finally appear on the poetry scene, enjoying unprecedented freedom and appearing in public social and literary gatherings—a profound change attributed by many to the Empress Wu Zetian (r. 690–705), China's first and only female monarch. As shown in Chapter 12 by Maija Samei, this newfound social freedom was used to advantage by a small class of women with problematic moral character—imperial consorts, Daoist nuns (often courtesans thinly disguised), and courtesans. Nonetheless, Confucian mores died hard. Women from noble families continued to pride themselves on being secluded from the public spheres and refrained from writing poetry for public circulation. For morally suspect women venturing into the male sphere, poetic excellence was the primary means of gaining patronage from emperors (including the Empress Wu Zetian, who assumed or "usurped" the role of Son of Heaven), high officials, or prominent literati poets like Bai Juyi (772–846) or Yuan Zhen (779–831), whose life stories are told in chapter 16 by Ao Wang, or of forging intellectual and emotional ties with civil service examination candidates.

Among the "successful" Tang woman poets, the most intriguing is Shangguan Wan'er (664?–710), who by her dazzling poetic talent earned the trust of Empress Wu Zetian and her son Emperor Zhongzong (r. 684, 705–710) and made herself the most influential woman after Empress Wu. Having beaten men at their own game of poetry composition, she was widely held to be the arbiter of literary taste in her time. The life stories of the Daoist nuns Li Ye (d. 784) and Yu Xuanji (844?–868) and of the famed courtesan Xue Tao (768–831) are almost equally dramatic and captivating. Ironically, what unifies the "success stories" of these female poetic talents is their tragic endings: Shangguan Wan'er, Li Ye, and Yu Xuanji all suffered gruesome executions for perceived political or legal transgressions. This attests to the high price Tang women poets paid for poetic fame.

FAMILY, COUNTRY, AND HISTORY

In various ways, we've seen how Chinese poetry manages to create its own world or sphere, which isn't necessarily that of the poet. In other words, its relation to the real world is often complex and is not always either direct or transparent. Nowhere is this more apparent than in the treatment of family. While the yearning of a wanderer (*youzi*) for home or the pining of a woman for the return of her absent husband appear perennially in Chinese poetry, the actual family life of the literati (for instance, intimate feelings for family members, especially parents and children) is a topic not eagerly broached in poetic works.

Instead, most poets assume the role of an invisible third person observing what's happening in families other than their own. So we have the anonymous "Old Poem Composed for the Wife of Jiao Zhongqing," discussed earlier. As shown in chapter 15 by Jack Chen, Du Fu, too, plays the role of a sympathetic observer, in "Three Officers" and "Three Partings." Unlike the anonymous poem, however, Du Fu isn't trying to portray particular people. Instead, he primarily aims to demonstrate how numerous commoners' families were destroyed or decimated by the protracted war with An Lushan rebels. So we get stories of the remaining man in a family being press-ganged for battle, or an old man's midnight escape, or a wife's plea to serve the troops as her husband's substitute—all meant to convey a sense of extreme agony and desperation over family destruction.

From the family, Du Fu works outward to the consequences of such destruction on society and the very existence of the country. Setting these six poems against a backdrop of constant war adds a sense of urgency and further amplifies his profound concern. Not surprisingly, their powerful expression of sociopolitical apprehension gave these six poems pride of place in mainland China for most of the twentieth century, as the apex of Du's poetic work. More recently, however, Du Fu's status as China's greatest poet is seen to rest more on other poems, where his personal experiences, his reflections on China's long history, and his Confucian worldview all coalesce into the most sublime poetic vision ever expressed in Chinese poetry (☞ *HTRCP* chap. 8 and 9). The title of "sage poet" is a fitting tribute to this unparalleled achievement.

*   *   *

These are all important facets of Chinese poetic culture from the earliest times through the Tang. For the journey of discovery ahead, we would like to offer you some suggestions. Rather than reading the book from cover to cover, you may focus instead on the areas of greatest interest to you, following the broad signposts provided in this introduction. Alternatively, you may follow the specific paths and byways charted out in the thematic table of contents for an in-depth exploration of certain topics and issues. Whichever route you choose for your journey, we would urge you to read as many poetic texts as you can in conjunction with the stories read, taking full advantage of the cross-references to the *Guided Anthology* (*HTRCP*) and the *Workbook* (*WKB*). The simultaneous use of these three books offers an optimal way to gain insight into the dynamic interplay of two mutually transforming forces—political and social circumstances shaping poetry and the ever-more-empowered poetry transforming, in turn, the sociopolitical world that shaped it.

ZONG-QI CAI

PART I
PRE-HAN TIMES

❖ I ❖
POETRY AND DIPLOMACY IN *ZUO TRADITION* (*ZUOZHUAN*)

The *Book of Poetry* (*Shijing*; ca. 1000–ca. 600 BCE), comprising 305 poems, is a foundational text in the Chinese tradition not only because of its antiquity and the range of human experience it encompasses but also because of its significance for understanding early thought, history, rituals, and politics. Scholars argue about the dating and origins of the *Poetry*; when, how, and why did this text come into being? What might have been the social, ritual, and political contexts for the performance of the poems that come to be collected in the *Poetry*?

Mencius (ca. fourth century BCE) claimed that the ideal interpreter of the *Poetry* "uses his mind to meet the intent [of the author]" (*yi yi ni zhi*; *Mengzi* 6A.4). The context of that remark is Mencius's critique of his interlocutor's wrong interpretation. This confirms how "authorial intention" is used to uphold one valid interpretation and to exclude other readings. The immensely influential Mao Preface to the *Poetry*, which cannot be dated with certainty but probably came into being no later than the first century, describes poetry as the product of affective response and inevitable expression. Predating reflections on authorial intention or the process of poetic creation, however, are instantiations of how poems that come to be collected in the *Poetry* can be used for political purposes.

Some of the earliest extant writings on Chinese literary thought thus pertain to the political functions of poetry. Confucius famously remarked, "If one does not study the *Poetry*, one does not have the wherewithal for proper speech" (*Analects* 16.13).[1] "Speech" here refers to political communication, as is evident in this explanation: "If, having recited three hundred poems, a person cannot achieve his goals when given a position of political responsibility, or if he cannot respond independently when being sent as envoy to domains in the four directions, then what purpose does it serve even if he knows many poems?" (*Analects* 13.5). These sayings attributed to the sage likely appear after, or may be inspired by, recorded instances of Eastern Zhou (770–256 BCE) aristocrats who recited the poems to convey their political vision, policy recommendation, or diplomatic finesse. Most of these examples are found in *Zuo Tradition* (*Zuozhuan*, hereafter *Zuo*), a vast repertoire of narratives and speeches related to events spanning 255 years (722–468 BCE) and traditionally understood as an exegetical tradition of the *Spring and Autumn Annals* (*Chunqiu*) (figure 1.1).

This was a period when many different domains vied for power and influence or struggled to survive, often through diplomatic rhetoric. Mastery of this language—what Confucius calls the competence to respond independently (*zhuandui*)—includes using apposite quotations from the *Poetry*, which are usually embedded in longer speeches, as well as the skill of *fushi*, variously translated as "reciting," "chanting," or "singing" the poems. The accounts of such performances would include

FIGURE 1.1 Rubbing from pictorial relief carving of four registers depicting mythical animals, female figures sitting and offering food in ceremony, and a procession of officers riding in horse-drawn vehicles; scenes are from the shrine of Wu Rong at the Wu Family Shrines, Jiaxiang, Shandong from the first year of Jianhe, Eastern Han dynasty (147). This rubbing of a Han relief carving (second century) gives us glimpses into how social, political, and ritual activities of the elite during the Spring and Autumn era might have been imagined. Courtesy of Special Collections, Fine Arts Library, Harvard University.

the terse formula of "X (subject) chants (*fu*) Y (a poem)," a concise delineation of the occasion and the context (usually a state visit, an interstate meeting, or a semiformal exchange between members of the elite), and the reaction of the addressee, often in the form of reciprocal *fushi*. On rare occasions, *fu* can mean "composition," but in most cases it refers to the appropriation of existing pieces. Many of these are found in the received text of the *Poetry*, and the few that are not are traditionally classified as "lost poems" (*yishi*). With rare exceptions, the actors in these stories are men.[2] In most cases, the poem is just mentioned by name rather than cited. This is cultural shorthand; the reader has to already know the *Poetry* in order to understand the import of the exchange.

Fushi in diplomatic context is first mentioned in *Zuo* Xi 23.6f (1:370–371 [637 BCE]) and last noted in *Zuo* Ding 4.3f (3:1760–1761 [506 BCE]), and most of the examples are concentrated in the sixth century BCE, especially during the reigns of Lord Xiang of Lu (572–542 BCE) and of Lord Zhao of Lu (541–510 BCE). We will never know for sure whether statesmen actually recited poems in diplomatic gatherings in the seventh and sixth centuries BCE, but what seems certain is that the competence to articulate aspirations and negotiate differences through common allegiance to a shared tradition is enshrined as a cultural ideal by the time of *Zuo*'s compilation.

The Han historian Ban Gu (32–92) describes the practice of *fushi* as the ideal synthesis of poetry and politics: "In ancient times, when princes, ministers, and high officers had dealings with neighboring domains, they used subtle words to sway each other. At the moment of bowing and politesse, they invariably cited the *Poetry* to convey their intent. For this was also the means whereby one could distinguish the worthy from the unworthy and observe rise and decline" (*Hanshu* 30.1755–1756). Proper *fushi* thus emphasizes effective communication through "subtle words" (*weiyan*), whose political function is a far cry from the usual associations of the phrase with indirect though pointedly conveyed moral intent (*weiyan dayi*), often linked to Confucius's putative authorship of the *Spring and Autumn Annals*. By "subtle words," Ban Gu seems to imply a language with an intrinsically flexible range of associations—something akin to what we would call symbolic or evocative language. Such finesse and polyvalence give a veneer of civility and ritual propriety to diplomatic transactions and mask (or ideally transform) raw power relations.

By invoking ancient exemplars and the affective contexts of the poems, one can indirectly articulate hopes, fears, and intent.[3] It is also the venue of judgment—through it the speaker expresses his judgment of political situations, and his competence or lack thereof in *fushi* also determines how others (including the implied reader) judge him. Failure to grasp the import of chanted poems addressed to them indicates moral blemish as well as intellectual inadequacy.[4] Similarly, *bulei* (chanting a poem inappropriate for the occasion or for the speaker's status and situation) invites criticism and punishment.[5] Ritual prescriptions define the propriety of the poems chanted; wise ministers decline to acknowledge poems implying honors beyond their due.[6] Yet *fushi* can be tied to the crucible of judgment precisely because ritual prescriptions are not stable and inflexible, for if they are, there is no room for statesmen to independently respond. A felicitous response has little regard for what might have been the "original" meaning of the poem; success depends on cutting the section (*duanzhang*) that can be tailored to the speaker's intent and context.[7] Yet if the ideal of *fushi* is seamless communication, the most interesting instances of the practice involve negotiating differences and debating interpretations, as the following examples will show.

BARBARIANS AND CULTURAL IDEALS

In a meeting summoned by the northern state Jin to mobilize support for an attack against the southern state Chu, a barbarian chief questions the boundaries separating the central domains from barbarian territories and the very definition of the barbarian as "cultural other" by reciting "Blue Flies" ("Qingying," Mao no. 219) from the *Poetry*.[8] The incident is described in *Zuo* Xiang 14.1 (2:1006–1011 [559 BCE]). The Jin minister Fan Xuanzi, who presides over the meeting, accuses Juzhi, the leader of the Rong barbarians, of leaking Jin's secrets and passing on rumors that undermine the princes' allegiance to Jin. Fan appeals to history; he claims that Jin saves the Rong from Qin's aggression:

Your ancestor Wuli, draped in a white rush cape and wearing a headdress made from brambles, came to our former ruler for protection. Though our former ruler, Lord Hui [r. 651–637 BCE] had but meager lands, he divided them with you to provide you with sustenance. Now the reason why the princes no longer serve our ruler in the same way as before is because words leaked out, and this could have happened only on account of you. You are not to take part in the event of the next morning. If you do, we shall have you arrested.

Juzhi, in response, proclaims Rong's allegiance to Jin but also stakes out its independence from Jin. Juzhi also qualifies Rong's indebtedness to Jin, claiming that the land Jin ceded to Rong was inhospitable wilderness, tamed only through Rong's efforts.

> He bestowed on us the lands of Jin's southern march, where foxes and wild cats dwelled, and where jackals and wolves howled. We, the various Rong, removed and cut down their brambles and drove away their foxes and wild cats, jackals and wolves, and became subjects of the former lord. Neither aggressive nor rebellious, we have been unwavering in our allegiance until now.

This is one of the rare occasions when the barbarian is given a voice. Far from being the "wild people," Rong is presented as the agent of civilization.

Instead of acknowledging Jin's protection of Rong against Qin, Juzhi emphasizes the contributions of Rong as Jin's ally in Qin–Jin conflicts, which are chronicled elsewhere: "Just as in the pursuit of a deer, the men of Jin seized its antlers, and the various Rong tribes caught its legs, and with Jin brought it to the ground."[9] Beyond past grudges or obligations, Juzhi probes the factors determining amity or confrontation between the central domains and barbarian realms. His approach is two-pronged. On the one hand, he emphasizes radical difference. Rong's culture (food, clothing, language) is so different that it is not capable of meddling in affairs of the central domains: "We do not exchange gifts with them, and our language and theirs do not allow communication. What harm can we possibly do?" Also, Rong's distinctiveness is such that isolation is no punishment, and it would not be moved by Jin's threat of removing it from the covenant meeting: "Not to participate in the meeting will be no cause for grief. He chanted 'Blue Flies' and withdrew."

On the other hand, Juzhi avers common roots with the central domains. Juzhi claims that, by helping the Rong, Lord Hui implicitly recognized them as "descendants of the lords of the Four Peaks," identified in various early texts as aides to the legendary sage kings Yao and Shun. This means that Rong deserves to be treated as Jin's equal. Most ironic of all, having emphasized cultural difference and obstacles to communication, Juzhi shows his mastery of a shared cultural heritage by chanting "Blue Flies," a poem that laments the perniciousness of slander:

	Buzzing blue flies	營營青蠅
2	Gather on the fence.	止於樊
	Joyous and civil is the noble man:	豈弟君子
4	He does not believe in words of slander.	無信讒言
	Buzzing blue flies	營營青蠅
6	Gather at the brambles.	止于棘
	The slander-mongers know no limit,	讒人罔極
8	And wreak havoc in domains on four sides.	交亂四國

	Buzzing blue lies	營營青蠅
10	Gather at the thickets.	止于榛
	The slander-mongers know no limit,	讒人罔極
12	And sow discord between you and me.	構我二人

[MSZY 2:489–490]

Commentators Zheng Xuan (127–200), Kong Yingda (574–648), and Zhu Xi (1130–1200) characterize "blue flies" as an affective, arousing image (*xing*) that prompts the poet to versify about the scourge of slander. Loathed for their propensity to "invert black and white," the blue flies may also bear a more direct metaphorical connection with "slander-mongers." By chanting "Blue Flies," Juzhi displaces the burden of cultural otherness to the instigators of discord. One may say that he erases Rong's status as cultural other by reciting a poem and by redefining amity in terms of shared values.[10] Juzhi's recitation apparently clinches the case for Fan Xuanzi, who "acknowledged his error and made Juzhi take part in affairs at the meeting, thus realizing the attributes of being 'joyous and civil.'" The *Zuo* passage ends thus: "From then on, the leaders of Jin reduced the obligatory contributions of Lu and treated its envoys with even greater respect." Fan Xuanzi might have been prompted to scale back demands on lesser domains because of Juzhi's speech. In this sense, Juzhi's chanting of "Blue Flies" is also effective remonstrance.

THE STRUGGLE FOR SUPREMACY

Juzhi recites "Blue Flies" to imply cultural common ground and also to assert the rights of the cultural other. There is, behind the recitation, a complex negotiation of demands and rebuttals, of self-definition and attempts to define the other, between the speaker and the addressee. Such negotiations often take place in the context of power struggles among various domains, for the period of *fushi* also coincides with the intense vying for the status of overlord (*ba*) or leader of the covenant (*mengzhu*). Indeed, the first instance of *fushi* takes place in the context of the quest of Chong'er (later Lord Wen of Jin, r. 636–628 BCE) to become Jin ruler and then overlord. In the course of his peregrinations upon being driven away from Jin, Chong'er comes to Qin, where the Qin ruler, Lord Mu (r. 659–621 BCE), treats him with courtesy and generosity. A ceremonial entertainment for Chong'er becomes the occasion to articulate ambitions and manipulate expectations.

One of Chong'er's main advisors, Hu Yan, excuses himself from attending the meeting: "I am not as cultured as Zhao Cui. Please have Zhao Cui accompany you." During the gathering, Chong'er recites "The Yellow River." The Qin ruler recites "The Sixth Month." Zhao Cui, true to his reputation for being "cultured," makes the most of this exchange. He says, "Chong'er bows in gratitude for the bestowed gift." Chong'er then descends and respectfully bows, touching his forehead to the ground. The Qin ruler descends one step and declines the honor. Zhao Cui explains, "You, my lord, have issued orders to Chong'er, claiming that he is one with the means to assist the Son of Heaven. Would Chong'er presume not to bow?" (*Zuo* Xi 23.6, 1:370–371 [637 BCE]).

Hu Yan is one of Chong'er's most resourceful advisors, but here he defers to Zhao Cui, whose greater "cultivation" (*wen*) or fuller mastery of ritual and textual traditions better equips him for diplomatic exchange. According to the *Zuo* scholar Du Yu (222–285), "The Yellow River" ("He Shui") is a lost poem that in this context implies comparison of Jin to the Yellow River and of Qin to the sea. In the parallel account of this anecdote in *Discourses of the States* (*Guoyu*, hereafter *Discourses*), the annotation of Wei Zhao (204–273) suggests that "River Mian" ("Mian Shui," Mao no. 183) includes appropriate lines on the river and the sea, and may indeed be the poem Chong'er recited. However, the fact that "The Yellow River" is also mentioned in a discussion of the *Poetry* in an excavated text seems to rule out Wei Zhao's speculation. (That text, included in the Shanghai Museum bamboo strip manuscript, comes to bear the title "Confucius's Discourse on Poetry" ["Kongzi shi lun"]).[11] In any case, the recitation was meant to honor the Qin ruler, Chong'er's host.

The Qin ruler recites "The Sixth Month" ("Liuyue," Mao no. 177), which praises the successful northern expeditions of the Zhou leader Yin Jifu against the Xianyun people during the reign of King Xuan of Zhou (r. 827–782 BCE).

	Disquiet and tumult in the sixth month:	六月棲棲
2	The chariots of war are already in order.	戎車既飭
	Our four steeds are strong and stalwart,	四牡騤騤
4	Our carts bear the customary gear of war.	載是常服
	The might of the Xianyun is ablaze,	玁狁孔熾
6	That is why we feel the urgency.	我是用急
	By royal command we are going to battle	王于出征
8	To save the king's realm.	以匡王國

[MSZY 2:357–358]

This is the first of six stanzas in the received text. As is often the case with battle poems in the *Poetry*, there is extensive description of the preparation for war and references to the outcome of the conflict and the postwar celebration, but the fighting itself is passed over quickly or in silence.[12] The Xianyun are traditionally identified as barbarians,[13] although the poem contains no denigrating references; it compares their might to a blazing fire and sounds the alarm for an urgent military response to their incursions deep into the central domains. The glory of the campaign seems to depend on the depiction of worthy enemies. The rest of the poem praises the dignity and martial prowess of the Zhou counterattack, although some details suggest a much more precarious and embattled situation for Zhou.

	Majestic and careful,	有嚴有翼
22	We respect martial endeavor,	共武之服
	Respect martial endeavor	共武之服
24	That brings order to the king's realm.	以定王國

Various place names in the poem suggest that the Xianyuns' incursions penetrate deeply into the Zhou domain. Instead of acknowledging this as a defensive campaign, however, the poem celebrates Zhou power, evident in its very insignia:

	Patterns of birds are emblazoned on banners,	織文鳥章
30	Silken streamers brightly shone.	白斾央央
	Ten charging war chariots:	元戎十乘
32	A spearhead prying open the enemy's ranks.	以先啟行

Despite the implied violence, the emphasis is on exemplary and orderly display based on perfect training. The hero of this poem is the Zhou leader Yin Jifu: "Cultured and martial is Jifu, / The exemplar for myriad domains" (*MSZY* 2:357–358).

When the Qin ruler recites "The Sixth Month," he is apparently invoking a vision of the princes rallying to defend Zhou against barbarian invasion. The poem ends with a feast, when Yin Jinfu celebrates his victory with the lords, including the "filial and fraternal" Zhang Zhong. Zhang Zhong is sometimes identified as Nan Zhong, the military commander in "Send Out the Chariot" ("Chuju," Mao no. 168) and "Abiding Martial Power" ("Changwu," Mao no. 263). Lord Mu of Qin may be implying analogies between himself and Yin Jifu, and between Chong'er and the virtuous Zhang Zhong. Zhao Cui, however, seizes the opportunity to redefine the meaning of "The Sixth Month" as Lord Mu's "gift" to Chong'er, his recognition of Chong'er as the leader who can "assist the Son of Heaven." He is referring to the end of the second stanza: "By royal command we are going to battle, / To assist the Son of Heaven." At this point Chong'er is but an itinerant prince seeking Qin's support for his claim to the Jin throne; by bowing to accept the "gift," he hopes to formalize Qin's assistance and recognition. The "cultured" Zhao Cui is adept at fashioning symbols; he turns the Qin ruler's general exhortation for common endeavor (or even self-praise) into an omen of Chong'er's greatness.

The omen is fulfilled two years later. One year after the *fushi* episode, the Zhou king is driven from the Zhou capital (*Zuo* Xi 24.2, 1:380–385 [636 BCE]) by his younger brother Dai, who has adulterous relations with the queen (a Di woman) and whose rebellion is fueled by Di troops. (Di is traditionally identified as one of the barbarian groups.) In the same year, Chong'er enters Jin and becomes the Jin ruler, posthumously honored as Lord Wen. After consolidating his position in Jin, Lord Wen comes to the assistance of the beleaguered Zhou king, defeats the Di forces, kills Dai, and reinstates the king in the Zhou capital (*Zuo* Xi 25.2, 1:388–391 [635 BCE]). This lays the foundation of his claim to become overlord. These developments seem to warrant the comparison of Lord Wen to Yin Jifu in "Sixth Month"; both are defending Zhou against barbarian incursions. (This may in fact be the reason why the anecdote about this poetic exchange is told in the first place.)

Closer inspection reveals a more complex and tangled scenario. Qin and Jin are vying for the role of the king's defender. Qin forces are stationed at the Yellow River, ready to assist the king, when the Jin ruler "declined the support of Qin troops and went down the river" (*Zuo* Xi 25.2, 1:390–391 [635 BCE]). According to Sima Qian's (ca. 145–86? BCE) *Records of the Historian* (*Shiji* 5.190), Lord Mu of Qin and Lord Wen of Jin join forces to defend the Zhou king, but the *Zuo* account points to their implicit competition. In some ways, Qin-Jin competition is already encoded in the *fushi* episode two years earlier.

In both "The Sixth Month" and the *Zuo* account, the restoration of order is premised on driving out barbarian invaders. Again, the actual boundaries and relations between central domains and barbarian domains are rather more complicated. The Zhou king marries a Di woman out of gratitude for Di's assistance in a punitive campaign against Zheng, a "brother domain" sharing the same clan name (*Zuo* Xi 24.2, 1:380–385 [636 BCE]). According to *Discourses*, Lord Wen of Jin succeeds in reinstating the Zhou king because of help from barbarians in the east (*Guoyu* Jinyu 4.5, 373). Indeed, the very model of central domains flanked by barbarian domains on the periphery does not do justice to the extent of admixture of peoples in this period. Three years before the *fushi* episode, "Qin and Jin moved the Rong of Luhun to River Yi" (*Zuo* Xi 22.4, 1:352–353 [638 BCE])—the Rong is moved from the northwestern territories of Qin and Jin to the environs of the Zhou capital, from "outside" to "inside." The proximity of the Rong is to pose a great threat for Zhou. In other words, the *fushi* episode, retroactively cast as an omen of Chong'er's greatness, proposes a vision of order (based on purgation of barbarians) that glosses over or suppresses compromises and conflicts of interests.

Zhao Cui's hastening to define the meaning of "The Sixth Month" dramatizes how a message about worthy purpose can be accepted yet manipulated. The opposite process, whereby one side articulates ambition through a poem only to be thwarted by a "counter poem," also appears in *Zuo*. One example is the exchange between a Chu prince (Gongzi Wei) and a Jin leader (Zhao Wu) in a meeting at Guo (in Zheng) in 541 BCE. During this gathering, "Gongzi Wei offered Zhao Wu a ceremonial toast and recited the first stanza of 'Great Brightness.' Zhao Wu recited the second stanza of 'Lesser'" (*Zuo* Zhao 1.3, 3:1312–1313 [541 BCE]). "Great Brightness" ("Daming," Mao no. 236) is one of six poems in the *Poetry* that tell of the rise of Zhou and of the Zhou conquest of Shang (ca. eleventh century BCE). Its first stanza, however, describes the challenges of kingship and the decline of Shang:

	Great brightness below,	明明在下
2	Blazing glory above.	赫赫在上
	Hard it is to trust in heaven,	天難忱斯
4	It is not easy to be king.	不易維王
	Heaven puts in place the heir of Yin,	天位殷適
6	And pries from him four sides of the realm.	使不挾四方

[*MSZY* 2:540]

According to Du Yu, Gongzi Wei is presumptuously "glorifying himself" as one comparable to King Wen of Zhou (r. 1099–1050 BCE), whose majesty and glory are praised in the first two lines. Since the stanza also refers to the unreliability of heaven's command and the fall of the last Shang king, Gongzi Wei may also be hinting at his ambition to usurp the Chu throne—his coup transpires a few months later (*Zuo* Zhao 1.13, 3:1332–1335 [541 BCE]). Instead of acceding to Gongzi Wei's use of Shang's decline to bask in the glory of Zhou's founding or to assert a bid for power, Zhao Wu reworks and elaborates the theme of uncertain mandate in "Great Brightness" and turns the perils of kingship into a warning for Gongzi Wei by reciting the second stanza of "Lesser" ("Xiaoyuan," Mao no. 196):

	The wise and worthy among men,	人之齊聖
8	Exercise restraint even as they drink.	飲酒溫克
	The benighted ones know nothing,	彼昏不知
10	Become drunk, and take in ever more.	壹醉日富

Let each be vigilant about his bearing,	各敬爾儀
12 Heaven's mandate does not come twice.	天命不又

[MSZY 2:419]

The Mao commentary identifies this poem as a minister's critique of the excesses of King You (r. 781–771 BCE). Zhu Xi disagrees and characterizes this as "a poem about officials who come upon the disorder of their times. Brothers caution each other so as to escape disaster."[14] The actual context of "brotherly admonition" may be open to debate, but there is little doubt that "Lesser" is a response to political turmoil. Images of disorder indeed dominate this poem. The second stanza describes how drunkenness imperils the claim to authority. Zhao Wu seems to be turning inebriation into a metaphor for all kinds of heedless excesses, thereby cautioning Gongzi Wei against the hubristic vision of emerging as the ultimate victor. Political ascendancy of one group must entail the decline and fall of another—Zhao Wu is urging Gongzi Wei to switch from self-congratulation to self-questioning, to ask whether he could be on the wrong side of history if "heaven's mandate is not constant." "Lesser" is one of four poems in the Xiaoya (lesser odes) section of *Poetry* that have the word *xiao* (little, lesser) in its title. The other three are "Lesser Heaven" ("Xiaomin," Mao no. 195), "Lesser Joy" ("Xiaopan," Mao no. 197), and "Lesser Brightness" ("Xiaoming," Mao no. 207). They all deal with the dislocation and sufferings of individuals in the context of political decline or familial conflicts. "Lesser" concludes with these lines: "Vigilant and careful, / As if coming to an abyss. / Fearful and wary, / As if treading on thin ice."[15] If Gongzi Wei is asserting ambitions for himself and for Chu, Zhao Wu is cautioning him to curb them.

The broader context of this poetic exchange is the struggle for power between Jin and Chu. Despite Zhao Wu's adept response in seeking to restrain Gongzi Wei's ambition, Jin is in fact powerless to counter Chu's bid to become the leader of the covenant in the mid-sixth century BCE. After the meeting, Zhao Wu analyzes the situation with another Jin minister, Shuxiang. Shuxiang predicts that the overreaching Gongzi Wei will prevail in the short run and Chu will eclipse Jin, but also that Gongzi Wei will eventually come to a disastrous end. "One who is unjust but strong is sure to meet a speedy death. As it says in the *Poetry*, 'Gloriously blazing was the ancestral Zhou: / Bao Si destroyed it'" (Zhao 1.3, 3:1312–1313 [541 BCE]).

Shuxiang is citing lines from "First Month" ("Zhengyue," Mao no. 192) to explain the inevitable demise of miscreant rulers. The evil queen Bao Si could bring down Zhou because she abetted King You of Zhou (r. 782–771 BCE) in indulging in excess. King You was later forced to abdicate.[16] (The emotional focus of "First Month" is the lamentation of the speaker, who is maligned, misunderstood, and unable to turn the tide of Zhou decline, but Shuxiang singles out the lines that pronounce Zhou's downfall from a more objective perspective.) Shuxiang offers a morally compelling explanation, but it is also used to hide the fact that Jin is powerless to intervene and has to let Gongzi Wei (later King Ling of Chu, r. 540–529 BCE) pave the way for his own downfall through the momentum of "accumulating transgressions." This is the first of many predictions of Gongzi Wei's demise, which will come about twelve years later (*Zuo* Zhao 13.2, 3:1488–1501 [529 BCE]).

In both *fushi* episodes (the poetic exchange between Lord Mu of Qin and Zhao Cui, and that between Gongzi Wei and Zhao Wu), separated by almost a century, contending political visions articulated through the recited poems determine the contours of power struggles. Whereas many *fushi* episodes in *Zuo Tradition* emphasize shared goals and mutual understanding, our examples here derive their momentum from "creative misinterpretation." Both Zhao Cui and his great grandson Zhao Wu impose limits on their respective counterparts through their deliberate misreading of their partners' intentions. For both Jin statesmen, *fushi* is also a kind of rhetorical compensation for actual weakness, with the difference that Jin glory lies ahead in the first story but has become a receding memory in the second one. Zhao Cui seizes the moment for his master Chong'er, turning "Sixth Month" into an omen of Chong'er's eventual greatness, despite his uncertain prospects at the moment of recitation. Zhao Wu for his part issues a moral warning to the overreaching Gongzi Wei by reciting "Lesser." In doing so, he seems to be making up for Jin weakness with his cultural competence. The political implications of this position will be further explored in the next section.

RITUAL PROPRIETY AND POLITICAL EFFICACY

In the examples given, cultural competence in reciting the *Poetry* is instrumental for asserting or resisting hegemonic ambitions. It is possible, however, to have a scenario whereby apparently seamless communication through skills in reciting or interpreting the *Poetry* masks betrayal or political failure, as when the aforementioned Zhao Wu meets the Lu minister Shusun Bao and the Zheng minister Han Hu shortly after his exchange with Gongzi Wei. In this gathering hosted by Zheng, Zhao Wu indicates his wish for a simple reception by reciting "Gourd Leaves" ("Hu ye," Mao no. 231), and the ministers of Lu and Zheng comply. Later, these ministers negotiate expectations with Zhao Wu through the exchanges of poems.

> Shusun Bao recited "Magpie's Nest." Zhao Wu said, "I am not worthy." Shusun Bao then recited "Picking Artemisia," saying, "The small domain is the artemisia. The great domain cherishes it and uses it sparingly. Can we fail to receive what you issue as anything but a command?" Han Hu recited the last stanza of "There Is a Dead Doe in the Wilds," and Zhao Wu recited "Plum Tree," saying, "If we brothers join together for peace, then we can keep the dog from howling." Shusun Bao, Han Hu, and the Cao high officer rose, bowed, raised their buffalo-horn goblets, and said, "The small domains rely upon you and know that they will be delivered from violence." They drank and made merry. When Zhao Wu exited, he said, "Never again am I to take such pleasure."
>
> [ZUO ZHAO 1.4, 3:1312–1315 (541 BCE)]

"Gourd Leaves" describes a simple feast. It begins with the image of picking and boiling gourd leaves. A rabbit is roasted, and the "noble men" drink in amity. The rhythm of pouring and tasting wine and of how host and guest honor each other suggests a single toast. Commentators discuss regulations for the number of toasts appropriate in entertaining guests of different ranks, as stated in ritual texts. According to Du Yu, five is the correct number for the minister of a great domain, and thus would be appropriate for Zhao Wu. Zhao Wu's request for a single toast can be interpreted as exemplary modesty. In political terms, however, this may mean that Jin is making less onerous demands on the smaller and weaker domains, as is indeed Zhao Wu's policy (*Zuo* Xiang 25.7, 2:1148–1149 [548 BCE]). Yet even as the smaller domains like Zheng and Lu fear an overbearing Jin, they also dread Jin's weakness and consequent failure to protect them from other aggressors, in this case Chu. To his audience, Zhao Wu's recitation of "Gourd Leaves" may thus seem to be a disquieting retreat from Jin's responsibility.

In this context, the Lu minister Shusun Bao's recitation of "Magpie's Nest" ("Que chao," Mao no. 12) seems to be an appeal to Jin to live up to its role as protector.[17] Most modern commentators consider this poem an epithalamium.

	The magpie has a nest,	維鵲有巢
2	But the cuckoo stays in it.	維鳩居之
	This girl is going to her mate's home,	之子于歸
4	A hundred carriages welcome her.	百兩御之
	The magpie has a nest,	維鵲有巢
6	But the cuckoo owns it.	維鳩方之
	This girl is going to her mate's home,	之子于歸
8	A hundred carriages escort her.	百兩將之
	The magpie has a nest,	維鵲有巢
10	But the cuckoo fills it.	維鳩盈之
	This girl is going to her mate's home,	之子于歸
12	A hundred carriages complete the ceremony.	百兩成之

[*MSZY* 2:46]

Later idiomatic usage turns the image of the cuckoo taking over the magpie's nest (*que chao jiu zhan*) into a metaphor for usurpation or intrusion, but there is little doubt that in its locus classicus this is an affective image that invokes associations with the bride entering her new home; it has no negative meanings. Shusun Bao is comparing himself and Lu to the cuckoo that needs a refuge, Zhao Wu and Jin to the magpie extending hospitality. Zhao Wu claims that he "is not worthy," because the implicit reference to marriage would place Jin in the superior position of a husband providing a home. As we shall see, the use of metaphors from courtship and marriage to negotiate power relations dominates this diplomatic occasion. Indeed, similar examples abound in *Zuo*.

As if to press the point, Shusun Bao recites "Picking Artemisia" ("Cai fan," Mao no. 13; ☞ *HTRCP* C1.9) and provides his own exegesis.

	Where does she pick artemisia?	于以采蘩
2	At the pool, at the pond.	于沼于沚
	For what will it be used?	于以用之
4	For the affairs of lords and princes.	公侯之事
	Where does she pick artemisia?	于以采蘩
6	In the middle of the stream.	于澗之中
	Where will it be used?	于以用之
8	At the temple of lords and princes.	公侯之宮

	With her hairpiece piled high,	被之僮僮
10	Day and night she is at the lord's hall.	夙夜在公
	With her hairpiece resplendent,	被之祁祁
12	She makes her way back.	薄言還歸

[MSZY 2:47]

Most commentators agree that the "affairs" in line four refer to sacrifices—the lady in the poem gathers humble plants to prepare for an august ritual that will take place in the ancestral hall or temple, and she does so with dignity and assiduity. How might this have been understood?

Following the gender analogy of "Magpie's Nest," this could have been interpreted as the dedication of a lesser domain (Lu) in serving a greater one (Jin) with ritual propriety. Shusun Bao, however, supplies his particular, corrective reading: "The small domain is the artemisia. The great domain cherishes it and uses it sparingly." Instead of being a simple profession of loyalty, it is another injunction that Jin should treat smaller domains with extreme care, "using" them sparingly and only for ritually proper purpose. If this condition is fulfilled, then Jin's allies will be willing to heed its every command. Yang Bojun notes that this is the only instance of someone "reciting a poem and supplying his own interpretation" (*zifu zijie*) in *Zuo* (*CQZZZ* 4:1209). Shusun Bao does so precisely because the other plausible reading would simply draw a parallel between Lu and the girl picking artemisia and flatter Jin with unconditional allegiance.

The Zheng minister Han Hu continues the feminine role or perspective developed in "Magpie's Nest" and "Picking Artemisia" by reciting the last stanza of "There Is a Dead Doe in the Wilds" ("Ye you sijun," Mao no. 23).

	There is a dead doe in the wilds,	野有死麕
2	White rushes wrap it.	白茅包之
	There is a girl longing for spring,	有女懷春
4	A fine man shows her the way.	吉士誘之
	There are oak and elm branches in the wood,	林有樸樕
6	There is a dead deer in the wilds.	野有死鹿
	White rushes bound and wrap it,	白茅純束
8	There is a girl just like jade.	有女如玉
	Slowly! Gently!	舒而脫脫兮
10	Do not ruffle my kerchief!	無感我帨兮
	Do not make the dog howl!	無使尨也吠

[MSZY 2:65]

The probable context for this poem has been construed variously as a successful or failed seduction, courtship, or marriage proposal. Depending on this context, the dead doe or deer wrapped in white rushes can be a gift of courtship or betrothal or it can be a metaphor for the "covering up" of lost innocence. All agree, however, that the speaker of the last stanza is the girl. Is her admonition serious, forbidding, playful, timid, or anxious? Du Yu interprets Han Hu's intent thus:

> This takes up the meaning that the noble man should approach slowly, abiding by ritual propriety. Do not make me lose integrity (or chastity) or startle the dog into barking: this is an analogy meaning that Zhao Wu should soothe the allies with a sense of proper duty. He is not to resort to ritual impropriety to impose on them.
>
> [ZZZY 4:701]

However, it is likely that the metaphor of "proper courtship" applies not only to Jin but also to Chu. (Throughout most of the period covered by *Zuo*, Zheng is hard pressed by both Jin and Chu and often becomes the proxy whereby Jin and Chu fight for supremacy.)

That seems to be the way Zhao Wu understands this as well. He recites "Plum Tree" ("Tang di," Mao no. 164), which celebrates brotherhood. The poem dwells on how danger and crisis draw brothers together: "The fear of death and mourning, / Makes brothers long for each other"; "The waterfowl is on the plain: / Brothers relieve the plight of each other"; "Brothers may quarrel within the walls, / But outside they fend off insults." The bond between brothers is also celebrated through a feast in the poem: "Set forth your food stands, / Drink wine to your fill."[18] The emphasis here is on how the "brother domains" (Jin, Lu, Zheng, and Cao share the clan name Ji and are related to the Zhou house by kinship ties) should join together to fend off outside threats. "If we brothers join together for peace, then we can keep the dog from howling" (Zhao 1.4, 3:1314–1315 [541 BCE]). If Jin confirms its alliance with the smaller domains, then it can keep Chu—the howling dog—at bay.

The feast apparently concludes with mutual understanding and perfect accord. Yet the account also ends on a note of foreboding. Zhao Wu declares that he will not experience such a pleasurable gathering again. This is one of several clues about his impending death—he dies eight months after the meeting with Lu and Zheng ministers (*Zuo* Zhao 1.15, 3:1334–1335). In the passages pertaining to Zhao Wu in *Zuo*, ritual expertise and political weakness are intertwined. As chief minister in Jin from 548 to 541 BCE, Zhao Wu's main goal is to achieve peace between Jin and Chu, yet this process, given a veneer of diplomatic finesse by Zhao Wu's skillful *fushi*, coincides with Jin's decline and inability to protect its allies. Zhao Wu has an excellent command of textual and ritual traditions—perhaps that is why his posthumous honorific is "Wenzi." As mentioned above, *wen* means "cultivation" or "culture" and implies mastery of ritual and textual traditions.

Besides the aforementioned episodes, Zhao Wu's competence in *fushi* is also evident in his meeting with seven Zheng ministers, whom he asks to recite poems so that "he can observe the seven fine men's aspirations" (*Zuo* Xiang 27.5, 2:1200–1203 [546 BCE]). His perceptive decoding of their political ambitions and accurate predictions are borne out by later events. This exchange takes place during the Covenant of Song (546 BCE), an attempt to negotiate cessation of conflicts between Jin and Chu. Zhao Wu's quest for peace is inseparable from his belief in the powers of words embodying cultural and ritual knowledge: "If we respectfully fulfill ritual propriety, and open the way with fine words of cultivation, thereby calming the princes, then military conflicts can be made to abate" (*Zuo* Xiang 25.7, 2:1148–1149 [548 BCE]).

Yet, from the beginning, the peace process is marred by the self-interest and mutual suspicions of the parties involved. Chu's assertiveness means that the laudable goal of halting conflict merely hides

Jin decline. Jin yields to Chu the position of de facto covenant chief, a status that will become evident in the gatherings of princes at Guo in 541 BCE (*Zuo* Zhao 1, 3:1302–1335 [541 BCE]), one of the occasions for *fushi* discussed earlier. Confucius is said to consider the Covenant of Song an occasion "replete with many fine words of cultivation" (*Zuo* Xiang 27.4b, 2:1194–1195 [546 BCE]). He notes the wealth of elaborate phrases in the diplomatic ritual, but its narrative context is the mutual suspicion of Jin and Chu.

Commentators differ as to whether Confucius is expressing praise or criticism. Considering the fact that the covenant does not lead to lasting peace and brings no tangible benefits, Confucius may indeed be voicing implicit criticism. The Covenant of Song only heightens the burden of court visits and offerings for the smaller domains, which are now required to send ministers to attend the courts not only of their protectors but also of their protectors' respective rivals. Song, the domain hosting the covenant, obtains no relief in the wake of its disastrous fire, despite empty pledges (*Zuo* Xiang 30.12, 2:1266–1269 [543 BCE]). Jin decline finds a palpable symbol in its chief minister Zhao Wu: for all his cultural competence, his words are said to be "torpid" (*Zuo* Xiang 31.1, 2:1272–1273 [542 BCE]). The self-exegesis and negotiations of meanings in the *fushi* episode cited earlier may thus betray awareness of the tension between ritual propriety and political efficacy or, more precisely, the suspicion that ritual propriety unsupported by political efficacy ultimately may be futile.

* * *

According to Ban Gu, the end of *fushi* marks the beginning of a new kind of poetry:

> After the Spring and Autumn Era, the way of Zhou gradually breaks down. Singing or reciting poems during diplomatic visits was no longer practiced among the various domains. Scholars learned in the *Poetry* found obscurity among commoners, and poetic expositions were created by worthy men whose will was thwarted. There were the great Confucian scholar Xun Qing (Xunzi) and the Chu minister Qu Yuan who encountered sorrow and felt anguish about his domain—both composed poetry to convey criticism. Their works all encompass the spirit of empathy like the poetry of ancient times.
>
> [*HANSHU*, 30.1756]

Political engagement by way of expressing discontent and lamentation is followed by excessive rhetoric: from late Warring States to Han, court poets "vied to create extravagant, ornate, grandiose, and overflowing phrases, losing the purpose of critique and instruction" (*Hanshu* 30.1756).

Irrespective of the historical accuracy of Ban Gu's account, it posits a compelling paradigm. *Fushi* is the seamless mergence of poetry and politics; perhaps the mergence is made possible by the way function displaces authorial intention as the prime focus. Once this real or imagined optimal moment recedes, however, poetry and politics may become too close or too far apart. We either regard disempowerment and alienation as the genesis of poetry (by far the more influential model) or consider poetry as being so embedded in the power structure that any articulation of critique or frustration is bound to be muted and indirect.

WAI-YEE LI

NOTES

1. All translations in this essay are mine.
2. The exceptions are Lady Mu of Xu and Mu Jiang, wife of Lord Xuan of Lu. The received text of *Zuo Tradition* is arranged chronologically, year by year, according to the reigns of twelve rulers of Lu. Citation in this chapter follows (or slightly modifies) *Zuo Tradition/Zuozhuan: Commentary on the "Spring and Autumn Annals,"* translated and annotated by Stephen Durrant, Wai-yee Li, and David Schaberg. For Lady Mu of Xu's composition of the poem "I Gallop" ("Zai chi," Mao no. 54), see *Zuo* Min 2.5b, 1:240–241, 637 BCE (i.e., entry 5b in the second year of Lord Min of Lu, vol. 1, 240–241). For Mu Jiang's recitation of the poem "Green Coat" ("Lüyi," Mao no. 27), see *Zuo* Xiang 9.5, 2:778–779, 582 BCE.
3. This version of "articulating intent" (*yanzhi*) is thus not about realizing intent through creating a poem but about using a poem for the purpose of self-revelation or communication.
4. See *Zuo* Xiang 27.2, 2:1188–1189 (546 BCE); 28.9e, 2:1224–1225 (545 BCE).
5. See *Zuo* Xiang 16.1, 2:1038–1039 (557 BCE).
6. See *Zuo* Wen 4.7, 1:484–485 (623 BCE); Xiang 4.3, 2:910–911 (569 BCE).
7. A Qi retainer, Lupu Gui, justifies his violation of the taboo against marrying someone with the same clan name: "Just as one breaks off stanzas when reciting the poems, I take what I seek. What do I know about common ancestors?" (*Zuo* Xiang 28.9, 2:1218–1219 [545 BCE]). Self-interest that overrides taboos is compared to the practice of breaking off stanzas to create meanings that fit the occasion during the recitation of poems. This indicates an awareness of how a poem can be used in different ways and an understanding of the gap between the performed and "originally intended" meanings of the poems.
8. We are giving the numbering according to the Mao Tradition of the *Poetry* (*Mao shi zhuan*), the received version of the anthology.
9. *Zuo* Xi 30.3, 1:434–435 (630 BCE); Xi 33.1, 33.3, 1:441–451 (627 BCE).
10. For other examples of the barbarian's mastery of ritual tradition and esoteric knowledge, see *Zuo* Xi 29.4, 1:430–431 (631 BCE); Zhao 17.3, 3:1544–1545 (525 BCE).
11. See Li Ling, *Shang bo Chu jian san pian jiaodu ji* (*Essays on Collating and Annotating Three Texts from the Shanghai Museum Chu Bamboo Strips*) (Beijing: Zhongguo renmin daxue chubanshe, 2007), 21, 148.
12. On this phenomenon, see David Keightley, "Clean Hands and Shining Helmets: Heroic Action in Early Chinese and Greek Culture," in *Religion and the Authority of the Past*, ed. Tobin Siebers (Ann Arbor: University of Michigan Press, 1993), 13–51.
13. Sima Qian identifies the Xianyun as one of the ancestors of the Xiongnu (*Shiji* 110.2879). Liu Xin also claims the Xianyun and the Xiongnu shared the same lineage (*Hanshu* 73.3125).
14. Zhu Xi, *Shi ji zhuan* (Nanjing: Fenghuang chubanshe, 2007), 160.
15. The final lines of "Xiao min" are very similar. Those lines are quoted in *Zuo* Xi 22.7, 1:354–355 (638 BCE); *Zuo* Xuan 16.1, 2:684–685 (593 BCE).
16. Their story is told in *Guoyu*, Zhengyu, 519; *Shiji* 4.147–149.
17. Shortly before this meeting, Zhao Wu intercedes with Chu and secures the release of Shusun Bao, whom Chu leaders arrested because they disapproved of Lu aggression against the small domain Ju (*Zuo* Zhao 1.2, 3:1308–1311 [541 BCE]). Shusun Bao may be reciting this poem in gratitude. In his mediatory efforts, however, Zhao Wu appeals to Chu as the leader of the covenant. Despite his success, Jin comes out as the weaker partner.
18. The Mao commentary reads *yu* as an informal feast where the guests would be more at ease: "Drink wine at this feast of ease."

PRIMARY SOURCES

Analects	*Lunyu yizhu* 論語譯註 (The *Analects*, with Translation into Modern Chinese and Annotations). Compiled by Yang Bojun 楊伯峻. Beijing: Zhonghua shuju, 2006.
CQZZZ	*Chunqiu Zuozhuan zhu* 春秋左傳注 (*Zuo Tradition* of the *Spring and Autumn Annals*, with Annotations). Compiled by Yang Bojun. 4 vols. Beijing: Zhonghua shuju, 2000 [1981].
Guoyu	*Guoyu* 國語 (Discourses of the States). Edited by Shanghai shifan daxue Guji zhengli zu 上海師範大學古籍整理組. Shanghai: Shanghai guji chubanshe, 1978.
Hanshu	Ban Gu 班固. *Xinjiao ben Hanshu jizhu* 新校本漢書集註 (Newly Collated Edition of *History of the Former Han*, with Collected Commentaries). Commentary by Yan Shigu 顏師古. Taipei: Dingwen shuju, 1986.
Mengzi	*Mengzi yizhu* 孟子譯註 (*Mencius*, with Translation into Modern Chinese and Annotations). Compiled by Yang Bojun. Hong Kong: Zhonghua shuju, 1984.
MSZY	*Mao shi zhengyi* 毛詩正義 (Correct Meanings of the Mao Text of the *Book of Poetry*). In *Chongkan Song ben Shisanjing zhushu fu jiaokan ji* 重刊宋本十三經註疏附校勘記 (Reproduction of the Song Edition of Commentaries and Subcommentaries on the Thirteen Classics, with Editorial Notes), compiled by Ruan Yuan 阮元 (1764–1849). 8 vols. Taipei: Yiwen yinshu guan, 1965.
Shiji	Sima Qian 司馬遷. *Xinjiao ben Shiji sanjia zhu* 新校本史記三家註 (Newly Collated Edition of *Records of the Historian*, with Three Commentaries). Commentaries by Pei Yin 裴駰, Sima Zhen 司馬貞, and Zhang Shoujie 張守節. Taipei: Dingwen shuju, 1981.
Zuo	*Zuo Tradition* (*Zuozhuan*): Commentary on the *Spring and Autumn Annals*. Translated and annotated by Stephen Durrant, Wai-yee Li, and David Schaberg. Bilingual edition. 3 vols. Seattle: University of Washington Press, 2016.
ZZZY	*Chunqiu Zuozhuan zhengyi* 春秋左傳正義 (Correct Meanings of *Zuo Tradition* of the *Spring and Autumn Annals*). In *Chongkan Song ben Shisanjing zhushu fu jiaokan ji*.

SUGGESTED READINGS

ENGLISH

Li, Wai-yee. *The Readability of the Past in Early Chinese Historiography*. Cambridge, MA: Harvard University Asia Center, 2007.

Schaberg, David. *A Patterned Past: Form and Thought in Early Chinese Historiography*. Cambridge, MA: Harvard University Asia Center, 2001.

Van Zoeren, Stephen. *Poetry and Personality: Reading, Exegesis, and Hermeneutics in Traditional China*. Stanford, CA: Stanford University Press, 1991.

CHINESE

Fu Daobin 傅道彬. *Shi keyi guan: liyue wenhua yu Zhoudai shixue jingshen* 詩可以觀: 禮樂文化與周代詩學精神 (The Poetry Can Be Used to Observe Mores: The Culture of Ritual and Music and the Spirit of Zhou Poetry). Beijing: Zhonghua shuju, 2010.

Mao Zhenhua 毛振華. *Zuozhuan fushi yanjiu* 左傳賦詩研究 (A Study of the Recitation of Poetry in *Zuozhuan*). Shanghai: Shanghai guji chubanshe, 2011.

Zhang Suqing 張素卿. *Zuozhuan chengshi yanjiu* 左傳稱詩研究 (A Study of the Uses of the Poetry in *Zuozhuan*). Taipei: Taiwan daxue chubanshe, 1991.

❀ 2 ❀

POETRY AND AUTHORSHIP

The *Songs of Chu* (*Chuci*)

The *Songs of Chu* (*Chuci*) is an anthology of poetry whose final version was compiled and annotated by Wang Yi (Eastern Han) around the turn of the second century but whose contents stretch from works by Wang Yi himself back to perhaps the fourth century BCE. Some contemporary scholars, trying to examine the evidence afresh, are uncertain what some of these poems are, when they were composed, and what they "mean." From the last century BCE on to the vast majority of contemporary East Asian scholars, there has been complete certainty about who wrote these poems and what they mean. There are local disputes about authorship and dating, but these occur on a background of shared premises. If we ask about their place in a literary culture, perhaps the best period to consider is the Han, when those now ossified premises were taking shape.

Many of the earliest poems and some of the clearly Han works invoke religious practices of the southern part of the Han Empire, the old kingdom of Chu. The Han court itself engaged in such religious practices, but these were not fully understood and often were despised by the literate elite of the Han court. In other words, we have the works of the *Chuci* as they entered a profoundly different intellectual climate, in which they needed a new context to make them comprehensible.

As the "meaning" of the poems of the *Book of Poetry* (*Shijing*) came to be dependent on the intentions of a putative editor, Confucius, so this body of southern poetry came to be dependent on an author, Qu Yuan, with all the works in the anthology attributed either to him, to supposed "disciples" like Song Yu, or to Han imitators. Without an author, no one would have known what to make of these poems; Qu Yuan as a historical person, whose experiences in the Chu court were the reason for composing his poems, was central to their Han interpretation. That need shaped the gradual formation of the story of Qu Yuan as much as the story of Qu Yuan shaped the new interpretation of the poems.

The story of Qu Yuan's life took shape gradually through the Han—indeed many central details of his life are still hotly contested. New attributions over the course of the first century BCE forced alterations in the biography, even as the interpretation of those poems was in turn shaped by the biography.

I will not venture dates for Qu Yuan, except to say that he was supposed to have lived in the last half of the fourth century BCE and may have lived into the early third century BCE. Qu Yuan does not appear in the extant historical record until about a century and half after his death. In the canonical account in Sima Qian's (ca. 145–ca. 85 BCE) *Records of the Historian* (*Shiji*), composed around the turn of the first century BCE, Qu Yuan's story is tied to the story of the brilliant young intellectual Jia Yi (200–168 BCE), who enjoyed a meteoric rise through the favor of the Han Emperor Wen (r. 180–157

BCE). Jia Yi soon incurred strong opposition from senior officials, who criticized him to the emperor. His fall was as meteoric as his rise: he was sent off to be tutor for the prince of Changsha, a place near the then southern border of the Han, which must have seemed the last outpost of civilization in the jungle (Guangdong was not conquered until 111 BCE). There, in roughly 174 BCE, he heard the story of Qu Yuan, an aristocrat of the pre-Qin kingdom of Chu (an inference from his surname, Qu), who had been slandered and had drowned himself in the Miluo River.

Jia Yi's "Lament for Qu Yuan" ("Diao Qu Yuan fu") gives no specifics about when Qu Yuan's suicide occurred or the circumstances leading up to it; it does not even say that he was banished. Qu Yuan is represented simply as a good man slandered and rejected, while the worst men flourished. Jia Yi was clearly speaking indirectly of his own case as much as he was about Qu Yuan's. The problem was that Qu Yuan's archetypal story came at last to suicide, a point where Jia Yi, still quite young, wanted alternatives. The second half of the "Lament" offers such an alternative: leaving the public world and living in isolation. For several centuries after this beginning, where Qu Yuan appears, the troubling question of his suicide is often close at hand.

Jia Yi refers to the story of Qu Yuan, but he does not mention any literary works by him. At one point he cites a version of a line now found in the coda of *Encountering Misery* (*Li Sao*), which suggests he heard some version of that work, but he does not mention it by name. The name and text of *Li Sao* appear in history about forty years later, in the 130s BCE, when the young Emperor Wu (r. 141–87 BCE) ordered his uncle Liu An (179–122 BCE), prince of Huainan, to write a prose account of *Li Sao*; this was almost certainly the moment the written text entered the imperial library. Only one paragraph survives that we can be certain comes from Liu An's account, and that paragraph does not mention exile.

Qu Yuan had been an aristocrat in the pre-Qin kingdom of Chu, centered in modern Hubei. The kingdom had grown to rule the land on either side of the Yangzi River all the way to the Pacific. Through political and military bungling, Chu gradually lost its territory to Qin, which eventually founded the first empire. When Qin conquered the old Chu capital of Ying (in modern Hubei), the kingdom moved east, finally establishing its capital in Shouchun, which would later become the capital of the Han principality of Huainan, ruled by Liu An. In other words, Liu An was ruling a territory with the last memories of Chu court culture. It seems likely that it was Liu An who introduced *Li Sao* to the Han court, most likely through a recitation, but accompanied by a text written out for deposit in the imperial library. There was a copy of *Li Sao* in the library later in Emperor Wu's reign, when it was read by Sima Qian, who was continuing a project begun by his father to write a history of China up to Emperor Wu's time.

Jia Yi's "Lament for Qu Yuan" echoed Jia Yi's own experience of slander and the consequent loss of imperial favor, but we have Jia Yi's own history and his "Lament," along with Qu Yuan's story, only because they were included in Sima Qian's history as a double biography. Both stories echoed Sima Qian's own experience, in which the loss of the ruler's favor, leading possibly to suicide, had a special resonance. Sima Qian, too, had suffered great injustice from Emperor Wu. Enraged by Sima Qian's defense of a defeated frontier general, Emperor Wu had ordered Sima Qian castrated, which was implicitly an invitation to commit suicide. Sima Qian had, instead, accepted the punishment in order to complete his history. As someone with such a background, his history was not simply a dry narrative but contained Sima Qian's own personal judgments and responses to figures from the past.

Sima Qian was, indeed, an "author" in a new sense, with a writing project that lasted many years. By his personal investment in the project—to the point of enduring humiliating punishment to complete it—he defined himself as an author. Without the book he left behind, there would be nothing particularly noteworthy about his life to deserve being remembered. It is not surprising that in his book Sima Qian returned again and again to figures who were not very important in the grand sweep of early Chinese political history but who suffered unjustly and composed memorable texts that expressed their suffering. In this process, Qu Yuan became an author, memorable because of the poetry he composed, which was in turn itself memorable because of his experiences.

The problem is that, from our very scant sources from before Sima Qian, it is not at all clear what Qu Yuan's experiences were. Indeed, when we read Sima Qian's biography of Qu Yuan, we see that Sima Qian, too, was having problems finding specifics. Sima Qian believed firmly that the life of an individual was meaningful through history, and he needed to find Qu Yuan in the historical record. Without going into the complex scholarly issues, we can simply say that Sima Qian identified Qu Yuan with a Chu courtier named Qu Ping, who seems to have played a minor role in a historically dubious narrative about the then famous political rhetorician Zhang Yi (?–310 BCE) and who seems to have suffered royal displeasure similar to what Qu Yuan's *Li Sao* described.

Here we might pause. The speaker in *Li Sao* gives no specifics. He does tell us the two names, given to him by his father—Zhengze (Upright Standard) and Lingjun (Holy Poise)—neither of which is Yuan or Ping. Commentators have standard explanations for this and other obvious anomalies, but there remain questions that require commentarial intervention. The speaker in the *Li Sao* was very much a mythic figure, and he remained something of a mythic figure in Jia Yi's "Lament." Part of Sima Qian's great historical work was taking all the myths and legends of China's past and locating them on a unified historical field with a specific historical context—in modern terms, translating them from "myth" into "history." A reading of *Li Sao* at the time it was composed might have yielded very different understandings of the text, but Sima Qian tied the poem to a historical author at a critical moment in the history of Chu, and whether this was true or not, Sima Qian's historicized Qu Yuan shaped the reading of the text ever thereafter. As the corpus of poems attributed to Qu Yuan grew, so the "author" grew in experience, which in turn became part of the understanding of those poems.

Sima Qian tells us that Qu Yuan initially lost favor through court rivalries, which we know from the *Li Sao* itself. Beyond that, everything is context. New variations on Qu Yuan's story continued to be introduced, so it is hard to tell the context as a single story. The improbable political follies of King Huai of Chu (?–296 BCE) have survived in large measure through the dubious narrative of Zhang Yi's power to persuade kings (notably King Huai) to do foolish things to the advantage of his true employer (Qin). Setting aside the reasons why political decisions were made, the large events in which the Qu Yuan story was set were general historical knowledge: Qin was expanding; Chu attacked Qin, with disastrous results; Chu undertook a general mobilization; Qin promised a treaty and tricked King Huai into a position in which he was taken hostage; King Huai died in captivity. Thereafter Chu, the only state with the resources to effectively block Qin's expansion, crumbled piece by piece. In Sima Qian's biography, Qu Yuan's voice is the sensible opposition to King Huai's misjudgments. The biography places his death during an exile in the reign of King Huai's successor,

King Qingxiang (r. 298–263 BCE). But the date of his death is adjusted to fit the content and interpretation of other poems attributed to him.

The main text, *Li Sao*, is in ninety-two four-line stanzas with a verse coda (☞ *HTRCP* C2.3). There is nothing like it earlier, and everything like it that was written later was composed in its shadow. He begins by telling of ancestry, birth, and nature. This was unprecedented in Chinese literature. We can read this as the statement of a historical person representing himself in figurative and mythic terms, but we can also read this in the voice of a reciter introducing himself in the voice of a possibly historical figure who has faded into myth. Despite the names and dates, nothing in the poem explicitly ties it to Chu in the fourth century BCE.

	Of the god-king Gaoyang I am the far offspring,	帝高陽之苗裔兮
2	my late honored sire bore the name of Boyong.	朕皇考曰伯庸
	The *sheti* stars aligned with the year's first month;	攝提貞于孟陬兮
4	*gengyin* was the day that I came down.	惟庚寅吾以降
	He scanned and he delved into my first measure,	皇覽揆余於初度兮
6	from the portents my sire gave these noble names:	肇錫余以嘉名
	The name that he gave me was Upright Standard;	名余曰正則兮
8	and my formal title was Holy Poise.	字余曰靈均
	Such bounty I had of beauty within,	紛吾既有此內美兮
10	this was doubled with fair appearance.	又重之以脩能
	I wore mantles of lovage and remote angelica,	扈江離與辟芷兮
12	strung autumn orchids to hang from my sash.	紉秋蘭以為佩

[*CCJJJS* 42–94]

Before we turn to the figure of Qu Yuan that was taking shape in the Han, we need to note a few things. The mythical ruler of high antiquity, Gaoyang, was one of the two lineages from which all the rulers and great aristocratic clans claimed descent (two were necessary for exogamy). Although this is alien to the meritocratic culture in which the Qu Yuan story developed, Qu Yuan's self-introduction is purely aristocratic, in a way that was as alien to Han intellectuals as it was to all later readers. He is "good" not for any specific moral quality but because of his lineage and the auspicious time of his birth. If Sima Qian attributes historically correct political judgment to him, that is Sima Qian and not *Li Sao*. He is a man utterly without particular virtues; his is an absolute "goodness," derived purely from his lineage and the astrological felicity of his birth.

His inner beauty is matched by wearing aromatic plants (figure 2.1), but this quickly shifts to the swift passage of time and the decay of plants; from his own aging, he shifts to worry about the aging of the "Fairest," taken as a figure for the king. This then turns to offering to lead the king on the right way. The king/beloved, however, believes slander and turns against Qu Yuan. Chinese does not mark gender, and we have here a good example of how the story shapes understanding. Although part of the following passage clearly refers to kings, other terms unmistakably suggest the courtship of a goddess ("the Holy One") and her fickleness; the Qu Yuan story makes these a figure for Qu Yuan's devotion to King Huai.

FIGURE 2.1 Qu Yuan's inner beauty matched by wearing aromatic plants (lines 9–12). Illustration by Men Yingzhao 門應兆 (fl. 1787), in *Qinding buhui Lisao quantu* 欽定補繪離騷全圖 (Complete Illustrations to *Lisao*, with supplements, made by imperial order), collected in *Siku quanshu*. Qing dynasty woodblock print. Reprinted in *Siku quanshu zhenben liu ji* 四庫全書珍本六集 (Rare Edition of *Siku Quanshu*), vol. 6 (Taipei: Taiwan shangwu yinshuguan, 1976).

	They fled swiftly from me, I could not catch them—	汨余若將不及兮
14	I feared the years passing would keep me no company.	恐年歲之不吾與
	At dawn I would pluck magnolia on bluffs,	朝搴阰之木蘭兮
16	In the twilight on isles I culled undying herbs.	夕攬洲之宿莽
	Days and months sped past, they did not long linger,	日月忽其不淹兮
18	springtimes and autumns altered in turn.	春與秋其代序
	I thought on things growing, on the fall of their leaves,	惟草木之零落兮
20	and feared for the Fairest, drawing toward dark.	恐美人之遲暮
	Cling to your prime, forsake what is rotting—	不撫壯而棄穢兮
22	why not change from this measure of yours?	何不改此度
	Drive a fine steed, go off at a gallop—	乘騏驥以馳騁兮
24	I will now take the lead, ride ahead on the road.	來吾道夫先路
	The Three Kings of old were pure and unblemished,	昔三后之純粹兮
26	where all things of sweet scent indeed were.	固眾芳之所在
	Shen's pepper was there, together with cassia,	雜申椒與菌桂兮
28	white angelica, basil were not strung alone.	豈維紉夫蕙茝
	Such shining grandeur had kings Yao and Shun;	彼堯舜之耿介兮
30	they went the true way, they found the path.	既遵道而得路
	But slouching and shambling were kings Jie and Zhou;	何桀紂之昌被兮
32	they walked at hazard on side-paths.	夫唯捷徑以窘步
	Those men of faction had ill-gotten pleasures,	惟夫黨人之偷樂兮

34	their road went in shadow,　narrow, unsafe.	路幽昧以險隘
	Not for myself　came this dread of doom—	豈余身之憚殃兮
36	I feared my king's chariot　soon would be tipped.	恐皇輿之敗績
	In haste I went dashing　in front and behind,	忽奔走以先後兮
38	till I came to the tracks　of our kings before.	及前王之踵武
	Lord Iris did not fathom　my nature within,	荃不察余之中情兮
40	instead he believed ill words,　he glowered in rage.	反信讒而齌怒
	I knew well artful words　had brought me these woes,	余固知謇謇之為患兮
42	yet I bore through it,　I could not forswear.	忍而不能舍也
	I pointed to Heaven　to serve as my warrant,	指九天以為正兮
44	it was all for the cause　of the Holy One.	夫唯靈脩之故也
	To me at first　firm word had been given,	初既與余成言兮
46	she regretted it later,　made excuses.	後悔遁而有他
	I made no grievance　at this break between us,	余既不難夫離別兮
48	but was hurt that the Holy One　so often changed.	傷靈脩之數化

[CCJJJS 94–172]

Qu Yuan then withdraws. We know that aromatic plants were planted near shrines to attract the god or goddess and used by religious practitioners (often described as "shamans" or female "shamakas," terms borrowed from Siberian religious practices). As in the preceding section, this religious theme alternates with the political, here a denunciation of the age. If Qu Yuan is "good" by birth, in an imagined polity where his position is guaranteed by "who he is," what he hates most is a world where people struggle to get ahead—whether by favor or merit—which was as much the Han world as it was the world of the late Warring States.

	I watered my orchids　in all their nine tracts,	余既滋蘭之九畹兮
50	and planted basil　in one hundred rods;	又樹蕙之百畝
	I made plots for paeonia　and for the wintergreen,	畦留夷與揭車兮
52	mixed with wild ginger　and sweet angelica.	雜杜衡與芳芷
	I wished stalks and leaves　would stand high and flourish,	冀枝葉之峻茂兮
54	I looked toward the season　when I might reap.	願竢時乎吾將刈
	If they withered and dried,　it would cause me no hurt,	雖萎絕其亦何傷兮
56	I would grieve if such sweetness　went rotting in weeds.	哀眾芳之蕪穢
	Throngs thrust themselves forward　in craving and greed,	眾皆競進以貪婪兮
58	they never are fully sated　in things that they seek.	憑不厭乎求索
	They show mercy to self,　by this measure others,	羌內恕己以量人兮
60	in them the heart stirs　to malice and spite.	各興心而嫉妒
	Such a headlong horse race,　each hot in pursuit,	忽馳騖以追逐兮
62	is not a thing　that thrills my own heart.	非余心之所急
	Old age comes on steadily,　soon will be here,	老冉冉其將至兮
64	I fear my fair name　will not be fixed firmly.	恐脩名之不立
	At dawn I drank dew　that dropped from magnolia,	朝飲木蘭之墜露兮

66	in twilight ate blooms from chrysanthemums shed.	夕餐秋菊之落英
	If my nature be truly comely, washed utterly pure,	苟余情其信姱以練要兮
68	what hurt can I have in long wanness from hunger?	長顑頷亦何傷

[*CCJJJS* 172–210]

After more lamenting his fate and refusing to change, he decides to go roaming. At this point he encounters a female figure, early interpreted as "sister"—though we do not know whether this is meant literally or figuratively.

	Then came the Sister, tender and enticing,	女嬃之嬋媛兮
130	mild of manner she upbraided me thus,	申申其詈余
	she said: "Gun was unyielding, he fled into hiding,	曰鯀婞直以亡身兮
132	at last died untimely on moors of Mount Yu.	終然殀乎羽之野
	Why such wide culling, such love of the fair,	汝何博謇而好脩兮
134	in you alone bounty of beautiful raiment?	紛獨有此姱節
	They stack stinkweed filling their rooms;	薋菉葹以盈室兮
136	you alone stand aloof and do not accept.	判獨離而不服
	No swaying the throngs person by person;	眾不可戶說兮
138	'no one discerns this my nature within!'	孰云察余之中情
	Now men rise together, each favors his friends,	世並舉而好朋兮
140	why do you stand alone— and not listen to me?"	夫何煢獨而不余聽

[*CCJJJS* 299–326]

FIGURE 2.2 The Sister criticizing Qu Yuan for his unbending nature (lines 129–140). Illustration by Men Yingzhao 門應兆 (fl. 1787), in *Qinding buhui Lisao quantu* 欽定補繪離騷全圖 (Complete Illustrations to *Lisao*, with supplements, made by imperial order), collected in *Siku quanshu*. Qing dynasty woodblock print. Reprinted in *Siku quanshu zhenben liu ji* 四庫全書珍本六集 (Rare Edition of *Siku Quanshu*), vol. 6 (Taipei: Taiwan shangwu yinshuguan, 1976).

Here, in the *Li Sao* itself, is the first in a long tradition of criticisms of Qu Yuan for his unbending nature (figure 2.2). Qu Yuan, however, goes for a second opinion to the deified sage-king Shun at his tomb in southern Chu. Qu Yuan cites a long string of historical examples showing that the wicked come to ruin and the virtuous prosper. He then sets off into flight on an airborne chariot, making a circuit of the cosmos in search of a mate—always a woman. This is understood as looking for a ruler who appreciates him.

	At dawn I loosed wheel block there by Cangwu,	朝發軔於蒼梧兮
186	and by twilight I reached the Gardens of Air.	夕余至乎縣圃
	I wished to bide a while by the windows of gods,	欲少留此靈瑣兮
188	but swift was the sun and it soon would be dusk.	日忽忽其將暮
	I bade sun driver Xihe to pause in her pace,	吾令羲和弭節兮
190	to stand off from Yanzi and not to draw nigh.	望崦嵫而勿迫
	On and on stretched my road, long it was and far,	路曼曼其脩遠兮
192	I would go high and go low in this search that I made.	吾將上下而求索
	I watered my horses in the Pool of Xian,	飲余馬於咸池兮
194	and twisted the reins on the tree Fusang,	總余轡乎扶桑
	snapped a branch of the Ruo tree to block out the sun,	折若木以拂日兮
196	I roamed freely the while and lingered there.	聊逍遙以相羊
	Ahead went Wang Shu to speed on before me,	前望舒使先驅兮
198	behind came Fei Lian, he dashed in my train.	後飛廉使奔屬
	Phoenix went first and warned of my coming,	鸞皇為余先戒兮
200	Thunder master told me that all was not set.	雷師告余以未具
	I bade my phoenixes to mount up in flight,	吾令鳳鳥飛騰兮
202	to continue their going both by day and by night.	繼之以日夜
	Then the whirlwinds massed, drawing together,	飄風屯其相離兮
204	they marshaled cloud-rainbows, came to withstand me.	帥雲霓而來御
	A bewildering tumult, first apart, then agreeing,	紛總總其離合兮
206	and they streamed flashing colors, high and then low.	斑陸離其上下
	I bade the God's gatekeeper to open the bar;	吾令帝閽開關兮
208	he stood blocking the gateway and stared at me.	倚閶闔而望予
	The moment grew dimmer, light soon would be done,	時曖曖其將罷兮
210	I plait orchids, standing there long.	結幽蘭而延佇
	An age foul and murky cannot tell things apart;	世溷濁而不分兮
212	it loves to block beauty from malice and spite.	好蔽美而嫉妒
	At dawn I set to fare across the White Waters,	朝吾將濟於白水兮
214	I climbed Mount Langfeng, there tethered my horses.	登閬風而緤馬
	All at once I looked back, my tears were streaming,	忽反顧以流涕兮
216	sad that the high hill lacked any woman.	哀高丘之無女
	At once I went roaming to the Palace of Spring,	溘吾遊此春宮兮
218	I snapped sprays of garnet to add to my pendants.	折瓊枝以繼佩
	Before the bloom's glory had fallen away,	及榮華之未落兮
220	I would divine a woman below on whom to bestow them.	相下女之可詒

[*CCJJJS* 411–475]

FIGURE 2.3 Qu Yuan bestowing sprays of garnet on "a woman below" (lines 217–220). Illustration by Men Yingzhao 門應兆 (fl. 1787), in *Qinding buhui Lisao quantu* 欽定補繪離騷全圖 (Complete Illustrations to *Lisao*, with supplements, made by imperial order), collected in *Siku quanshu*. Qing dynasty woodblock print. Reprinted in *Siku quanshu zhenben liu ji* 四庫全書珍本六集 (Rare Edition of *Siku Quanshu*), vol. 6 (Taipei: Taiwan shangwu yinshuguan, 1976).

He is moving in time as well as space. A series of proposed matches with "women below" all fail and all involve women of legendary antiquity, including one of his own female ancestors in the Gaoyang lineage (figure 2.3). After these failures he is filled with doubts and consults a shaman, Holy Fen, who tells him to continue his search. Again he seeks a second opinion, from another deified shaman, Shaman Xian, who descends from heaven and also tells him to continue his search, this time with a series of examples of rulers who found worthy ministers. Even in the *Li Sao* itself we have the parallel between seeking a woman as a mate and a ruler finding a worthy minister. This is followed by one of the darker passages, in which the aromatic plants, always the symbol of virtue, change.

	My pendants of garnet, how they dangle down from me—	何瓊佩之偃蹇兮
302	yet the throngs would dim them, cover them over.	眾薆然而蔽之
	These men of faction are wanting in faith,	惟此黨人之不諒兮
304	I fear their spite and malice, that they will break them.	恐嫉妒而折之
	The times are in tumult, ever transforming.	時繽紛其變易兮
306	how then may a man linger here long?	又何可以淹留
	Orchid, angelica change, they become sweet no more;	蘭芷變而不芳兮
308	iris and basil alter, they turn into straw.	荃蕙化而為茅
	How do plants that smelled sweet in days gone by	何昔日之芳草兮
310	now straightaway become but stinking weeds?	今直為此蕭艾也
	Can there be any reason other than this?—	豈其有他故兮
312	the harm that is worked by no love for the fair.	莫好脩之害也

	I once thought that Orchid could be steadfast:	余以蘭為可恃兮
314	it bore me no fruit, it was all show.	羌無實而容長
	Forsaking its beauty, it followed the common;	委厥美以從俗兮
316	it wrongly is ranked in the hosts of sweet scent.	苟得列乎眾芳
	Pepper is master of fawning, it is swaggering, reckless,	椒專佞以慢慆兮
318	only mock-pepper stuffs sachets hung from waists.	樧又欲充夫佩幃
	It pressed hard to advance, it struggled for favor,	既干進而務入兮
320	what sweet scent remains that is able to spread?	又何芳之能祇
	Truly, ways of these times are willful and loose,	固時俗之流從兮
322	who now is able to avoid being changed?	又孰能無變化
	Viewing orchid and pepper, seeing them thus,	覽椒蘭其若茲兮
324	will less be true of lovage and wintergreen?	又況揭車與江離

[*CCJJJS* 612–638]

At this point Qu Yuan sets off into flight again with his entourage of deities. But on the point of ascent, he looks back, unable to go on. Then comes the coda, with its final decision to go "where Peng Xian dwells." The Qu Yuan "story" that developed in the Han seems to have generated a legend that Peng Xian was an ancient worthy who drowned himself, thus anticipating Qu Yuan's own suicide. But Peng Xian might also be "Peng and Xian," both deified shamans, one of whom, Shaman Xian, had just descended from heaven earlier in the poem. If this is the case, instead of drowning himself, he decides to go upward (figure 2.4).

FIGURE 2.4 Qu Yuan roaming the heavens (lines 357–364). Illustration by Men Yingzhao 門應兆 (fl. 1787), in *Qinding buhui Lisao quantu* 欽定補繪離騷全圖 (Complete Illustrations to *Lisao*, with supplements, made by imperial order), collected in *Siku quanshu*. Qing dynasty woodblock print. Reprinted in *Siku quanshu zhenben liu ji* 四庫全書珍本六集 (Rare Edition of *Siku Quanshu*), vol. 6 (Taipei: Taiwan shangwu yinshuguan, 1976).

	Then I massed all my chariots,　a thousand strong,	屯余車其千乘兮
358	jade hubs lined even,　we galloped together.	齊玉軑而並馳
	I hitched my eight dragons,　heaving and coiling,	駕八龍之婉婉兮
360	and bore my cloud banners　streaming behind.	載雲旗之委蛇
	I then quelled my will　and slackened my pace;	抑志而弭節兮
362	the gods galloped high　far to the distance,	神高馳之邈邈
	they were playing Nine Songs　and dancing the Shao,	奏九歌而舞韶兮
364	making use of this day　to take their delight.	聊假日以媮樂
	I was mounting aloft　to such dazzling splendor—	陟陞皇之赫戲兮
366	all at once I peered down　to my homeland of old.	忽臨睨夫舊鄉
	My driver grew sad,　my horses felt care,	僕夫悲余馬懷兮
368	they flexed looking backward　and would not go on.	蜷局顧而不行
	The Coda: It is done now forever!	亂曰: 已矣哉
	In the domain there is no one,　no one who knows me,	國無人兮莫我知兮
370	then why should I cherish　that city, my home?	又何懷乎故都
	Since no one can join me　in making good rule,	既莫足與為美政兮
372	I will go off to seek　where Peng Xian dwells.	吾將從彭咸之所居

[CCJJJS 681–708]

It is a strange, passionately intense poem, mixing religious myth with judgments of contemporary political mores. Sima Qian's "Qu Yuan story" was constructed on very shaky grounds, but if one believed it, it provided a context to make some sense of the poem, with all its religious dimensions explained as figurative references to Qu Yuan's political misfortunes. In the Han context, its impact was obvious: the utter dependence of the fickle favor of an absolute ruler and the mortal fear of disfavor were close enough to permit them to read themselves into Qu Yuan's story.

The Qu Yuan story given by Sima Qian was already hard-pressed to explain *Li Sao*, but that story had to extend to accommodate a growing number of poems attributed to Qu Yuan. In his comment on the Qu Yuan biography, Sima Qian tells us that he personally read four works by Qu Yuan: *Li Sao*, *Heaven Questions* (*Tian wen*), *Summoning the Soul* (*Zhao hun*), and "Lament for Ying" ("Ai Ying"). He also quotes "Embracing the Sand" ("Huaisha") in its entirety in the biography and includes a poetic dialogue between Qu Yuan and a Daoist fisherman, "The Fisherman" ("Yufu"), as part of the narrative.

Sima Qian worked in the imperial library, and we can presume that he read *all* the works by Qu Yuan that were contained in the imperial library early in the first century BCE. Over the course of that century, there was considerable interest in Qu Yuan, with imitations and, in one case, a very old man invited to court because he could "do *Chuci*." If certain kinds of works were popular in court, those who had books would often send them to the imperial library to gain favor. This seems to have happened. Toward the end of the century, when Liu Xiang did an inventory of the imperial library, he counted not six but twenty-five works by Qu Yuan. He did not name these in his bibliography, but they were certainly the core of his anthology *Chuci*, consisting of works by Qu Yuan and by his supposed disciple Song Yu, and Han imitations, including Liu Xiang's own verses. This was the anthology for which Wang Yi wrote a commentary and added a set of his own verses, which is the version that survives.

Some modern scholars doubt Qu Yuan's authorship of some or all of the works attributed to him, but they were all accepted as genuine before the twentieth century and still are by most scholars and readers. Wang Yi or his predecessors had to find a place for all of these works in Qu Yuan's life. Jia Yi had heard a simple story of a good man slandered, leaving court, and committing suicide in despair. Sima Qian combed through his texts and inserted that story in the larger context of the decline of the kingdom of Chu. Now all the other texts had to be explained by new moments in Qu Yuan's life. The ingenuity of Wang Yi or of a commentarial tradition he inherited was remarkable.

The *Heaven Questions* is a series of questions about cosmology and mythology, blurring into history (the two were not then distinct). Here is the opening:

At the very beginning of ancient days,	曰: 遂古之初
who passed on word of them?	誰傳道之
Before what was higher and lower took form	上下未形
how did anyone find out about it?	何由考之

[*CCJJJS* 1008–1011]

From the beginning of the world, the questions move to myth and history. These questions have no clear order, but they do seem to move roughly chronologically. This work was in the imperial library early in the first century BCE, and Sima Qian, whether by tradition or supposition, believed it was by Qu Yuan. But what does this text have to do with the good man slandered? This was how Wang Yi explained the work, even offering a reason for the confused sequence of the questions:

When Qu Yuan was exiled, his troubled heart was sorely grieved. He roamed about marshes and mountains; he passed over hills and flatlands. With a groan he cried out to the vault of the sky; looking up to Heaven he heaved a sigh. He saw the temple to the former kings of Chu and the shrines to its lords and grandees. It was painted with the gods and spirits of Heaven and Earth and of the mountains and rivers, marvelous and strange, along with the deeds of ancient sages and worthies and weird beings. Weary of his travels, he rested under them. He looked up and saw the paintings, then wrote this on the wall, shouting and questioning it [Heaven], to vent his torment and divulge his sorrowful thoughts. The people of Chu pitied Qu Yuan, so they joined to transmit and explain it, which is why the sense of the text is out of order.

[*CCJJJS* 1003]

Sima Qian also mentions the "Lament for Ying" among Qu Yuan's works. Now included as one of the *Nine Stanzas* (*Jiu zhang*), the "Lament for Ying" describes catastrophe and an exodus from the old Chu capital. Without Qu Yuan's name as the author, any reader would take it as a lament for the Qin sack of the Chu capital in 278 BCE, after which the court moved to the eastern part of the kingdom. Indeed, it is one of several pieces of evidence that the earliest works in the Han library came from Huainan, the last independent part of the old Chu kingdom. Since the speaker in the poem refers to this event happening nine years earlier, this is far too late for Qu Yuan. Commentators have exercised great ingenuity in trying to reconcile the text of the poem with Qu Yuan's authorship.

The *Nine Songs* (*Jiuge*) is not the ritual sequence referred to at the end of the *Li Sao*, but that name was borrowed for these eleven songs, ten to deities and one a ritual coda (for two of these eleven songs, ☞ *HTRCP* C2.1, C2.2). Since their rhymes are close to the *Book of Poetry* rhymes, they were either very old or very late, normalized by Han ritualists. The first deity is Donghuang Taiyi, "the Emperor of the East; the Supreme One." The "Supreme One" was mentioned before the Han as an intellectual principle, but as a deity, his cult was first established in Han Emperor Wu's reign as the theological counterpart of Emperor Wu's centralization of imperial power. If this set of songs had been archeologically recovered without an author, scholars would certainly have dated it to Emperor Wu's reign in the Han. Appearing after *Li Sao* in Wang Yi's anthology as Qu Yuan's composition, however, the antiquity of the songs is left unquestioned. Certainly, the *Nine Songs* represent archaic practice and are closely related to *Li Sao*, but we don't know when these particular texts were composed. As with the *Heaven Questions*, a story was needed to bring these obviously religious texts into the Qu Yuan story. Since the songs present some clear textual problems, Wang Yi is no less ingenious here:

> Of old in the city of Southern Ying in the Kingdom of Chu, around the Yuan and Xiang Rivers, the local customs involved belief in spirits and they liked worship them with ceremonies. In these ceremonies there would always be song and music, drumming and dancing to delight all the deities. When Qu Yuan was banished, he hid himself away in this region; the cares on his mind consumed him with bitterness, and his sad thoughts swelled within. Going forth he witnessed the rituals the commoners performed and the music of their songs and dances. The phrasing was uncouth, so he composed the *Nine Songs* for them. On one level they demonstrate reverence in serving the deities; on another level they reveal his own sense of having been wronged that knotted within him, and he invested them with criticism. Thus their meanings are not unified, and their exposition is all mixed up, developing different significances.
>
> [*CCJJJS* 713]

Even Wang Yi cannot fully allegorize these texts, so he allows them a double intention: celebrating the deities and expressing his grievances against King Huai. Although a southerner, Wang Yi was an Eastern Han intellectual; it did not trouble him that local temples were devoted to single deities or closely associated deities. The only site where one can imagine such diverse deities being brought together is in a political center—possibly the capital of Chu (though there is no evidence), but certainly in the Han Chang'an of Emperor Wu.

The following is the "Mountain Spirit" ("Shan gui"):

	It seemed there was someone in the cleft of the hills,	若有人兮山之阿
2	mantled in climbing fig, she was girded with ivy,	被薜荔兮帶女羅
	with a sidelong glance, her mouth formed a smile:	既含睇兮又宜笑
4	"You yearn for me, good at being comely—	子慕予兮善窈窕
	I drive the red leopards, I have striped wildcats follow me,	乘赤豹兮從文貍
6	with magnolia-wood wagon, my flags, plaited cassia,	辛夷車兮結桂旗
	mantled in rock orchid, girded with asarum,	被石蘭兮帶杜衡

8	I snap the sweet fragrance, gift for the one that I love.	折芳馨兮遺所思
	I dwell in bamboo's darkness, never see sky;	余處幽篁兮終不見天
10	the way is steep and hard, came late and alone."	路險難兮獨後來
	Alone she stands forth, on the height of the hill,	表獨立兮山之上
12	with clouds' rolling billows there down below;	雲容容兮而在下
	sunken in darkness, daylight dims,	杳冥冥兮羌晝晦
14	in gustings of eastwind the goddess rains.	東風飄兮神靈雨
	I remain for the holy one, transfixed, forget going,	留靈脩兮憺忘歸
16	the year has grown late, who will clothe me in flowers?	歲既晏兮孰華予
	I picked three-bloom mushroom out in the hills,	采三秀兮於山間
18	stones rough and rocky, vines spreading tangles;	石磊磊兮葛蔓蔓
	reproaching the Lady, I in grief forget going,	怨公子兮悵忘歸
20	for though the lady may love me, she does not find time.	君思我兮不得閒
	In the hills there is someone, sweet smell of galangal,	山中人兮芳杜若
22	she drinks from the stone-springs in shadow of cypress and pines.	飲石泉兮蔭松柏
	. . .	□□□□□□
24	though the lady may love me, she holds back unsure.	君思我兮然疑作
	The sky shakes in thunder, the rain brings darkness,	雷填填兮雨冥冥
26	the apes are all wailing, in the night monkeys moan;	猿啾啾兮狖又夜鳴
	the whistling of winds that howl through the trees;	風颯颯兮木蕭蕭
28	I long for the Lady, fruitless torment I find.	思公子兮徒離憂

[*CCJJJS* 952–973]

Wang Yi is hard put to find Qu Yuan here, but the line "mantled in rock orchid, girded with asarum," similar to the recurrent flower clothing in *Li Sao*, leads him to identify the speaker with Qu Yuan. In this and a few other lines, he discovers Qu Yuan talking about himself and his longing for the return of King Huai's favor, but he cannot offer an overall figurative interpretation—but then Wang Yi tells us that the *Nine Songs* are confusing because each has two incommensurate purposes.

Wang Yi's accounts that try to integrate the *Heaven Questions* and the *Nine Songs* into the Qu Yuan story are well known, because they tell a story that is marginally plausible. Although there are still many Chinese scholars who accept its attribution to Qu Yuan, "Far Roaming" ("Yuan you") simply cannot have been written by Qu Yuan. Not only does it mention a known figure who lived almost a century after Qu Yuan and used terminology of Han Daoism that is not attested earlier but also it explicitly rejects Qu Yuan's world of early antiquity in favor of famous immortals popular in the Han. If *Li Sao* begins by claiming descent from Gaoyang, the speaker in "Far Roaming" declares:

Remote is Gaoyang, too faint in the distance,	高陽邈以遠兮
from whom would I take my model?	余將焉所程

[*CCJJJS* 1923–1924]

He answers his question by saying he will follow Qiao the Prince, one of the immortals who became famous in the Han. The entire poem is filled with the technical language of Daoist self-cultivation, and, in striking contrast to *Li Sao*, it is generally optimistic. It uses the machinery of the "heavenly journey" from *Li Sao*, but, in a telling moment, the gates of heaven are opened for this protagonist rather than left closed, as they were in the *Li Sao*. Although the speaker in "Far Roaming" does briefly think on old acquaintances and brush away tears, he cheerfully continues the ascent to transcendence and eventually achieves it. In the process, Gaoyang, Qu Yuan's ancestor, reappears again as one of the speaker's attendant minions, but under his other name, Zhuan Xu, the cosmic emperor of the north. The poem ends in Daoist transcendence:

Vertiginous depths below me where no land was,	下崢嶸而無地兮
a cavernous emptiness above where was no sky.	上廖廓而無天
It flashed where I looked, but I saw nothing,	視儵忽乎而無見兮
a blurred rumble when I listened, but I heard nothing.	聽惝怳而無聞
I passed beyond nonacting, I reached to the Clear,	超無為以至清兮
the Very Beginning became my neighbor.	與泰初而為鄰

[*CCJJJS* 1983–1987]

Wang Yi clearly does not know what to do with such an upbeat poem that so contradicts his image of Qu Yuan. His preface reiterates his version of Qu Yuan, with a few gestures to the text, but in the final part he simply ignores the text.

> Qu Yuan was straight and upright in his doings and was not tolerated by his age. On one level he was slandered by devious and unctuous men; on another level he was driven to the utmost hardship by the common sort. He roamed about marshes and mountains, with nowhere to state his complaint. Then he thought deeply on the origins of being, and held to tranquility. Longing to save the age, his thoughts burst forth in a passion; elegant writing spread out, in a sequence of wondrous thoughts. He formed a match with the immortals, and traveled with them for sport; he traversed all Heaven and Earth, and there was nowhere he did not go. Nevertheless the Kingdom of Chu was still in his thoughts, and he yearned for those he used to know; this is his steadfastness in loyalty and the depth of his humaneness and sense of right. For this reason the good man treasures his aims and celebrates his words.

[*CCJJJS* 1895]

Qu Yuan's was a resonant story that did not quite fit many of the older texts gathered under his name. Those texts that fit perfectly were probably composed with a knowledge of both *Li Sao* and the Qu Yuan story.

What was the context of Han literary culture in which the *Chuci* was gathered and so obviously admired? We cannot know clearly because we are heavily dependent on writing. Writing was then not a mere skill; it was, as elsewhere in the ancient world, learned in conjunction with texts that inculcated certain values, most of which we would now call "Confucian." They did not like local religion and mysterious old myths. Where they could, they assimilated older material in terms of their own values, which is what we see in the development of the Qu Yuan story.

Not everyone in the Han court was like them; many probably heard something in these texts which they may have no longer fully understood but which was still immensely resonant. When his favorite

Lady Li died, Emperor Wu composed (or had someone compose) a "Lament," the first part of which was essentially *Chuci*, with the bereft emperor seeking her fugitive soul as the devotee seeks the goddess. We have this text only because it was preserved by the first-century historian Ban Gu (32–92) as an example of Emperor Wu's folly in doting on a woman who was a mere commoner by birth.

There is much in the *Chuci* (and in a long panegyric to Emperor Wu by the court poet Sima Xiangru [ca. 179–118 BCE], which overlaps with "Far Roaming") to suggest that being a ruler in a non-Confucian sense may have involved the spiritual power to fly to every corner of the heavens, seeking an elusive woman. Such memories of an older cultural world survived in the Western Han, but we can see that archaic world only through what the new, more rational intellectuals preserved and explained in their own terms. However forced the interpretations of the *Chuci* may be, the Qu Yuan story brought those texts into the new world that intellectuals could understand (☞ *HTRCP* chap. 2).

There was, however, one thing those new intellectuals could not accept: suicide. They did not reflect on the number of stories of characters in ancient China who drowned themselves (or were posthumously submerged) and who became deities. Qu Yuan may have been an exemplar of misunderstood virtue, but in the Han imagination, his was a virtue flawed by its own perfection. The proper response to being at odds with the political world was to withdraw from public life, perhaps to await better times. In one variation, the "recluse" should pretend to go along with the world while actually being aloof from it. From this perspective, Qu Yuan's determination not to be corrupted by the world became stubbornness that inevitably led him to suicide.

The criticism begins in *Li Sao* itself, with the "Sister," who brings up the case of his inflexible ancestor Gun, who died because of his stubbornness. Jia Yi softly echoes such criticism when he says:

He went through the Nine Regions and served his lord,	歷九州而相其君兮
why did he have to have this great city always on his mind?	何必懷此都也

[QHFPZ 6]

In a China divided into many kingdoms, he might look for another ruler who could appreciate his worth—but Jia Yi could not understand that this could not have been a choice for Qu Yuan, who hated people who sought higher position, and he kept faith with a world in which one's position was that into which one was born. "Seeking a position" was indeed the standard interpretation of the parts of *Li Sao* in which he traveled through the heavens seeking an appropriate mate—but those same commentators would also praise his unwavering loyalty to the foolish and unworthy King Huai. In short, Qu Yuan suffered from the peculiar problem that any virtue, carried to the extreme, can turn into a shortcoming.

The criticism turned almost satirical in its Daoist iteration in "The Fisherman," strangely cited in Sima Qian as a historical event rather than a poem; no less strangely, it was preserved as Qu Yuan's own composition. Encountering the Daoist fisherman, Qu Yuan states his standard complaint:

	"The whole of this age is filthy,	舉世皆濁
10	and I alone am clean.	我獨清
	The crowds of men are all drunk,	眾人皆醉
12	and I alone am sober.	我獨醒
	For this I have been cast out."	是以見放

The fisherman is not impressed:

14	"A Sage does not get bogged down in things,	聖人不凝滯於物
	he is able to shift and get by with his age.	而能與世推移
16	If all the men in this age are filthy,	世人皆濁
	why not stir their mud and rise with the wave?	何不淈其泥而揚其波
18	If the crowds of men are all drunk,	眾人皆醉
	why not feed on the mash and sip the foam?"	何不餔其糟而歠其醨

[*CCJJJS* 2022–2027]

But Qu Yuan maintains his inflexible virtue, and in the end the fisherman smirks and goes his way.

As Confucian values became increasingly normalized in the last part of the first century BCE and into the first century CE, Qu Yuan came under more criticism. The famous Confucian scholar Yang Xiong (53 BCE–18 CE) composed an *Anti-Li Sao* (*Fan Li Sao*), in which he goes through a series of moments in the poem and suggests what Qu Yuan should have done instead. The historian Ban Gu, sympathetic to Qu Yuan in some contexts, wrote a "Preface to the *Chuci*," criticizing Qu Yuan rather harshly for boasting, intolerance, and, of course, his suicide. The Han initially turned Qu Yuan from a mythic figure into a fully historical figure; then, as times changed, discovered they could not entirely approve of the character they had created.

The criticism died down, and Qu Yuan retained his status as an icon of virtue. "Icons of virtue" are usually rather uninteresting; Qu Yuan remained interesting, in part, precisely because his virtues were so extreme that they could never be perfectly reconciled to all the dominant values of the civilization. Perhaps even more than that, the speaker in the *Li Sao* was more than could be completely contained by the historical figure of Qu Yuan.

In the last passage quoted from the *Li Sao*, he begins, "Then I massed all my chariots, a thousand strong." That is not a simple hyperbole. "A thousand chariots" is the standard mark of a king—indeed "a thousand chariots" was a way to refer to the ruler of a domain. Ancestry from either Gaoyang or Gao Xin was necessary to be a king. Seeking a woman as a mate was a far more appropriate figure for a ruler seeking a loyal minister than a minister looking for a ruler to appreciate him.

Parts of the *Li Sao* match the Qu Yuan story very well; other parts do not fit at all. When Sima Xiangru praises Han Emperor Wu, it is not as a Confucian ruler but as a god-king, on the model of the traveler in "Far Roaming," which in turn is modeled on *Li Sao*. There is, as we suggested earlier, an archaic surplus in *Li Sao* that resists easy integration into the Qu Yuan story. We don't know quite what it means, but the echoes are there—very resonant still in the Western Han, and perhaps always resonant. The name that he tells us his father gave him, Lingjun (Holy Poise), is not an ordinary name. The prefix "*Ling*" is restricted to shamans—or, more precisely stated, to those who have the power to move between the divine and human realm, as Qu Yuan does.

Sima Qian wanted to make Qu Yuan an "author" like himself. He succeeded. But there was a divine world that may have touched human history but was beyond it; we still hear its echoes when we read *Li Sao*.

I have been describing Qu Yuan as a name to which works were gathered, and a life that grew in specificity to contain those works and to fit into an account of a larger history of China at the time.

Once this process was completed and the *Chuci* achieved its final form, then the works were swallowed up by their putative author. Qu Yuan became an icon of many things: inflexible virtue, loyalty to a dynasty, and even, in modern times, "patriotism."

The interpretive strategies used by Wang Yi around the turn of the second century grafted the impassioned erotics and divine aura of the *Chuci* texts onto the centrality of the minister–ruler relationship. Ever thereafter, the invocation of "the Fair One [especially a beautiful woman] and aromatic plants" (*meiren xiangcao*) recalled Wang Yi's interpretation of *Chuci*. The aromatic plants represented virtues, and the "Fair One" might be the desired ruler or the spurned minister. Often this mode of interpretation was routine, but in some of the most interesting cases, the venture into the magical world of *Chuci* overwhelmed interpretive routine and made it strange.

STEPHEN OWEN

PRIMARY SOURCES

CCJJJS   Cui Fuzhang 崔富章 and Li Daming 李大明, eds. *Chuci jijiao jishi* 楚辭集校集釋 (Collected Collations and Commentaries on the *Chuci*). Vols. 1–2 of Cui Fuzhang, ed. *Chuci xue wenku* 楚辭學文庫 (Compendium of *Chuci* Studies). 5 vols. Wuhan: Hubei jiaoyu chubanshe, 2003.

QHFPZ   Kong Kechang 龔克昌 et al. *Quan Han fu pingzhu* 全漢賦評注 (Complete Han *Fu*, with Annotations and Commentaries). 3 vols. Shijiazhuang: Huashan wenyi chubanshe, 2003.

SUGGESTED READINGS

ENGLISH

Hawkes, David. "The Quest of the Goddess." *Asia Major* 13, no. 1–2 (1967). Reprinted in Cyril Birch, ed. *Studies in Chinese Literary Genres*. Berkeley: University of California Press, 1974.

———. *The Songs of the South*. Rev. ed. London: Penguin, 1985.

Walker, Galal LeRoy. "Toward a Formal History of the 'Chuci.'" PhD diss., Cornell University, 1982.

CHINESE

Cui Fuzhang 崔富章, ed. *Chuci xue wenku* 楚辭學文庫 (Compendium of *Chuci* Studies). 5 vols. Wuhan: Hubei jiaoyu chubanshe, 2003. The first two volumes are the most thorough compilation of premodern and modern commentaries, with critical judgments. The third volume is a compilation of premodern and modern comments and essays. The fourth volume contains discussions of scholarly and critical books, and the final volume is a lexicon of various topics.

Lin Geng 林庚. *Shiren Qu Yuan ji qi zuopin yanjiu* 詩人屈原及其作品研究 (Studies on Qu Yuan the Poet and His Works). Shanghai: Shanghai guji chubanshe, 1981.

Wen Yiduo 聞一多. *Chuci jiaobu* 楚辭校補 (*Chuci*, with Collations and Additions). Chengdu: Bashu shushe, 2002.

PART II
THE HAN DYNASTY

❀ 3 ❀

EMPIRE IN TEXT

Sima Xiangru's "Sir Vacuous/Imperial Park Rhapsody" ("Zixu/Shanglin fu")

Although there were numerous kingdoms and dynasties of various sizes throughout Chinese history, the Western and Eastern Han dynasties (206 BCE–220 CE), from which we derive the common terms for the Chinese language and majority ethnicity (*Hanyu* and *Han ren*), to a large extent provided the foundations for China's politics, society, and culture and determined the course of their development. The Han, which followed upon the unification of the empire by the Qin (221–206 BCE), was the longest-lived of all the dynasties. At its height under the reign of Emperor Wu (r. 141–87 BCE), grain storehouses were full and talented men were employed in large numbers. Internally, feudatory states were weakened through the implementation of the "county-commandery system" of administration (*junxian zhi*); externally, campaigns against the Xiongnu peoples opened the western frontier and relentlessly expanded into new territory. The question of how to maintain conditions for a unified *tianxia* ("all under heaven") thus became Emperor Wu's lifelong concern.

It may be difficult for inhabitants of the twenty-first century—Internet and smartphone users for whom the circulation of information and assertion of power is so convenient—to imagine life in the year 141 BCE, the year Emperor Wu ascended the throne. Bamboo strips and silk, inscribed with knives and fur-tipped brushes, still served as the primary tools for storing and communicating information. Given the impossibility of rapid, easy, and universal communication—paper was not ready to hand, and not everyone carried a written manuscript—writers could not easily correct their compositions as they wrote, and readers could not browse ahead or review preceding text. However, despite the limitations of their writing technologies, the Western Han court produced "great rhapsodies" (*da fu*) of several thousand characters. This surprises us, and it invites us to imagine how the authors of these great rhapsodies composed and edited in their minds—reflecting, remembering, mulling over words—prior to the act of writing. The audience must also have first acquired a certain degree of shared knowledge, for otherwise they would have had great difficulty understanding the words in the instant before they vanished (☞ *HTRCP* chap. 3).

Let us now look at the famous "Sir Vacuous/Imperial Park Rhapsody" ("Zixu/Shanglin fu") by Sima Xiangru (179–127 BCE), the most important Western Han author. Besides its length (over 3,500 characters), perhaps most striking for today's readers are the great rhapsody's abundance of allusions, its florid language, and its many sonorous phrases involving verbal repetition and rhyme—all of which requires significant effort to decipher. One wonders how the rulers and ministers in the courts of those days understood and, moreover, appreciated works like the great rhapsody. Was it necessary to understand each and every word, phrase, and passage? If not everyone had a written copy at hand, then would this not have required formidable powers of recitation and listening? We could well imagine that the great rhapsody would call upon the collective memory, or that which everyone knew by heart. We can also imagine the erudition of this courtly milieu, and how the great rhapsody accorded with the age's ideals of "broad learning" (*bo xue*). As it flourished during the great unified Han Empire, we may ask what sort of relation this ornate and learned form had with contemporary notions of *tianxia*.

THE STORYTELLER BESIDE THE KING

Every literary form develops over a long period of time, and much cultural preparation is required for it to become recognized and understood. In a period before the division of writings into the "four departments" of classics, histories, philosophers, and literary collections; before the distinction was drawn between "collected works" and the "separate collection," between poetry and prose, or between the *sao* (also called *ci*) and the rhapsody, it was not necessary for rhapsody writers to self-consciously delimit the boundaries of the genre. There was no need to treat the rhapsody as a kind of *wenxue* ("literature") and thus distinguish it from other fields of study. In other words, the author of the "Sir Vacuous/Imperial Park Rhapsody" did not write with our modern conceptions of the rhapsody or of genre in mind, but within a discursive field that was comparatively fluid. Sima Xiangru's writing can also be seen as a continuation of various oral and written types and topics of the pre-Qin period. The origins of the Han rhapsody (*Han fu*), as David Knechtges believes, may lie in the *Songs of Chu* (*Chuci*) tradition associated with the names of Qu Yuan (ca. 340–278 BCE) and Song Yu (ca. 298–222 BCE), or it might have developed out of the rhetorical arts of the "traveling persuaders" (*you shui*) of the Warring States period (ca. 476–221 BCE).[1]

Born in the Shu (modern Sichuan) region in 179 BCE, Sima Xiangru studied literature and swordsmanship, mastering both civil and military arts. Admiring the wisdom and bravery of Lin Xiangru, who saved the state of Zhao (403–222 BCE) with his rhetorical skills and negotiated with the powerful state of Qin (778–207 BCE), he decided to do away with his childhood name Quanzi (Puppy) and rename himself Xiangru. In ancient times, the civil service examination system was as yet undeveloped, and the primary division of skill was between administration (*zhi guo*) and warfare (*yong bing*). In the former category, literary elegance, like that of the intrepid Lin Xiangru, was most prized. Such figures were innumerable in pre-Qin times, including names like Zichan (d. 522 BCE), Yan Ying (d. 500 BCE), Su Qin (d. 317 BCE), and Zhang Yi (d. 310). From records contained in the *Rites of Zhou* (*Zhouli*), *Discourses of the States* (*Guoyu*), and *Zuo Tradition* (*Zuozhuan*), we see that the nobles, ministers, historians, entertainers and others who gathered around the rulers "all had cultivated literary abilities, and possessed rich stores of cultural knowledge. Without exception, they were well versed in imperial genealogies, plants and animals, natural phenomena, history, and more. . . . They were able to chant poems and recite rhapsodies, and occasionally would toss out a witty admonition."[2] Rulers might accept their counsel, but they would also listen with pleasure to lively historical legends or fantastic tales of faraway exotic lands.

Although these kings enjoyed listening to stories, their counselors had to consider what kind of story, told in what way, would best capture the ruler's attention. When Sima Xiangru gained admittance to the entourage of Prince Xiao of Liang (168–143 BCE), he joined the company of eminent traveling scholars and rhapsodists like Mei Sheng (d. ca. 140 BCE), Zou Yang (?–?), Zhuang Ji (?–?), and others. He not only resided in the lavish halls of the prince but also regularly came into contact with rhapsodies like Mei Sheng's "Seven Stimuli" ("Qi fa"), which he had ample opportunity to study and emulate. At first glance, "Seven Stimuli" seems like a dialogue between a doctor and a patient. Following an initial diagnosis, the "guest from Wu" presents a series of remedies, which include listening to music, eating and drinking, riding in carriages, banquet outings, hunting parties, ocean viewing, and other activities—all in order to gauge the reactions of the patient, a "Chu crown prince." In the end, it is only the discourses of the philosophers, the last of the rhapsody's remedies, that finally cures the prince's afflictions. Clearly, the moral is that the prince must not excessively indulge in sensual pleasures, must rid himself of his desires, and must seek out bodily balance and moderation. The message is not at all mysterious; it is quite clear and easily understood. But if the Chu prince could not miss the meaning, why must the "guest from Wu" test him with all manner of sensory enjoyments?

AN EVOCATIVE EXPERIENCE OF DESIRE

In fact, the rhetorical strategy of "Seven Stimuli," in which descriptions of sensual pleasure are employed to attract the prince's attention, was used by Yi Yin of the Shang dynasty. The "Original Flavor" ("Ben wei") chapter of *The Annals of Lü Buwei* (*Lüshi chunqiu*) records that Yi Yin used just such descriptions of the world's delicacies to move Tang, the Shang king, including "the beauty of meats," "the beauty of fish," "the beauty of vegetables," "the beauty of blended flavors," "the beauty of rice," "the beauty of water," and more. The section on food and drink in the "Seven Stimuli" can thus be seen as a distillation of the "Original Flavor" chapter. Mei Sheng also wrote, "Summon Yi Yin to do the cooking and boiling, and Yi Ya to blend and harmonize it."

We could almost say that this amassing and categorizing of great numbers of things provides the blueprint for the later great rhapsody. Yi Yin's elaborate story is filled with all sorts of strange and exotic things, such as the *yao*, which looks like a carp but has wings and "often flies at night from the Western Sea to wander in the Eastern Sea." He also tells of plants that ease the body, prevent death, and make one immortal, such as the *ping* of Kunlun, the flowers of the tree of longevity, the leaves of red and black trees, and the *gan lu*, an otherwise unknown fruit. It is hard to believe that King Tang, who only heard Yi Yin's oral performance, could have completely understood every word or recognized each thing described. How could he capture the interest of a king who did not understand all his words?

It was likely a sense of novelty and overabundance that was the first step in attracting King Tang. In this connection, Yi Yin's discussion of cooking deserves attention. Before describing the many pleasures under the sun, Yi Yin first gives the following presentation of culinary art:

As a general rule, the fundamental rule in preparing flavors is that water is the first ingredient. For the five tastes and the three materials, as well as the nine simmerings and nine transformations, fire serves as the regulator. At times quick and at times slow, it eliminates fishiness, removes rankness, and eradicates fetidness. One must be sure that while these are overcome, one does not lose the inherent qualities of flavor. In the task of harmonizing and blending one must use the sweet, sour, bitter, acrid, and salty. The balancing of what should be added first or last, and of whether to use more or less, is very subtle, as each variation gives rise to its own effect. The transformation within the cauldron is quintessential, marvelous, extremely fine, and delicate. The mouth cannot describe it; the mind cannot find an illustrative example. It is like the subtle arts of archery and horsemanship, the products of the mixing of Yin and Yang, and the different methods practiced in the four seasons. Thus it keeps for a long time and does not ruin, is thoroughly cooked but not mushy, sweet but not cloying, sour but not excessively so, salty but not deadening, acrid but not caustic, mild but not bland, rich with fats but not greasy.

[*LSCQ/S* 14.739–741; TRANS. KNOBLOCK AND RIEGEL, 309]

If we simply examine the various kinds of food (meat, fish, vegetables, fruits, and so forth), the emphasis is placed on their rarity and exotic value. However, with an eye to their culinary preparation, Yi Yin no longer merely presents the ingredients one by one but rather as purified, boiled, and blended. He thus not only presents "flavor" as deriving from a "thing" itself but also implicates the water, fire, and wood (the "three materials") of the cooking process. For something to qualify as "lovely flavor" (*mei wei*) requires not only the qualities of the single ingredients (sweet, sour, fatty, or bland tastes, for instance) but also the transformation resulting from their combination with the workings of water, fire, and wood.

When Yi Yin comes to this "indescribable," inexhaustible "transformation within the cauldron" (*ding zhong zhi bian*), it is not only to display the chef's skill but also to lure the listener into an imaginative experience of exquisite "taste" (*pin wei*). This is precisely the technique of "connecting kinds" (*lianlei*)—not simply proceeding from meat to fish to vegetables but also showing how it is only through the cross-kind interactions among these ingredients and water, fire, and so on that the dominant qualities of each reach a beauty of balance and harmony, becoming "sweet but not cloying," "sour but not excessively so." Only this allows the one-dimensional presentation of ingredients to be refined into a "depth" of taste and to become the "perfect flavor" (*zhi wei*).

In this discussion of flavor, Yi Yin does not clearly point out whether the "Way" he wishes King Tang to understand is in fact the way of "benevolence and righteousness" or the Daoist way of "naturalness." Yet, on the basis of an experience of the "harmonious balance" of flavor, he can indirectly indicate the benefits of universal cooperation and the beauty of mutual completion. This is similar to the way of "kingly governance" (*wang zhi*), which involved bringing together heaven and earth with the "ten thousand things" (*wan wu*) and with humankind to achieve a state of harmony. Yi Yin's technique of indirect criticism does not require affiliation with a particular school of thought or code of ethics, but rather he is able to move the king, and possibly spur him to self-examination, through a practice of imaginative association and the skillful connection of kinds.

THE ATMOSPHERIC STATE OF RELYING ON SOUND TO CONVEY MEANING

Of course, this way of speaking is rather circuitous. Just as ministers did not explain their ideas or principles directly, kings were even less like today's readers, who can check dictionaries and commentaries as much as they like. In other words, understanding via manner and affect may have been more important than interpretation via the meaning of single words or phrases. From the division of the topic of "lovely flavor" into sections on meat, fish, vegetables, blends, rice, water, and fruits, or "Seven Stimuli's" division of "sensual desire" (*shi yu*) into music, food and drink, carriage riding, banquet excursions, hunting, wave viewing, and so forth, all the way to Sima Xiangru's "Sir Vacuous/Imperial Park Rhapsody," which is organized into waters and marshes, mountains and tombs, palaces and towers, plants and animals, hunting and mounted archery, banquets and entertainment, and the final exhortation to frugality—it can be seen that all of these are composed of connected individual units. We may suppose that these units were part of a storehouse of memory that had gradually accumulated through a process of repeated transmission. In such an era of inconvenient writing, it is very likely that these sections were only memorized after repeated recitations.

This memory archive could display many aspects of a single topic. On one hand, it allowed for the material to be arranged into a main thread and made it easier for a speaker to produce a coherent, integrated piece on the spot. For instance, on the topic of "lovely flavor," one would start with meat, fish, vegetables, and so on, and then connect them to rice, fruits, and similar ingredients. On the other hand, if listeners knew these sections of parallel amplification by heart, they would be expected to imaginatively join in and to readily appreciate the repeated hints contained in the layering and amplification. For example, like the cooking of ingredients, which refines them into a balanced and harmonious taste, the listener must overlook the words and things he does not understand and smoothly grasp the whole topic that emerges after the individual units are connected.

Besides familiarity on the part of rulers and ministers, another important condition for the mutual intelligibility of orally recited, extended pieces like the rhapsody can perhaps be explained through the prevalence in them of reduplicative binomes (*lianmian ci*). Such terms are extremely common in pre-Qin sources, especially in those from the period when orality was the primary medium of cultural communication. The great rhapsodies of the Western Han, which were often recited orally, were in even greater need of a language suitable for aural appreciation. These reduplicative binomes fundamentally "relied on sound to convey meaning" (*ping yin da yi*). When they were recited, they often had no fixed written characters, each therefore having to be identified based on sound. In some cases, the character forms differed yet the binome's meaning could be understood based on the information provided by its sound and by the context of the surrounding words. Of course, the understanding of such phrases would not have been as precise as that of other words or objects and instead would have constituted a contrasting background atmosphere. Echoing our earlier discussion, the king would not necessarily recognize each and every strange word or exotic thing but would still be able to fully enjoy the experience of "connecting kinds."

Reading Sima Xiangru's "Sir Vacuous/Imperial Park Rhapsody," it is clear that he borrowed many contrasting and atmospheric reduplicative binomes from the *Book of Poetry* (*Shijing*) and the *Songs of Chu* (*Chuci*). These adjectival phrases do not clearly define boundaries, directions, measurements, or forms. The same phrase, such as *cui wei* ("tall and towering"), can be applied to anything high up. It can be used to describe mountains or clouds just as readily as the tall hats of officials. Although they apply to things of different kinds—the dazzle of light and color, the fragrance that fills the air, the ceaseless undulation of waves, or a forest's depth and mystery—these can give rise to bodily experiences that cannot be precisely measured or defined. In other words, when the listening king does not approach external things from their established definitions, he in fact lets himself inhabit an imaginative, associative state that transcends established categories of things.

TIANXIA: THE DISCOURSE OF THE UNIFIED EMPIRE

Sima Xiangru was of course very conscious that his audience was Emperor Wu of Han, the most ambitious ruler since the founding of the dynasty. The great ministers and generals at his court included the renowned Confucian classicist Dong Zhongshu (179–104 BCE), the intrepid explorer of western lands Zhang Qian (200–114 BCE) (figure 3.1), and the valiant scourges of the northern Xiongnu: Li Guang (d. 119 BCE), Wei Qing (d. 106 BCE), and Huo Qubing (140–117 BCE). Sima Xiangru himself, we should remember, also led campaigns on behalf of Emperor Wu to pacify the tribes of the Ba-Shu region in the southwest. It is insufficient to conceive of Sima Xiangru as merely a man of letters; we should ask how his rhapsodies participated in and contributed to his flourishing age.

In 221 BCE, the first emperor of Qin completed his political unification of China. His foremost administrative task was to convert a "feudal" system into a centrally controlled system of counties and commanderies, the significance of which was to integrate the many polities of the Warring States period into a single *tianxia* controlled by the Qin. The concept of *tianxia* existed already in the Spring and Autumn period (ca. 771–476 BCE) and can even be found in earlier sources. On one hand, it had a religious significance, as everything was presided over by the Son of Heaven (*tianzi*), the earthly representative of God on High (*shangdi*). On the other hand, there was the *tianxia* that was made up of the Central States and the Four Directions—the cultural mission to integrate these directions, spaces, and peoples.

By the Spring and Autumn period, both senses of the term were well established; the Zhou king's status as the Son of Heaven was supported by each individual state. However, after the unification by the Qin and Han, when *tianxia* was moving toward an "absolutist" suppression of all political difference, the court's most urgent task was to find a discourse appropriate to a *tianxia* ruled by a single family. Along with laws and institutions, it was essential that language respond to the age's defining transformations.

FIGURE 3.1 Emperor Wu sending explorer Zhang Qian on a mission to Central Asia. Detail of an eighth-century painting from the Mogao Caves, Dunhuang.

In the early Han, the county-commandery and fiefdom systems coexisted. Families of empresses and imperial consorts, high officials, and princes all wielded great power. Emperor Wu decisively reduced the influence of the affinal families and weakened the princes' power bases. Also of lasting influence was Dong Zhongshu's proposal, in response to Emperor Wu's edict, to "honor classicist teachings alone." Basing himself on the concept of Great Unity (*da yitong*) from the *Spring and Autumn Annals* (*Chunqiu*), Dong Zhongshu addressed the exigencies of the time in the following way:

> Teachers of the present day follow different paths, and people's discourses are diverse. The hundred schools from the various regions point to meanings that are not the same. Therefore those above have no means of grasping unification. Laws and statutes repeatedly change, so those below know not what to obey. Your servant humbly proposes, regarding all those who do not practice the Six Arts and the teachings of Confucius, that their doctrines be cut off and that they not be allowed to continue side by side. Only after wicked and outlandish sayings are exterminated can governance be unified and laws and regulations be made clear. Then the common people will know what to follow.
>
> [HS 56.2523]

This passage is clearly a response to Emperor Wu, concerning the parameters and essentials of securing political order; it is not a purely philosophical discussion. For Dong, what is most important is the establishment of a philosophical orthodoxy for the unified empire. "Honoring classicist teachings alone" provided classical sanction and a discursive foundation for the consolidated power of the Han dynasty.

THE "RHAPSODY ON THE IMPERIAL PARK" AS STATEMENT OF CENTRALIZED POWER

From this point, "enriching clerical tasks with classical discourse" became the guiding administrative principle at the court of Emperor Wu. Naturally, "after this there was an abundance of literary men among the officials of all ranks" (*SJ* 117.3119–3120). The meaning of "literature" (*wenxue*) here was quite broad. The study and implementation of classicist teachings, as well as various kinds of discourse on and interpretation of classical texts, became criteria for promotion at court. From this point of view, the reason for the imperial favor enjoyed by Sima Xiangru cannot be reduced to his literary abilities, narrowly understood. The discourse promoted by Han ministers to legitimize Han Great Unity took a wide variety of forms. In his "Sir Vacuous/Imperial Park Rhapsody," Sima Xiangru adopted a question-and-answer format and, through a dispute between representatives of the feudal domains and the central court, demonstrated the latter's unchallengeable authority.

The "Sir Vacuous/Imperial Park Rhapsody" features three fictional characters. In the first half, which in the *Anthology of Refined Literature* (*Wenxuan*) appears separately as the "Sir Vacuous Rhapsody," the eponymous ambassador from the state of Chu arrives in the state of Qi. After attending a hunt meant to display the great size and wealth of Qi's lands, Sir Vacuous informs his counterpart, "Master Improbable," that even Yunmeng Marsh, the smallest of Chu's seven marshes, would be enough to outdo the whole of Qi.

The rhapsody does not describe the lands of Qi, as if to make Yunmeng Marsh representative of the great gardens in all feudal domains. Before he unfolds his dazzling portrayal of hunting excursions and banquet entertainments, there is first a summary account of the marsh, which employs a center-periphery structure characteristic of representations of *tianxia*. First, it describes the central mountains, emphasizing the quality of their soil and rock. Following this are sections on the east, south, west, and north, which tell of plains, waters, fragrant plants, flowering trees, and native animals.

Now, we know that the *tianxia* of this time could only be that of the Liu family or of Emperor Wu himself. The regional parks represented by the state of Chu could not and must not compete with the Son of Heaven's imperial Shanglin Park. Therefore, in the rhapsody's second half, listed separately in the *Wenxuan* as the "Imperial Park Rhapsody" (☞ *HTRCP* C3.1), another character—"Duke No-such"—begins to speak on behalf of the Son of Heaven.

As soon as he opens his mouth, Duke No-such argues that the states of Qi and Chu should not boast of their strength, because:

> having the vassal lords present tribute is not for the articles and presents themselves, but is a means for them to report on the administration of their offices. Setting up boundaries and drawing borders are not for protection of defense, but are a means of curbing excess. Now Qi has been placed as the eastern defensive barrier. Yet externally it secretly consorts with Sushen, abandons its own territory, goes beyond its borders, crosses the sea to hunt. In terms of its vassal duty, such things certainly should not be allowed. Moreover, in your speeches, both of you gentlemen do not strive to elucidate the duties of ruler and subject or to correct the ritual behavior of the vassal lords. You merely devote yourselves to competing over the pleasures of excursions and games, the size of parks and preserves, wishing to overwhelm each other with wasteful ostentation and surpass one another in wild excesses. These things cannot serve to spread fame or enhance a reputation, but are enough to defame your rulers and do injury to yourselves.
>
> [*SJ* 117.3016; TRANS. KNECHTGES, "*FU* POETRY," 61]

We know that, from the pre-Qin period, the concept of sensual pleasure was always central to the admonitory discourse of itinerant rhetoricians. It was a topic that both officials and rulers were familiar with, and one to which the latter would be receptive. In the richly elaborate descriptions of the "Sir Vacuous/Imperial Park Rhapsody," the basic form has not changed. Both are composed of sequential units treating forms of mountains and rivers, plants and animals, palaces and parks, traveling and hunting, and banquet entertainments, followed by a final exhortation to frugality. However, in the "Imperial Park Rhapsody," the powers of the subject who enjoys have changed, and, accordingly, so have the symbolic meanings of the objects and affairs having to do with sensual pleasure.

Starting with the possession of territory, the demarcation of feudal domains served internally to protect the royal clan and externally to separate Chinese from barbarian. If the state of Qi not only had its own interactions with the peoples to the northeast but also even crossed its borders to hold hunting expeditions on the Verdant Hills, this not only would be a failure to uphold the responsibilities of a feudal lord but also would reveal an illicit intention to encroach on imperial authority. Second, the feudal lords were obligated to submit tribute to the central court. They were to treat all their land's wealth and all authority as belonging to the ruler and were not to consume and enjoy it as they wished. Finally, because of this, these domains, pleasure parks, and their resources did not have to do only with enjoyment and display.

When Duke No-such renders his judgment on proprietary rights, the form is the same as that of the discourse on sensual pleasure dating from pre-Qin times. However, here it becomes a statement of the power of the central government. The reason that the hunting trips and feasts of the "Imperial Park Rhapsody" carry more legitimacy than those of the "Sir Vacuous Rhapsody" is entirely because they accord with tenets of Confucian political hierarchy, such as "the righteousness of the ruler–subject relation" (*jun chen zhi yi*) and "the proper ritual etiquette of the feudal lords" (*zhu hou zhi li*). In other words, the discourse on sensual pleasure was sufficient to represent normative relations between status groups. The "huge and gorgeous" (*ju li*) garden of the "Imperial Park Rhapsody" is a microcosm of the power of the Han (Liu) family's *tianxia*; it is a map, presented by Sima Xiangru to Emperor Wu, of the great unified territory of his desire.

"FOLLOWING THE RULER'S DESIRES" AS A MODEL FOR WRITING

The challenge faced by Sima Xiangru was not merely to describe the ruler's possessions but also to portray what the ruler longed for—an almost limitless project that may be called "following the ruler's desires" (*cong jun suo yu*). Sima Xiangru could not have been without help in this task. The writings left behind by itinerant rhetoricians and court storytellers made up an archive that must have assisted him in producing his map of desired territory. Earlier, we discussed the rhetorical technique of "connecting kinds," used by traditional elites in their writings and oral discourse, in which things of a kind were linked to make up a topic (for instance, the topic of "lovely flavor" linked meat, fish, fruit, and so on), and by which divisions between kinds could be transcended to produce a greater significance (for instance, lovely flavor required the "balanced harmony" [*zhong he*] produced by the cooking process).

Sima Xiangru applied this model to his project of following the ruler's desires. On one hand, we see that in every unit he amasses an exorbitant number of elements, and although in the end these combined elements can be said to express a meaning, there is no necessary relation of cause and effect in their sequence. For example, the section on the excessive luxury of the emperor's hunting excursions ends with an exhortation to reflect on the virtues of frugality and moderation. However, was it necessary to describe the architecture of palaces and parks in the section recounting a hunt? It is hard to see the functional role of undersea beasts and treasures or alpine flora to a section on the slaughtering of animals. On the other hand, with such endless accumulation in no necessary order, the rhapsody repeatedly employs the connective phrase "And then . . . ," when in fact spatiality takes precedence over temporality here.

To use a comparison from modern narrative literature, the effect produced by descriptive passages in just about every section of the great rhapsodies is the temporary suspension of time and the progress of the plot. In this state of suspended time, there is no modulation in feeling brought on by the gains and losses associated with historical change. Everything is before one's eyes in the moment, nearby and ready to hand. To suggest another contemporary comparison, Sima Xiangru's "Imperial Park Rhapsody" presented the emperor with a device through which a comprehensive picture could be grasped, surveyed, manipulated, and erased at will.

NAMING AND POSSESSING THINGS

We can imagine how a ruler might become bored with a story that always remained the same. Sima Xiangru therefore had to strive for novelty. In addressing the size of Shanglin Park, for example, he twice readjusts his focus. At the beginning, we read:

> To its left is Cangwu, to its right is Western Limits; the Cinnabar River traverses its south, the Purple Gulf intersects its north.
>
> [*SJ* 117.3017; TRANS. KNECHTGES, "*FU* POETRY," 61]

If "Western Limits" refers to Bin, the residence of the Zhou dynasty founder, King Tai, then it would be located to the northwest of the capital, Chang'an. However, none of the referents proposed for Cangwu place it to Chang'an's east. Even less could it make up a four-directional boundary between the Western Limits and the Cinnabar River or Purple Gulf, both of which flowed near the capital. Such an ambiguous and unverifiable Four Directions takes on a more fantastic form in the rhapsody's middle section:

> And then, gazing round, broadly viewing, one sees such plenteous profusion, such a vast vista, he becomes dizzy and dazed, confounded and confused. Look at it, and it has no beginning; examine it, and it has no end. The sun rises from its eastern pond, sets at its western dike. To the south, in deepest winter there are germination and growth, bubbling waters, and surging waves. Its animals are: the zebu, hairy yak, tapir, grunting ox, plunging bull, sambar, elaphure, redhead, roundhoof, extreme extraordinaire, elephant, and rhinoceros. To the north in full summer it is enveloped in a freezing cold that cleaves the ground; one just lifts his skirt to cross the iced-over streams. Its animals are: the unicorn, horn-snout, tarpan, camel, chigetai, kulan, hinny, ass, and mule.
>
> [*SJ* 117.3025; TRANS. KNECHTGES, "*FU* POETRY," 64–65]

This "eastern pond" and "western dike" could be located in the city of Chang'an or in Shanglin Park. However, the eastern pond could also refer to the mythical Sunrise Valley (*yang gu*), and no place names at all are given for the south and north. The park's southern region is described as never freezing, its plants not even withering in the depths of winter; likewise, in the north at the height of summer there is ice all around. This ingenious evocation of the weather in remote places highlights the extreme distance between north and south in Shanglin Park.

Whether it includes Sunrise Valley or other extremely distant places, such stage settings anticipate a performance transcending space and time. Emperor Wu rebuilt Shanglin Park on the foundations of the Qin dynasty's old palace park, referring to it as the Seventy Detached Palaces and Separate Lodges. However, he had certainly never seen a palace park in which shooting stars, rainbows, immortals, and divine creatures arrived and danced about:

> Downward through the deep darkness nothing can be seen; upward, one may clutch the rafters to touch the sky. Shooting stars pass through doors and wickets; arching rainbows stretch over the rails and porches. A green dragon curls and coils in the eastern chamber; the elephant carriage twists and

turns through the western repose. Hordes of immortals rest in the leisure lodges; Wo Quan and his kind sun themselves in the southern eaves.

[*SJ* 117.3026; TRANS. KNECHTGES, "*FU* POETRY," 65]

This imperial palace park, which is continuous with the heavenly abode of immortals, dazzles the eyes with its blending of the real and the fantastic. However, even more fascinating are the rare kinds of things linked together and presented using abstruse language, such as exotic fish, birds, fragrant plants, jade stones, fruits, and more. It resembles an encyclopedia that can always be added to and never read to its end.

For example, there are the beasts of Shanglin Park's northern and southern regions, auspicious animals like the mythical unicorn (*qilin*), which only appears with the coming of a sage. Then there is the *mo*, the giant panda that still survives in today's Sichuan. And again, there are precious fruits and exotic trees, which include, in addition to pomelos, dates, peaches, and pears, the grapes whose appearance in China predated Zhang Qian's travels to western lands. As for trees and plants that supply dyes, medicine, and materials for tools, they are beyond enumeration.

As the scroll unfurls, there appear a profusion of "things" (*wu*), characters with radicals for "horse," "fish," and "wood." Later readers believed Sima Xiangru to have been a skilled linguist or philologist, which explained his ability to employ such abstruse vocabulary and his familiarity with such a range of living things. However, we must recognize that in the "Imperial Park Rhapsody," or in any other piece of this kind, Sima Xiangru's purpose was not simply to display his own erudition or to seek out abstruse principles. Sima Xiangru was indeed the speaker and narrator, but there is another main character behind the curtain: Emperor Wu, the single listener he was serving. He enabled this illustrious Son of Heaven to hear the "ten thousand things" pronounced and named, one after another. It is in the moment that these things were given names that they entered the expansive territory taken in by the emperor's vision. They were thereby discovered, categorized, and vividly, concretely touched and taken hold of. It was ultimately this godlike Son of Heaven who, in bestowing names upon things, proclaimed the advent of an unprecedented "huge and gorgeous" world (figure 3.2).

THE EMPIRE OF ENCYCLOPEDIC ERUDITION

From this we are led to reexamine the relation between *wenxue* and *tianxia*, literature and empire. If the "Imperial Park Rhapsody" offered Emperor Wu a space in which to proclaim his sovereignty over *tianxia* and to survey the "ten thousand things" as his possessions, then it is not simply the product of an individual author's imagination. Rather, this is an oral and written form, in which words and phrases are connected in a vast fabric, composing, as if on blank canvas, a three-dimensional, all-encompassing vision. This is why readers, especially we who live two millennia later, see before us the "giant text" of the Han Empire. Sima Xiangru no doubt pondered and reflected Emperor Wu's desires. However, it is also conversely true that the "Imperial Park Rhapsody" constructed, in the space of the text, a Han Empire for eternity.

This relation of interdependence made the great Han rhapsody not merely a kind of hyperbolic literary genre or a (perhaps not terribly effective) mode of remonstration. It has substantive meaning

FIGURE 3.2 Emperor Wu hunting in Shanglin Park. Detail of *Shanglin* 上林圖, by Qiu Ying 仇英 (c. 1494–c. 1552). Courtesy of National Palace Museum, Taipei.

for cultural history because its oral/literary model made possible the construction not only of a Han Empire but also, more importantly, of a knowledge system that was transmitted over centuries.

Scholars observed long ago that the rhapsody was the precursor of the *leishu* (encyclopedia). Such *leishu* gather from a multitude of books and are organized according to "kinds" (*lei*), without distinguishing between classics, histories, philosophers, or literary collections. The most common sequential order of "kinds" is the following: heaven, earth, people, affairs, and things. Under each section heading are found not only various definitions and explanations but also relevant excerpts from poetry and prose.

In the East Asian sinographic sphere, prior to the arrival of encyclopedias from the West, these *leishu* were vital treasuries of knowledge. The compilation of such books required the support of the court—its authority, human labor, and material resources—and could only be accomplished after the appearance of more accessible and convenient tools for writing. As it happened, just when paper was replacing bamboo as a primary writing surface, Cao Pi (Emperor Wen of Wei [r. 220–226]) compiled China's first *leishu*—*The Imperial Reader* (*Huang lan*). After this there appeared works like the *Collection of Literature Arranged by Kind* (*Yiwen leiju*) of the Tang dynasty, *An Imperial Reader of the Taiping Era* (*Taiping yulan*) of the Song, up to the *Yongle Encyclopedia* (*Yongle dadian*), the compilation of which was overseen by the Ming Emperor, Yongle (r. 1402–1424), and the *Complete Collection of Illustrations and Writings from Past and Present* (*Gujin tushu jicheng*), completed during the reign of the Qing Yongzheng emperor (r. 1722–1735). Since the Han, each significant unifying dynasty has used the compilation of massive encyclopedias as proof of its glorious achievements.

The records contained in the various categories of such gigantic works (3.7 million characters in the original *Yongle dadian*; 1.7 million in the *Gujin tushu jicheng*) encompassed practically the entire universe of their day and connected the present to the remotest antiquity. They very much resembled the encyclopedias on which we rely today, especially those online. Today we use knowledge from the Internet to construct our worldviews and to organize the schedules of our lives. Just like the empire of the Internet that invisibly traverses the globe, these rulers and administrators of "Great Unity" dynasties also used the gathering and ordering of information to create the knowledge system of their time. While compiling and transmitting the past, they also inscribed onto this system the imagination of empire, or *tianxia*, which transcended temporal and spatial distances. To hold in one's hands this sea of knowledge was to bring forth the endless desire of "embracing *tianxia* from where you sit" (*zuo yong tianxia*).

Sima Xiangru was not necessarily aware that the written model of his rhapsodies was laying down a blueprint for future empires. He appears to have been aloof and indifferent to the reports of distant battles that often arrived at the court of Emperor Wu, to the exotic treasures that made their way as tribute, and to the storytellers who came bearing marvelous tales. He seems not to have been moved by the rise and fall of events but to have fallen asleep one moment and awoken the next, having woven a great dream—the beautiful dream longed for by Dong Zhongshu, Li Guang, Zhang Qian, and Emperor Wu.

YU-YU CHENG AND GREGORY PATTERSON

NOTES

1. David Knechtges, "Han Fu," in *Ancient and Early Medieval Chinese Literature: A Reference Guide, Part One*, ed. David Knechtges and Taiping Chang (Leiden: Brill, 2010), 317–319.
2. Shi Shu, "Exploring the Background of the 'Nine Songs,' 'Questioning Heaven,' and the Spirit of *Chuci* Literature," *Wenshi congkan* 31 (1969): 50–52.

PRIMARY SOURCES

HS	Ban Gu 班固 (32–92 CE). *Han shu* 漢書 (History of the Former Han). 4 vols. Beijing: Zhonghua shuju, 1995.
LSCQJS	Chen Qiyou 陳奇猷, ed. *Lüshi chunqiu jiaoshi* 呂氏春秋校釋 (The Annals of Lü Buwei, with Collation and Explication). Taibei: Huazheng shuju, 1984.
SJ	Sima Qian 司馬遷 (ca. 145–ca. 86 BCE). *Shiji* 史記 (Records of the Grand Historian). 3 vols. Beijing: Zhonghua shuju, 1995.

SUGGESTED READINGS

ENGLISH

Chin, Tamara. *Savage Exchange: Han Imperialism, Chinese Literary Style, and the Economic Imagination*. Cambridge, MA: Harvard University Press, 2014.

Gong Kechang. *Studies on the Han Fu*. Trans. and ed. David R. Knechtges et al. New Haven, CT: American Oriental Society, 1997.

Knechtges, David R. "*Fu* Poetry: An Ancient-Style Rhapsody." In *How to Read Chinese Poetry: A Guided Anthology*, ed. Zong-qi Cai, 59–83. New York: Columbia University Press, 2008.

———. *The Han Rhapsody: A Study of the Fu of Yang Hsiung (53 BCE–A.D. 18)*. Cambridge: Cambridge University Press, 1976.

Knoblock, John, and Jeffrey Riegel, trans. *The Annals of Lü Buwei: A Complete Translation and Study*. Stanford, CA: Stanford University Press, 2000.

Lewis, Mark Edward. *Writing and Authority in Early China*. Albany: State University of New York Press, 1999 (esp. 317–325).

Scott, John, trans. "Seven Stimuli." In *Classical Chinese Literature, An Anthology of Translations*, ed. John Minford and Joseph S. M. Lau, 281–292. New York: Columbia University Press, 2000.

CHINESE

Hsing I-tien 刑義田. "Cong gudai tianxia guankan Qin-Han changcheng de xiangzheng yiyi" 從古代天下觀看秦漢長城的象徵意義 (The Symbolic Significance of the Great Wall from the Perspective of the Early Chinese Political Worldview). *Yanjing xuebao* 燕京學報 (Yenching Journal of Chinese Studies) 13 (November 2002): 15–64.

Kan Huai-chen 甘懷真. "Qin-Han de 'tianxia' zhengti—yi jiaosi li gaige wei zhongxin" 秦漢的「天下」政體—以郊祀禮改革為中心 (The Polity of "Tianxia" in the Qin-Han Period: The Rituals of Suburban Sacrifice). *Xin shixue* 新史學 (The New History) 16, no. 4 (December 2005): 13–56.

❋ 4 ❋

POETRY AND IDEOLOGY

The Canonization of the *Book of Poetry* (*Shijing*) During the Han

The remaking of the *Book of Poetry* (*Shijing*) as a Confucian canon is an intriguing story of Han poetic culture. By now we are all familiar with the *Poetry* and the use of it before the Han (206 BCE–220 CE). We know the various stories told in the *Poetry* itself, and how ingeniously some *Shijing* poems were presented and performed on diplomatic occasions to express analogically the intentions of given states or their high officials. The story you will hear now is of a different kind: of an extraordinary transformation of lively, often erotic love songs into didactic tales by Han compilers and commentators, with the literary imagination ironically fired by such seemingly dull allegory. Their imaginative exercise anticipates the ways Tang poets tap the evocative power of linguistic ambiguities and poetic images.

Let us begin by looking at what Han commentators made out of "Ospreys" ("Guan ju,"  *WKB* P01), the first and most discussed of the 305 *Shijing* poems.

"Ospreys" is the beginning of the airs; it is that by which the customs of the world are influenced and the husband–wife relationship is rectified. . . . "Ospreys" celebrates the finding of a virtuous woman to match a lord. She worried about the worthy not being promoted and did not indulge in her own sensuality. She grieved over the neglect of the beautiful, yearned for the worthy, and did not harbor anything that is against the good. This is the meaning of "Ospreys."

OSPREYS	關雎
"Guan, guan," cry the Ospreys,	關關雎鳩
2 On the islet in the river.	在河之洲
Graceful is this fair maiden,	窈窕淑女
4 A fine bride for a gentleman.	君子好逑
Thick and thin grows the water mallow,	參差荇菜
6 Left and right one gets it in the flow.	左右流之
Graceful is this fair maiden,	窈窕淑女
8 Awake or asleep, I am seeking her.	寤寐求之

	Seeking though I was, I could not possess her,	求之不得
10	Awake or asleep I was longing for her.	寤寐思服
	Alas, longing and forlorn	悠哉悠哉
12	I tossed and turned in bed.	輾轉反側
	Thick and thin grows the water mallow,	參差荇菜
14	Left and right one plucks it.	左右采之
	Graceful is the fair maiden,	窈窕淑女
16	With zither and zithern I will befriend her.	琴瑟友之
	Thick and thin grows the water mallow,	參差荇菜
18	Left and right one gathers it.	左右芼之
	Graceful is this fair maiden,	窈窕淑女
20	With bells and drums I will gladden her.	鐘鼓樂之

[MAO NO. 1, *MSZY* 1:273–276; MY TRANSLATION]

This poem and its preface are cited from the Mao Text of the *Book of Poetry* (*Mao shi*), one major edition of the *Poetry*, compiled by someone surnamed Mao living during the Former Han (206 BCE–8 CE). This compiler has been taken to be either Mao Heng of the Lu region or the younger Mao Chang of the Shao region. The Mao Text is made up of two closely integrated parts: the 305 poems and as many prefaces. The preface to the first poem is known as the Major Preface because the bulk of it (omitted above) elaborates on the provenance, creative process, and functions of the *Poetry* as a whole. The prefaces to the other 304 poems are known as Minor Prefaces. The major and minor prefaces are together known as the "Mao Prefaces" ("Mao xu"), even though they were probably not authored by Mao himself. These prefaces are believed by some scholars to have existed as a self-contained text appended to the *Poetry* before Mao took them apart and reintegrated them with the poems proper. Different parts of the prefaces have been attributed to historical figures living several hundred years apart from one another, ranging from Confucius's disciple Zixia (507 BCE–?) to Mao Heng or Mao Chang of the Former Han to a Later Han scholar called Wei Hong (fl. 25–57). Thanks in part to this alleged illustrious lineage direct from Confucius, "Prefaces" acquired canonical status almost equal to that of the *Poetry* itself shortly after the Han.

Reading the first poem and its preface together, what strikes us most is a glaring disconnect between the two. The poem depicts the wooing of a graceful young lady by a male speaker. The first stanza presents a graceful lady set against the singing ospreys on an islet. The other four stanzas offer snapshots of the speaker pining for the lady day and night and trying to gladden her with music, juxtaposed with recurring scenes of harvesting water plants. The "Prefaces" author, however, completely ignores all these vivid details of courtship and takes the husband–wife relationship—not courtship—as the poem's theme. Moreover, he changes the gender of the speaker from male to female, identifying her as the main wife of a lord seeking other worthy females to serve her lord as concubines.

Why does the "Prefaces" author turn a blind eye to what is actually described in the poem and willfully change the theme and the speaker's gender? An answer may be found by looking at the opening paragraph of the Major Preface:

"Ospreys" is the beginning of the airs; it is that by which the customs of the world are influenced and by which the husband–wife relationship is rectified. Therefore, it is applied to the commoners and to the states. The airs are to influence like a wind and to teach. To influence like a wind is to move, teach, and transform people.

[*MSZY* 1:269; MY TRANSLATION]

This paragraph leaves little doubt about the author's ethico-sociopolitical agenda in interpreting the *Poetry*. He is less interested in what the poems say than in how they can be made into a comprehensive guidebook for ethical conduct and proper sociopolitical action by rulers and commoners alike. He goes on to explain that all the *Shijing* poems accurately portray good or bad governance and its praise or censure by people at the time. According to him, airs or folk songs (*feng*) in the *Poetry* are particularly effective in providing a perfect channel of communication between rulers and commoners. Thanks to the subtle and indirect expressive style of these airs, commoners can air their grievances with impunity while rulers can discern and correct their own errors without losing face.

In commenting on "Ospreys" and other airs, the "Prefaces" author spares no effort to reveal the ethico-sociopolitical discourse hidden beneath the textual surface. Typically, he seeks to conceive the underlying intent of a poem by tracing its provenance and tying it to a prominent political figure from a particular period of the Zhou dynasty. Indeed, in the Major Preface, he explicitly speaks of "the affairs of a given state being tied to one specific person" and mentions the first two groups of airs, "Zhou South" ("Zhou nan") and "Shao South" ("Shao nan"), as being tied to the luminous Duke Zhou and King Shao. If a political figure with whom a given poem is tied is laudable, he tends to describe the poem as praising his or her moral conduct and influence. Conversely, if the figure is despicable, he usually characterizes the poem as a censure of his or her evil conduct and influence. Pursuing this agenda, it is only natural that the "Prefaces" author would completely ignore the first poem's apparent depiction of courtship and instead give a purely ethico-sociopolitical reading.

How does the "Prefaces" author typically pursue his reading? To answer this second question, let me try to reconstruct his interpretive process, again using "Ospreys" as an example. In my opinion, the "Prefaces" author has gone through three main steps to reach his conclusion about the meaning of "Ospreys." First, he identifies the provenance of "Zhou South" and "Shao South," the first two groups of the airs, as the former fiefdoms of early Zhou kings. Consequently, he assumes that "Ospreys" and all other airs of the two groups praise the virtues and accomplishments of the early Zhou kings.

Next, he proceeds to tie "Ospreys" to King Wen, the founder and the first king of Zhou. As King Wen or his kingly way is believed by all Confucians to be the moral foundation of the entire Zhou dynasty, he believes that "Ospreys," the first poem of the *Poetry*, can only be an encomium on the most important of King Wen's moral virtues: a harmonious husband–wife relationship. While we moderns regard spousal relationships as a private domestic issue, the ancient Confucians considered it the very foundation of moral government, lying at the heart of concentric circles of human relationship. This point is made perfectly clear by the "Prefaces" author himself when he claims that "[with the *Poetry*] the early kings regulated the husband–wife relationship, instituted filial piety and reverence, dignified human relations, perfected moral edification, and transformed social customs" (*MSZY* 1:270–271).

Finally, he seeks to demonstrate "Ospreys" as exemplifying the ideal husband–wife relationship. This is no easy task. The description of a prenuptial courtship hardly squares with anyone's notion of the conjugal state. Even if the two parties in this courtship can be taken to symbolize husband and wife, there is still an insurmountable difficulty in identifying King Wen, a venerated Confucian sage-king, with a young man infatuated with a beautiful girl. Nevertheless, the "Prefaces" author comes up with an ingenious solution: identify the speaker with the main wife of a lord and the graceful lady as someone being recruited by her to serve as a concubine. This re-identification of the two parties enables the "Prefaces" author to turn a sensuous courtship into a moral tale of a selfless, devoted wife who "worried about the worthy not being promoted and did not indulge in her own sensuality." Of course, this praise of a lord's wife is ultimately praise of the lord. The virtues of a lord's wife are invariably credited to the moral influence and cultivation by her lord. Although the "Prefaces" author himself doesn't explicitly do so, many later commentators identify this virtuous wife with Tai Si, the main wife of King Wen.

This kind of reading of "Ospreys" and other airs in "Prefaces" undoubtedly strikes us as very far-fetched. But Han readers had no problem embracing it. To them, both the major and minor prefaces were as convincing and insightful as they were edifying. By deftly integrating these prefaces with the 305 *Shijing* poems, the compiler Mao accomplished something truly remarkable: elevation of his text of the *Poetry* above other competing texts, toward canonical status.

In Han times, there were four major texts of the *Poetry*, and attendant schools of learning. Besides the Mao Text, there were the Qi, the Lu, and the Han texts of the *Poetry*. These three texts were each formally sanctioned by the Han court, but the Mao Text was not. Nonetheless, the Mao Text had a much more profound influence than the other three texts on how the *Poetry* was read and interpreted after the Han. There are extrinsic and intrinsic reasons for this. Extrinsically, the other three texts were all lost after the Han, and the Mao Text alone survived. Intrinsically, the Mao Text bested its rivals in transforming the *Poetry* into a Confucian classic.

The rise to prominence of the four texts of the *Poetry* was no doubt a response to the adoption of Confucianism as the state ideology during Emperor Wu's reign (141–87 BCE). In 136 BCE, Emperor Wu formalized the Confucian canon with five classical texts long used and praised by Confucius and his followers (the *Book of Changes*, the *Book of Poetry*, the *Book of Documents*, the *Book of Rites*, and the *Spring and Autumn Annals*), establishing chairs for each of them. These chairs, known as "erudites" (*bo shi*), were the highest scholarly degree or honor conferred by the imperial court (figure 4.1).

Canonization of the *Poetry* entailed a codification of scattered interpretive remarks on the *Poetry* by Confucius and later Confucians, within a cogent, all-encompassing interpretive framework. The Mao Text was much better suited to this task than the other three texts. Its Major Preface established a framework of ethico-sociopolitical interpretation, while its Minor Prefaces interpreted each poem within that framework, consistently characterizing them as works of praise or censure. By contrast, as some scholars argue, the other three texts may not have had prefaces at all, let alone anything like the well-integrated network of prefaces seen in the Mao Text.

There is evidence that "Prefaces" had already acquired considerable canonical authority during the Han (figure 4.2). For instance, the famous "Mao Commentaries" ("Mao zhuan"), generally attributed to Mao Heng, seldom deviates from the readings established by "Prefaces." Nor do the equally important commentaries by Zheng Xuan (127–200), collectively known as "Zheng Annotations" ("Zheng jian"). In many ways, both "Mao Commentaries" and "Zheng Annotations" may be seen as footnotes to "Prefaces" in that they go all out to justify its strained ethico-sociopolitical interpretations.

FIGURE 4.1 A fragment of the Xiping Stone Classics. Confucian classics were carved in stone in 172–178 BCE. The third column of characters from the right reads, "The erudites of the Five Classics." The fragment could be part of a document on the establishment of the erudites.

Just as the "Prefaces" author is audacious in making his strained claims for the 305 poems, Mao and Zheng are resourceful in finding ways to support those claims despite an absence of credible textual evidence. Having reconstructed the interpretive process behind "Prefaces," let me now examine three of the many interpretive strategies employed by Mao and Zheng to rationalize the readings given by "Prefaces."

The first strategy is that of allegorizing nature images. In annotating "Ospreys," Mao labels the depiction of the ospreys as *xing*, or an "affective image." The word "*xing*" literally means "to inspire" or "to evoke." While Confucius spoke of the *Poetry* as being capable of inspiring (*Shi keyi xing*), Mao is probably the first to use *xing* as a noun to denote nature images placed at the beginning of a stanza in a *Shijing* poem. Typically, an affective image is juxtaposed with emotive statements that follow it. It displays little logical relationship with ensuing emotive statements, although a vague analogy may be at times construed between the two.

If post-Han critics tend to explore an affective image's aesthetic effect, Mao is only interested in its analogical relevance to ensuing statements. Indeed, when annotating the first stanza of "Ospreys," he takes the description of ospreys in the next two lines as an encomium to Hou Fei, presumably King Wen's main wife. He explains:

Ospreys are the finest of their kind. They form devoted couples and yet maintain a proper distance from each other.... Hou Fei delights in her lord's virtues and lives in perfect harmony with him. She doesn't show off her beauty and maintains a cautious and reclusive demeanor, just as ospreys keep company with their mates. Consequently, she is capable of influencing all under heaven.

[*MSZY* 1:273]

FIGURE 4.2 Teaching of Confucian classics in the Han. Rubbing of a portrait engraved on bricks. Sitting on the raised platform, the teacher is giving a lesson to his pupils sitting on mats. Each student is holding a booklet—a stack of stringed bamboo strips carved with characters. One student (the first from the lower right) is wearing on his waist a "writing knife," which is used for carving characters on a bamboo strip. 40 by 45.8 cm. Unearthed in Chengdu, Sichuan Province.

By drawing such an analogy between ospreys' and Hou Fei's lifestyles, Mao manages to transform ospreys into an allegorical symbol of Hou Fei's moral virtues, lending support to the ethico-sociopolitical reading given in "Prefaces."

The second strategy is a modified exercise of "cutting a section off a *Shijing* poem to conceive a meaning" (*duanzhang quyi*). This phrase refers to the old practice of taking lines of a *Shijing* poem out of their original context and making them expressive of a state's or courtier's intent on a diplomatic occasion. When so presented, these lines yield new meaning that has little do with the original text and has to be construed in the new context of an ongoing diplomatic conversation. Zheng Xuan's annotations on "I Beg of You, Zhong Zi" ("Jiang Zhong Zi," ☞ *HTRCP* C1.4) constitute a clever adaptation of this old practice of deconstructing *Shijing* lines.

> "I Beg of You, Zhong Zi" is a satire of Duke Zhuang. He could not restrain his mother, nor could he keep his brother out of harm's way. When his brother Shuduan of Gong went astray, he did not stop him. Zhai Zhong remonstrated with him but he wouldn't listen. His intolerance of mild criticism eventually led to great calamities.

I BEG OF YOU, ZHONG ZI 將仲子

	I beg of you, Zhong Zi,	將仲子兮
2	Don't cross into my hamlet.	無踰我里
	Don't break my planted willows,	無折我樹杞
4	Could I care so much for them?	豈敢愛之
	It's father and mother I dread.	畏我父母
6	Zhong, you're embraceable . . .	仲可懷也
	But the talk of my father and mother is	父母之言
8	Indeed something dreadful.	亦可畏也
	I beg of you, Zhong Zi,	將仲子兮
10	Don't climb over my wall.	無踰我牆
	Don't break my planted mulberries.	無折我樹桑
12	Could I care so much for them?	豈敢愛之
	It's all my brothers I dread.	畏我諸兄
14	Zhong, you're embraceable . . .	仲可懷也
	But the talk of all my brothers is	諸兄之言
16	Indeed something dreadful.	亦可畏也
	I beg of you, Zhong Zi,	將仲子兮
18	Don't leap into my garden.	無踰我園
	Don't break my planted hardwoods.	無折我樹檀
20	Could I care so much for them?	豈敢愛之
	I dread others will talk too much.	畏人之多言
22	Zhong, you're embraceable . . .	仲可懷也
	But others' talking too much is	人之多言
24	Indeed something dreadful.	亦可畏也

[MAO NO. 76, *MSZY* 1:337; TRANS. NIENHAUSER, 18–20]

Read against the poem proper, this preface looks even more unlikely than the preface to "Ospreys" discussed earlier. We can't help but wonder what on earth this erotic love poem has to do with a censure of Duke Zhuang of Zheng (757–701 BCE) for condoning the evil conduct of his younger brother Shuduan of Gong (754 BCE–?).

The poem features a young woman addressing in her mind her lover, whom she imagines or actually sees crashing through one barrier after another and getting closer and closer to her. Her speech is made up of a plea ("I beg of you, Zhong Zi"), a warning ("Don't . . . / Don't . . ."), a rhetorical question and clarification ("Could I care so much for them? / "It's . . . I fear"), and an expression of love and fear ("Zhong, you are embraceable / but the talk of . . ."). If these sentences aptly convey her complex feelings of fear, yearning, and worry, an incremental repetition (a repetition with variation) amplifies them most dramatically. The shift of location in line 2 of the three stanzas—from the hamlet to the hall of a family compound to an inner garden—captures an inbound physical movement of her lover penetrating layers of barriers and getting closer and closer to her.

Then the variation of the people mentioned in lines 5, 13, and 21 and 7, 15, and 23 reveals an opposite, outbound movement of the mind: her fear of accusers widening from her parents to her brothers to all people in the hamlet. In the *Poetry*, and in fact in folk songs of any time and place, it is very rare to see incremental repetition generating two simultaneous crescendos of movement (physical versus mental) in opposite directions (inbound versus outbound) to produce such a riveting effect. For this reason, "I Beg of You, Zhong Zi" is one of the most memorable airs in the *Poetry*.

Completely ignoring this dramatic description of a pending tryst, the author of "Prefaces" takes "I Beg of You, Zhong Zi" to be an allegorical account of Duke Zhuang's ill-advised rejection of his minister Zhai Zhong's remonstration. To justify this strained allegorization, Zheng Xuan does some bold gender switching of his own. He identifies the speaker, obviously a young woman passionately in love, with Duke Zhuang, while accordingly changing the addressee from the woman's lover to Zhai Zhong.

With the speaker and the addressee so replaced, Zheng Xuan proceeds to cut a section off a *Shijing* poem to conceive a meaning. First, he cuts off lines 2–3 ("Don't cross into my hamlet. / Don't break my planted willows") and transplants them into the scene of confrontation between Duke Zhuang and Zhai Zhong. This enables him to read the two lines as Duke Zhuang's rebuff of Zhai Zhong: "Don't impose on my relatives" and "Don't harm my brothers." By recontextualizing lines 4–8 in the same fashion, Zheng turns these lines into Duke Zhuang's explanation of the reasons for condoning his evildoing brother: "My brother Duan is causing troubles. How dare I love him and spare his punishment? It is because of my parents that I do not punish him. . . . Pressured by my parents, I cannot follow your advice" (*MSZY* 1:337). By cutting all these lines from "I Beg of You, Zhong Zi" and drawing a one-to-one correspondence between them and the words spoken by two historical figures, Zheng Xuan has effectively turned the entire poem into a bona fide political allegory.

The third strategy is that of interiorizing a poem or parts of it—that is, reading it as fragments of imagination by a speaker rather than as a description of an actual scene or event. Zheng Xuan's annotations on "There Is a Dead Doe in the Wilds" ("Ye you sijun") is an excellent case in point:

"There Is a Dead Doe in the Wilds" expresses abhorrence at impropriety. As the world was in turmoil, acts of violence were inflicted on people and licentious conduct became rampant. But thanks to the transforming influence of King Wen, people still abhorred impropriety even in this time of chaos.

	In the wilds there is a dead doe;	野有死麕
2	With white rushes we cover her.	白茅包之
	There was a lady longing for the spring;	有女懷春
4	A fair knight seduced her.	吉士誘之
	In the wood there is a clump of oaks,	林有樸樕
6	And in the wilds a dead deer	野有死鹿
	With white rushes well bound;	白茅純束
8	There was a lady fair as jade.	有女如玉

"Heigh, not so hasty, not so rough;	舒而脫脫兮
10 Heigh, do not touch my handkerchief.	無感我帨兮
Take care, or the dog will bark."	無使尨也吠

[MAO NO. 23, *MSZY* 1:292–293; TRANS. WALEY, 60]

Here, the mismatch between preface and text proper is even more glaring than in the previous two poems. The preface says exactly the opposite of what is described in the poem. The poem gives an account of a tryst in action (as opposed to a pending one in "I Beg of You, Zhong Zi"), climaxed by the girl's halfhearted protest at being caressed by her lover. The preface, however, considers the poem an expression of abhorrence at licentious conduct. This counterintuitive reading is obviously dictated by the "Preface" author's belief in historical-geographical determinism. Since this poem is an air from Shao Nan, the home region of King Shao, he must have reasoned that it couldn't be anything but an encomium to the fine social customs observed there. Hence, he offers laudatory comments on the poem but, as usual, doesn't deign to explain.

The task of explanation is left to two prominent Han exegetes, Mao and Zheng Xuan. To justify the far-fetched preface, Mao takes the initial step of identifying a transgression of proper rituals implied in the poem: "The impropriety at issue refers to the practices of doing away with matchmaking, not sending [the betrothal gifts of] wild geese and silk, and kidnapping and coercing women into marriages. It was the time of Zhou [the last king of the Shang dynasty]" (*MSZY* 1:292). He also observes, "In time of calamities and famine, betrothal gifts were reduced but were still made. The dead doe in the wild was the spoil of hunting. It was carved up so that its meat could be shared. The white rushes were used to wrap its meat because it was clean and pure."

Following Mao's glosses and notes, Zheng Xuan goes one step further to explain each line of the poem as indicative of either a transgression or an observance of proper rituals. Echoing what Mao has said about forced marriages, he takes the last two lines of the poem, literally a halfhearted reprimand for a lover's caress, to be a resolute expression of abhorrence at the kidnapping and coercion of women by violent men. It is much harder, however, to read the other lines of the poem in the same vein. In the preceding line, the speaker obviously speaks in a tone of gentle, loving persuasion. In line 4, the young suitor is called "a fair knight," and it is impossible to imagine this appellation being applied to a kidnapper of women.

How to smooth out these contradictions and make the poem fit what is said in "Prefaces"? Zheng comes up with a most ingenious solution: take all but the last two lines as flashes of imagination by someone yearning for ideal marriage rituals. According to Zheng, the dead doe in the wild depicted in lines 1–2 and 5–6 is in fact envisioned by "a virtuous woman wishing to see someone come with a share of a hunted doe's meat as a betrothal gift" (*MSZY* 1:292). Similarly, the beautiful woman depicted in lines 3–4 and 7–8 is an inward image of "a virtuous woman yearning to meet a fine man in accordance with rituals during midspring, a meeting properly made possible by a matchmaker sent by the man." To emphasize these scenes as imagined rather than actual, Zheng adds that "all this was said to disapprove the practice of impropriety at the time." In other words, these scenes are imagined not only to fulfill an unobtainable wish but also to convey social criticism. Zheng's "interiorization" of these lines may very well be the best rationalization one could possibly produce in support of the strained reading given in "Prefaces."

Through witnessing the transformation of three love poems into positive or negative historical examples of personal conduct and state governance, we gain insight into the Han exegetes' ambitious attempt to canonize the *Poetry*, and the array of interpretive strategies they deployed for achieving that goal. Judging by the unchallenged canonical status accorded the *Poetry* since the Han, these Han exegetes achieved their goal most impressively. However, insofar as the *Poetry* is also a literary work in its own right, "Prefaces," "Mao Commentaries," and "Zheng Annotations" inevitably invite evaluation as works of literary criticism as well. Judged in terms of aesthetic and critical sensibility, the three commentaries fare rather poorly. Understandably, they have long been deplored for their obliviousness to the beauty of such lively, spontaneous love poems as they unsympathetically reduce them to dull, tone-deaf moral exemplars. This uncomplimentary view of the three texts is widely held among premodern and modern literary critics alike. Few if any pause to consider whether these three texts might have some undiscovered literary value.

True, the ethico-sociopolitical readings of *Shijing* love poems in these three texts are implausible, boring, and hard to defend. But these readings hide an ironic, completely overlooked fact: the interpretive process that yields such readings is itself an admirable exercise of literary imagination. The imagination so exercised is "literary" in that it is primed by a conscious exploitation of rich semantic and syntactic ambiguities, now generally deemed a crucial aspect of the "literariness" of a poetic text.

Just recall how the "Prefaces" author and Zheng Xuan take advantage of the absence of personal pronouns to change the gender of poetic speakers—a lovesick young man in "Ospreys" to Hou Fei, and a young woman passionately in love in "I Beg of You, Zhong Zi" to Duke Zhuang. Without exploiting the ambiguities arising from the omission of pronouns, the "Prefaces" author and Zheng Xuan could not possibly have allegorized the two poems in the ways they did. If the "Prefaces" author and Zheng Xuan were to use a language like English, in which no sentences make sense without a stated subject or an unambiguously implied one (such as the implied "you" in an imperative sentence like "Open the window"), would they be able to change the genders of poetic speakers at will to facilitate their allegorizing endeavors? Definitely not. They would be just as hamstrung as Western allegorists by the mandatory subject-plus-predicate syntax and deprived of their unique privilege for indulging in gender switching.

This brings us to a prominent issue of Chinese literary scholarship: the inherent relationship between the noninflectional, ambiguity-rich Chinese language and Chinese poetic art. In the Western-language scholarship on Chinese poetry, much has been said about the aesthetic effects obtained by the customary omission of personal pronouns in classical Chinese poems, especially those composed in highly condensed, regulated styles during and after the Tang. Great poets like Du Fu (712–770) consciously exploit the truncated, subjectless sentences to generate multiple readings of a parallel couplet, each of which enhances the poetic theme in its own way.[1] What has so far escaped notice is that such an exploitation of ambiguities begins with the pre-Han and Han exegetes of the *Poetry*, not with Tang poets who come five centuries later.

Another kind of ambiguity consistently exploited by Mao and Zheng Xuan involves indefinite referents of nature images. In the airs of the *Poetry*, nature images are usually neither grouped together to coherently depict a scene nor tightly woven into a narrative. More often than not, they occur in the first two lines of a stanza, followed by two or more lines of emotive statements. This juxtaposition of two apparently unrelated parts gives rise to abundant ambiguities. What did the poet intend to convey by juxtaposing nature images and emotive statements?

This question is apparently of no concern to the "Prefaces" author. In his view, nature images are interpretively irrelevant and hence are seldom if ever mentioned in the prefaces. However, in amplifying the ethico-sociopolitical readings of "Prefaces," Mao attaches great importance to nature images, labeling them *xing* or "affective images." In glossing "affective images," he seeks to show how they evoke or call up a visual analogue of the ethico-sociopolitical significance proclaimed by "Prefaces." His gloss of "Ospreys," noted earlier, is an excellent case in point.

Of course, not all nature images lend themselves so readily to an analogical interpretation. For instance, is it possible to make the "dead doe" into an analogue of matchmaking and presenting betrothal gifts? Probably not—and hence no gloss by Mao. However, while Mao considers this image "un-analogizable" or conceptually unexplainable, Zheng Xuan finds it stunningly evocative: it calls up an imagined scene or fantasy in the mind of a lovesick girl. Zheng's reading of the "dead doe" presages how later critics would handle "un-analogizable" images: not responding to them conceptually but emotively and imaginatively. Shortly after Mao and Zheng, Chinese critics begin to differentiate between "analogizable" and "un-analogizable" images. They label the former *bi* (analogues) while reserving the term *xing* (affective images) for the latter. Anything in between they call *bixing* (analogical-affective images).

On a more theoretical level, the allegorization of three love poems by Han exegetes reveals a dynamic, symbiotic relationship between the ethico-sociopolitical and the literary in Han poetic culture. We have noted that the canonization of the *Poetry*, a court-sanctioned endeavor, is achieved largely through a dexterous exploitation of its inherent literary qualities, especially its reservoir of syntactic and structural ambiguities. In claiming that the airs "employ indirect expressions to make subtle remonstrance" (*zhu wen jue jian*) in the Major Preface, the "Prefaces" author himself seems to acknowledge the pivotal importance of indirection or ambiguities for his purposes. The consistent exploitation of ambiguities by the "Prefaces" author, Mao, and Zheng amounts to nothing less than a genuine imaginative exercise.

Considering the symbiotic relationship between the ethico-sociopolitical and the literary in "Prefaces," "Mao Commentaries," and "Zheng Annotations," we may wonder how these *Shijing* commentaries got admitted into the Confucian canon by themselves. In his famed *Correct Meanings of the Mao Text of the* Book of Poetry (*Mao shi zheng yi*), Kong Yingda (574–648) treats "Prefaces" practically the same way he does the *Poetry* itself, writing equally copious commentary on both (figure 4.3). Clearly this is the best testament to the canonical status accorded the "Prefaces" and, by extension, its attendant "Mao Commentaries" and "Zheng Annotations." By contrast, these three texts are considered by most to be of small literary value, except for a theoretical exposition on the *Poetry*'s provenance and functions in the Major Preface. But given the symbiosis noted above, this long-accepted view should be challenged. In my opinion, they merit serious reevaluation on account of their positive influence on poetry, criticism, and aesthetic theory.

In terms of poetics, it is not difficult to see a connection between the Han exegetes' exploitation of ambiguity in their commentaries and the linguistic maneuvers performed by masterful Tang poets like Du Fu in their poetic works. After all, the Mao Text of the *Book of Poetry* and the three commentaries are the Confucian canonical texts on which these poets were reared. Repeated readings of the three *Shijing* commentaries must have left an indelible impression on these poets' supple creative minds. These poets would have inherited from the Han exegetic masters a keen sensitivity to the

FIGURE 4.3 A woodblock print of "Major Preface to the Mao Text of the *Book of Poetry*."

expressive potential of ambiguity in the Chinese language, and they must have acquired the skill to exploit these to the best possible effect. In any case, their acts of poetic creation represent in many ways a replication of the Han exegetes' acts of creative interpretation.

In the realm of poetry criticism, Zheng Xuan's interiorizing of nature images like the dead doe marked the beginning of an abiding preoccupation with *xing* (affective images) in traditional Chinese poetics. Since the Han, the discussion about the distinction of *xing* from *bi* (analogues) and the former's unparalleled aesthetic effect has taken on a life of its own and in fact continues to this day. In modern Chinese literary scholarship, *xing* has been rightly regarded as a hallmark of Chinese poetic art and has been insightfully compared to the juxtapositional modes developed in Western modernist poetry. But it has so far gone unnoticed that this millennia-old fascination with *xing* actually begins with Zheng Xuan's pioneering exploration of it as images of the mind.

In the more rarefied realm of aesthetic theory, we note a thought-provoking irony. The far-fetched and seemingly unaesthetic readings of the *Poetry* in "Prefaces" offer an alternative or complementary version of the Chinese aesthetic ideal of "meaning beyond words" (*yan wai zhi yi*). Almost invariably, this ideal has been traced to Laozi's and Zhuangzi's remarks on the existence of Dao, or ultimate reality beyond words. But the Han exegetes' interpretive practices point to a Confucian source for the "meaning beyond words" ideal. Less metaphysically or more practically, they have successfully constructed and projected an ethico-sociopolitical intent beyond the textual meaning. Notably, many later Confucian-minded poets not only would follow the Han exegetes' footsteps in their poetic creation but also would theorize about their allegorist practices in terms of a quest for meanings beyond words. Such theorization was apparently calculated to compete with the dominant Daoist version of "meanings beyond words." All this said, I can now end my own quest for meanings beyond words: the far-reaching literary implications behind the Han commentaries' allegorization of the *Shijing* love poems. (For more *Shijing* poems, ☞ *HTRCP* chap. 1).

ZONG-QI CAI

NOTES

1. A classic example is Du Fu's famous couplet "feel time flower shed tears / hate separation bird startle heart" (word-for-word translation) in "Spring Scene." This couplet generates as many as five different readings, each of which enables us to empathize with the grieving poet from a unique angle. See my discussion of this couplet in Zong-qi Cai, ed., *How to Read Chinese Poetry: A Guided Anthology* (New York: Columbia University Press, 2008), 165–167 and 387.

PRIMARY SOURCE

MSZY *Mao shi zhengyi* 毛詩正義 (Correct Meanings of the Mao Text of the *Book of Poetry*). In Ruan Yuan (1764–1849), *Shisanjing zhushu* 十三經註疏 (Commentaries and Subcommentaries on the Thirteen Classics), 1:259–630. 2 vols. Beijing: Zhonghua shuju, 1977.

SUGGESTED READINGS

ENGLISH

Legge, James. *The Chinese Classics, with a Translation, Critical and Exegetical Notes, Prolegmena, and Copious Indexes*. Vol. 4, *The She King*. Taipei: SMC Publishing, 1994.
Nienhauser, William H. "Tetrasyllabic *Shi* Poetry: *The Book of Poetry (Shijing)*." In *How to Read Chinese Poetry: A Guided Anthology*, ed. Zong-qi Cai, 13–35. New York: Columbia University Press, 2008.
Waley, Arthur, trans. *The Book of Songs*. New York: Grove Press, 1960.

CHINESE

Chen Zizhan 陳子展. *Shijing zhijie* 詩經直解 (The *Book of Poetry* Straightforwardly Understood). 2 vols. Shanghai: Fudan daxue chubanshe, 1983.
Mao shi Zheng jian 毛詩鄭箋 (Zheng Annotations on the Mao Text of the *Book of Poetry*). Sibu beiyao edition.
Xiang Xi 向熹. *Shijing cidian* 詩經詞典 (Dictionary for the *Book of Poetry*). Rev. ed. Beijing: Shangwu yinshuguan, 2014.

5

LOVE BEYOND THE GRAVE

A Tragic Tale of Love and Marriage in Han China

"Old Poem Composed for the Wife of Jiao Zhongqing" ("Gushi wei Jiao Zhongqing qi zuo") is a long narrative poem in pentasyllabic verse by an unknown author, dated usually to the last years of the Han dynasty (206 BCE–220 CE). In written sources, it first appeared in the early sixth-century anthology *New Songs from a Jade Terrace* (*Yu tai xin yong*), known as a repository of poems standing outside the orthodox tradition and dealing particularly with women and love. Editors of the anthology provided the poem with a preface claiming that it is based on a real story that happened "in the end of the Han during the Jian'an era [196–220] in the prefecture of Lujiang," and that it was composed shortly afterwards. However, this claim may itself be a fiction; the poem might have been created at any time before it was recorded in written form.

There is a long and ongoing academic discussion about the dating; recently, linguistic data such as specific vocabulary or the nature of the rhymes have been given as evidence, with the prevailing opinion dating the poem's origin to the late Han or early Wei (220–265). If this is true, the poem must have circulated in oral form for a long time before it was recorded. This assumption is quite plausible; we know of similar practices of oral transmission in other cultures, perhaps most notably the works of Homer. On account of its likely origin in the oral tradition, this poem is generally considered a *yuefu* poem, a work in the style of folk songs collected by the Han Music Bureau (Han Yuefu). Recent research positions the origin of the poem among professional singers and storytellers performing in the houses of noble families on festive occasions.[1]

The poem tells the tragic story of the broken marriage of Jiao Zhongqing, a petty clerk in the prefectural office, and his wife Liu Lanzhi (Orchid Liu). Lanzhi, a beautiful and talented young woman, does not get along well with her mother-in-law. As a result, she is eventually divorced from her loving husband, and later, after being sent home, she is forced by her older brother to remarry. Lanzhi and Zhongqing still feel a deep affection for each other, and when it becomes clear they will not be reunited, they decide that they would rather die than live apart.

The poem begins with an "affective image" (*xing*) of the flying peacock, which gives the poem its alternative and today generally used title, "Southeast Flies the Peacock" ("Kongque dong nan fei"). This affective image, a popular poetic device originating in the ancient songs of the *Book of Poetry* (*Shijing*), sets the mood at the very beginning of the poem, though the exact meaning of the peacock motif remains ambiguous, bringing into the poem a vague theme of hesitation, difficult decision making, perhaps also a parting, and an overall air of melancholy. We will see another bird image at the end of the poem, where it will bring back the bird symbolism and evoke further meanings related to it.

The story has become one of the best-known love stories in Chinese literature. In the past, mainly since the Ming (1368–1644) and Qing (1644–1911) dynasties, it was popularized among wide audiences through theater. During the republican period, the story was embraced by the young generation aspiring for free marriage and love, and it was adapted several times for Western-style theater. Recently it was adapted again, as a melodramatic TV movie.[2] The prevailing understanding of the story today is as a criticism of the old society governed by Confucian orthodoxy and lacking the freedom to love. Hans Frankel, in the most detailed study of the poem in a Western language, also characterizes it as a "protest against the prevailing absolute authority of the family elders in matrimonial matters," further elaborating on its supposedly "Freudian slant."[3]

A careful reading of the poem, however, including a richer consideration of both its provenance and its historical and social contexts, also reveals other kinds of meaning and thus opens the poem to a range of possible interpretations. Before looking further into its theme and form, let us first read the entire poem.

	Southeast flies the peacock,	孔雀東南飛
2	Every five miles it hesitates for a while.	五里一徘徊
	"At thirteen I could weave silk,	十三能織素
4	At fourteen I learnt how to tailor clothes,	十四學裁衣
	At fifteen I played the harp,	十五彈箜篌
6	At sixteen I recited the *Songs* and the *Documents*.	十六誦詩書
	Since at seventeen I became your wife,	十七為君婦
8	In my heart I have always felt bitterness and sorrow;	心中常苦悲
	After you, my lord, have become a prefectural clerk,	君既為府吏
10	You keep to your duties, not moved by love;	守節情不移
	I remain in an empty room,	賤妾留空房
12	Only rarely do we see each other.[4]	相見常日稀
	When the cock crows I sit by the loom to weave,	雞鳴入機織
14	Night after night without rest.	夜夜不得息
	In three days I finish five bolts of silk,	三日斷五疋
16	But the Great One, your mother, still reproaches me as being too slow.	大人故嫌遲
	It's not that my weaving is slow,	非為織作遲
18	But in your family it's hard to be a daughter-in-law.	君家婦難為
	I cannot bear to be ordered about,	妾不堪驅使
20	In vain I remain here, good for nothing.	徒留無所施
	You can tell my mother-in-law now:	便可白公姥
22	Please send me back without delay."	及時相遣歸
	When the prefectural clerk heard this,	府吏得聞之
24	He went up to the hall and told his mother:	堂上啟阿母
	"Your son has been born with an unhappy lot,	兒已薄祿相
26	But I was fortunate to get this wife.	幸復得此婦
	Newly wed, we have shared pillow and mat,	結髮同枕席
28	Beneath the Yellow Springs we will remain companions;	黃泉共為友
	We have lived together for two, three years,	共事二三年

30	It has not been long yet;	始爾未為久
	In her behavior was nothing improper,	女行無偏斜
32	How would I have thought you would not like her?"	何意致不厚
	Mother said to the clerk:	阿母謂府吏
34	"How can you be so stupid?	何乃太區區
	This wife shows no politeness or restraint,	此婦無禮節
36	In her behavior she does as she wants,	舉動自專由
	I have long been angry with her.	吾意久懷忿
38	How can you dare to disobey?	汝豈得自由
	Our neighbors to the east have a virtuous daughter	東家有賢女
40	Who calls herself Qin Luofu.	自名秦羅敷
	She is lovely, her appearance without peer,	可憐體無比
42	Mother will ask for her for you.	阿母為汝求
	Quickly send your wife away.	便可速遣之
44	Send her off! Beware of keeping her!"	遣去慎莫留
	The clerk long knelt and begged,	府吏長跪告
46	Bowing down and in deep thought, he announced to his mother:	伏惟啟阿母
	"If you now send this wife away,	今若遣此婦
48	Till my death I'll never marry again."	終老不復取
	When Mother heard this,	阿母得聞之
50	She pounded her seat and flew into a rage:	槌牀便大怒
	"You, little boy, have no respect at all,	小子無所畏
52	How dare you speak up for your wife?	何敢助婦語
	I have already lost all affection for her,	吾已失恩義
54	I will most certainly not agree to what you say."	會不相從許
	The clerk was silent and made no sound,	府吏默無聲
56	He bowed twice and went back to his rooms.	再拜還入戶
	He started to talk about this to his young wife,	舉言謂新婦
58	Choking with grief, he could hardly speak:	哽咽不能語
	"I myself would not drive you out, my dear,	我自不驅卿
60	It is my mother who is forcing me.	逼迫有阿母
	My dear, just return home for the time being,	卿但暫還家
62	And I'll report for now to my office.	吾今且報府
	Before long I will return,	不久當歸還
64	And when I return, I'll certainly bring you back.	還必相迎取
	For that sake please put up with it,	以此下心意
66	And please do not act against my words."	慎勿違吾語
	The young wife told the clerk:	新婦謂府吏
68	"Please do not trouble yourself anymore.	勿復重紛紜
	Some time ago, in late winter,	往昔初陽歲
70	I parted with my home and came to your noble house.	謝家來貴門
	I served my mother-in-law and obeyed her,	奉事循公姥

72	How would I dare decide on my own in anything I did?	進止敢自專
	Day and night I labored diligently,	晝夜勤作息
74	Lonely entwined in hard work.	伶俜縈苦辛
	I believe I committed no fault,	謂言無罪過
76	I took good care of her to repay her great kindness;	供養卒大恩
	Despite that, I am being expelled,	仍更被驅遣
78	Why talk about bringing me back?	何言復來還
	I have an embroidered waist jacket,	妾有繡腰襦
80	Gorgeous, all shining on its own;	葳蕤自生光
	A doubly thick red-gauze bed curtain	紅羅復斗帳
82	With sachets suspended at four corners;	四角垂香囊
	Sixty or seventy chests and cases,	箱帘六七十
84	Tied up with bluish-green silk strings,	綠碧青絲繩
	Each piece different from another,	物物各自異
86	With all kinds of things inside.	種種在其中
	Once one becomes unworthy, one's belongings also lose value,	人賤物亦鄙
88	They are not good enough to welcome my successor.	不足迎後人
	Keep them as something given away,	留待作遺施
90	From now on we'll have no chance to meet again.	於今無會因
	From time to time draw consolation from them,	時時為安慰
92	And never forget about me."	久久莫相忘
	The cock crowed, outside it was about to get bright,	雞鳴外欲曙
94	The young wife rose and started carefully to dress.	新婦起嚴妝
	"I put on my embroidered lined skirt."	著我繡夾裙
96	Every piece she tried on four or five times.	事事四五通
	On her feet she put silk shoes,	足下躡絲履
98	On her head a shiny tortoise shell ornament, shone	頭上瑇瑁光
	Around her waist a stream of white silk,	腰若流紈素
100	On her ears she wore bright-moon pearl earrings.	耳著明月璫
	Her fingers were like peeled tender onion stems,	指如削蔥根
102	Her mouth like holding a piece of cinnabar.	口如含朱丹
	Delicately she took tiny steps,	纖纖作細步
104	Exquisite, without equal in the world.	精妙世無雙
	She went up to the hall and bowed to Mother,	上堂拜阿母
106	Mother listened but did not keep her from going.	母聽去不止
	"In the past, as a child,	昔作女兒時
108	I grew up in village backwaters.	生小出野里
	I never had fine breeding,	本自無教訓
110	And I felt more ashamed when married to the son of a noble family.	兼愧貴家子
	I received much money and silk from you, Mother,	受母錢帛多
112	But I was unable to live up to your orders.	不堪母驅使
	Today I go back to my home,	今日還家去

114	I think of you toiling in the house."	念母勞家裏
	Then she parted with her little sister-in-law,	卻與小姑別
116	Her tears fell like strings of pearls:	淚落連珠子
	"When I first came as a bride,	新婦初來時
118	You, my little sister, had just learned to walk, leaning on the bed.	小姑始扶牀
	Now when I am being expelled,	今日被驅遣
120	You are nearly as tall as I.[5]	小姑如我長
	Exert yourself and provide for my mother-in-law,	勤心養公姥
122	Take good care of her.	好自相扶將
	On the seventh day of the seventh month and each nineteenth day,	初七及下九
124	When you play and celebrate, don't forget me."[6]	嬉戲莫相忘
	She left the house and mounted her carriage,	出門登車去
126	Her tears falling in hundreds of rows.	涕落百餘行
	The prefectural clerk's horse was in front,	府吏馬在前
128	The young wife's carriage behind;	新婦車在後
	Yin yin, it sounded, and *dian dian*,	隱隱何甸甸
130	Both stopped at the main road corner.	俱會大道口
	He got off the horse and entered the carriage,	下馬入車中
132	Lowered his head and whispered in her ear:	低頭共耳語
	"I swear I won't abandon you, dear,	誓不相隔卿
134	But for now go back to your family,	且暫還家去
	And I'll go to my office for the time being,	吾今且赴府
136	But before long I'll be sure to return.	不久當還歸
	I swear to Heaven I won't betray you."	誓天不相負
138	The young wife said to the prefectural clerk:	新婦謂府吏
	"I thank you, my lord, for your affectionate concern.	感君區區懷
140	As you remember me so well,	君既若見錄
	I'll expect you to come soon.	不久望君來
142	You must be like a rock, my lord,	君當作磐石
	I, your servant, must be like a reed;	妾當作蒲葦
144	The reed is tough and pliable as silk,	蒲葦紉如絲
	The rock neither turns nor moves.	磐石無轉移
146	But I have an elder brother,	我有親父兄
	By nature as fierce as thunder;	性行暴如雷
148	I fear he will not let me do as I wish,	恐不任我意
	When I think of it my bosom boils!"	逆以煎我懷
150	They raised their hands in a long, painful farewell,	舉手長勞勞
	Both were loath to part.	二情同依依
152	She entered the door and went up to the main hall of her family house,	入門上家堂
	At a loss what to do, she was ashamed of herself.	進退無顏儀
154	Her mother wrung her hands:	阿母大拊掌
	"I did not expect you would return by yourself, my daughter!	不圖子自歸

156	At thirteen I taught you to weave silk,	十三教汝織
	At fourteen you knew how to tailor clothes,	十四能裁衣
158	At fifteen you played the harp,	十五彈箜篌
	At sixteen you knew etiquette and propriety,	十六知禮儀
160	At seventeen I sent you away to marry,	十七遣汝嫁
	And I believed you would do no wrong.	謂言無誓違
162	What fault did you commit,	汝今何罪過
	That now you return alone without being invited?"	不迎而自歸
164	Lanzhi was ashamed to face her mother:	蘭芝慙阿母
	"Your daughter really has done no wrong."	兒實無罪過
166	Mother was overcome with sorrow.	阿母大悲摧
	Ten-odd days after she returned home,	還家十餘日
168	The district magistrate sent a matchmaker	縣令遣媒來
	He said: "The magistrate has a third son,	云有第三郎
170	So handsome, he has no equal in the world.	窈窕世無雙
	He is just eighteen or nineteen years old,	年始十八九
172	Well-spoken, and with many talents."	便言多令才
	The mother said to her daughter:	阿母謂阿女
174	"You may go and promise yourself to him."	汝可去應之
	The daughter answered in tears:	阿女含淚答
176	"When Lanzhi was returning home	蘭芝初還時
	The prefectural clerk exhorted over and again	府吏見丁寧
178	That we swear not to forsake each other.	結誓不別離
	If now I act against our love,	今日違情義
180	I am afraid this would not be good.	恐此事非奇
	You may send back the messenger,	自可斷來信
182	Tell him: 'Slowly, slowly—we'll talk about it later.'"	徐徐更謂之
	The mother said to the matchmaker:	阿母白媒人
184	"We, a poor and humble family, have this daughter.	貧賤有此女
	Shortly after we married her, she was sent back home.	始適還家門
186	Unfit to be a clerk's wife,	不堪吏人婦
	How could she be a match for your young lord?	豈合令郎君
188	Fortunately you can direct your inquiries widely around,	幸可廣問訊
	I can't just say yes to your proposal."	不得便相許
190	A few days after the matchmaker had gone,	媒人去數日
	Before long, the magistrate's adjutant was sent to pay a call on the prefect and returned:	尋遣丞請還
192	"I told the prefect about this girl Lanzhi,[7]	說有蘭家女
	Whose family inherited the status of high officials.	承籍有宦官
194	They told me there is the prefect's fifth son,	云有第五郎
	Dainty and elegant, not yet married,	嬌逸未有婚
196	And sent me to act as a matchmaker.	遣丞為媒人

	His secretary had passed the prefect's word to me."	主簿通語言
198	Coming to the point, he said to the mother: "In the prefect's family	直說太守家
	There is this young gentleman.	有此令郎君
200	Since they want to tie up with you the bond of kinship,	既欲結大義
	They have sent me to your noble house."	故遣來貴門
202	Mother told the matchmaker:	阿母謝媒人
	"My daughter has sworn an oath,	女子先有誓
204	How could I, an old lady, speak about it?"	老姥豈敢言
	But when the elder brother heard this	阿兄得聞之
206	He was displeased and annoyed in his heart.	悵然心中煩
	He started to speak to his younger sister:	舉言謂阿妹
208	"When making decisions, why don't you think it over?	作計何不量
	First you married a prefectural clerk,	先嫁得府吏
210	In your next marriage you can have a noble lord.	後嫁得郎君
	One was bad fortune and the other is good—the difference between heaven and earth.	否泰如天地
212	It's enough to bring you distinction of a lifetime!	足以榮汝身
	If you don't marry this righteous gentleman,	不嫁義郎體
214	What do you hope for in the future?"	其往欲何云
	Lanzhi raised her head and replied:	蘭芝仰頭答
216	"It truly is as you, my elder brother, say.	理實如兄言
	I left home to serve my husband	謝家事夫壻
218	But returned midway to my brother's house.	中道還兄門
	In everything to be settled I'll comply with my brother's view,	處分適兄意
220	How could I assert my own wish?	那得自任專
	Though I gave my oath to the prefectural clerk,	雖與府吏要
222	We are destined never to meet again.	渠會永無緣
	You may agree to the marriage at once,	登即相許和
224	So the wedding may be arranged."	便可作婚姻
	The matchmaker got off his seat,	媒人下牀去
226	He was all "Yes, yes," and again "So be it, so be it."	諾諾復爾爾
	Having returned to the office he told the prefect:	還部白府君
228	"Your lowly official by your command	下官奉使命
	Negotiated and had good fortune."	言談大有緣
230	When the prefect heard this	府君得聞之
	He was very pleased in his heart.	心中大歡喜
232	He examined the calendar and again opened the books:	視曆復開書
	"Fortunately in this month	便利此月內
234	All six combinations are fitting.	六合正相應
	The lucky day is the thirtieth,	良吉三十日
236	Today is already the twenty-seventh.	今已二十七

	Go ahead and prepare the wedding."	卿可去成婚
238	They passed on the message to hurry up and prepare everything,	交語速裝束
	Moving fast here and there like floating clouds.	駱驛如浮雲
240	Blue bird and white swan boat,	青雀白鵠舫
	With dragon banners in four corners,	四角龍子幡
242	Flap, flap, turning with the wind;	婀娜隨風轉
	Golden carriages with wheels of jade;	金車玉作輪
244	Piebald horses pacing up and down;	躑躅青驄馬
	Tasseled saddles with inlays of gold;	流蘇金鏤鞍
246	Betrothal money of three million coins,	齎錢三百萬
	All strung on green silk strings.	皆用青絲穿
248	Of colored silks three hundred bolts;	雜綵三百疋
	Fish and delicacies bought in Jiao and Guang.	交廣市鮭珍
250	Escort of four, five hundred men	從人四五百
	Overflowing from the prefect's gate.	鬱鬱登郡門
252	Mother said to her daughter:	阿母謂阿女
	"I have just received a letter from the prefect,	適得府君書
254	Tomorrow they will come and welcome you.	明日來迎汝
	Why don't you make your clothes?	何不作衣裳
256	Don't let this marriage fail!"	莫令事不舉
	The daughter was silent and made no sound;	阿女默無聲
258	With her handkerchief she covered her mouth and cried,	手巾掩口啼
	Tears falling, immediately pouring down.	淚落便如瀉
260	"Move my crystal-decorated *ta* stool,	移我琉璃榻
	Take it out and place it by the front window."	出置前窗下
262	With her left hand she held scissors and measure,	左手持刀尺
	With her right she took silk and gauze.	右手執綾羅
264	In the morning she finished an embroidered lined skirt,	朝成繡袷裙
	By the evening she had finished a thin gauze shirt.	晚成單羅衫
266	Gloomy, gloomy, the sun was about to set,	晻晻日欲暝
	Full of grief she went out of the door and cried.	愁思出門啼
268	When the prefectural clerk heard of this twist of events,	府吏聞此變
	He requested a leave to return home.	因求假暫歸
270	Two, three miles before he arrived	未至二三里
	He was so mournful, even his horse neighed sorrowfully.	摧藏馬悲哀
272	The young wife, recognizing the horse's voice,	新婦識馬聲
	Stepped into her shoes and went to meet him.	躡履相逢迎
274	In anguish, she looked out for him into the distance,	悵然遙相望
	She knew it was her former husband coming.	知是故人來
276	She raised her hand and stroked the horse's saddle,	舉手拍馬鞍
	Her sighs would have made a heart break:	嗟歎使心傷

278	"Since you have left me,	自君別我后
	Events have been unexpected;	人事不可量
280	Not indeed as we would have wished,	果不如先願
	Nor do you know all the details.	又非君所詳
282	I have my own mother,	我有親父母
	Who, together with my elder brother, forced me,	逼迫兼弟兄
284	Promised me to another man.	以我應他人
	What hope is there for you, my lord, to return?"	君還何所望
286	The prefectural clerk said to the young wife:	府吏謂新婦
	"I congratulate you, dear, for your lofty advancement!	賀卿得高遷
288	The rock is square and thick,	磐石方且厚
	It can last a thousand years.	可以卒千年
290	The reed was tough and pliable for a while,	蒲葦一時紉
	Just from dawn to dusk.	便作旦夕間
292	You'll be nobler from day to day,	卿當日勝貴
	I will go alone to the Yellow Springs."	吾獨向黃泉
294	The young wife said to the prefectural clerk:	新婦謂府吏
	"Why do you say such things?	何意出此言
296	We have been both forced,	同是被逼迫
	It is like this for you, my lord, and also for me.	君爾妾亦然
298	Beneath the Yellow Springs we'll see each other,	黃泉下相見
	Let's not betray the words of today."	勿違今日言
300	They clasped hands and went their separate ways,	執手分道去
	Each of them returned to his house.	各各還家門
302	Still alive, they parted for death.	生人作死別
	Their resentment, how could it be described?	恨恨那可論
304	They thought about parting from the world,	念與世間辭
	On no account could they be saved.	千萬不復全
306	The prefectural clerk went back to his home,	府吏還家去
	Went up to the hall, and bowed to his mother.	上堂拜阿母
308	"Today the great wind is cold,	今日大風寒
	The cold wind breaks the trees,	寒風摧樹木
310	Severe frost forms on the orchids in the courtyard.	嚴霜結庭蘭
	Your son is like the setting sun today,	兒今日冥冥
312	I will leave you, mother, behind alone.	令母在後單
	I have myself decided on this unkind design,	故作不良計
314	Do not blame ghosts or spirits.	勿復怨鬼神
	May your life last like the rocks of South Mountain,	命如南山石
315	May your four limbs be healthy and straight."	四體康且直
	When his mother heard this,	阿母得聞之
316	Shedding tears, she replied:	零淚應聲落
	"You are the son of a great family	汝是大家子

318	That served in the imperial office.	仕宦於臺閣
	You must not die for a woman.	慎勿為婦死
320	How could it be heartless if one is base, the other noble?	貴賤情何薄
	Our neighbors to the east have a virtuous daughter,	東家有賢女
322	Graceful, the prettiest in the city.	窈窕艷城郭
	Mother will ask for her for you,	阿母為汝求
324	It'll take no longer than from dawn to dusk."	便復在旦夕
	The prefectural clerk bowed twice and returned.	府吏再拜還
326	Long he sighed in the empty room.	長歎空房中
	He made his decision, and thus it would be done.	作計乃爾立
328	He turned his head toward the inner chamber,	轉頭向戶裏
	Bit by bit overcome by grief.	漸見愁煎迫
330	On that day, cows lowed and horses whinnied,	其日馬牛嘶
	As the young wife entered the green wedding tent.	新婦入青廬
332	It was gloomy, gloomy, after dusk,	奄奄黃昏後
	It was quiet, quiet, when everyone began to settle down:	寂寂人定初
334	"My life will be cut off today,	我命絕今日
	My soul will depart, my corpse long remain."	魂去尸長留
336	She grasped her skirt, took off her silk shoes,	攬裙脫絲履
	Raised her body, and plunged into the clear pond.	舉身赴清池
338	When the prefectural clerk heard of the event	府吏聞此事
	He knew in his heart it was parting forever.	心知長別離
340	He paced back and forth under the courtyard trees,	徘徊庭樹下
	Then hanged himself from the southeastern branch.	自掛東南枝
342	Their two families asked for joint burial,	兩家求合葬
	And jointly they were buried, beside the Flowery Mountain.	合葬華山傍
344	East and west they planted pines and cypresses,	東西植松栢
	Left and right grew *wutong* trees,	左右種梧桐
346	Branch upon branch, covering each other,	枝枝相覆蓋
	Leaf upon leaf intertwined.	葉葉相交通
348	Amidst it all a pair of flying birds,	中有雙飛鳥
	Called mandarin ducks,	自名為鴛鴦
350	Who raised their heads to call to each other,	仰頭相向鳴
	Every night, until the fifth watch.[8]	夜夜達五更
352	Passersby stopped and listened;	行人駐足聽
	Widows arose and paced about.	寡婦起彷徨
354	Beware, O ye of later times,	多謝後世人
	Take this warning: be sure never to forget.	戒之慎勿忘

[YTXY 1:42–64][9]

PORTRAIT OF A YOUNG WIFE—BETWEEN SENSE AND SENSIBILITY

The narrator concludes with a direct warning to the audience, thus turning the poem into an exemplum. The didactic message, though explicitly enunciated, is left unclear. Could a Han dynasty song performed in houses of Confucian nobles be a warning against the older generation meddling in love affairs of their children? Or even an attack against a feudal morality, as modern Chinese readers would most probably say? It is hard to believe, and we have to explore other possibilities.

The key to the meaning of the story is in the personality of the main female protagonist. Through her speeches and actions in interaction with other characters, we get a complex portrait of a beautiful and talented young woman from a noble family who is caught up, first, between the love of her husband and the resentment of her mother-in-law, and, later, between her love and her sense of duty toward her own family. Within these conflicts and contradictions, Lanzhi is revealed as a well-educated young woman who is capable of independent decisions and knows how to face life in a pragmatic way. Her independent mind drives Lanzhi into conflict with conventional morality prescribing young wives to obey their mothers-in-law, which she "cannot bear" (line 19). She is also inclined to rash decisions; after complaining about the bad treatment she receives in her husband's family, she herself asks to be sent back to her parents, despite her love for her husband (line 18–22). It is in fact these ill-considered words that trigger further events.

Several scenes in the story show Lanzhi's sudden twists of mood, wavering between outbursts of emotions and perfect composure and rational assessment of the situation. The narrator uses observations about her behavior to demonstrate the ambivalence of her feelings. When her husband comes to tell her the wish of his mother to send her away and at the same time expresses his hope that he will soon bring her back, he is so overcome with grief that he can hardly speak (line 58). By contrast, Lanzhi gets her emotions under control and in the end replies in a matter-of-fact manner, reminding her husband that her return to his side is not possible (lines 68–78). The next day, when preparing herself to leave her husband's home, she is at first so agitated that she tries on every piece "four or five times" before she gets dressed (line 96), but shortly afterward, when she goes to take leave of her mother-in-law, she is again in perfect control of herself and speaks in an exemplary manner as a humble and obedient daughter-in-law (lines 107–114), only to succumb to her emotions again when later parting with her younger sister-in-law (lines 115–126).

Contradictory emotions and rash decisions also guide the events after Lanzhi returns home, and eventually culminate in her death. Her sudden obedience to her elder brother, following her previous passionate refusal to remarry, cannot be explained only by her natural inclination to abrupt changes of mind or a sudden awakening to her sense of family duty. A Qing dynasty critic, Zhang Yugu (1721–1780), commented still differently on Lanzhi's gesture of raising her head when she replies to her brother (line 215). According to him, Lanzhi must have first listened to her brother with her head bowed, humbly yet in defiance; by raising her head, she shows that she has given up her resistance to her brother's wish for her to remarry and at the same time has made a firm decision to end her life, as she has come to the conclusion that she is "destined never" to meet with her beloved husband anymore (line 222). Whether we accept this reading or not, it is interesting as an example of the intense care traditional readers have given to small details in behavior, and also as a testimony to a variety of possible readings.

Both Lanzhi's personal character and her social position are revealed indirectly through the precious objects, mostly silk, but also coins or rare delicacies associated with her person. These objects indirectly express Lanzhi's beauty, dignity, and social superiority. The narrator always pays attention to how carefully Lanzhi dresses herself; she, in her own words, measures her value by the expensive silks she fashions, by what she wears and with what she covers her bed, and by the bluish-green silk cords with which she binds up her chests and cases, "each piece different from another, / with all kinds of [treasures] inside" (lines 79–86). By giving away the precious silks, she displays her pride, her firm conviction (or at that moment perhaps even decision?) that she will never return, but also her love for her husband, including a hint of jealousy against his imagined future new wife (line 88). Silk is briefly mentioned even as Lanzhi is getting ready to die, taking off her silk shoes and grasping her (presumably silk) skirt (line 336).

The prefect measures Lanzhi's value by sending a splendid retinue with marvelous steeds and painted boats adorned with silk banners, bringing rich betrothal gifts, all sorts of rare and valuable objects (lines 240–251). The extravagant display of precious gifts given as a price for Lanzhi demonstrates how rich her would-be new husband was and how much he valued her. When contrasted with her decision to die rather than to marry him, the riches of the gifts also indirectly demonstrate how great was Lanzhi's love for her first husband.

In the end, Lanzhi acts resolutely and with dignity. As she promised, she goes to end her life without looking back, and in this behavior she differs from her hesitant husband. Zhongqing's hesitation is first effectively expressed in the moment when "long he sighed in the empty room" (line 326), suffering with grief over leaving his mother behind alone. Later, upon hearing about Lanzhi's death, "he paced back and forth under the courtyard trees" (line 340) before he too ends his life. The verb *paihuai*, literally "to walk back and forth," is used here metaphorically to mean "to hesitate," thus reinforcing the contrast with the resolute Lanzhi.

It remains ambiguous how these differences between the deaths of the wife and the husband would have been judged by contemporary audiences. Notwithstanding the evident compassion with the couple's gloomy fate, expressed already in the preface to the poem in the *New Songs from a Jade Terrace*, was Lanzhi perceived as more courageous and decisive than her husband? Or was she rather regarded as acting impetuously and without a proper sense of her responsibilities, unlike her husband, who, as a filial son, was until his last moments thinking about his obligations toward his old mother? It should be taken into consideration that, from the Eastern Han (25–220) through the early medieval period, filial piety (*xiao*) was the preeminent virtue in elite society, and this must be considered an important theme in the poem.

WOMEN AND MARRIAGE IN CHINESE SOCIETY

The story vividly dramatizes a conflict between a young couple yearning for love and the family elders who impose on them their power and the authority of established values. As such, it has a universal appeal, going beyond ages and cultures. But there also are aspects related to the traditions of ancient China, which give the tragic love story further dimensions and meanings that are less evident to today's reader. Given the social environment in which the poem was circulated, it is highly improbable that the exclamation at the end of the poem would challenge the established social order. Considerations of the meaning of the concluding couplet and of the whole poem must take into account contemporary social values and customs related to the social morality usually identified as Confucian.

The story of Lanzhi unfolds in the social milieu of noble families whose male members were involved on various levels in the complex bureaucratic system, the highest being the offices of the central government at court. These families derived their social position and authority from the generations of successful officials that they produced. Indispensable for such a career was a thorough education in Confucian classics and formalized behavior in accordance with the ritual prescriptions contained in the Confucian canon. Filial piety was among the most important virtues to be displayed in this society, and its importance was growing, particularly during the Eastern Han and in the period afterwards.

In matters of marriage, equal status between the families of husband and wife was requisite. In the poem, this is witnessed in the words of the matchmaker, who, when suggesting that Lanzhi would be a good match for the prefect's son, speaks first of all about her family, which has "inherited the status of high officials" (line 193). Also, the oppressive mother-in-law, when comforting her son Zhongqing, who is pining for Lanzhi, and promising to give him a better wife, stresses that he is "the son of a great family" (*da jia*; line 317)—a family with a member who served at court in the past.

The position and behavior of women in the upper society of the Han and early medieval China was governed by patriarchal norms and values as they are summarized in the *Book of Rites* (*Liji*). Another important text asserting the subjugation of women to male dominance is *Admonitions for Women* (*Nü jie*), written during the Eastern Han by a noted female scholar, Ban Zhao (ca. 45–20).[10] The orthodox demand speaks of triple subordination (*san cong*) of a woman to a man, first summarized in the *Book of Rites*: "The woman follows (and obeys) the man: in her youth, she follows her father and elder brother; when married, she follows her husband; when her husband is dead, she follows her son."[11] According to the orthodoxy, her position is limited to the household and she is not required to have the same education as a man.

However, the *Book of Rites* and *Admonitions for Women* are usually regarded as more prescriptive than descriptive of the actual situation. Other sources, such as the *Collected Life Stories of Exemplary Women* (*Lienü zhuan*) attributed to Liu Xiang (77–6 BCE), women's biographies in dynastic histories, and the recently excavated sources on Chinese law suggest that women in elite society during the Han and shortly afterwards not only obeyed their parents and husbands and occupied themselves with needlework and other feminine works but also received education in Confucian literature and played important roles in relation to men: they educated their sons (future high officials), advised their husbands and remonstrated with them if they decided on a morally wrong decision, and made decisions about all sorts of family matters.[12] The author of *Admonitions for Women* herself received the same education as the male members of her family and was able to become an important author and instructor. Yan Zhitui, a late sixth-century conservative scholar and proponent of Confucian orthodoxy, living a few decades after the poem about Liu Lanzhi was first recorded, also testifies that practices regarding the position of women in family and society may have differed significantly from the canonical prescriptions. He comments on women who appear frequently in public and intervene in public matters concerning their husbands and sons. As an orthodox scholar, he disapproves of that, yet he admits that this is a widespread habit, especially in the city of Ye and in northern China in general (*YSJX* 18–19).

Modern research on marriage and divorce in Han China, based on legal and other documents, also suggests, not altogether surprisingly, that actual practices differed from the prescriptions offered by the orthodoxy, and that these differed considerably among regions.[13] Girls were married quite early, in their teens, and the marriages were arranged by the parents of the future couple or other older relatives, sometimes with the help of a matchmaker. Though young people usually did not decide on their future partner on their own, they could express their preferences, and it was a rule that the parents required their consent. This is also the case in our poem, when the matchmaker comes to ask for Lanzhi; when her mother learns that Lanzhi does not want to marry the proposed husband, she follows her daughter's wish and declines the offer with a polite excuse (lines 175–189).

An indispensable part of the marriage ritual was the exchange of betrothal gifts, sent by the husband's family, and the dowry, brought to the marriage by the wife. The exchanged marriage gifts and dowry could be of great value, and a marriage had an important impact on the economy of both families. The property provided by both families usually would be specified in a written agreement between the two parties, in a manner of a business deal. Thus, marriage was in a certain sense an act of buying the bride. The dowry remained the wife's property, and in case of divorce she would take it away with her. Thus, the gesture of Liu Lanzhi leaving her dowry behind for her husband is unusual and can be seen as a gesture of despair and anger as well as a corroboration of her attachment to her husband, which is so deep that she does not want to keep the objects that would painfully remind her of her past marriage.

According to ritual prescriptions, divorce was understood as a great disgrace. According to the *Book of Rites*, a woman could be divorced under seven conditions, the first among them being disobedience to her parents-in-law and another being the loss of affection on the part of the parents-in-law. These are indeed the reasons that Lanzhi's mother-in-law insists that Lanzhi should be sent back. Once again, however, Han dynasty historical sources reveal incongruity between the orthodox prescriptions and actual social practices. Divorces, and remarriages of divorced wives, were common during the Han and mostly did not harm the reputation of a woman in the way that became common in later periods. This also would conform to the story of Lanzhi, who, despite being divorced, still remains a desirable match.

The case of Liu Lanzhi may provide another small testimony about the actual degree of independence of women in noble families in early Chinese society, as opposed to the prescriptions of the Confucian canon. Two key motifs are repeatedly used to characterize Lanzhi in the story: her excellent education and her independent mind. Apart from traditional feminine skills related to silk making, sewing, and playing music, we are told that Lanzhi's education was similar to the education of boys. She has studied the canonical books—the *Book of Documents* (*Shang shu*) and the *Book of Poetry*—and also proper behavior, "etiquette and propriety" (*li yi*; line 159), as demanded of men.

Confucian upbringing asks a young wife for modesty and obedience to her husband, and even more so to the parents-in-law; this finds expression in the way Lanzhi uses the modest self-address of *qie* ("concubine" or "female servant," usually translated simply as "I"). On several occasions, Lanzhi displays perfect Confucian manners. This is most remarkable in her composure and polite words when parting with her mother-in-law; despite previous complaints, she modestly thanks her mother-in-law for her generosity and expresses anxiety about her having to toil by herself after her daughter-in-law is no longer around to help (line 114). Facing her mother-in-law, Lanzhi speaks humbly, as appropriate, noting that she "grew up in village backwaters" and "never had fine breeding," and she expresses her gratitude for the money and silks her mother-in-law provided for her (lines 107–111).

If we read this display of exemplary humility and obedience against other parts of the poem (especially the opening monologue, where Lanzhi praises herself for her upbringing and complains about her mother-in-law), it can be perceived as a proud demonstration of correct manners. Contrasted with the scene in which she is giving away her rich dowry (lines 79–89), a bitter irony emerges from Lanzhi's polite words, and her feeling of superiority over the old lady becomes apparent as well. Lanzhi generally gives the impression of being a self-confident woman used to making her own decisions; this independence is first accentuated in a significant manner in the very beginning of the poem, when she prides herself on her skills and education, complains of the lack of respect from her mother-in-law, and suggests that she would herself divorce her husband.

There are some indications that Lanzhi's assertive behavior might have been conditioned by her family background. It is suggested that her family status was higher than her husband's, or at least that the Liu family was more affluent and socially on the rise, unlike the Jiaos, who seem to be in decline. The most conspicuous pronouncement of this situation is in the way Zhongqing is named all through the story as *fuli* (a petty clerk in a district or prefecture). This means that he holds a subordinate and dependent position in the local bureaucracy and so, for example, he must stay in the office and cannot leave of his own will. His relatively low position is further contrasted with the elevated position of Lanzhi's second proposed husband, who is a son of the prefect, the highest official in the neighborhood (and most probably Zhongqing's superior in the office). There are other indirect hints suggesting the possibility of Lanzhi's higher status: her extraordinary education (mentioned twice in the poem), her refusal to listen to the commands of her mother-in-law, and her voluntary decision to go back to her family. The dowry Lanzhi leaves behind when parting with Zhongqing also suggests her rich family background.

Placed in the context of late Han and early Six Dynasties (220–581) and the meager evidence we have about women in upper society, the case of Liu Lanzhi may provide another small testimony about the social position of women from noble families. The poem illustrates well the tension between canonical prescriptions and the actual reality of women's lives, and it deserves closer examination along this line.

GENRE AND SOME FORMAL ASPECTS

The poem is unusually long, compared to the majority of Chinese pentasyllabic poetry, and it presents a question of authorship and genre affiliation. When it was first recorded, it was categorized as an "ancient-style poem" (*gushi*). During the Song period (960–1279), the poem was included in Guo Maoqian's (1041–1099) *Collection of Yuefu Poems* (*Yuefu shi ji*), and in literary histories and anthologies it is still placed among other Han *yuefu* (Music Bureau poems of the Han), sometimes also referred to as "Han *yuefu* ballads."

The poem has some features typical of the *yuefu* genre, starting with the striking "affective image" in the opening line and its use of hyperbole, vivid dialogue, and many exclamations and rhetorical questions. Other devices typical of the *yuefu* are used as well, the most prominent being prefabricated formulae; stock phrases, including the name of Qin Luofu, the proverbial beauty of the well-known song "Mulberry Along the Lane" ("Moshang sang") (☞ *HTRCP* C4.8); numerical series; and repetitions.[14]

The enumerations of luxurious objects, however, bear also a certain affinity with the rhapsodies (*fu*), which were a popular entertainment genre during the Eastern Han. These enumerations contribute to the beauty of the poem and must have made it attractive to the audiences when performed; the singers could certainly elaborate on such descriptions, making variations according to their imaginations and the mood of the occasion. Such opportunities are found, for example, in the passage in which Lanzhi gives away her rich dowry before leaving her husband and enumerates her silk dresses and elaborate bed coverlet (lines 79–86), or again when Lanzhi carefully dresses and adorns herself before she goes to take leave of her mother-in-law (line 95–104). In both passages, although the silks and other precise objects contribute to the characterization of Lanzhi and her dealings with the other characters, they also serve to indulge the audience's fascination with luxury and beautiful things. The same fascination for beautiful things is most elaborate in lines 240–251, where the procession of marriage gifts sent by the prefect's son is vividly described.

Compared to other *yuefu* works, this poem is narrated in a concise and coherent manner; it lacks abrupt transitions in the narrative and also has no prominent lyrical parts. It is told by an omniscient narrator in a simple chronological order, unfolding in eleven suggestively presented scenes, each consisting of a vivid dialogue occasionally interspersed with a short description of the action. Considerable tension is created, culminating in the death of the lovers. At this point, the narrator cuts off the dramatic form of presentation, and after a brief description of the burial and grave of the lovers, with intertwined trees and mandarin ducks as symbols of conjugal love, he (or she, because the person singing this song might have been a female entertainer as well) addresses the audience in a didactic manner.

The poem is also quite exceptional in the complexity of the main character's psychology. Direct speeches move action and reveal relationships, emotions, and the complex psychology of the protagonists, contributing to their individualized portraits and presenting the complexity of the decision-making process. All this gives the poem, despite its stylized language and hyperbole, a touch of realism. As a result, the poem can easily be visualized and followed like a performance on stage or in film.

Complex character psychology, its impact on decisions made and on the events following them, and preoccupation with the conflict between individual emotions and socially endorsed propriety and family interests position the topic of the poem close to some aspects of Chinese historiography. It conforms to the Han Confucian elite's general interest in the results of individual decisions and the reasons for the outcomes of important events in history, this time projected into the intimate sphere of their own family lives.

In Chinese literary history, the term "folk" (*minjian*) is usually included among the characteristics of the poem (and the Han *yuefu* in general), and its origin among ordinary folk is emphasized. But contrary to such expectation, the story in fact reflects the life and moral concerns not of ordinary folk but rather of the noble families whose male members served on various levels of the bureaucratic system and who professed a Confucian morality. The language, some stylistic features, and the pentasyllabic form, together with the mode of presentation, suggest that the poem was created by anonymous professional entertainers to be performed during banquets in houses of the upper society. This would give it a measure of folk quality not usually associated with a pure literati composition.

OLGA LOMOVÁ

NOTES

1. For the topic of professional singers and storytellers during the Han, see Gao Lifen, *Juechang: Han dai geshi renleixue* (Perfect Songs: Anthropology of the Han Song Poetry) (Taibei: Le jin, 2007). The author includes "Old Poem Composed for the Wife of Jiao Zhongqing" in her discussion.
2. *Kongque dongnan fei*, a TV series in thirty-six episodes, directed by Wang Wenjie (Beijing: CCTV Splendid TV and Film Corp., 2009). http://www.youku.com/show_page/id_zcbffb7e6962411de83b1.html.
3. Hans Frankel, "The Chinese Ballad 'Southeast Fly the Peacocks,'" *Harvard Journal of Asiatic Studies* 34 (1974): 266.
4. In some editions, lines 11 and 12 are missing, and they may be a later interpolation.
5. This statement is incongruous with the short period Lanzhi spent in the Jiao family, as indicated earlier in the poem. Chinese commentators either explain this as a supposed corruption of the text or understand the statement as a hyperbolic expression of the passage of time.
6. The seventh day of the seventh month is the day when, according to Chinese folklore, the legendary Cowherd and the Weaving Maid once a year meet in heaven. The day was a women's festival and, together with the nineteenth day of every month, was a time when girls and women did not have to work and could enjoy themselves.
7. The verse in original speaks about a girl "from the Lan family"; we suspect the text was corrupted here and it should be "family with the daughter named Lan."
8. *Geng*, or night watch, is an old Chinese term of time, referring to one of the five two-hour periods into which the night (approximately seven p.m. to five a.m.) was divided. The fifth watch, or *wugeng*, therefore, is just before dawn, from approximately three a.m. to five a.m.
9. My translation, after consulting and sometimes adapting the rendering of Frankel, "The Chinese Ballad." The translation also benefitted from comments and corrections by the editor.
10. For an English translation with commentary, see Nancy Lee Swann, *Pan Chao: Foremost Woman Scholar of China, First Century AD* (New York: Century, 1932). Ban Zhao and her book also are discussed in Lisa Raphals, *Sharing the Light: Representations of Women and Virtue in Early China* (Albany: State University of New York Press, 1998), 236–246.
11. *Liji* (*Book of Rites*), Jiao Te Sheng 35 (Chinese Texts Project, http://ctext.org/liji/jiao-te-sheng). For further accounts about the prescriptions for women in the *Book of Rites*, see Robin Wang, *Images of Women in Chinese Thought and Culture: Writings from the Pre-Qin Period Through the Song Dynasty* (Indianapolis, IN: Hackett, 2003), 48–60.
12. For a complex study of the treatment of women in early Chinese texts, see Raphals, *Sharing the Light*.
13. See, for instance, Jack Dull, "Marriage and Divorce in Han China: A Glimpse at 'Pre-Confucian' Society," in *Chinese Family Law and Social Change in Historical and Comparative Perspective*, ed. David C. Buxbaum (Seattle: University of Washington Press, 1978), 23–74.
14. For detailed formal analysis of the poem, stressing the presence of the *yuefu* generic features, see Frankel, "The Chinese Ballad." See also the studies of Han *yuefu* in Zong-qi Cai, *The Matrix of Lyric Transformation: Self-Presentation and Poetic Modes in Early Chinese Pentasyllabic Poetry* (Ann Arbor: University of Michigan Center for Chinese Studies, 1996), 21–59; and Jui-lung Su, "*Shi* Poetry: Music Bureau Poems (*Yuefu*)," in *How to Read Chinese Poetry: A Guided Anthology*, ed. Zong-qi Cai (New York: Columbia University Press), 84–102.

PRIMARY SOURCES

YSJX   Yen Chih-tui (Yan Zhitui). *Yan shi jiaxun* 顏氏家訓 (Family Instructions for the Yan Clan: Yen-shih chia-hsun). Trans. Teng Ssu-yü. *T'oung Pao Monographie* 4. Leiden: Brill, 1968.

YTXY   *Yutai xinyong* 玉臺新詠箋注 (New Songs from a Jade Terrace Annotated). 2 vols. Beijing: Zhonghua shuju, 1999.

SUGGESTED READINGS

ENGLISH

Birrell, Anne. *New Songs from a Jade Terrace: An Anthology of Early Chinese Love Poetry*. London: George Allen and Unwin, 1982.

Cai, Zong-qi. *The Matrix of Lyric Transformation: Poetic Modes and Self-Presentation in Early Chinese Pentasyllabic Poetry*. Ann Arbor: University of Michigan Center for Chinese Studies, 1996.

Dull, Jack. "Marriage and Divorce in Han China: A Glimpse at 'Pre-Confucian' Society." In *Chinese Family Law and Social Change in Historical and Comparative Perspective*, ed. David C. Buxbaum, 23–74. Seattle: University of Washington Press, 1978.

Frankel, Hans. "The Chinese Ballad 'Southeast Fly the Peacocks.'" In *Harvard Journal of Asiatic Studies* 34 (1974): 248–271.

Nylan, Michael. *Five "Confucian" Classics*. New Haven, CT: Yale University Press, 2001.

Raphals, Lisa. *Sharing the Light: Representations of Women and Virtue in Early China*. Albany: State University of New York Press, 1998.

Su, Jui-lung. "*Shi* Poetry: Music Bureau Poems (*Yuefu*)." In *How to Read Chinese Poetry: A Guided Anthology*, ed. Zong-qi Cai, 84–102. New York: Columbia University Press, 2008.

Swann, Nancy Lee. *Pan Chao: Foremost Woman Scholar of China, First Century AD*. New York: Century, 1932.

Wang, Robin. *Images of Women in Chinese Thought and Culture: Writings from the Pre-Qin Period Through the Song Dynasty*. Indianapolis, IN: Hackett, 2003.

CHINESE

Gao Lifen 高莉芬. *Juechang: Han dai geshi renleixue* 絕唱：漢代歌詩人類學 (Perfect Songs: Anthropology of the Han Song Poetry). Taibei: Le jin, 2007.

Ke Qingming 柯慶明. "Ku'nan yu xushishi de liang xing: lun Cai Yan 'Beifen shi' yu 'Gushi wei Jiao Zhongqing qi zuo.'" 苦難與敘事詩的兩型—論蔡琰「悲憤詩」與「古詩為焦仲卿妻作」 ("Suffering and Two Types of Narrative Poems: On Cai Yan's 'Poem of Grief and Indignation' and 'Old Poem Composed for the Wife of Jiao Zhongqing'"). In *Wenxue mei zonglun* 文學美綜論 (Collection of Writings on Literary Aesthetics), 83–150. Taibei: Da'an chubanshe, 2009.

PART III
THE SIX DYNASTIES

6

HEROES FROM CHAOTIC TIMES

The Three Caos

In China, instead of saying "Speak of the devil" when one is surprised by the unexpected appearance of the "devil" of one's conversation, one would say "Speak of Cao Cao and he doth appear." What kind of character, one might wonder, could manage to have his notoriety perpetuated in such a devilish manner?

The historical figure who bore the name Cao Cao (155–220) was a sagacious warlord, an insightful statesman and military strategist, and a shrewd sovereign whose deeds not only helped shape the history of his time but also made a far-reaching impact on the centuries to come. He also proved to be a great poet and, in addition to poetic works, produced two poets in his sons Cao Pi (187–226) and Cao Zhi (192–232). The trio of father and sons, known as the Three Caos (*San Cao*), set the tone for the literature of the Jian'an era (196–220) around the time of the last reign in the Han dynasty (206 BCE–220 CE), which marked the beginning of a new phase in the evolution of Chinese poetry.

Though he was one of the most controversial figures in Chinese history, Cao Cao's admirers and his detractors agreed on one thing: that one might like him or hate him, but there was no way to ignore the vital force emanating from his personality. One story tells how, as the ruler of northern China, Cao Cao once had an audience with a Xiongnu envoy. Fearing that his appearance and stature were not imposing enough to inspire awe in the barbarian guest, Cao arranged for one of his subordinates, who was known for majestic bearing and manner, to sit on the throne, while he himself stood by the side as the attendant, with a broad sword in hand. After the audience, Cao sent a spy to ask the envoy, "How did our king look?"

"His Majesty was extraordinarily elegant," replied the envoy. "But it was the man holding the sword by his side that was truly heroic." When Cao Cao heard the report, he ordered his man to overtake the homeward-bound envoy and kill him (*SSXYJJ* 2:333).

Unlike most hostile accounts of Cao Cao in popular literature, exemplified by the well-known narrative *Romance of the Three Kingdoms* (*Sanguo yanyi*) or the cartoonish Beijing opera face painting, which indisputably determines Cao's identity as a villain by its clear-cut white color, this story tries to reveal the complexity of a charismatic figure. The vestiges of the character's trademark cunning calculation and suspicious vigilance, capable of the senseless brutality suggested by the ending of the story, recede into the background; what is foregrounded is the irresistible aura of ebullient heroism surrounding the character, which denied the carefully wrought camouflage scheme.

The validity of this story, like that of other stories about Cao, is in doubt, yet even the most serious historians cannot resist the appeal of the apocryphal anecdotes and hearsay accounts of this nature, so much so that the true picture of Cao Cao (if such a thing ever exists) becomes blurred. Fortunately, as sophisticated readers in this post-deconstructionist age, and aided by several educated grains of salt, we can hope to see through these stories and get close to a "real" Cao Cao.

Cao Cao was born in the county of Qiao (present-day Bozhou, Anhui) in 155. His father Cao Song was a foster son of Cao Teng, a powerful eunuch in the imperial court. Biographical accounts of Cao Cao's early life present a picture of an unscrupulous hooligan. It was said, for instance, that a nosy uncle tried time and again to bring the misconduct of the young rogue to his father's attention. Cao did not like this, and he decided to solve the problem once and for all. One day, when he ran into his uncle on the road, Cao twisted his face in such a painful way that the uncle was terrified and asked him what had happened. Cao told his uncle that he might be suffering from some kind of facial palsy. The uncle alerted Cao's father, who instantly summoned Cao, only to find his health entirely normal.

"But your uncle told me that you had a fit," said the father.

"Nothing happened," Cao replied. "I know my uncle never likes me and always makes up stories about me whenever he has a chance." The uncle thus lost his credibility, and Cao could carry on unchecked (*SGZ* 2).

Several friendly sources, however, tell of a very different Cao Cao, a diligent young man who perused books, especially books on military affairs. This is attested to by Cao's commentary on Sunzi's *Art of War* (*Sunzi bingfa*), which today is still included in the classical annotations of the text. Reading became Cao's lifelong habit. According to recollections of his sons and those who followed him through his long military career, even during campaigns Cao did not let a day pass without books. He "elucidated military strategies during the day and meditated on classics at night" (*SGZ* 38).

Several notables of the day perceived Cao's talent, saying that this was a person to watch. One of them, the supreme advisor on military affairs to the Han court, referred Cao to Xu Shao (150–195), a well-known "character judge" of the time, for a prediction of his future. At first Xu refused to see Cao, possibly because of his questionable reputation. However, Cao would not give up, and he pestered Xu until the latter eventually gave in, saying, "You will be a treacherous minister in peaceful times but a hero in a chaotic world" (*HHS* 8:2234).

At age twenty, Cao was appointed northern district commandant of the capital city of Luoyang. On the day he assumed the post, Cao displayed outside his office the tools he promised to use for law enforcement: rows of multicolored, heavy sticks. It so happened that an uncle of one of the most powerful eunuchs of the day refused to pay any heed to the young captain, challenging his authority by deliberately breaching the evening curfew. Cao's reaction was swift and decisive; he had the offender beaten to death (*SGZ* 2).

The way the young Cao exercised his power as a junior security official smacked more of "a hero in a chaotic world" than "a treacherous minister in peaceful times." And a chaotic world it certainly was. Harassed by the nomadic tribes from the north and plagued with domestic social unrest and ugly power struggles in court, the Han dynasty began to lose its grip on control of the country. In 184, when Cao was twenty-nine, the Yellow Turban Rebellion broke out. No sooner had that happened than a power struggle in court, between the eunuchs and the imperial relatives, came to a head. Warlords took advantage of the situation to expand their power and influence, and the country was thrown into ceaseless wars.

Cao Cao's time had come. He was first summoned by the court to participate in the effort to quell the yellow turbans and maintain order. Then, in 190, after the powerful warlord Dong Zhuo (d. 192) carried out his plans to usurp the Han throne, Cao joined the anti-Dong alliance and involved himself ever more deeply in the big game of power struggle that eventually brought down the Han dynasty. By skillfully maneuvering among competing warlords, expanding his power through accumulation of small wins on the battlefield, and consolidating his own military and political base through implementation of wise policies (especially those promoting agricultural production), he gradually established his local hegemony, leaving himself well poised for the final round of the rivalry. In 196, he convinced Emperor Xian (181–234; r. 189–220) to move the court to his territory and thus had the throne under his firm control. During the following decade, he defeated his remaining rivals in the north, one by one, and by 207 he had become the virtual ruler of northern China.

Amazingly, Cao never forgot to write poetry. His experiences in the long political and military struggle are recorded in several poems, such as "Graveyard Song," possibly written sometime after 197:

GRAVEYARD SONG 蒿里行

East of the Passes there were loyal knights, 關東有義士
2 Who rose in arms to crush all wickedness. 興兵討群凶
They were meant to meet together in Mengjin, 初期會盟津
4 To set their hearts on getting to Xianyang. 乃心在咸陽
Yet the allied armies would not pull together, 軍合力不齊
6 But marched about like lines of aimless geese. 躊躇而雁行
A lust for power led them at last to wrangle, 勢利使人爭
8 In a little while they were at each other's throats. 嗣還自相戕
A young man was styled emperor in Huainan. 淮南弟稱號
10 An imperial seal was carved out in the north. 刻璽於北方
Their armor was alive with breeding lice, 鎧甲生蟣虱
12 Ten thousand families were all wiped out. 萬姓以死亡
Their white bones lay and bleached in the wilderness, 白骨露於野
14 For a thousand leagues not a cock was heard to crow. 千里無雞鳴
Of the people, barely one in a hundred survived, 生民百遺一
16 Remembering this is enough to break your heart.[1] 念之斷人腸

[HWLCSX 93]

To narrate the war waged by the "loyal knights" of the allied forces against the "wickedness" of Dong Zhuo, Cao Cao alludes to the famous war between the alliance led by King Wu of Zhou (d. 1043 BCE) and the tyrannical King Zhou of Shang (d. 1046 BCE), which had happened thirteen centuries before (line 3), and to the battles during the final years of the Qin (221–206 BCE), which toppled the dynasty (line 4). The analogy of the conflicts between good and evil is thus self-evident. What follows in the poem, however, does not show much good or righteousness in the war. If the internecine strife presented in lines 5–8 is still a general reference to the chaotic situation within the anti-Dong alliance, the documentary of betrayal and conspiracy in lines 9–10 unmistakably points to actual historical events. Thanks to its incisive reflection on history, the poem is known today as an example of "poetic chronicle." As the "chronicler" himself was an important player in the events depicted, his lament on people's suffering carries historical weight, and his sympathy sounds unaffected.

This poetic chronicle of Cao's differs from factual history in that it is not a record of contemporary events but a "virtual" living experience of moods, sentiments, and feelings. In a book of conventional history, what happened in the coldest beginning months of the year 206 might only occupy one line, reporting in an indifferent voice a military campaign against a certain General Gao, a nephew of one of Cao Cao's major rivals. Not to be found in it will be the unbearable coldness and the hardship of the journey endured by the common soldiers, which can be more painful than bloody death on a battlefield and which is visible and palpable only in a straightforward "micro-narrative" by a poetic persona, as is shown in the following lines:

SONG ON ENDURING THE COLD 苦寒行

North we climb the Taihang mountains; 北上太行山
2 the going's hard on these steep heights! 艱哉何巍巍
Sheep Gut Slope dips and doubles, 羊腸坂詰屈
4 enough to make the cartwheels crack. 車輪為之摧
Stark and stiff the forest trees, 樹木何蕭蕭
6 the voice of the north wind sad; 北風聲正悲
crouching bears, black and brown, watch us pass; 熊羆對我蹲
8 tigers and leopards howl beside the trail. 虎豹夾路啼
Few men live in these valleys and ravines 谿谷少人民
10 where snow falls thick and blinding. 雪落何霏霏
With a long sigh I stretch my neck; 延頸長歎息
12 a distant campaign gives you much to think of. 遠行多所懷
Why is my heart so downcast and sad? 我心何怫鬱
14 All I want is to go back east, 思欲一東歸
but waters are deep and bridges broken; 水深橋梁絕
16 halfway up, I stumble to a halt. 中路正徘徊
Dazed and uncertain, I've lost the old road, 迷惑失故路
18 night bearing down but nowhere to shelter; 薄暮無宿棲
on and on, each day farther, 行行日已遠
20 men and horses starving as one. 人馬同時飢
Shouldering packs, we snatch firewood as we go, 擔囊行取薪
22 chop ice to use in boiling our gruel— 斧冰持作糜
That song of the Eastern Hills is sad, 悲彼東山詩
24 a troubled tale that fills me with grief.[2] 悠悠使我哀

[HWLCSX 96]

The poem is told in the first person—in the original, *wo* ("I") is used three times to emphasize the presence of the persona. The "I" who quotes from the *Shijing* (*Book of Poetry*) at the end is the same "I" who bears brunt of the north wind (line 6), faces the bears and tigers (lines 7–8), sighs (line 11), and feels sad (line 13). Cao Cao, the commander of his army, is feeling the pain felt by each and every member of the rank and file. This empathetic merging of a general with his men reminds one of the famous story—the meaning of which is often intentionally misread—about how Cao Cao told his thirsty soldiers on a difficult journey that not far ahead of them was a patch of plum trees with juicy fruits. The tantalizing news brought water to the soldiers' mouths and gave them several ounces of strength to go some extra miles (*SSXYJJ* 2:455). A cunning mind without heart is not capable of this kind of psychology.

The allusion to the *Shijing* at the end of the poem deserves a further look. Since the "Eastern Hills" ("Dong shan," Mao no. 156) is a song mainly about the hardship of a military campaign let by the Duke of Zhou (fl. 1100 BCE), the legendary ancient leader who helped consolidate the Zhou state, the comparison between the two campaigns, as well as between the two leaders, is implied. What interests us more, however, is Cao Cao's rereading of the canonical text. Cao refers to the *Shijing* not to give a halfhearted salute to the didactic tradition built on the text, a practice sanctioned by the state ideology of the Han, but to trace back—skipping the Han—to the time of the *Shijing* before its canonization, to rediscover the life force and artistic verve imbued in the original poetic situations, and to revitalize them in the poetic expressions of his personal feelings here and now. Cao's iconoclastic gesture well signifies his intent to separate poetry from the institutionalized Confucian ideology.

Cao Cao revisited the *Shijing* in another poem, "Short Song," probably written while he was drinking with a group of guests. By shedding the traditional moralistic exegesis of its banquet ritual and the far-fetched scholastic interpretation of the poem, Cao borrows from the song "Deer" ("Lu ming," Mao no. 161) the setup of an ancient picnic on the meadow (lines 11–14), giving himself an excuse to go over his brooding thoughts:

SHORT SONG 短歌行

	The wine before me as I sing:	對酒當歌
2	how long can a man's life last?	人生幾何
	I liken it to morning's dew,	譬如朝露
4	and the days now past are too many.	去日苦多
	The feeling is strong in me,	慨當以慷
6	brooding thoughts I can't ignore.	憂思難忘
	How can I banish melancholy?—	何以解憂
8	by Du Kang's gift of wine.	唯有杜康
	"Blue, blue are your gown's folds,	青青子衿
10	ever you are in my heart,"	悠悠我心
	and only because of you,	但為君故
12	my concerns keep on till now.	沉吟至今
	"Yoo, yoo" cry the deer,	呦呦鹿鳴
14	eating the shoots in the meadow:	食野之苹
	Worthy guests are here with me	我有嘉賓
16	so play the harp and blow the pipes."	鼓瑟吹笙
	Bright and full is the moon—	明明如月

18	when will its passage cease?	何時可輟
	Cares come from deep within,	憂從中來
20	nor can they be halted.	不可斷絕
	You crossed the paths and lanes,	越陌度阡
22	taking the trouble to visit me,	枉用相存
	now feasting and chatting after hard times,	契闊談讌
24	your hearts consider old kindness done.	心念舊恩
	The moon is bright, the stars are few,	月明星稀
26	and magpies come flying south,	烏鵲南飛
	three times around they circle the tree,	繞樹三匝
28	where is the branch on which to roost?	何枝可依
	The mountain does not mind its height,	山不厭高
30	the ocean does not mind its depth.	海不厭深
	The Duke of Zhou broke off his meals,	周公吐哺
32	and all the world turned to him in their hearts.[3]	天下歸心

[*HWLCSX* 94–95]

There lingers a trace of sadness in the poem (lines 1–6 and 17–20), reminiscent of the "carpe diem" motif characteristic of the "Nineteen Old Poems" ("Gushi shijiu shou"). Yet the poet refuses to become a victim of time. For him, "seizing the day" does not need to be a desperate chase after fleeting time but can be the substantiation of one's limited share, with accomplishments tangible enough to be measured by the depth of seas and the height of mountains. The span and scope of an individual life is limited, but the joint efforts of many lives and talents can overcome the tyranny of time and space. Therefore, the poet calls for comrades from all over the land to join his grand cause. The lively human experience in the *Shijing*, again, comes to his aid: the intensity in the yearning for a lover/friend expressed in "Blue Are Your Gown's Folds" ("Zijin," Mao no. 91) provides him a "coordinate" for the persona's craving for talents (lines 9–10).

At the end of the poem, the poet holds up the ancient sage Duke of Zhou as an example to emulate. In fact, as Cao Cao once declared—in his response to those who urged him to take the imperial title—if heaven's mandate truly rested with him, then he would rather be the Duke of Zhou, the powerful statesman without a crown (*SGZ* 38). With the real power already in his grip, Cao did not need the title. He just wanted to achieve what the Duke of Zhou had achieved—to gather around him all the capable people under heaven. Cao proclaimed that—so long as they had employable skill—men of no good conduct, who had been disgraced, or who proved themselves no filial sons should be nominated to offices (*CCJ* 48–49). Even loyalty was not a requirement. Cao employed as his personal secretary a literary genius who had served his enemy and who had once called Cao "a descendent of castrates" in a proclamation of war (*SGZ* 148, 447). Thanks to his all-embracing big heart, comparable to that of the Duke of Zhou, Cao gathered under his banner all sorts of capable people, including literary talents of the day. The seven most outstanding of these, known as the Seven Talents of the Jian'an era (*Jian'an qizi*), have gone down in history together with the Three Caos.

In the early autumn of 207, on his way to a campaign against the northern nomadic Wuhuan, Cao Cao passed Jieshi by the Bohai Sea. Standing on the ridge where land and sea met and where heaven and earth joined, his heart was full, and he wrote down these lines:

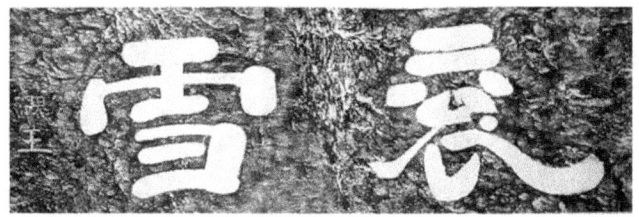

FIGURE 6.1 "Rolling Snow" ("Gunxue"). Calligraphy attributed to Cao Cao. Exact date unknown; possibly 215. Stone rubbing of an inscription on the surface of a rock (now on display at the Hanzhong City Museum) in the Bao River inside present-day Liuba County, Hanzhong, Shaanxi Province. 67 cm by 148 cm.

VIEWING THE OCEAN	觀滄海
East looking down from Jieshi	東臨碣石
2 I scan the endless ocean:	以觀滄海
waters endlessly seething,	水何澹澹
4 mountained islands jutting up,	山島竦峙
trees growing in clusters,	樹木叢生
6 a hundred grasses, rich and lush,	百草豐茂
Autumn wind shrills and sighs,	秋風蕭瑟
8 great waves churn and leap skyward.	洪波湧起
Sun and moon in their journeying	日月之行
10 seem to rise from its midst,	若出其中
stars and Milky Way, brightly gleaming,	星漢燦爛
12 seem to emerge from its depths.	若出其裏
How great is my delight!	幸甚至哉
14 I sing of it in this song.[4]	歌以詠志

[HWLCSX 97]

It is unlikely that Cao did not know that the first emperors of the Qin and the Han had been to Jieshi and had stood at exactly the spot where he now was. But he chose not to say anything about them. This was his moment. Years before, when he had to resign from office and retreat for a short period to his native village, wondering about his future, he cherished a dream that, when he died, his gravestone would be engraved with these words: "Tomb of Marquis Cao, the Grand Han General Lording Over the West" (*CCJ* 41). The dream had almost become reality. Now he was a powerful leader who could proclaim without exaggeration that "had the state not had me, heaven knows how many men would have called themselves emperors and kings" (*CCJ* 42). As if it was not, as the Chinese saying goes, that the time made a hero, but that the hero saved the time (figure 6.1).

Therefore, what Cao Cao does with his heroic outburst of sentiments is not really "writing" poetry. He just allows his ego and personality to overflow into verse by simply letting his thoughts and feelings follow his eyes from the scenes around him to the agitations of nature in the distance, all the way to the ins and outs of the heavenly bodies and to the pulsating movements of the universe. The sublime grandeur of his poetic world, which is forged out of simplicity, is sustained by the balanced rhythm of the stately four-character lines. The secret of Cao's technique seems to lie in having no technique.

A larger-than-life hero, Cao Cao can enthrall his life-size readers with both his composed dignity and his gracious humbleness, as is exemplified in the following poem:

THOUGH TORTOISE LIVES LONG	龜雖壽
Though the tortoise lives long,	神龜雖壽
2 Time will come when it meets its end.	猶有竟時
Though the dragon can rise high in the mist,	騰蛇乘霧
4 To dust it will eventually turn.	終為土灰
The old steed may be in the stable,	老驥伏櫪
6 Its heart gallops thousands of miles away.	志在千里
A hero may get old,	烈士暮年
8 Never will his ambition abate,	壯心不已
One's days can be long or short,	盈縮之期
10 Yet all is not up to heaven.	不但在天
Take good care of yourself,	養頤之福
12 And your fair share will be prolonged.	可得永年
How great is my fortune!	幸甚至哉
14 I sing of it in this song.	歌以詠志

[*HWLCSX* 98]

This is a hero who knows his limits but can also face his lot with courage. Imaged as a tenacious old steed, the aging hero touches readers' heart with both his undying fighting spirit and his humbleness. At a time when the heartrending laments on the transiency of human existence typical of the "Nineteen Old Poems" are still vivid in the collective memory of his contemporaries, Cao's heartwarming tragic heroism energizes the scene of poetry.

Cao Cao nearly changed the course of history. But when his fleet of thousands of ships, arranged in battle formation and ready to take his force across the Yangzi River to southern China, were burned to ashes by the allied forces of Sun Quan (182–252) and Liu Bei (161–223) in Chibi (Red Cliff) one afternoon at the end of year 208, Cao realized that he had lost his last chance to unite China. In the years that followed, having reassessed his ambition, he refocused his time and energy on consolidating his rule in northern China. After his death in 220, his successor, Cao Pi, forced Emperor Xian to abdicate, replaced the dynasty with the state of Wei, made himself the "Emperor of Culture," and honored his father Cao Cao with the posthumous title of Emperor of Prowess. With Cao's kingdom of Wei in the north and Sun Quan's and Liu Bei's power bases in the south and the southwest, the Three Kingdoms Period (220–280) began.

As a believer in meritocracy, Cao Cao did not care too much for primogeniture when the question of succession was brought onto his agenda. He would just give his power to the most capable of his sons. The most capable, of course, might not always be the eldest. Actually, in the case of the Cao family, the brightest happened to be the youngest, Cao Chong (196–208). Legend has it that Cao Cao once received a gift of an elephant and wondered how he could find out the weight of that huge animal. Cao Chong, only five or six at the time, came up with an idea. He led the elephant aboard a boat and marked the location of the waterline on the boat's side. He then replaced the elephant with rocks of manageable sizes until the mark of the waterline touched the surface of the water again. The problem was solved once he had the rocks weighed and put the numbers together (*SGZ* 433).

Unfortunately, the Archimedean prodigy died young, and Cao Cao had to go back and choose between Cao Pi, the second-eldest son (the eldest had died in a battle), and Cao Zhi, the remaining brightest. To make up his mind, Cao Cao weighed and pondered back and forth for almost ten years, and many ugly things happened during that long period of time. In the rivalry, Cao Pi seemed to receive more help from associates and advisors, many of whom had Cao Cao's ear. Once, before Cao Cao set out for a military expedition, both brothers went to see their father off. Being a master of words, Cao Zhi was able to make an enthusiastic and somewhat flattering speech on the spot. His father was pleased, while Cao Pi was understandably worried. One of his men told Cao Pi not to worry, advising him that the most proper thing for a son to do on this occasion was not to talk but to show his filial feelings. Cao Pi took the hint. He managed to have tears gushing from his eyes at the very moment his father's chariot lurched forth. The expression of emotion moved everyone present, and turned the younger brother's flowery speech into an insincere ploy (*SGZ* 455).

The story, however, sounds biased against Cao Pi. Actually, quite a few biographical accounts, stories from various sources, and interpersonal writings by Cao Pi himself reveal a congenial and amiable character. For instance, one story tells that, at the funeral of one of the Seven Talents, Cao Pi said to the other mourners, "Since our friend liked to listen to donkey's brays, we may each make a long bray to see him off" (*SSXYJJ* 2:347–348). Sure enough, the graveyard resonated with a donkey's brays. And this unprincely thing is said to have happened after Cao Pi was chosen to be the heir apparent. There also are records showing how the two Cao brothers enjoyed each other's company when hosting the gatherings of the literary salon in Ye, the city of their father's headquarters.

Definitely overshadowed by his father's multifaceted talent on the one side and probably eclipsed by his younger brother's literary achievements on the other, Prince Cao Pi nevertheless did make some marks on the development of Chinese literature. Among these is his all-important thesis "On Literature" ("Lun wen"). In it Cao Pi argues that, more than anything else, it is the various forms of life force or vital energy (*qi*) of individual writers that gives literature its rich diversity, and hence its true life. In line with this, Cao Pi further declares that literature is a great undertaking comparable to the management of state affairs. A writer can achieve immortality through his writing: "Effortlessly, his name gets known by the later generations, without needing any help from great historians or influential political promoters."[5]

Cao Pi's own literary practice verifies his theory. Take, for example, the following:

SONG OF YAN 燕歌行

   Autumn winds whistle sadly, the air grows chill, 秋風蕭瑟天氣涼
2 Plants wither, leaves fall, dew turns to frost. 草木搖落露為霜
   Swallows fly homeward, geese wing south; 群燕辭歸鵠南翔

4	I think of your distant wandering and am filled with love.	念君客遊多思腸
	Longingly you think of returning to your old home,	慊慊思歸戀故鄉
6	Why linger on in remote places?	君何淹留寄他方
	Forlorn, your wife keeps to the deserted room;	賤妾煢煢守空房
8	Misery cannot make me forget my love.	憂來思君不敢忘
	Unaware of the tears that moisten my gown,	不覺淚下沾衣裳
10	I play zither tunes in the *qing shang* mode,	援琴鳴絃發清商
	The songs are brief, the breath, weak—nothing lasts.	短歌微吟不能長
12	The brilliant moon shines upon my bed,	明月皎皎照我床
	Stars, the Milky Way, stream westward; the night not even half over.	星漢西流夜未央
14	Herd Boy and Weaving Maid, you gaze at each other from afar,	牽牛織女遙相望
	Why are you confined alone to the "river" bridge?[6]	爾獨何辜限河梁

[HWLCSX 99]

Had the author not been emperor of the Wei kingdom, or had he not written anything else, his name would still be handed down to posterity because of this poem alone. The piece is the earliest existing complete poem in heptasyllabic lines, a witness to the author's pioneering contribution to the development of poetic forms.

In "On Literature," when trying to identify the most distinctive trait of poetry as a genre, in contrast with other "practical" genres such as memorial, inscription, epistle, and so forth, Cao Pi observes that poetic works should "aspire to be beautiful"—glaringly beautiful, that is.[7] What he exactly means by "beautiful" (*li*) is not very clear. But when one reads his "Song of Yan" closely, one gets some idea. Before Cao Pi, many songs in the "Music Bureau" (*yuefu*) and the "ancient-style poems" (*gushi*) traditions had been written about wives longing for their husbands abroad. The female persona in Cao Pi's piece differs from other pining wives before her in that she does not simply speak out her feelings straightforwardly. With the beginning of the poem densely packed with images—not only visual but also audial and tactile—of the effects of seasonal changes, she shows how impossible it is not to long for her loved one at this time of year. Though her person is here, her heart and mind are distant, somewhere with her husband. This makes it hard to face the reality of being alone in an empty room. She just does not know how to manage herself; even music or singing cannot ease her pain. The image of the bright moon reveals many things: the lonely shadow cast on her bed, the enduring sleepless night, and the thought of another longing person trying to communicate with the persona via the same moon, from a different locale, not to mention the Milky Way by the side of the moon, which conveniently brings forth the beautiful story about the separation of the mythical loving couple.

Cao Pi's skill in creating the image of a longing wife makes it look easier to present a lonely traveler:

	UNTITLED VERSE, NO. 2 OF 2	雜詩（二之二）
	Deep and boundless, the long autumn night,	漫漫秋夜長
2	Fierce and cutting, the chill northern wind.	烈烈北風涼
	I toss and turn, unable to sleep;	展轉不能寐

4	Putting on a robe, I rise and pace	披衣起彷徨
	Back and forth; suddenly it is late;	彷徨忽已久
6	White dew moistens my gown.	白露沾我裳
	I gaze down at the clear rippling water,	俯視清水波
8	Glance up at the brilliant moonlight.	仰看明月光
	The "Heavenly River" steams back westward,	天漢迴西流
10	Countless stars glitter in every direction.	三五正縱橫
	How melancholy the cry of the insects!	草蟲鳴何悲
12	A solitary goose wings southward;	孤雁獨南翔
	Heavy are the thoughts inside me,	鬱鬱多悲思
14	Endlessly I think of home.	綿綿思故鄉
	I long to fly away, yet have no wings—	願飛安得翼
16	I long to cross the river, yet there's no bridge.	欲濟河無梁
	Facing the wind, my sighs pour forth,	向風長嘆息
18	A broken spirit knows only torment![8]	斷絕我中腸

[HWLCSX 101]

It seems that, to complete his task, Cao Pi does not have too many "props" at his disposal. Notice how many images, present in the previous piece, he has to recycle: the chilling autumn wind, the cold dews, the migrating birds, the same bed that makes one sleepless, and the same bright moon with its multiple functions. Even the association of the Milky Way is hinted at by the mention of a river without a bridge. In fact, these are all stock images frequently used in the *yuefu* and the *gushi* traditions. When Cao Pi reuses them in his poem, he creates a lyrical sequence of his own that permits the liveliness lying dormant inside them to rekindle. The effect is anything but trite. The tone of the persona remains as candid as that of the travelers from the *yuefu* poems, the feelings as sincere, but the way they are presented is no longer simple and straightforward. The twists and turns of the traveler's sentiments are brought out with fresh detail. This is *li*, disturbingly beautiful.

As noted earlier, Cao Cao does not *write* but just *is* poetry. It is the magnetic field of his overpowering personality that makes his kind of poetry possible. In comparison, Cao Pi's art is different. He is at his best when writing about the experiences of others—he creates. In this sense he is a "professional" writer. The blue blood in his veins means that, no matter what, he has already secured a place in history. As if to prove that he does not need any help from historians to obtain a spot in history, he creates poetry. Imagine a prince-emperor writing airs of longing wives and heartbroken travelers! He simply needs to see to it that his name is known by later generations not because of his emperorship but because of his poetry.

Ironically, it is also poetry, or the legends of poetry, that drags Cao Pi's name through the mud of history. It is said that, after becoming the emperor of Wei, Cao Pi did everything he could to pay back his brother Cao Zhi for all the miserable and ignoble feelings resulting from their battle for succession. A household story tells that, one day, Cao Pi ordered his younger brother to compose a poem and threatened to deal him capital punishment if he could not finish in the time it would take to walk seven steps. On the spur of the moment, Cao Zhi wrote this verse: "Beanstalks feed the fire to boil the beans, / While the beans in the pot weep: / 'Stemming from the same roots we are, / Why would you burn your siblings with such earnest?'" (*SSXYJJ* 1:134).

There is also a poetic legend—again at the expense of Cao Pi—about the romantic relationship between Cao Zhi and the beautiful and talented Lady Zhen (183–221), Cao Pi's wife and Cao Zhi's sister-in-law. Despite the convincing evidence that the story was created by a Tang (618–907) annotator who twisted the meaning of Cao Zhi's story of his platonic encounter with the mythical goddess of the Luo River, eponym of his celebrated poetic prose, later generations nevertheless chose to believe that beautiful fiction of an incestuous nature.

The reason that Cao Zhi has been generously compensated with sympathy from all kinds of popular literature and unofficial history is that he is believed to be a victim of his brother's treachery and shrewdness. Actually, Zhi's failure was not all Pi's fault; it was partly of the younger brother's own making. According to official historical accounts, very early on, Cao Zhi had won his father's favor with his agile intellectual capacity and his unadorned, straight character. With a purposeful plan in mind, the father created every opportunity for the son to temper his mind and body in preparation for a possible future leading role, bringing the teenager along on military campaigns and, after the lad reached twenty, assigning him responsibilities only a seasoned administrator could shoulder (*SGZ* 416–417). The young man, however, had a personality too impetuous and a disposition too hedonistic to fit into his father's design. The problem with Cao Zhi was that what he was naturally inclined to do often happened to be things that he had better not do. He knew it, but could hardly help himself. A good example can be found in the contradiction between, on the one hand, his solemn denouncement of drinking as the source of many evils—in an exposition in response to his father's strict prohibition policy—and, on the other hand, his uncontrollable drinking habit.⁹

At the end of 217, after many years of hesitation, Cao Cao made his elder son the heir prince. Curious historians might want to know, had Cao Cao's decision gone the other way, how he would have reacted several months later, when Cao Zhi, intelligent as he was, negligently and unscrupulously forced his carriage right through the front gate of his father's palace and down the speedway, the central path reserved for the sovereign. This encroachment upon his father's authority was no small offense. Cao Cao was enraged. "At first I thought this son of mine was the one most worthy of grand duties," sighed Cao Cao. "From this day on I cannot but treat him differently" (*SGZ* 417).

Unlike his elder brother, who does not reveal much about himself in poetry, many of Cao Zhi's poems can be read as autobiographical accounts, as is seen in the following examples:

WHITE HORSE 白馬篇

	The white horse adorned with a gold bridle,	白馬飾金羈
2	Gallops in a winged flight toward the northwest.	連翩西北馳
	May I ask, whose household the rider is from?	借問誰家子
4	He is a knight-errant from You and Bing.	幽并遊俠兒
	At an early age he left his hometown,	少小去鄉邑
6	And made his name known across the desert frontier.	揚聲沙漠垂
	For many years he has carried his fine bow,	宿昔秉良弓
8	See his *hu* arrows—long and short!	楛矢何參差
	Drawing his bow, he shatters the left target,	控弦破左的

10	Shooting right, he smashes the *yuezhi* [target].	右發摧月支
	Lifting his hand, he shoots into a flying monkey,	仰手接飛猱
12	Bending down, he breaks up the horse hoof [targets],	俯身散馬蹄
	More nimble and speedy than a monkey or ape,	狡捷過猴猿
14	And as fierce and fleet-footed as a leopard or a dragon-like beast.	勇剽若豹螭
	Many a time the border towns are on alert,	邊城多警急
16	The mounted barbarians are often on the move.	虜騎數遷移
	A feathered dispatch comes from the north,	羽檄從北來
18	And he gallops off to a high embankment.	厲馬登高隄
	On and on he charges to crush the Xiongnu,	長驅蹈匈奴
20	Turning to the left, he overruns the Xianbei.	左顧凌鮮卑
	He would throw himself onto the tip of a blade,	棄身鋒刃端
22	His life—how little he cherishes it!	性命安可懷
	He does not even think of his father and mother,	父母且不顧
24	Not to mention his sons and wife!	何言子與妻
	With his name in the book of brave soldiers,	名編壯士籍
26	He cannot think of himself.	不得中顧私
	He lays down his life to relieve his country's woes,	捐軀赴國難
28	Seeing death as just a matter of going home.¹⁰	視死忽如歸

[HWLCSX 117]

Yet to be found is a better soldier and leader, with martial skills of this caliber and a determination so resolute to lay down his life for his country! But what if he is also the "I" presented in the following poem?

FAMOUS CAPITAL　　　　　　　　　　　　　　　　名都篇

	A famous capital has many bewitching girls,	名都多妖女
2	From the Capital of Luo come many young men.	京洛出少年
	Their precious swords are worth a thousand in gold,	寶劍直千金
4	Their clothes are beautiful and bright.	被服麗且鮮
	They fight cocks on the road to the eastern suburb.	鬥雞東郊道
6	They race their horses between tall catalpas.	走馬長楸間
	I have not galloped half through the course,	馳騁未能半
8	When I see two rabbits dash out before me.	雙兔過我前
	I grab my bow, draw out a whistling arrow,	攬弓捷鳴鏑
10	And race in pursuit of them up Southern Mountain.	長驅上南山
	On the left I draw my bow, to the right I shoot;	左挽因右發
12	A single arrow shoots through both rabbits.	一縱兩禽連
	Before the remaining feats are performed,	餘巧未及展
14	I raise my hands and shoot right into a flying kite.	仰手接飛鳶
	All the spectators say my skills are excellent,	觀者咸稱善

16	The expert bowmen lavish praise upon me.	眾工歸我妍
	We return and feast at the Pingle Gate Tower,	我歸宴平樂
18	The fine wine costs ten thousand a quarter gallon.	美酒斗十千
	The minced carp and stewed shelled prawn,	膾鯉臇胎鰕
20	Roast turtles and broiled bear paws.	炮鱉炙熊蹯
	I called out loud for my companions,	鳴儔嘯匹侶
22	And we sit in a row, filling the long mat.	列坐竟長筵
	Then we dash back and forth, kicking a ball and tossing woodpegs,	連翩擊鞠壤
24	Quick and nimble we play, in ten thousand ways.	巧捷惟萬端
	The white sun rushes to the southwest,	白日西南馳
26	Time cannot be brought to a halt.	光景不可攀
	We go back to the city, scattering like clouds,	雲散還城邑
28	But come morning we will return again.[11]	清晨復來還

[HWLCSX 113–114]

Many traditional commentators and modern scholars refuse to believe that the second poem presents a self-image of the poet and insist that it is Cao Zhi's sarcastic criticism of the playboys of his day, thus saving their hero from falling into ignominy. The more closely we read the images in both poems and the more carefully we compare them side by side, however, the more we are amazed by the similarities between the two poetic characters. The patriotic proclamation by the former and the dissipation flaunted by the latter, sincere or affected as they might be, are gestures and attitudes that can be displayed in a very conscious manner. By contrast, the physical feats of the young men, so meticulously presented in both poems, belong to the realm of the automatic and subconscious. The two characters are thus identical in one thing: their martial skill. For good or for bad, the actions of the two are automatic, and their reactions to outside stimuli are continuous and unmediated by calculation. Indeed, it takes little imagination to associate the nimbleness of bodily execution of the archer on horseback in the poems here with Cao Zhi's demoniac skill—if the legendary story is to be believed—of completing a poetic rhapsody in an instant during a competition of talents with his brothers on the Bronze Bird Terrace, under their father's watchful eyes. The spontaneity demonstrated by Cao Zhi's poetic characters epitomizes the intuitive side of the poet's own character.

Both the valiant knight-errant from the You and Bing and the profligate son from the famous capital are fascinatingly attractive. But suppose you are Cao Cao, needing to choose an heir who is to be trusted with the life and death of the family and of the country. This explains why, eventually, Cao Zhi's much less attractive brother was chosen. It was also why, when the wavering Cao Cao sought opinions on this issue from an advisor known for his rectitude and unbiased judgment, the advisor made his pick against Cao Zhi, without hesitation. This advisor was none other than the uncle of Cao Zhi's wife (*SGZ* 278).

In 219, two years after Cao Cao picked the elder son as his successor, he gave the younger son yet another, and final, chance. In response to an unexpected military crisis, he made Cao Zhi the commander of an army to rescue his brother Cao Ren (168–223), besieged by an enemy. Cao Zhi let everybody down. For some reason, he got so drunk that he failed to answer his father's call for a last-minute consultation before departure (*SGZ* 417). One year later, his father died, and suddenly Cao Zhi found himself on his own.

In 223, Cao Zhi and his two half brothers, Prince Rencheng and Prince Baima, who by Emperor Cao Pi's orders were also restricted to their remote and isolated fiefs, went to the capital for the annual autumnal ritual. Not long after his arrival, Prince Rencheng died of suspicious causes. On the journey back to their fiefs, Cao Zhi and Prince Baima—still trying to recover from their grief—wished to accompany each other as far as they could. However, the court official who supervised the trips, whether following the strict tradition handed down from the Han court or taking special orders from Cao Pi, would not allow the two brothers to do so. Forced to bid a heartbroken farewell to his brother in the circumstances, and not knowing when and if ever they might see each other again, Cao Zhi wrote a long poem, "To Cao Biao, the Prince of Baima" ("Zeng Baimawang Biao"), to express his bitterness and resentment (*SGZ* 422). The following is the fourth of the seven sections of the poem:

	Hesitate to go on, but why stay here?	踟躕亦何留
2	My loving thoughts of you are endless.	相思無終極
	Autumn wind brings a light touch of chill,	秋風發微涼
4	Cold cicadas are chirping by my side;	寒蟬鳴我側
	The vast wilderness, how bleak and desolate!	原野何蕭條
6	The white sun suddenly hides in the west.	白日忽西匿
	Homing birds fly into the tall trees,	歸鳥赴喬林
8	Their swift wings flapping and flapping.	翩翩厲羽翼
	A lone animal roves in search of its mates,	孤獸走索群
10	Having no time even to eat the grass in its jaws.	銜草不遑食
	Moved by them, my chest fills with anguish,	感物傷我懷
12	I pass my hand over my heart and heave a long sigh.[12]	撫心長太息

[*HWLCSX* 128]

It is bitterly ironic that Cao Zhi's poetic art, represented here, is reminiscent of that of his elder brother (who is responsible for his suffering), as seen in his depictions of the longing wives and sad travelers, discussed earlier. Like his brother, Cao Zhi also creates a lyrical situation of his own to accommodate and re-enliven the stock images from the *yuefu* and the *gushi* traditions he has to use. In trying to make these old images merge into the new context, he pays meticulous attention to even the minutest details. For instance, instead of the generally "cold" wind, it is a very slight touch of the chill (*weiliang*; line 3) at the turn of the season that stirs the overly susceptible nerve of the persona. The synesthesia of the "cold cicada" is already sharp enough to catch the tactile effect of the insect's chirping on the persona, but what is even sharper is the elusive source of the chirping—"by my side"(line 4) or yonder?—that conjures up a realistic experience of the sad and disoriented traveler. And with the right word "suddenly" (*hu*; line 6) in the right place, the poet turns the sun from a static spatial image into a flowing temporal process by which the vivid tempo of the persona's experience is measured. The vivid sense of immediacy thus created makes the persona's experience intimately accessible to the reader. The significance of Cao Zhi's innovative use of the minute details of poetic images can never be overemphasized. Not only do they give life to the narrative but also they contribute to the buildup of an intense and exquisite lyrical ambience in his poems, something new to the *yuefu* tradition but to be seen more and more often in the new lyrical modes that were yet to come.

It is said that Xie Lingyun (385–433), the so-called father of Chinese landscape poetry and an overzealous admirer of Cao Zhi, once claimed, "There are only ten bushels of talent under heaven, of which Cao Zhi takes eight, I get one, and the rest of the world share what remains." A more balanced assessment, however, might still place the youngest Cao among the famous trio and in the context of that juncture of history in which the father and sons of the Caos found themselves. Each of the three is a giant figure carrying his special weight. But what is truly beyond measurement is the accomplishment of the joint efforts of the Three Caos, together with that of the Seven Talents and many others in the Jian'an era: the amelioration of the pentasyllabic poetic form; the establishment of a masculine, heroic poetic style of "air and bone" (*fenggu*)—tinged with a tragic strain—that immortalizes the era; and the expansion of the scope of poetic topics. It is amazing that one can pinpoint the exact moment in history—the chaotic years around the Jian'an era—during which a great rhetorical turn opened up many exciting new possibilities in the development of Chinese poetry.

XINDA LIAN

NOTES

1. Translation by John Frodsham. See John Minford and Joseph S. M. Lau, eds., *An Anthology of Translations: Classical Chinese Literature*, vol. 1, *From Antiquity to the Tang Dynasty* (New York: Columbia University Press, 2000), 419–420.
2. Translation by Burton Watson. See Burton Watson, ed., *The Columbia Book of Chinese Poetry: From Early Times to Thirteenth Century* (New York: Columbia University Press, 1984), 104.
3. Translation by Stephen Owen. See Stephen Owen, ed. and trans., *An Anthology of Chinese Literature: Beginnings to 1911* (New York: Norton, 1996), 280–281.
4. Translation by Burton Watson. See Watson, *The Columbia Book of Chinese Poetry*, 105.
5. Guo Shaoyu, *Zhongguo lidai wenlun xuan* (Selected Texts of Chinese Literary Thoughts). 4 vols. (Shanghai: Shanghai guji chubanshe, 1980), 158–159.
6. Translation by Ronald C. Miao. See Wu-chi Liu and Irving Yucheng Lo, eds., *Sunflower Splendor: Three Thousand Years of Chinese Poetry* (Bloomington: Indiana University Press, 1975), 46.
7. Guo Shaoyu, *Zhongguo lidai wenlun xuan*, 158.
8. Translation by Ronald C. Miao. See Guo Shaoyu, *Zhongguo lidai wenlun xuan*, 44.
9. See Cao Zhi, "Jiu fu," in *Cao Zhi ji jiaozhu* (Annotated Collected Works of Cao Zhi), annotated by Zhao Youwen (Beijing: Renmin wenxue chubanshe, 1998), 124–125.
10. Translation by Zong-qi Cai. See Zong-qi Cai, *The Matrix of Lyric Transformation: Poetic Modes and Self-Presentation in Early Chinese Pentasyllabic Poetry* (Ann Arbor: University of Michigan, Center for Chinese Studies, 1996), 115.
11. Translation by Zong-qi Cai, in *The Matrix of Lyric Transformation*, 113.
12. Translation by Zong-qi Cai, in *The Matrix of Lyric Transformation*, 122.

PRIMARY SOURCES

CCJ	Cao Cao 曹操. *Cao Cao ji* 曹操集 (Collected Works of Cao Cao). Beijing: Zhonghua shuju, 1959.
HHS	Fan Ye 范曄 (398–445). *Hou Han shu* 後漢書 (History of the Later Han), with commentary compiled by Li Xian 李賢 (654–684). Beijing: Zhonghua shuju, 1965.

HWLCSX	Yu Guanying 余冠英. *Han Wei Liuchao shixuan* 漢魏六朝詩選 (Selected Poems from the Han, Wei, and Six Dynasties). Beijing: Renmin wenxue chubanshe, 1978.
SGZ	Chen Shou 陳壽 (233–297). *Sanguo zhi* 三國志 (Records of the Three Kingdoms), with commentary compiled by Pei Songzhi 裴松之 (372–451). Beijing: Zhonghua shuju, 1959.
SSXYJJ	Xu Zhen'e 徐震堮. *Shishuo xinyu jiaojian* 世說新語校箋 (Annotated Text of *A New Account of Tales of the World*). Beijing: Zhonghua shuju, 1984.

SUGGESTED READINGS

ENGLISH

Besio, Kimberley Ann, and Constantine Tung, eds. *Three Kingdoms and Chinese Culture*. Albany: State University of New York Press, 2007.

Cai, Zong-qi. *The Matrix of Lyric Transformation: Poetic Modes and Self-Presentation in Early Chinese Pentasyllabic Poetry*. Ann Arbor: University of Michigan, Center for Chinese Studies, 1996.

de Crespigny, Rafe. *Imperial Warlord: A Biography of Cao Cao 155–220 AD*. Leiden: Koninklijke Brill NV, 2010.

Dunn, Hugh. *Cao Zhi: The Life of a Princely Chinese Poet*. Beijing: New World Press, 1983.

Mather, Richard B., trans. *Shih-shuo Hsin-yü: A New Account of Tales of the World*. Minneapolis: University of Minnesota Press, 1976.

CHINESE

Cao Cao 曹操. *Cao Cao ji* 曹操集 (Collected Works of Cao Cao). Beijing: Zhonghua shuju, 1959.

Cao Zhi 曹植. *Cao Zhi ji jiaozhu* 曹植集校注 (Annotated Collected Works of Cao Zhi). Annotated by Zhao Youwen 趙幼文. Beijing: Renmin wenxue chubanshe, 1998.

Guo Shaoyu 郭紹虞. *Zhongguo lidai wenlun xuan* 中國歷代文論選 (Selected Texts of Chinese Literary Thoughts). 4 vols. Shanghai: Shanghai guji chubanshe, 1980.

Sun Mingjun 孫明君. *San Cao yu Zhongguo shishi* 三曹與中國詩史 (The Three Caos and the History of Chinese Poetry). Beijing: Qinghua daxue chubanshe, 1999.

Wu Huaidong 吳懷東. *San Cao yu Wei Jin wenxue yanjiu* 三曹與魏晉文學研究 (The Three Caos and the Study on the Wei and Jin Period Literature). Hefei: Anhui wenyi chubanshe, 2011.

THE WORTHIES OF THE BAMBOO GROVE

Whether the "Seven Worthies of the Bamboo Grove" (*Zhulin qixian*) ever existed as a group is a matter of some debate; the important point is that it served as a tangible symbol of the Wei-Jin spirit of freedom. Composed of Wei-Jin gentry, the group included Ji Kang (223–262), Ruan Ji (210–263), Liu Ling (d. after 265), Xiang Xiu (ca. 221–ca. 300), Shan Tao (205–283), Wang Rong (234–305), and Ruan Xian (234–305) (figures 7.1 and 7.2). Stories of their lives and influence, whether authentic or legendary, were widely recorded by contemporary scholars. *A New Account of Tales of the World* (*Shishuo xinyu*), compiled by the Liu-Song prince Liu Yiqing (403–444) and his staff around 430, preserved and sometimes recast these stories. And the *Shishuo* in turn formed the basis for the extensive and collaborative commentary of Liu Jun (courtesy name Xiaobiao, 462–521).

The fame of the illustrious Seven Worthies spread with the rise of the Wei-Jin *Xuanxue* (Abstruse Learning, also known as Dark Learning or Mysterious Learning). This philosophical school took shape after New Text Confucianism collapsed with the fall of the Han. Subsequently, the legalist policy of Cao Cao (155–220) and the Wei regime (220–265) he founded gave way to the Sima-led Jin dynasty (265–420). In the process, the scholastic metaphysics of New Text Confucianism was eclipsed by the new trend of ideas and notions known in the *Xuanxue*, whose major philosophical sources included the *Book of Changes* (*Yijing*), the *Laozi*, and the *Zhuangzi*. Trapped in the power struggle between the Cao-Wei regime and the Sima clan, the Seven Worthies sought safety in seclusion.

They also found themselves in need of philosophical refuge as the Simas reintroduced Confucian rituals in order to persecute political opponents. For this, the Worthies turned to the *Zhuangzi*, drawing inspiration especially from its idealized personalities: the Perfected Person (*zhiren*), the Spiritual Person (*shenren*), the Sage (*shengren*), and the Great Person (*daren*). All of these are "in fact one" (see Cheng Xuanying's *shu* commentary, *ZZJS* 2:395). They make their first collective appearance in the "Free Roaming" ("Xiaoyao you") chapter of the *Zhuangzi*, where this person is described as the embodiment of spiritual freedom: dependent on nothing, only following the natural course and changes—"availing of the right course [*zheng*] of Heaven and Earth, riding the changes of the six vital energies [*qi*], and . . . thus able to wander the cosmos without any constraints or limitations" (*ZZJS* 1:17).

This ideal person also possesses special qualities and capacities, elaborated by Zhuangzi (ca. 369–ca. 286 BCE) in his discussion of the Spiritual Person, a being

> with skin like ice or snow, and gentle and shy like a virgin girl. The Person doesn't eat the five grains, but sucks the wind, drinks the dew, climbs up on the clouds and mist, rides a flying dragon, and wan-

ders beyond the four seas. By concentrating his/her spirit, the Person can protect creatures from sickness and plague and make the harvest plentiful.

[ZZJS 1:28; TRANS. WATSON, 33 (MODIFIED)]

Through an ethereal taking in of natural essences and concentration of spirit, this person develops benevolent powers over the natural world. Accompanying the idea of transformative cosmic power is a suggestion of the feminine—expressed in delicate physical beauty, gentleness, and nurturing, generative tendencies. (This might suggest that such spiritual perfection and human efficacy is equally attainable by women as well as men. With this in mind, I render *ren* as "person" rather than "man.") For this ideal person, "rites are but something created by the vulgar men of the world." As one who "follows rules of Heaven and prizes genuineness," the person "does not allow himself/herself to be cramped by the vulgar" (ZZJS 4:1032). The ideal personalities in the *Zhuangzi* inspired the Seven Worthies both metaphysically and experientially. Metaphysically, they invoked the concept of a freewheeling

FIGURE 7.1 *The Seven Worthies of the Bamboo Grove and Rong Qiqi*. Rubbing of a brick relief. South wall, tomb at Xishanqiao, Nanjing, Jiangsu. Late fourth to early fifth century. From left to right: Ji Kang, Ruan Ji, Shan Tao, and Wang Rong. Nanjing Museum. Photograph courtesy of Audrey Spiro.

FIGURE 7.2 *The Seven Worthies of the Bamboo Grove and Rong Qiqi*. Rubbing of a brick relief. North wall, tomb at Xishanqiao, Nanjing, Jiangsu. Late fourth to early fifth century. From left to right: Rong Qiqi (an ancient recluse mentioned in Ji Kang's "Rhyme-Prose on the Zither" ["Qinfu"] as Rong Qi, placed here for purposes of symmetry), Ruan Xian, Liu Ling, and Xiang Xiu. Nanjing Museum. Photograph courtesy of Audrey Spiro.

spiritual self. Sustained by such a self, the Worthies could defy the repressive Confucian rituals in favor of a free, aesthetic lifestyle that nurtured artistic and poetic beauty.

In this chapter, I will show how Zhuangzi's ideal personalities loomed large in the lives and works of the Bamboo Grove worthies, focusing mainly on Ji Kang, along with Ruan Ji, Liu Ling, and Xiang Xiu. These four associated themselves more closely with the *Zhuangzi* and were more poetically creative than the rest of the group. I shall devote a section to each figure, beginning each section with a story that depicts a defining moment in the man's life and interpreting that moment with support from his poetic works. Using this approach, I hope to explore how the Worthies of the Bamboo Grove drew on the Wei-Jin *Xuanxue* to fashion their poetic personae, themes, and vision.

JI KANG

The most remarkable moment of Ji Kang's life came when it was about to end. As described in the *Shishuo*: "On the eve of Ji Kang's execution in the Eastern Marketplace of Luoyang (in 262), his spirit and bearing showed no change. Taking out his zither (*qin*), he plucked the strings and played the 'Melody of Guangling' ('Guangling san')" (*SSXYJS* 1:344). Ji Kang was executed as punishment for his unyielding defiance of the Sima clan. This heartrending moment completed Ji Kang's lifelong effort to cultivate himself into a Perfected Person, for the expression "his spirit and bearing showed no change" resembles the person in the "Tian Zifang" chapter of the *Zhuangzi*. This person possesses such great spiritual strength that he/she may "peep into the blue heavens above, dive into the Yellow Springs below, and roam freely to the end of the eight directions," all while "keeping his/her spirit and bearing no change" (*ZZJS* 3:725).

Indeed, throughout Ji Kang's poetic corpus, he expresses his admiration for the ideal personalities in the *Zhuangzi*, the Perfected Person in particular. In an early poem, number nineteen of his poetic series "To My Elder Brother the Lord Xiucai on His Joining the Army" ("Xiong Xiucai gong rujun zengshi"), Ji Kang chants:

	The vulgar public are difficult to enlighten;	流俗難悟
2	They pursue material gain, and cannot return.	逐物不還
	[In contrast,] the Perfected Person is farsighted	至人遠鑒
4	And will eventually return to Nature.	歸之自然
	He sees myriad things as one,	萬物為一
6	And four seas belong to the same family.	四海同宅
	If only I could share the same destiny with him,	與彼共之
8	What else do I have to treasure?	予何所惜
	Life is like a floating, temporary lodging;	生若浮寄
10	It emerges briefly, then suddenly disappears.	暫見忽終
	The world affairs are in chaos,	世故紛紜
12	I abandon them to eight directions.	棄之八成[戎]
	Although the swamp pheasant is hungry	澤雉雖饑

14	It does not want to be kept in a garden orchard.	不願園林
	How can I serve as a horse on a chariot,	安能服禦
16	Wearing out my body, grieving my heart?	勞形苦心
	My person is precious, whereas fame is of no importance,	身貴名賤
18	Glory and disgrace, who cares for their whereabouts?	榮辱何在
	All I value is that my intent can roam freely,	貴得肆志
20	And let my heart/mind gallop as it will, with no regrets!	縱心無悔

[*JKJJZ* 1.19–20]

Drawing broadly on the *Zhuangzi*, Ji Kang summarizes the image of the Perfected Person as the emblem of nature, who transcends the confinement of the profane world. In identifying himself with the person, Ji Kang thus bases his lifestyle on his philosophical understanding and aspiration.

While the young Ji Kang hoped to live according to his free will, the pressures of political reality often disturbed his attempts at the ideal life. To gain support for their usurpation of imperial power, the Simas endeavored to tempt scholar-officials into their camp. As one of the outstanding *Xuanxue* thinkers, poets, and musicians of his time, Ji Kang with his scholarly and artistic achievements and exemplary manner won great admiration from the Wei gentry and made him a highly desirable target for the Simas. Ji Kang's intensely honest character and marriage to a daughter of the Cao-Wei royal clan, however, kept him from yielding to their pressure. The *Shishuo* records several of his confrontations with the Simas and their followers.

One such exchange occurred between Ji Kang and Zhong Hui (225–264), a close associate to the powerful Sima Zhao (posthumously titled Emperor Wen of the Jin; 211–265). Desiring acquaintance with Ji Kang, Zhong Hui paid him a visit with a group of impressive gentlemen. Ji Kang was found forging metal beneath a tree and totally ignored Zhong Hui's presence. When Zhong Hui finally rose to go, Ji Kang asked him, "What had you heard that made you come, and what have you seen that makes you leave?" (*He suo wen er lai, he suo jian er qu*). Zhong Hui replied, "I heard what I heard so I came, and I saw what I have seen so I am leaving" (*Wen suo wen er lai, jian suo jian er qu*) (*SSXYJS* 2:766).

The repeating syntactical structure of Zhong Hui's response might indicate his admiration for Ji Kang, in that he wishes to imitate his speech. Yet Zhong Hui also feels humiliated in having been so ignored. By changing only two of Ji Kang's original words—"what" (*he*) to "hear" (*wen*), and "what" (*he*) to "see" (*jian*)—Zhong Hui refuses to specify what he heard and saw and totally alters the mood of the sentence. If before the statement sounded haughty and somewhat satirical, like Ji Kang's own personality, it now becomes resentful and threatening, revealing two of Zhong Hui's prominent character traits, which would soon after prove deadly.

In addition to fending off temptations and threat from the Sima camp, Ji Kang also had to deal with worldly hassles from his friends. Another *Shishuo* episode tells us that Shan Tao recommended Ji Kang as his replacement as head of the selection bureau, in 262. Ji Kang responded with a letter to announce the breaking off of their friendship (*SSXYJS* 2:651). Though he could easily have refused him in private, Ji Kang chose to send Shan Tao a public rebuke in which he severely attacked the contemporary moral-political system as confining human nature. He thereby offended the dominant Sima clan, which was then reaffirming Confucian moral teachings as the basis of governance in an effort to conceal their intended usurpation of the Wei throne—a betrayal of the very essence of Confucian moral teachings. In this sense, Ji Kang was not so much breaking off from Shan Tao as using the opportunity to expose the Simas' hypocritical moral-political system and signal his own unyielding integrity.

Ji Kang's defiance of prevailing norms resulted from his philosophical attachment to the Perfected Person ideal, which inspired him "to transcend the Confucian moral teaching and follow one's natural inclinations [*ziran*]" (*JKJJZ* 6.234). Ji Kang rejected Confucian teaching insofar as it subscribes to standard moral and social norms. He was instead in favor of a life lived according to one's own inner dictates and expressive of what one genuinely feels. He comes to this attitude from what he sees as the intrinsic needs of human nature:

> The Six Confucian Classics teach us above all to restrain and guide [human nature], yet a human being by nature only feels happy by following its desire. To restrain and guide human nature goes against one's will, whereas by following one's desire one can retain one's natural inclinations. Thus, to retain one's natural inclinations, one should not follow the restraining Six Classics; to maintain one's natural intake, one does not need ritual and rules that offend human feelings.
>
> [*JKJJZ* 7.261]

Facing temptation and threat from the Sima camp, Ji Kang insisted upon living according to his Perfected Person ideal. He believed that this ideal could guard his integrity from the encroachments of the dangerous, mundane world. As he wrote in the third of "In Reply to the Two Guos, Three Poems" ("Da er Guo shi san shou"):

	Carefully observing the world's affairs,	詳觀凌世務
2	I see they are full of sorrows and unpredictable dangers.	屯險多憂虞
	People give favors in exchange for benefits;	施報更相市
4	The Great Way is hidden, not able to unfold.	大道匿不舒
	The smooth roads are planted with thorny bushes;	夷路值[殖]枳棘
6	I want to walk at ease, but where can I go?	安步將焉如
	The powerful and intelligent are fighting with one another;	權智相傾奪
8	One should not possess fame and position.	名位不可居
	A phoenix avoids web and net,	鸞鳳避罻羅
10	And flies far away to Mount Kunlun.	遠托昆侖墟
	Zhuang Zhou mourns the dead divine tortoise [treasured in the king's ancestral temple];	莊周悼靈龜
12	Prince Sou of Yue laments being forced to the throne.	越稷[搜]嗟王輿
	The Perfected Person preserves his/her self.	至人存諸己
14	Like an unpolished jade, happy with the mysterious and the void.	隱璞樂玄虛
	Deeds and fame are not worth dying for;	功名何足殉
16	Who wants to leave records in blocks and books?	乃欲列簡書
	What I like shines so brightly to signal my direction;	所好亮若茲

18	[No need to be like] Master Yang, who sighs at forked roads.	楊氏歎交衢
	Going on and on, to follow my intent,	去去從所志
20	How dare I excuse myself not to go with the Dao?	敢謝道不俱

[JKJJZ 1.64–65]

Ji Kang tried to stay away from politics and live as a recluse, but ultimately his passionate and unyielding personality prevented him from "preserving his self." Ji Kang and Lü An were close friends. Later, Lü An's beautiful wife was raped by his brother Lü Xun, a Sima Zhao follower. Fearing that Lü An would condemn him publicly, Lü Xun turned Lü An in to prison under the false accusation of beating their mother. When Ji Kang went to the court to defend and clear his friend, Zhong Hui publicly slandered Ji Kang as "unprofitable to the present age and a baneful influence on its morals." He urged Sima Zhao to execute Ji Kang along with Lü An to "purify the Royal Way" (*SSXYJS* 1:344–349).

In prison, Ji Kang wrote the poem "On Sorrow" ("Youfen shi") as a retrospective of his life. He recalls how he developed a Daoist approach to life:

	As I have reached adulthood	爰及冠帶
10	Doted on by my family, I behave without restraint.	馮寵自放
	With mind lofty, I admire ancient worthies,	抗心希古
12	And follow what they upheld.	任其所尚
	I have favored the ideas in the *Laozi* and the *Zhuangzi*,	託好老莊
14	Depreciating material life but prizing my person.	賤物貴身
	I have been willing to guard my plainness	志在守樸
16	Cultivating my purity and keeping my genuineness intact.	養素全真

Even with such an aloof approach to life, Ji Kang finds himself accused and in prison. Aware of his naive innocence, he admits: "Yet I am not smart, / Too kind to see the evil in people" (lines 17–18). This is in part a reference to Lü Xun, whose evil so exceeds Ji Kang's imagination that Ji Kang is unprepared to protect either Lü An or himself from such harm. He also admits that, "being impatient by nature, / I have been eager to show my approval and disapproval [of others]" (lines 25–26). Thus,

	I have tried to refrain from making mistakes,	欲寡其過
30	Yet slanders against me rise like boiling water.	謗議沸騰
	By nature I never hurt other people,	性不傷物
32	Yet I have frequently caused resentment and hatred.	頻致怨憎
	I feel uneasy facing Liu[xia] Hui in the past,	昔慚柳[下]惠
34	And Sun Deng in the present.	今愧孫登
	Looking inward I haven't lived up to my own expectations;	內負宿心
36	Looking outward I feel I have let my good friends down.	外恧良朋

Liuxia Hui, although thrice dismissed as a judge, refused to bend the Way (*LYYZ* 192). Sun Deng, a Daoist living in reclusion in the Ji mountains, had advised Ji Kang to "protect his life" (*SSXYJS*

2:648–649). Ji Kang now felt in a bind because he could not simultaneously follow both principles. Unable to anticipate that Sima Zhao and Zhong Hui could put him to death (another proof of his being too trusting to see the evil in his enemies), Ji Kang promised himself:

	I wish to try harder in the future	庶勗將來
82	Wafting neither fragrance nor stench.	無馨無臭
	I'll pick up woodland ferns in the fold of the mountain,	採薇山阿
84	Letting my hair down as I dwell in a cliff cave.	散髮巖岫
	With prolonged whistling and chanting	永嘯長吟
86	I nourish my nature to acquire longevity.	頤性養壽

[JKJJZ 1.25–35]

Sima Zhao might not have wanted to kill Ji Kang. But when three thousand scholars of the Grand Academy petitioned for Ji Kang's release and appointment as their teacher, Sima Zhao must have felt threatened. Fearing that Ji Kang's popularity could subvert his own dominant position, Sima Zhao ordered his execution, only to repent of it later (*SSXYJS* 1:344).

As for Ji Kang, he found composure in the Perfected Person ideal, calmly playing the zither in the last moments of his life. He had earlier composed his "Rhyme-Prose on the Zither" ("Qinfu"), in which he argued that the zither was invented by such Perfected Persons as Rong Qi and Qi Ji, "who have fled from the world." "Realizing the abundant burdens of the profane world, / They emulate the remaining glory of Ji Mountain" (lines 71–72), where the ancient sage Xu You had lived as a recluse after declining the sage-king Yao's offer of the throne. These Perfected Persons take a young bough from a paulownia tree, making it into an "elegant zither" (*yaqin*) to "release their thoughts" (*shusi*) (*JKJJZ* 2.88–90).

Seen in this light, the coda (*luan*) of Ji Kang's "Rhyme-Prose on the Zither" seems to foreshadow the ending of his own life:

	Harmonious and peaceful is the virtue of the zither,	愔愔琴德
348	Which cannot be fathomed.	不可測兮
	Pure is the body of the zither, and aloof its mind,	體清心遠
350	Both of which are extremely difficult to comprehend.	邈難極兮
	The instrument of good quality and the fine player	良質美手
352	Meet in this age.	遇今世兮
	Its rich and symphonic sound	紛綸翕響
354	Surpasses all other arts.	冠衆藝兮
	Yet very few can understand its music,	識音者希
356	So who will treasure it?	孰能珍兮。
	The one who can fully reveal the beauty of the elegant zither,	能盡雅琴
358	Is only the Perfected Person.	唯至人兮

[*WX* 1:259; *JKJJZ* 2.109]

Since few in the mundane world could understand him, why not leave it? The virtue of the zither quietly and gently accompanied Ji Kang's spirit into eternal nature, where the Perfected Person, now Ji Kang himself, could enjoy the peaceful and pure life he had longed for.

RUAN JI

The Seven Worthies were more or less addicted to wine, but Ruan Ji was undoubtedly the most famous drunkard among them. Sima Zhao once wanted to marry his son to Ruan Ji's daughter but could not find an opportunity to propose the marriage because Ruan Ji was drunk for sixty days! Several times, Zhong Hui attempted to check on Ruan Ji's political attitudes, looking for a way to implicate him; every time Ruan Ji eluded him by getting drunk. Ruan Ji had no interest in public office: he requested the position of infantry commandant only because he had heard that the office had a great storage of wine.

To be sure, Ruan Ji "originally had the intent to benefit the world." Discovering, however, that "few famous gentlemen could maintain their lives intact" (*quan*) during the Wei-Jin transition, he kept away from political affairs, indulging himself instead in books, especially the *Laozi* and the *Zhuangzi*, and in wine (*JS* 5:1359–1360). His addiction to wine was very likely based on his emulation of the ideal personalities in the *Zhuangzi*. The chapter "Mastering Life" ("Dasheng") in the *Zhuangzi* likens a drunken person to the Sage: the former preserves his spirit intact in wine, and the latter in nature (*ZZJS* 3:636).

To protect himself, Ruan Ji discussed only abstruse topics, never allowing himself to be drawn into individual character appraisals. Still, he openly invoked another ideal personality, similar to the Perfected Person in the *Zhuangzi*—the Great Person—to refute the Simas' Confucian ritual model, the "superior man" (*junzi*). In his famous essay "Biography of the Great Person" ("Daren xiansheng zhuan"), Ruan Ji accuses the superior man of "establishing ritual rules to control people," for these ritual rules are "indeed the tactics of brutalizing inferior people and creating chaos, danger, and death" (*RJJ* A.66). In contrast, the Great Person "shares the same body with Nature the Creator, is born with Heaven and Earth, roams above the world, and thus completes self-fashioning together with the Dao" (*RJJ* A.64).

Ruan Ji's critique of the superior man was directed less toward the essential moral teachings of Confucius (to which he remained sincerely loyal) than toward the Simas' manipulation and distortion of them. His own elaboration of the ideal personalities in the *Zhuangzi* even incorporates certain Confucian values. He points out, for instance, that "the Perfected Person ... with his/her spiritual and noble Dao preserved within, transforms myriad things beyond Heaven" and that "this is why all under Heaven receives its nourishment and myriad things grow vigorously" (*RJJ* A.68). His argument is built on the function of the person's spirit (*shen*), depicted in the *Zhuangzi*'s "Free Roaming," but also incorporates the quality of the Confucian Sage "being able to assist in the transforming and nourishing powers of Heaven and Earth," from the "Doctrine of the Mean" ("Zhongyong") in the Confucian classic *Book of Rites* (*Liji*) (*LJZY* 2:1632).

For Ruan Ji, what negotiates between Daoist naturalness and Confucian moral teaching is *zhen* (genuineness). Again from the *Zhuangzi*:

By genuineness I mean purity and sincerity in their highest degree. One who lacks purity and sincerity cannot move others. . . . [Therefore,] when one has sincerity within oneself, one's spirit will manifest one's sincerity to others. That is why genuineness is to be prized! When genuineness is applied to human principles, in the service of parents, it is love and filial piety; in the service of the ruler, it is loyalty and integrity; in festive wine drinking, it is merriment and joy; in periods of mourning, it is sadness and grief.

[*ZZJS* 4:1032]

The genuineness prized by the Sage explains Ruan Ji's "uninhibited and eccentric" (*rendan*) behavior. His conduct upon losing his mother serves as an example. According to the *Shishuo* records, Ruan Ji drank wine and ate meat during the mourning period for his mother, thus offending Confucian burial rituals and earning the censure of "superior men" who demanded that Sima Zhao "banish Ruan Ji beyond the sea to set right the Confucian moral teaching." Yet, as Ruan Ji was about to bury his mother, he cried to the point of spitting up blood (*SSXYJS* 2:727, 731). For Ruan Ji, mourning a parent's death involved spontaneous expression of genuine feelings rather than observing dictated rituals.

Ji Kang and Ruan Ji ended their lives in keeping with their different addictions—the former to the "five-mineral powder" (*wushi san*), the latter to wine. Ji Kang took drugs to achieve immortality (as only an immortal can disdain the mundane world), whereas Ruan Ji drank wine to intoxicate himself and so avoid facing the world seriously. Being perceived as a threat to the reigning powers, the sober Ji Kang was consequently executed. Ruan Ji, meanwhile, eluded those powers by drowning his resistance in wine. Although Ruan Ji escaped execution, we can wonder whether all his repressed anxiety and sorrow was the reason he survived Ji Kang by only a year. Poem 33 from his poetic series "Poems Singing of My Innermost Thoughts" ("Yonghuai shi") reflects his intense feelings:

	A day is followed by another night;	一日復一夕
2	A night followed by another morning.	一夕復一朝
	My complexion changes its original color,	顏色改平常
4	And my spirit has lost its vigor.	精神自損消
	My bosom is filled with burning fire and boiling water,	胸中懷湯火
6	As I am constantly affected by the changes of the world	變化故相招
	Myriad things disturb me endlessly;	萬事無窮極
8	Sadly I do not have enough wisdom to cope.	知謀苦不饒
	I am only afraid that in no time	但恐須臾間
10	The ether of my soul will be swept away by the wind;	魂氣隨風飄
	All of my life I will tread on thin ice	終身履薄冰
12	Who could know that my heart is on fire?	誰知我心焦

[*RBBYHSZ* 43]

Ruan Ji's inner torment, described as an unquenchable fire consuming his soul, seems to be caused by an internalization of "myriad things"—the "changes of the world" and his own losses—and his powerlessness even to cope with them. Poem 34, whose opening couplets closely resemble those of poem 33, expresses his grief for old friends who lost their lives because of their "lofty behavior."

Without them, Ruan Ji laments (*RBBYHSZ* 43–44), "who will be with me to guard our genuineness?" This poem surely refers to Ji Kang; after all, they had built their friendship upon their shared emulation of the ideal personalities in the *Zhuangzi*.

LIU LING

Whereas Ruan Ji gets drunk to evade and conceal his anger toward the hypocritical "superior men," Liu Ling becomes explicitly defiant of conventional norms while drunk. The *Shishuo* records that Liu Ling once, upon becoming drunk, took off his clothes and sat naked in his room. When people saw him and chided him, Liu Ling retorted, "I take heaven and earth for my pillars and roof, and my house for my pants and coat. Why do you gentlemen come into my pants?" (*SSXYJS* 2:730).

Liu Ling's eccentric behavior again resulted from his emulation of the ideal personalities in the *Zhuangzi*, in this case the Great Person. In his "Eulogy to the Virtue of Wine" ("Jiude song"), he describes the Great Person as one for whom

	Heaven and earth are as brief as but one morning,	以天地為一朝
2	Ten thousand ages but a trice,	萬期為須臾
	The sun and the moon but his door and window,	日月為扃牖
4	And the eight directions but the paths in his courtyard.	八荒為庭衢
	He leaves neither tracks nor traces behind while traveling,	行無轍跡
6	And lives in neither house nor hut.	居無室廬
	He has sky for curtain and earth for mat,	幕天席地
8	And he abandons his ideas to wherever they like to go.	縱意所如
	As he rests, he holds a goblet or a cup;	止則操卮執觚
12	While he moves, he carries a jug or a pot.	動則挈榼提壺
	He takes drinking wine as his only task;	唯酒是務
14	What else should he care to know?	焉知其餘

[*SSXYJS* 1:250]

Clearly, the Great Person is a portrait of Liu Ling himself. To identify with the Great Person, Liu Ling transcends mundane space and enters the spiritual void, where his mind can travel beyond all confinement. Only under such free and natural conditions could his "self" grow of its own accord.

Liu Ling thus enrages the ritual-abiding men: with angry looks and gnashing teeth, "they lecture him on ritual, / Stirring up sharp arguments on right and wrong" (lines 19–22). In the face of this, Liu Ling

	Listens quietly, but hears no crashing noises of thunder,	靜聽不聞雷霆之聲
32	And gazes attentively, but sees not even the form of Mount Tai.	熟視不睹泰山之形
	He does not feel penetrating coldness or burning heat;	不覺寒暑之切肌
34	Stirred by neither profit nor desire.	利欲之感情

[*SSXYJS* 1:250]

As the Great Person, Liu Ling has merged with nature; detaching himself from worldly disturbances, he is not affected by these gentlemen's attacks.

XIANG XIU

Xiang Xiu was close to Ji Kang. He would assist in Ji Kang's metal forging by working the bellows (*SSXYJS* 2:766) and debate with him on philosophical topics "in order to expand Ji Kang's profound ideas" (*JS* 5:1374). After Ji Kang was executed, Xiang Xiu was forced to serve under the Simas. On his way to the capital Luoyang, he passed by Ji Kang's former residence and wrote the famous rhyme-prose "Recalling Old Friends" ("Sijiu fu"). This piece contains his profound and touching tribute to his friend's last moments:

	I grieve that when Master Ji bid farewell to this world,	悼嵇生之永辭兮
18	He looked back at his shadow in the sun and played the zither.	顧日影而彈琴
	Entrusting his destiny to his [philosophical] understanding,	託運遇於領會兮
20	He placed [the meaning of] his remaining life on this brief moment.	寄餘命於寸陰

[*WX* 1:230]

Xiang Xiu lamented Ji Kang's tragic ending and understood how Ji Kang coped with his impending death by drawing on his philosophical beliefs. He did not, however, share Ji Kang's devotion to the Perfected Person ideal. When Xiang Xiu arrived in Luoyang, Sima Zhao asked him, "I heard you had [Xu You's] ambition of retiring to Ji Mountain. What are you doing here?" Xiang Xiu responded that Xu You was "narrow-minded and stubborn" and that he "could not fully understand Yao's intention when he offered the throne, not worthy of emulation!" (*JS* 5:1375). Xiang Xiu's response has been read as reluctant self-defense, since he well knew that Ji Kang had lost his life precisely because he emulated Xu You. Although there may be some truth in this, as Yu Jiaxi (1884–1955) suggests, Xiang Xiu eventually held office because his philosophical attitude differed from that of Ji Kang (*SSXYJS* 1:80).

Like Ji Kang, Xiang Xiu was passionate about the *Laozi* and the *Zhuangzi*. Feeling that previous commentators had failed to understand the *Zhuangzi* fully, Xiang Xiu wrote his own explanatory interpretation, whose subtle analysis greatly increased the popularity of the Abstruse Learning. However, Xiang Xiu's commentary also revealed the sharp divergence between his readings of the *Zhuangzi* and that of Ji Kang. Whereas Ji Kang understood Zhuangzi's "free roaming" as an ideal embodied in the lofty Perfected Person, who is free from mundane constraints, Xiang Xiu defines "free roaming" as "self-contentment" (*zizu*). For Xiang Xiu, one can achieve spiritual freedom as long as one is content in one's position, be it ruling on a throne or wandering on Ji Mountain. It was with this philosophical belief that Xiang Xiu reconciled himself to his sociopolitical circumstances and yielded to the Sima regime.

Eventually, though, Ji Kang's view of the Perfected Person would triumph, closely heeded by *Xuanxue* adepts in the Eastern Jin (317–420), especially an eminent gentry group active in the mid-third century and led by the Buddhist monk Zhi Dun (314–366). An adept of Mahāyāna Buddhism and *Xuanxue*, Zhi Dun combined the two and enriched both, drawing on the *Zhuangzi* to interpret the Prajñāpāramitā Sūtras and vice versa. He dispatched his most influential argument on the *Zhuangzi* against Xiang Xiu's interpretation of "free roaming" as "each creature acts according to its nature." Zhi Dun questions this premise, asking whether we must then consider the brutal rule of tyrants Jie and Zhou also free roaming, since they are by nature cruel (*GSZ* 4.160). Such an essentially nonmoral conception obviously affects the Buddhist belief in a universe dominated by moral law. Zhi Dun employs the Perfected Person to expound further on the true nature of freedom in his "On Free Roaming" ("Xiaoyao lun"):

> Free roaming manifests the heart/mind status of the Perfected Person . . . The Perfected Person, riding upon the correctness of Heaven, soars aloft, wandering infinitely in unfettered freedom. Since the Person treats objects as objects, without being treated as an object by other objects, therefore in his/her roaming s/he is not self-satisfied; being mystically in communion with the universe, the Person does not act purposefully. S/he is not hurried, yet moves swiftly. Therefore in his/her freedom the Person goes everywhere. This is how it becomes "free roaming."
>
> But if, on the other hand, one has desire to fulfill one's own contentment, and to be content with one's own contentment, such a man in his happiness has something like natural simplicity, like a hungry man once he is satiated, or a thirsty man once his thirst is quenched. But would such a man forthwith forget all about cooking and eating in the presence of grains and cereals, or put an end to all further toasting and pledging in the presence of wines and liquors? Unless it is perfect contentment (*zhizu*), how can it be a means to free roaming?
>
> [*SSXYJS* 1:220; TRANS. MATHER, 109–110 (MODIFIED)]

In place of Xiang Xiu's "self-contentment," which still relies on outside conditions to satisfy desires, Zhi Dun proposes "perfect contentment," a transcendence of all mundane entanglements that mystically merges the self with the Great Way of Nature. Only then can one achieve "free roaming" and become the Spiritual Person who "doesn't eat the five grains but sucks the wind, drinks the dew" and "wanders through the boundless," dependent on nothing.

Scholars have argued that Zhi Dun's more metaphysical interpretation of "free roaming" reflects his Buddhist background. Yet his use of the Perfected Person as the emblem of "perfect contentment" surely also drew upon Ji Kang, Ruan Ji, and Liu Ling's poetic elaborations as well as their attempts to personify the ideal personalities in the *Zhuangzi*. Through the Seven Worthies, Zhuangzi's ideal exerted strong influence on Eastern Jin *Xuanxue*. The major *Xuanxue* practice of "character appraisal" (*renlun jianshi*), for instance, evaluated human character using these ideals as standards and described more abstract, inner qualities through images borrowed from nature. In this way, character appraisal contributed to the formation of landscape poetry in the Eastern Jin.

Another important legacy of the Seven Worthies was their "Bamboo Grove aura" (*Linxia fengqi*), which represents the most respected of Wei-Jin character traits—philosophical depth, poetic talent, artistic expertise, and, above all, a free, unrestrained spirit. This aura extended to the famous Wei-Jin "worthy ladies" (*xianyuan*) and became the epithet for these women and their later followers. As portrayed in the chapter "Xianyuan" in the *Shishuo xinyu*, these women were said to embody every aspect of the Perfected Person ideal. Women in subsequent periods would repeatedly invoke *xianyuan* as the earliest and perhaps most admirable examples of the talented Chinese woman (*cainü*). The legacy of the Seven Worthies of the Bamboo Grove, with their poetic elaboration of Zhuangzi's ideal personalities, clearly opens onto a wide variety of fascinating research topics as well as remaining a rich focus of study in its own right.

NANXIU QIAN

PRIMARY SOURCES

GSZ	Hui Jiao 慧皎. *Gaoseng zhuan* 高僧傳 (Biographies of Eminent Monks). Collation and commentary by Tang Yongtong 湯用彤. Beijing: Zhonghua shuju, 1992.
JKJJZ	Ji Kang 嵇康. *Ji Kang ji jiaozhu* 嵇康集[校注] ([Collation and Commentary on the] *Collected Works of Ji Kang*). Collation and commentary by Dai Mingyang 戴明揚. Beijing: Renmin wenxue chubanshe, 1962.
JS	Fang Xuanling 房玄齡 et al. *Jinshu* 晉書 (History of the Jin). 10 vols. Beijing: Zhonghua shuju, 1974.
LJZY	*Liji* [*zhengyi*] 禮記[正義] ([Orthodox Commentary on the] *Book of Rites*). In *Shisanjing zhushu* 十三經註疏 (Commentaries on the Thirteen Chinese Classics). Ed. Ruan Yuan 阮元. 2 vols. 1826; reprint Beijing: Zhonghua shuju, 1979.
LYYZ	*Lunyu* [*yizhu*] 論語[譯註] ([Annotated Translation of the] *Analects of Confucius*). Annotation and translation from classical into modern Chinese by Yang Bojun 楊伯峻. Beijing: Zhonghua shuju, 1980.
RBBYHSZ	Ruan Ji 阮籍. *Ruan Bubing Yonghuai shi* [*zhu*] 阮步兵詠懷詩[註] ([Commentary on the] "Poems Singing of My Innermost Thoughts" by Ruan Ji). Commentary by Huang Jie 黃節. Beijing: Renmin wenxue chubanshe, 1984.
RJJ	*Ruan Ji ji* 阮籍集 (Collected Works of Ruan Ji). Shanghai: Shanghai guji chubanshe, 1978.
SSXYJS	Liu Yiqing 劉義慶. *Shishuo xinyu* [*jianshu*] 世說新語[箋疏] ([Commentary on the] *Shishuo xinyu*). Commentary by Yu Jiaxi 余嘉錫. 2 vols. Shanghai: Shanghai guji chubanshe, 1993.
WX	Xiao Tong 蕭統, ed. *Wenxuan* 文選 (Selections of Refined Literature). 3 vols. Beijing: Zhonghua shuju, 1977.
ZZJS	*Zhuangzi* [*jishi*] 莊子[集釋] ([Collected Commentary on] *Zhuangzi*). Compiled by Guo Qingfan 郭慶藩. 4 vols. Beijing: Zhonghua shuju, 1961.

SUGGESTED READINGS

ENGLISH

Henricks, Robert G., trans. *Philosophy and Argumentation in Third-Century China: The Essays of Hsi K'ang*. Princeton, NJ: Princeton University Press, 1983.

Holzman, Donald. *Poetry and Politics: The Life and Works of Juan Chi (A.D. 210–263)*. Cambridge: Cambridge University Press, 1976.

Mather, Richard B., trans. *Shih-shuo Hsin-yü: A New Account of Tales of the World*. Minneapolis: University of Minnesota Press, 1976.

Qian, Nanxiu. *Spirit and Self in Medieval China: The* Shi-shuo hsin-yü *and Its Legacy*. Honolulu: University of Hawai'i Press, 2001.

Rushton, Peter. "An Interpretation of Hsi K'ang's Eighteen Poems Presented to Hsi Hsi on His Entry into the Army." *Journal of the American Oriental Society* 99, no. 2 (1979): 175–190.

CHINESE

Chen Yike 陳寅恪. "'Xiaoyao you' Xiang-Guo yi ji Zhi Dun yi tanyuan" 逍遙游向郭義及支遁義探源 (Tracking the Origins of Xiang-Guo's and Zhi Dun's Interpretations of "Free Roaming"). In *Jinmingguan conggao erbian* 金明館叢稿二編 (Collected Essays from Jinming Studio). Shanghai: Shanghai guji chupanshe, 1980. See especially 83–89.

He Qimin 何啓明. *Zhulin qixian yanjiu* 竹林七賢研究 (A Study of the Seven Worthies of the Bamboo Grove). Taipei: Zhongguo xueshu zhuzuo jiangzhu weiyuanhui, 1966.

Liu Liangjian 劉梁劍. "'Xiaoyao you' Xiang-Guo yi yu Zhi Dun yi kanhui"《逍遙游》向[秀]郭[象]義與支遁義勘會 (A Comparative Study Between Xiang [Xiu]-Guo [Xiang]'s and Zhi Dun's Interpretations of "Free Roaming"). *Huadong shifan daxue xuebao* 華東師範大學學報 (Social Sciences) 3 (2010): 26–31.

Lu Xun 魯迅. "Wei-Jin fengdu ji wenzhang yu yao ji jiu zhi guanxi" 魏晉風度及文章與藥及酒之關係 (Wei-Jin Manners, Literature, Drugs, and Wine). *Lu Xun quanji* 魯迅全集 (Complete Works of Lu Xun). 18 vols. Beijing: Renmin wenxue chupanshe, 2005. See especially 3:523–553.

Tang Yongtong 湯用彤. *Wei-Jin Xuanxue lungao* 魏晉玄學論稿 (Preliminary Studies of Wei-Jin *Xuanxue*). Beijing: Renmin wenxue chubanshe, 1957.

8

THE POETRY OF RECLUSION

Tao Qian

Tao Qian (365–427) is ubiquitous. Beginning in the Tang dynasty, and especially enhanced and formulated during the Song, a sort of Tao Qian consciousness became a part of literati culture, and over the centuries a certain something about him so imbued Chinese mentality that many characteristic cultural traits that now may seem to be archetypically Chinese actually develop from Tao Qian and his writings. Tao Qian, also known by his byname Tao Yuanming,[1] may not be ranked as the finest of China's poets of all time—this honor is usually given to Du Fu (712–770) or Li Bai (701–762), with Bai Juyi (772–846) and Su Shi (1037–1101) close behind (Su Shi himself ranked Tao Yuanming above Li Bai and Du Fu). But his influence on Chinese sensibilities has been particularly profound and pervasive, for Tao Qian's life and writings have played a foundational and indelible role in the alluring portrayal of reclusion, especially in terms of both the circumstances and the quality of private life. Tao Qian took a path all his own, choosing a humble life, farming the countryside, yet rich with the humanistic values that literati cherish. His writings, especially his poetry, depict the joys and concerns of an alternative lifestyle alongside the ease and the burdens of self-determination and introspection, and a deeply philosophical outlook on the natural processes of life.

One would think that the life and times of Tao Yuanming would be easy to recite, since there are elegant writings about him by prominent literati, dating from within a century of his death. These include a rich funerary elegy by Tao's erudite friend Yan Yanzhi (384–456), a biography for the dynastic history of the Song period by the eminent scholar-official Shen Yue (441–513), as well as another biography and a preface to his collected writings by Xiao Tong (501–531), crown prince of the Liang dynasty and compiler of the *Anthology of Refined Literature* (*Wenxuan*), which included nine of Tao's poems. But, actually, the biographies add little beyond several of Tao's own pieces about himself, and besides the frame of a few historical facts, Tao Yuanming's own corpus of writings, especially his poems, have served over the centuries as the primary sources for envisioning the man.

Indeed, the early biographies invariably note the fitting likeness of probably the most famous short self-portrayal ever, "Biography of Master Five Willows" ("Wuliu xiansheng zhuan"), Tao's own innovative mode of autofictography. In a pastiche of images without real biographical substance, he constructs a character that has resonated with Chinese sensibilities, one that Tao Yuanming himself also draws upon and amplifies in a number of his writings. The following translation shows the recurring themes of equanimity and independence from conventional pursuits and views, and of the richness of poverty, books, friendship, and wine:

Where this gentleman was born is not known, nor is one sure of his name, but beside his house were five willow trees, from which he took his nickname. He was a man of tranquil disposition and few words, and did not seek fame or fortune. He was fond of reading, but did not look for a recondite explication. When he came across something to his liking he would be so delighted that he would forget to eat. By nature he liked wine, but being poor could not always come by it. Knowing the circumstances, his friends and relatives would at times set out wine and invite him over. He could not drink without emptying his cup, and always ended up drunk, after which he would retire, without a thought about whether to stay or to leave. His hut was spare, and did not shelter against rain and sun. His short tunic was torn and patched, and his vessels for food and drink frequently empty, but he was unperturbed. He often composed writings for his own amusement, and in them are revealed his ideas about things. He had no concern for worldly success, and so he ended his days.

[TYMJJZ 502]

Although this self-caricature is blatantly imagistic, readers over the centuries have consistently commented that Tao Qian's writings possess the quality of "genuineness," and the quasi-equivalence of poet and poetic content was highlighted early on by Zhong Rong (468–518) in his evaluation of poets from the Han into the Liang, *Grading of Poets* (*Shi pin*): "With each reading of his writings, one is reminded of his virtuous conduct as a person."[2] Zhong Rong also deemed Tao "the patriarch of poets of reclusion, past and present," and much of Tao's writing really does describe his version of life in reclusion. While some imagery may ultimately derive from literary stock, Tao Yuanming both vivifies it and personalizes it in a mode completely uncharacteristic of his day.

One should not generally look to a person's name to find the person's character reflected therein, but in this case there is the scent of correspondence. "Yuanming" indicates "deep and perspicacious," "Qian" indicates "hidden," and his posthumous appellation was "A Man of Tranquility and Integrity" (*Jingjie xiansheng*). Tao Yuanming's grandfather had been commander-in-chief of the Eastern Jin (317–420), and Tao Yuanming served in a few relatively minor posts in his thirties before leaving official service for good in December of 405, at age forty, for the rural life of a gentleman-scholar in retirement.

Since the *History of the Liu Song Dynasty* (*Song shu*) biography of him in the sixth century, a good many have argued that Tao Yuanming was a loyalist to the fallen Jin dynasty. On the face of it, this may seem to fit the facts: early on, Tao had served Liu Yu (363–422), the man who eventually deposed the Jin emperor to found his own new dynasty, the Song, but he declined Liu's later summons to take an office in the new dynasty; on account of this, Tao is often referred to as "Summoned Scholar Tao" (*Tao zhengjun*). Some have argued that it was then that he adopted the name Qian, as an indication of his refusal to serve in the official bureaucracy of a successor dynasty, choosing instead to live in reclusion in the Chinese sense. But in terms of Tao Yuanming's character, it may be most important to bear in mind that Tao had already left his final office fifteen years prior to the founding of the Liu-Song in 420, and he tells us why throughout his corpus, most pointedly in the preface to one of his best-remembered and most endearing poems, "Leaving for Home!" ("Guiqulai xi ci"), a poem so poignant in its imagery that it has been depicted as a narrative painting on scrolls since at least the thirteenth century and continues to be an artistic motif as well as a fixture in the zither (*qin*) repertoire.

This poem, written in the long, expository *fu* form, is a self-narrative about Tao Yuanming's return home after quitting his position as magistrate of Pengze, a regional center not far from his native home in rural Jiangxi. He has spent just over eighty days on the job and is distressed at having "made my heart my body's slave," as he tells in his poem. He writes in his preface to the poem that he had taken the minor post in part to support himself and his family and in part because the yield from the fields would produce a sufficient quantity of wine. Accounts of his resignation say that he quit after being told by a functionary that he needed to straighten up his appearance and pay respects to a visiting inspector: "How could I, for the sake of five pecks of rice, bow at the waist before some country bumpkin?"[3] He writes, "My inner disposition is what it is naturally, and not got from effort or discipline. Hunger and cold might be cutting, but to defy myself just makes me sick. I tried the official's life in the service of others, but it always has been as the slave to my mouth and stomach" (*TYMJJZ* 460–461).

In the poem, Tao writes endearingly about the joys of being home: his children; his books, his zither, and a cup of wine; his unhurried outings; his pleasures and duties to fields and garden; and most of all, the natural world and its seasonality. The latter brings on a meditation about his own seasonality and what is important for him in life: following his heart and, in accord with the immutable changes, to face his ultimate homecoming, death, with equanimity. Tao Yuanming's poem captures the essence of an earnest and estimable life in reclusion, and as the scholar A. R. Davis writes, "Here he seems above all concerned with the establishment of his hermit image, and for subsequent Chinese literature he succeeded completely."[4]

Tao Yuanming went into reclusion at this juncture because he felt he was compromising his personal ideals and inner nature. The literal meaning of "reclusion" (*yin*) is "hiding," both in terms of disengagement from the mainstream pursuits of the scholar-official and in terms of withholding one's talents from the state. Reclusion is often seen as the antipode of an appointment as a scholar-official in the bureaucracy, with political overtones of disengaging from the system. One's reason may indeed be oppositional: refusing to serve an undeserving superior or an illegitimate regime or, as some have imputed to Tao Qian, refusing to give allegiance to a second dynastic house or a conqueror. But the crux is more a sort of individualism in conducting one's life and in not compromising one's principled conduct. Rising above the affairs of the "world of dust," practitioners of reclusion sometimes are called "high-minded men" (*gao shi*).

By Tao Yuanming's time, a good number of literati chose to forego official service in favor of a private life, some out of philosophical or religious beliefs, others out of dedication to teaching and scholarship, and others simply in order to lead a quiet, satisfying "retired" existence, usually distant from the hustle and hassle of the urban centers, and often in the mountains. All three biographical accounts of Tao Yuanming in the dynastic histories appear in the sections devoted to reclusion, and a number of writings speak of Tao as one of his day's Three Hermits of Xunyang, Tao's native home. This being the case, it is of fundamental importance to note that reclusion in China does not necessarily indicate that one is keeping to a state of self-imposed solitude and asceticism, and so while the English word "hermit" is often used for Chinese men in reclusion, not all men in reclusion were hermits; indeed, the vast majority were not, and the reclusion of Tao Qian was not eremitism.

Even before returning home for good, Tao Qian had written about his urge for farming, as in the last lines of a poem composed in 401, "Written in the Seventh Month of the Year *Xinchou* in Tukou

While Traveling at Night Returning to Jiangling After Leave" ("Xinchou sui qiyue fujia huan Jiangling yexing Tukou"):

	Self-promotion is not my thing;	商歌非吾事
16	I only yearn to be a plow-mate,	依依在耦耕
	To discard my official's cap, return to my old abode,	投冠旋舊墟
18	And not be bound by love of rank,	不為好爵榮
	To nourish my true nature in a thatched hut,	養真衡茅下
20	And aspire to respect myself for virtuousness.	庶以善自名

[*TYMJJZ* 194]

Tao Yuanming left for home to cultivate his life and to cultivate his fields in the company of his family and his neighbors. His own poetic record of his pursuits and concerns is redolent with a sympathetic description that has been the subject of empathy and emulation by posterity. He wrote about many aspects of rural life, both as a direct participant and as a reflective scholar, and this resonated with many scholar-officials who might experience this sort of existence only in poetry.

Another of his great writings, a set of five poems on "Returning to Dwell in My Gardens and Fields" ("Gui yuan tian ju"), composed in 406, the summer after he left for home and life in reclusion, describes both his outer and his inner life. The first of these poems, translated in full here, tells about heart (☞ *HTRCP* C6.1; *WKB* P10):

	Out of tune with the crowd even while young,	少無適俗韻
2	By nature I love the hills and mountains,	性本愛丘山
	By mischance I fell into the dusty net,	誤落塵網中
4	And once gone, away for thirteen years.	一去十三年
	The confined bird pines for its native forest,	羈鳥戀舊林
6	The pond fish longs for its former deep waters.	池魚思故淵
	I've now cleared land at the southern edge of town, and	開荒南野際
8	With simplicity intact I return to garden and field.	守拙歸園田
	My domain is just a few acres square,	方宅十餘畝
10	My thatched hut but several room-measures big.	草屋八九間
	Elm and willow shade the back eaves,	榆柳蔭後檐
12	Peach and plum array before the hall.	桃李羅堂前
	Dim and vague the village of men far distant,	曖曖遠人村
14	Faint and hazy the smoke from their hamlet.	依依墟里煙
	Dogs bark amid the deep alleyways,	狗吠深巷中
16	Roosters crow atop the mulberry trees.	雞鳴桑樹巔
	My abode is without dust or disturbance,	戶庭無塵雜
18	My rooms are spare, but full with ample leisure.	虛室有餘閑
	Long fenced up inside a cage,	久在樊籠裏
20	I again can return to the way it should be.	復得返自然

[*TYMJJZ* 76]

Tao Yuanming writes of his personal fulfillment in farming the land, but he does not shy from describing the strenuousness of the work and the worries about the outcome. And in these poems too, he inevitably will ponder some of the bigger questions of life and one's values. He writes, "Is the farmer's life not bitter? / No way to avoid these hardships" (*TYMJJZ* 227). Yet he is not bitter about his hardships, for it is "the work itself" that provides fulfillment, as he writes in 403, in the second of two poems titled "Remembering the Ancients on My Farm in Early Spring in the Year *Guimao*" ("Guimao sui shichun huaigu tianshe"):

Although I've not yet measured the harvest yield,	雖未量歲功
In the work itself there is much to enjoy.	即事多所欣

[*TYMJJZ* 203]

And for him there is also the constancy of other fulfilling pursuits and personal gratifications. Several of these are ubiquitous in his poems. One example is from "In Reply to Aide Pang" ("Da Pang canjun"):

	Inside my rustic home,	衡門之下
2	There is a *qin*, there are books.	有琴有書
	Now I strum the *qin*, now I intone the writings,	載彈載詠
4	And in this I find my joy.	爰得我娛
	How could I not have other interests?	豈無他好
6	My pleasure is this, the secluded life.	樂是幽居
	In the morning I water my garden,	朝為灌園
8	In the evening I rest in my hut.	夕偃蓬廬

[*TYMJJZ* 26–27]

And in the first of thirteen poems titled "On Reading the *Classic of Mountains and Seas*" ("Du *Shanhai jing*"), he puts reading into the context of his life in reclusion:

	Early summer, plants in their growth,	孟夏草木長
2	Encircling my house, the trees are lush.	繞屋樹扶疏
	The birds are happy with their roost,	眾鳥欣有托
4	And I too love my cottage.	吾亦愛吾廬
	Plowing finished, and planting also done,	既耕亦已種
6	Time again for me to read my books.	時還讀我書

[*TYMJJZ* 393]

Perhaps most memorable of Tao Yuanming's pastimes is what he famously calls "the thing in the cup" (*TYMJJZ* 304) and "the thing for forgetting worry" (*TYMJJZ* 252). Indeed, one can hardly imagine a description of Tao Yuanming without the mention of wine. But there is rarely disproval in the portrayal of drink in Chinese literature, with the possible exception of certain intentionally trashy tales. On the contrary, tippling often is considered a welcome trait that brings out a depth of character. As Tao Yuanming himself tells it, "In wine there is a taste of profundity" (*TYMJJZ* 268).[5]

For Tao Yuanming, wine is both a worldly pleasure and an inspiration for reflection. In a poem titled "Drinking Alone in Incessant Rains" ("Lian yu du yin"), composed around 407, he writes:

	My elder friend offers wine, and	故老贈余酒
6	Says drinking will confer a freeness of being.	乃言飲得仙
	I try a serving and all cares are distant;	試酌百情遠
8	Another round, poof! the whole world is gone.	重觴忽忘天

[*TYMJJZ* 125]

In a series of twenty poems titled simply "Drinking Wine" ("Yin jiu"), Tao addresses some of life's questions for an introspective and deep-thinking individual, such as success and failure, right and wrong, mortality, individualism and reclusion. He also sings of conviviality with sympathetic friends and, of course, wine. His preface to the poems is itself rightfully memorable, for it lays out another component of the Tao Yuanming loved by posterity. It was probably written in 417, when he was fifty-three years old and had been in reclusion for more than fifteen years:

I live in retirement with fewer sources of pleasure, and now with the autumn nights already long, I just happen to have some prized wine, and there is not an evening I don't imbibe. In the company of my shadow I empty my cups alone, and of a sudden I am tipsy again. Once I get tipsy, I invariably compose a number of lines for my own amusement. The pages I have inked accordingly have become many, but the verses remained unedited and unarranged. After a time I asked a close friend to copy them out into something we can laugh at with pleasure.

[*TYMJJZ* 235]

Tao Yuanming was happy when tippling in company, and inspired when imbibing in solitude. Although the poems in the series are diverse, two are especially evocative. In poem 14 (poem 5 is addressed below), he writes of wine as a vehicle for communion with friends and also with the universe:

	Old friends appreciate my tastes,	故人賞我趣
2	And with wine jar in hand come to visit.	挈壺相與至
	Setting out mats, we sit beneath the pines, and	班荊坐松下
4	After several pourings we once again are tipsy.	數斟已複醉
	Oldsters and elders interject chatter and gossip,	父老雜亂言
6	And all order is lost in pouring out wine.	觴酌失行次
	No longer aware of any sense of self,	不覺知有我
8	How to put a value on material things?	安知物為貴
	Disengaged, afar, lost from any fixed place,	悠悠迷所留
10	In wine there is a taste of profundity.	酒中有深味

[*TYMJJZ* 268]

Besides the many references to wine in Tao Yuanming's poetry—nearly all positive—he also wrote "An Account of Wine" ("Shu jiu," *TYMJJZ* 286–287), which oddly enough has nothing at all of the tippler in it, and, according to James Hightower, "is notoriously one of the most difficult poems in Chinese."[6] Much scholarship has tried to explicate the poem as a veiled political commentary through the vehicle of a death potion—literally a killer wine and thus not the sort of thing in Mr. Five Willows's cup. This poem is exceptional and uncharacteristic, but another one is a tongue-in-cheek tour de force titled "Stopping Wine" ("Zhi jiu"; *TYMJJZ* 286–287). In this poem, the word "stop" occurs in every line, a remarkable poetic innovation, but the word carries a range of connotations, from "ending" to "abiding in," and even while he writes at one point "This morning I really did stop," in the end the irony is that he really has no intention whatsoever in stopping.

The enduring image of Tao Yuanming as a tippler has a fair amount of support directly in his poems and in the earliest writings about him. Both early sixth-century biographies mention that, when he served briefly in Pengze, he wished to plant his entitlement only with sorghum, for making liquor, and shared the fields with food rice only at the insistence of his wife and children. And they include the story of the scholar-official Yan Yanzhi, Tao's good friend and drinking companion, who, when leaving for another posting, left Tao 20,000 cash, which Tao promptly put toward a tab at the tavern (*TYMJJZ* 607–608, 611–612).

To view Tao Yuanming as carefree, however, is both simplistic and unfair. His poems also show that he is very much concerned with doing what is right and with how one lives in an impermanent world. This is especially true of his post–"Leaving for Home!" writings, and since most of his writings are from his later period, this means that most of his writings contain, to one extent or another, philosophical probing. And this is fundamental to the perception of "genuineness" in Tao's work: his writings capture the range and fullness of the real sentiments of someone one would like to get to know better, someone who has put into words and images many of the things on one's own mind, someone who offers an alternative to one's own dusty cage, at least in literary portrayal.

Toward the close of his life, Tao Qian composed another brilliant self-portrayal, in which he both affirmed his life and ways and clearly stated his philosophy. He did so in the equally innovative format of a funeral elegy to himself, "Sacrificial Offering to Myself" ("Zi ji wen"). This, along with "Leaving for Home!," is Tao Qian's own figurative narrative of Tao Yuanming. Probably writing two months before his death, he tells of Master Tao's departure from the traveler's lodge of life and his permanent return to his original home, the very earth into which his body is to be consigned. "Alas and woe!" he wails in standard plaint. But while in life he met with poverty (little food, thin winter clothing), he was happy hauling water and carrying firewood, living in a secluded home. He continues:

	As springs and autumns passed in alternation,	春秋代謝
14	There was always work in my central garden,	有務中園
	Sometimes weeding, sometimes hoeing,	載耘載耔
16	Now cultivating, now nurturing.	乃育乃繁
	I found joy in books and writings,	欣以素牘
18	And peace in my seven-string *qin*.	和以七弦
	. . .	. . . . . .
	Content with my heavenly-appointed lot,	樂天委分
24	So did I arrive at my "hundred years."	以至百年

As he relates, men all fear life without success and lament the passage of time, but he has gone his own, alternative way, unconcerned about praise or censure. Rather:

	Off aloof in my poor hut,	捽兀窮廬
36	I enjoyed my drink and wrote my poetry.	酣飲賦詩
	...	......
	Now in this ultimate transformation,	余今斯化
40	I am able to have no regret.	可以無恨
	In my long life, a hundred years,	壽涉百齡
42	I have only prized reclusion.	身慕肥遁
	That I meet my end old in age,	從老得終
44	What more could I desire?	奚所復戀

Since life is for the living, and death for the dead, he asks to go on without ado. Alive, he never cared for acclaim; why would he value songs of praise when gone? He ends:

	The life of a man is surely hard,	人生實難
62	What can one do about death?	死如之何
	Alas and woe!	嗚呼哀哉

[TYMJJZ 555–556]

Tao Qian writes about mortality and death in a number of poems, most of these also from his later days, and in most it is pretty clear that he accepts his lot. In a set of well-known poems in the tradition of imitations of an old threnody, titled "In Imitation of the Lyrics of the 'Song of the Coffin Bearers'" ("Ni wange ci") but innovatively written in his own voice, Tao Qian's persona (albeit the persona of a recently deceased Tao Qian) again rings forth, and thus we get a further bit of his story. Some have suggested that these songs, similar to his "Sacrificial Offering to Myself," may have been his envisioning of what ought to be sung in his own funeral cortege, but that is pure surmise, because imitations of these songs are generic; in any case, the persona fits. Here are a few choice lines from the first poem:

	When there is life, there must be death	有生必有死
2	An early end is not fate's haste	早終非命促
	...	......
	In a thousand autumns, ten thousand years,	千秋萬歲後
12	Who will know my fame or failure?	誰知榮與辱
	I only regret when in the world,	但恨在世時
14	In drink I never got my fill.	飲酒不得足

[TYMJJZ 420]

And a few more selected lines, drawn from the second:

	In the past I had no wine to drink,	在昔無酒飲
2	Now only now they fill my empty cup.	今但湛空觴
	...	......
	I want to speak, but my mouth lacks sound,	欲語口無音
8	I want to see, but my eyes lack sight.	欲視眼無光
	...	......
	One morning I went out the gate,	一朝出門去
14	With no return from this everlasting night.	歸來良未央

[*TYMJJZ* 423]

Tao Qian's most explicit philosophical poem is again one that has been a magnet for attention from the outset. It is an interior conversation between three versions of himself, titled "Body, Shadow, Spirit" ("Xing ying shen"), also commonly translated as "Substance, Shadow, and Spirit." In a preface we learn that the subject is the universal concern about life—about not losing it—and that the author does not find this concern reasonable. So, after presenting the "bitter words" between Body and Shadow, Spirit will resolve the matter with remarks about "naturalness" (literally *ziran*, "the way it all is on its own"). In the first section, "Body Presents to Shadow" ("Xing zeng ying"), Body has the view of the immediacy of the physical side of the man and says to Shadow that, since man cannot avoid the inevitable obliteration of death:

I wish for you to trust in my words:	願君取吾言
When wine is at hand, never say no.	得酒莫苟辭

[*TYMJJZ* 59]

In the next section, "Shadow Replies to Body" ("Ying da xing"), Shadow responds to Body as the immaterial but ever so tangible reflection of a person—how one is seen by others and what one projects through the illuminating backdrop of centuries of human society. *You and I are one*, it says, *and when you go I go*, so instead of drinking wine to dissolve care:

With goodness established, one's legacy is love;	立善有遺愛
How could one not put all effort into this?	胡為不自竭

[*TYMJJZ* 64]

In the final section, "Spirit Resolves" ("Shen shi"), Spirit resolves the issue as one of the triad, linked in life but also linked with heaven and earth. It relates that dying old or dying young both are equally death; whether one is wise or foolish, there will never be a second reckoning. Drinking might help one forget, but will it not just rush one's years by more quickly? Establishing a reputation is desirable, but who will sing one's praises? The resolution is:

	Thinking too deeply harms our life,	甚念傷吾生
20	Best to entrust to the natural cycle,	正宜委運去
	Carried on waves in the Universal Changes,	縱浪大化中

22	Not in happiness, but neither in fear.	不喜亦不懼
	When time for the end, then we must end,	應盡便須盡
24	With never again this unnecessary fuss.	無復獨多慮

[*TYMJJZ* 67]

One of Tao Qian's most widely appreciated so-called philosophical poems is the fifth in the "Drinking Wine" series. It embodies a quintessential aspect of both the inner architecture of Tao Yuanming and the outer currents of the thought of his time, and it must be one of the most exceptional and memorable poems ever written. The reader is likely to find it in any anthology of Chinese poetry (☞ *HTRCP* C6.2; *WKB* P11). The poem frames a deep insight under a placid surface, and while it is ostensibly written with the enhancement of wine, what is described in the poem is not the outcome of imbibing, although it could be that wine may act as a sort of poetic catalyst. It begins:

	I build my hut where people dwell, yet	結廬在人境
2	There is no clamor of carts and horses.	而無車馬喧
	One asks how can this be so?	問君何能爾
4	With the mind detached, the place becomes remote.	心遠地自偏

When Tao Qian writes "With the mind detached, the place becomes remote," he writes of the detachment of what, for some, would be the highest state of reclusion: the crux of the matter is found first of all in oneself and not in external things and thus is a matter of heart and mind and not of space and time. One need not be far in the mountains to have that remote mountain presence of disengagement.

The closing lines of the poem are also full of signification and implication. He writes of picking chrysanthemums and seeing the Southern Mountain in the distance, and of the loveliness of the mountain air at sunset and the return of birds flocked together. His remarkable conclusion is:

	In these things there is genuine meaning;	此中有真意
10	I would explain but I have forgotten the words.	欲辨已忘言

[*TYMJJZ* 247]

There is here an unmistakable allusion to a famous pronouncement in the *Zhuangzi*: "The point of words lies in their meaning; when the meaning is got, one can forget the words" (*TYMJJZ* 249).

One must suppose that Tao Qian's meaning was clear without telling, yet interpretations of the poem vary widely. Is he saying that the natural world is simply something lovely, on its own, and that he can appreciate it without distraction because he has "got the meaning"? Or is it that his "return" will be as natural as geese flying home, undertaken in the company of all who once had life, and that he is not distracted by the world of men? Or something else? I will leave it to the reader to ponder with a cup of wine.

The opening lines of "Drinking Wine, Number 5" tell us that it is the essence that counts and not material circumstances. Along these lines, Tao Qian's earliest biographical accounts include the following iconographic anecdote, with the bracketed addition from his mid-seventh-century biography in the *History of Jin* (*Jin shu*):

> Qian had no understanding of music, but he kept an unadorned *qin* that was without strings. Whenever he had wine and company, he would play it and therein project his mind. [. . . He would strum it and harmonize, saying, "I am attuned only to the expressive gist from within the *qin*; why should I be weary about the sounds of the strings?"][7]

Tao Qian's writings present a number of resolutions to abiding conflicts about how to understand the life of man and natural processes, and, with more immediacy and greater attention, how to live *his* life in *this* world. He states that he followed his nature and endeavored to lead a life that accorded with the naturalness of the world, yet he appears not to have fully achieved a blissfully resolved state of peace with himself or the world. Besides his wrangling with his ever-looming mortality, a number of his poems reveal an unsettled concern about his decision to withdraw from serving in office, some about doing good and leaving behind a good name, some about the material consequences of his homestead life in reclusion.

In many of his poems, Tao Yuanming looks to the past for models of resilience, partly because he is acting on his own in his own time. Yet in a number of poems he also laments that the good of the past was not present in his present. And in what must be the absolutely best-known piece of Chinese literature, he imagines a utopian past existing parallel to his own problematic contemporary times. This is the "Account of Peach Blossom Spring" ("Taohua yuan ji"), also translated as "Peach Blossom Source." The "Account" is more rightly the preface to a companion poem, "Peach Blossom Fountainhead" ("Taohua yuan shi"), but it is by far the much more famous and influential piece. It has been the subject of or been alluded to in countless writings and has become a traditional subject for artistic depiction; indeed, it would be difficult to mention "peach blossoms" without Tao Qian coming to mind.

The "Account" begins by relating how, in the late fourth century (Tao Qian's own era), a nameless fisherman goes far, far upstream and finds himself in groves of blossoming peach trees, which lead to a mountain and to the fountainhead source of the stream. It continues:

> The mountain had a small opening, through which there seemed to be light. Leaving his boat behind, he entered the opening, at first quite narrow and barely passable, then several tens of paces later suddenly opening to a broad expanse of level open land with houses in orderly arrangement. There were rich fields and lovely ponds, as well as mulberry, bamboo, and such; the field-paths crossed and led through, chickens and dogs were heard from one hamlet to another. Coming and going, planting and working, were men and women dressed just like those on the outside. Old folks and young children all were happily amusing themselves. When they saw the fisherman they were greatly surprised, and asked where he had come from. . . . They said that their ancestors had fled the troubled times of the Qin dynasty along with their wives, children, and townspeople, coming to this cutoff region and never again venturing beyond, thenceforth remaining separated from the world outside.
>
> [TYMJJZ 479]

The fisherman tells them of the vicissitudes of the world outside during the previous five hundred years, and they eagerly entertain him hospitably for several days. As he prepares to depart, he is told "There is no reason to speak of this to the people outside." He heads back downstream, carefully marking his trail, and of course he tells the governor. But, as the reader already knows, the ensuing search for the utopia is unsuccessful and the land remains lost.

One tries in vain to disassociate an analogy to the great Dao, the Way, which cannot be found by looking, but that would be an extreme overinterpretation of Tao Qian. Tao Qian probably adapted a current tale, but he personalized it and focused it on a reality that contrasted with that of his time. He does not expect to find anyone of the same mind in this world, and perhaps when seen in the context of his own reclusion, his personal idealism and willful individualism are all the more clear.

Tao Qian's writings are replete with ethical and philosophical dimensions, and reading Tao Qian, many have asked, *Was he a Daoist? Was he a Confucian? Was he . . . ?* A facile reply would be simplistic and unfair, for the views and values expressed in his writings ring with the contextual complexity of his moment and resonate with the wide-ranging scope of medieval Chinese cultural capital. In his writings, Tao Qian ponders mortality and life, history and mankind, and his poetry is full of moral exemplars. He may be selective, and in this way laying a foundation of precedent and self-justification, but the men of the past that inspire his present are invariably far from obscure and would have been an integral component of the scholar-official's basic curriculum. I would suggest that we keep in mind that Tao Qian, like many others, deeply embodies in his writings and conduct a spectrum of the literary and cultural repertoire of the scholar-official, manifesting different aspects when moved or when fitting. Some writings or acts may not always seem to be congruent with others, and indeed may be wholly contradictory, but in this diversity can be seen the fullness of the man, a complex individual in a complex life in a complex cultural moment.

Over the years, Tao Qian often has been viewed as a representative exponent of the Confucian tradition, steeped in the classics and humanely, responsibly responsive to situations in his human world. This is seen in his reclusion, which is a moral response to an ethical problem; in his acceptance of poverty, which is the noble alternative (he even has a series of seven poems "In Praise of Impoverished Gentlemen" ["Yong pinshi"; *TYMJJZ* 364–379]); in his elevation of good men of the past, as allusions and as poetic subjects; and in the cultivated pursuits of the cultivated individual, such as reading the great books of old or playing the *qin* (figure 8.1). Yan Yanzhi's "Elegy for the Summoned Scholar Known Posthumously as the Man of Tranquility and Integrity" ("Jingjie zhengshi lei") also points out his filial support of his elderly mother and his attentiveness to the needs of his young sons (*TYMJJZ* 605).

By at least the early eighth century, a tradition arose that represented the deep and friendly exchange among the three principal currents of thought and religious practice, depicting Tao Qian as the quintessential Confucian, in the company of the eminent Buddhist monk Huiyuan (334–416) and the scholarly Daoist practitioner Lu Xiujing (406–477). Though the story is fabricated and historically impossible, the point here is that Tao Qian, the summoned scholar who declined the life of the scholar-official, clearly was the Confucian in the group and thus is a clear model for Confucian conduct and values. One might observe without reservation that scholar-officials could easily embrace Tao Qian's legacy as something they too might emulate, when Tao Qian is viewed as a Confucian exemplar. But it may be more important to see that, in this representational mode, Tao Qian at the very least provided an example of an appropriate and outstanding alternative for the scholar-official: engaging in literary composition and a lifestyle that puts value on pursuits outside of officialdom, focusing instead on the good and respectable pleasures of "the work itself."

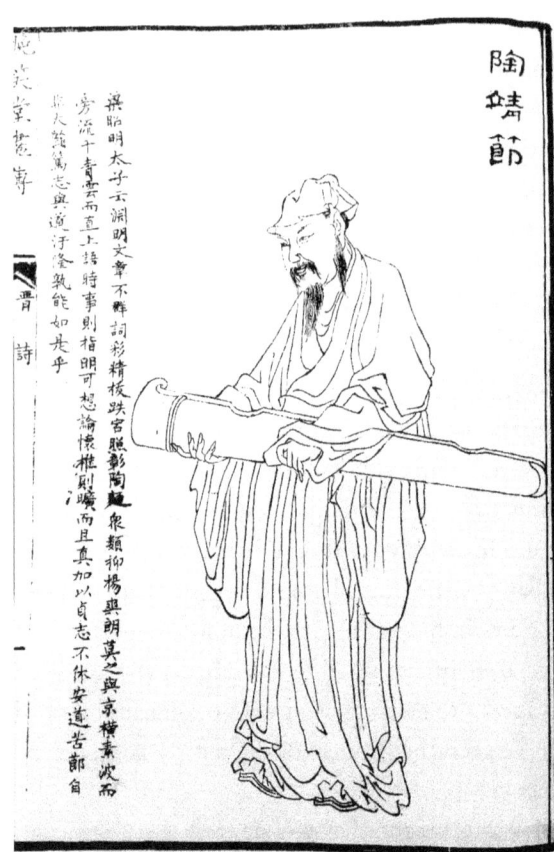

FIGURE 8.1 Tao Jingjie (aka Tao Qian or Tao Yuanming), by Shangguan Zhou 上官周 (1665–1752?) in *Portraits from the Hall of Late Blossoming* 晚笑堂畫傳 (Wanxiao tang hua zhuan). Qing dynasty woodblock print edition (1743), reprinted by the *Shanghai Journal* Office 申報館 (*Shenbao* guan) as *Zhu Zhuang's Portraits from the Hall of Late Blossoming* 晚笑堂竹莊畫傳 (Wanxiao tang zhuzhuang hua zhuan) (1921).

In contrast, many discussions—probably the great majority—have presented Tao Qian as Daoist, and much of his writing and his life as it has been represented certainly could demonstrate some general Daoist characteristics, even without consensus on what is meant by "Daoist." After all, among other things, there are more than a few likenesses to the *Zhuangzi* in his writing, and he portrayed himself as living a private life in reclusion in a rural setting, attending to the seasonal work of the poor farmer, communing with his rustic neighbors, playing his *qin*, reading and composing, spontaneous in action, unworried about material conditions, strongly individualistic, and, of course, drinking to drunkenness, musing on the great Dao, accepting his lot, and facing death with equanimity. This, too, is Tao Yuanming, and some of his most iconographic portrayals and most repeated lines issue from this context. The Daoist religion has recorded Tao Qian biographical accounts in several specifically Daoist hagiographical compilations. And even his "Mr. Five Willows," entirely fictive and not specifically Daoist at all, so fit a sort of idealized composite "Daoist" persona that, by the late Tang period, Mr. Five Willows was canonized as a god in the broad pantheon of the Daoist religion, with sway over one of the minor Daoist terrestrial heavens—which just happened to be Tao Qian's home.

Tao Qian's style has often been characterized as overtly unembellished in diction, straightforward in exposition, and quite free of the ornate encumbrances of many of the writings of his contemporaries. This may contribute to helping readers feel closer to the writer and not distanced through allusive and ornate "constructed" lines. Similarly, his candid exposition of his lifeways over the years encouraged readers to see a genuineness in his writings that they could relate to. Did Tao Qian himself have this in mind? In the "Elegy" by his friend Yan Yanzhi, Yan quotes him as saying:

| If one's person and talents are not real, | 身才非實 |
| One's glory and fame will come to an end. | 榮聲有歇 |

[TYMJJZ 606]

Tao Qian's life and writings reveal an individual who tried to be true to himself and thus genuine toward his contemporaries and to posterity. Yet they also show a man a bit out of step with his time. There is even a long composition in the *fu* form, precisely on this subject, that is attributed to him: "Moved by the Scholar Not Meeting His Time" ("Gan shi bu yu fu"; *TYMJJZ* 431–433). Still, he had a few contemporary admirers, as mentioned in his biographies and in his writings, and in his preface to the first collection of Tao's collected works ("*Tao Yuanming wenji* xu"), Xiao Tong writes about his sincere admiration for the man: "I love to savor his writing, and cannot put it off my hands. And moreover, when I reflect upon his virtuous nature, I bemoan not being born in his time" (*TYMJJZ* 614).

Nevertheless, widespread recognition of the greatness of Tao Qian did not come until centuries after his death, when he met with a sympathetic audience who saw in the man, as reflected in his writing, a paradigmatic, culturally appropriate model. This may stem in part from the recension process of his writings. Already in the sixth century, it had been observed that editions of his collected works (excepting that of Xiao Tong) were inconsistent and disorganized, and it was feared that this would result in the loss of his poems (*TYMJJZ* 614). By the time of Su Shi, some five hundred years later, Tao Qian's writings were a focus of discussion and editorial decision, through which variant readings of his poems were chosen to best conform with a vision of the author as icon.

Tao Qian was remarkable, certainly, but his enduring cultural role also owes a bit to the attentions of his later promoters. Along the way, the real Tao Qian may have suffered some "displacement," but his legacy remains deep and vibrant. The genuineness that was sensed in his life and words has been closely experienced personally, and on occasion emulated publicly, as a literary and culturally appropriate exemplar. Tao Yuanming led his life in reclusion, disengaged so to speak, but he has been consistently seen as a model of positive engagement, especially with himself vis-à-vis the world, and this is quite unlike the many moral models of the past, who are remembered for lamenting their lack of recognition. Indeed, Tao Yuanming is always "here" (it begins and ends with his unvarying integrity and personal sense of home) and "now" (he does what he does, fully engaged in his moment in the flow of life).

Tao Yuanming was deemed "the patriarch of poets of reclusion, past and present," and a great many of Tao's poems address the joys of his life in reclusion. He writes of home and family, of farming his fields and gardens, of convivial get-togethers with friends and neighbors, of talk of chrysanthemum and mulberry, of reading books and writing poetry, of drinking wine and playing the *qin*, and of other facets of the quiet, private life distant from the hubbub of the metropolis and the tasks of the scholar-official (☞ *HTRCP* chap. 6). Tao Yuanming's poetic lines and evocative images all have contributed to the ready repertoire of later scholars, echoing in the background of the literary topos about life in reclusion.

Jiang Yan (444–505) may have been the first to directly imitate in content and phraseology what must already have been seen as the distinct "Tao Qian" style, in this case mostly about the work of farming.[8] And since the expression of sentiment seems so genuine, it has been easy, when one sees fit to identify with Tao Yuanming, to adopt a Tao Yuanming persona, whether for solace or for joy or merely for a poetic moment, and a number of famous poets have matched Tao Yuanming's poems over the centuries as an indication of their solidarity with the man.

The best, fullest, and most appreciated example is without doubt Su Shi, who wrote more than a hundred poems matching the rhymes in Tao's poems. About these compositions, Su Shi wrote to his younger brother Su Che (1039–1112), who also matched many of Tao Yuanming's poems, "How could it be that I merely admired his poems? I truly have been affected by the way he conducted himself as a person."[9]

Donald Holzman has written that Tao Yuanming and the lifestyle he portrays in his writings mark a change in Chinese cultural attitudes, providing the literati with a new and enduring legitimate model for living the private life and engaging in "the work itself."[10] It is this model that has so deeply imbued the sensibilities and panorama of Chinese culture that it sometimes seems like it has always been there. As Yan Yanzhi wrote in his "Elegy" for his friend Tao Yuanming: "Alas for the pure and true man!" (*TYMJJZ* 605).

ALAN BERKOWITZ

NOTES

1. In this essay, the names Tao Qian and Tao Yuanming both are used, as has been the case in writings from the fifth century on. Unless specifically noted, all translations are mine, after consulting and sometimes adapting the erudite and felicitous renderings of James Hightower, A. R. Davis, and others. I am grateful for their guidance in interpretive issues and hope that my iteration of their words demonstrates both my respect and their own flawless richness.
2. Beijing daxue and Beijing shifan daxue Zhongwen xi, eds., *Gudian wenxue yanjiu ziliao huibian: Tao Yuanming juan* (Shanghai: Zhonghua shuju, 1965), 9.
3. Beijing daxue, *Gudian wenxue yanjiu*, 3, 7, 9, 12.
4. A. R. Davis, trans., *Tao Yüan-ming (A.D. 365–427): His Works and Their Meaning* (Cambridge: Cambridge University Press, 1983), 194.
5. One might note here that, because the usual alcoholic beverage of the time was made from fermented grain rather than fruit, some might prefer the word "beer." But that word may unnecessarily distort the reading context, thus the more conventional word "wine" is customarily used to render the broadly contoured Chinese word for "alcoholic beverage."
6. James Robert Hightower, trans., *The Poetry of Tao Qian* (Oxford: Clarendon Press, 1970), 159.
7. Beijing daxue, *Gudian wenxue yanjiu*, 4, 7.
8. Beijing daxue, *Gudian wenxue yanjiu*, 6.
9. Beijing daxue, *Gudian wenxue yanjiu*, 35.
10. Quoted in Alan Berkowitz, *Patterns of Disengagement: The Practice and Portrayal of Reclusion in Early Medieval China* (Stanford, CA: Stanford University Press, 2000), 222.

PRIMARY SOURCE

TYMJJZ   Yuan Xingpei 袁行霈, ed. *Tao Yuanming ji jianzhu* 陶淵明集箋注 (The Collected Works of Tao Yuanming, with Notes and Commentary). Beijing: Zhonghua shuju, 2003.

SUGGESTED READINGS

ENGLISH

Ashmore, Robert. *The Transport of Reading: Text and Understanding in the World of Tao Qian (365–427)*. Cambridge, MA: Harvard University Asian Center, 2010.

Berkowitz, Alan. *Patterns of Disengagement: The Practice and Portrayal of Reclusion in Early Medieval China*. Stanford, CA: Stanford University Press, 2000.

Davis, A. R., trans. *T'ao Yüan-ming (A.D. 365–427): His Works and Their Meaning*. 2 vols. Cambridge: Cambridge University Press, 1983.

Hightower, James Robert, trans. *The Poetry of Tao Qian*. Oxford: Clarendon Press, 1970.

Swartz, Wendy. *Reading Tao Yuanming: Shifting Paradigms of Historical Reception (427–1900)*. Cambridge, MA: Harvard University Asian Center, 2008.

Tian, Xiaofei. *Tao Yuanming & Manuscript Culture: The Record of a Dusty Table*. Seattle: University of Washington Press, 2005.

CHINESE

Beijing daxue, and Beijing shifan daxue Zhongwen xi 北京大學北京師範大學中文系, eds. *Tao Yuanming juan* 陶淵明卷 (Section on Tao Yuanming), in *Gudian wenxue yanjiu ziliao huibian* 古典文學研究資料彙編 (Collected Research Materials on Classical Literature). 2 vols. Shanghai: Zhonghua shuju, 1965.

Cai Yu 蔡瑜. *Tao Yuanming de renjing shixue* 陶淵明的人境詩學 (Poetic Studies on the Human Realm of Tao Yuanming). Taipei: Lianjing, 2012.

Gong Bin 龔斌, ed. *Tao Yuanming ji jiaojian* 陶淵明集校箋 (The Collected Works of Tao Yuanming with Collation Notes). Shanghai: Shanghai guji chubanshe, 1996.

Hu Bugui 胡不歸. *Du Tao Yuanming ji zhaji* 讀陶淵明集札記 (Notes on Reading the *Collected Works of Tao Yuanming*). Shanghai: Huadong Shifan daxue, 2007.

Lu Qinli 逯欽立, ed. *Tao Yuanming ji* 陶淵明集 (The Collected Works of Tao Yuanming). Beijing: Xinhua shudian, 1982.

Wang Guoying 王國瓔. *Gujin yinyi shiren zhi zong: Tao Yuanming lunxi* 古今隱逸詩人之宗: 陶淵明論析 (The Patriarch of Poets of Reclusion Past and Present: Discussion and Interpretation of Tao Yuanming). Taipei: Yunchen, 1999.

Wang Shumin 王叔岷, ed. *Tao Yuanming shi jianzheng gao* 陶淵明詩箋證稿 (The Poetry of Tao Yuanming with Draft Collation Notes). Taipei: Yiwen, 1999.

Wang Yao 王瑤, ed. *Tao Yuanming ji* 陶淵明集 (The Collected Works of Tao Yuanming). Beijing: Renmin wenxue chubanshe, 1983.

Yang Yong 楊勇, ed. *Tao Yuanming ji jiaojian* 陶淵明集校箋 (The Collected Works of Tao Yuanming with Collation Notes). Taipei: Zhengwen shuju, 1976.

Xu Yimin 許逸民, ed. *Tao Yuanming nianpu* 陶淵明年譜 (Chronological Biographies of Tao Yuanming). Beijing: Zhonghua shuju, 1986.

9

THE STRUGGLING BUDDHIST MIND

Shen Yue

Famed as "the supreme master of literature" (*cizong*), Shen Yue (441–513) was a mirror of Southern Dynasties (420–589) elite culture. Serving the central court through three dynasties (Song, Qi, and Liang) and living to seventy-two years of age at a time when his contemporary courtiers typically died before turning forty, he was an embodiment of all the major shifts of his time, whether sociopolitical, intellectual, religious, or literary. As one might imagine, such a life was also filled with conflicts. Here we will explore one dimension of his complex life: his struggling Buddhist mind. Through one of his most famous works—a *fu* totaling 452 lines[1]—we will hear the story not just of an individual but also of an era when Buddhism first took hold in elite culture, ultimately influencing poetry composition.

An episode that took place during Shen Yue's later years serves as a prelude to the larger story. He had reached the peak of his official career and was spending most of his time at his garden estate. It was during this period that he composed his magnum opus as a poet, entitled "*Fu* on Living in the Suburbs" ("Jiaoju fu"). Shen Yue apparently expended a good amount of time and energy on the piece, and before he was completely done, he showed it to Wang Yun (481–549), a younger poet whom he greatly admired and had taken under his wing. The episode is recorded in the official history of the Liang dynasty:

Shen Yue had composed a "*Fu* on Living in the Suburbs," for which he had labored his thoughts for a lengthy period of time. When he still had not yet finalized it, he invited Wang Yun and showed him the draft. When Wang Yun reached the line "*ciye lianjuan*" ("the joined arc of the Female Rainbow") in his recitation, Shen Yue, clapping his hands, said excitedly: "I'm always afraid that people will pronounce *ye* as *ni*!" Next when it came to "*zhuishi duixing*" ("The fallen rocks are piled up to the stars"), as well as to "*bing xuan kan er dai chi*" ("Ice hangs in the dips and encircles the isles"), Wang Yun, without fail, beat rhythmically and gave high praises. Shen Yue said: "'One who truly knows sounds' is rare and true appreciation has all but vanished. The reason that I invited you was for none other than these few lines."

[LS 33.485]

The mutual admiration of the pair was evident. But why did it have to hinge on "these few lines," particularly given the lengthiness of the piece? A fuller understanding of what transpired between the two poets in this episode requires a closer reading of the *fu*.

REFLECTION IN THE SUBURBS

Shen Yue's garden estate was named the Eastern Field (Dongtian), due perhaps to its location just northeast of the capital city. From 507, when he was sixty-seven years old, until the end of his life, it was his refuge, allowing him leisure and the time to think and write. His "*Fu* on Living in the Suburbs" was closely tied to the garden estate; not only was it composed there but also it was composed *for* it. Part autobiography, part historical evaluation, it is for the most part contemplative, revealing the thoughts and emotions that had led the poet to building the Eastern Field and residing there. The past is at the center of the piece. There is, in the earlier part, a recollection of his family history:

In the past, at the end of the Western Han,	昔西漢之標季
22　The relocation of our family began.	余播遷之云始
Abandoning "the benefits from appointing [aides]"[2] in Haihun,	違利建於海昏
24　They started "planting mulberries"[3] along the tributaries of Jiang.	創惟桑於江汜
Like the Yellow River and Ji River, crisscrossing for generations,	同河濟之重世
26　They surpassed ten decades of Bans.	踰班生之十紀
Some, forfeiting their official salary, returned to farming;	或辭祿而反耕
28　Others, dusting off their official caps, came to take office.	或彈冠而來仕

[LS 13.236]

Haihun was in modern Jiangxi, southwest of Shanghai, and "the tributaries of Jiang" ("Jiang si") refers broadly to the region southeast of the Jiang (also called the Yangzi River). Here, recounting the experience of his ancestors during the Western Han dynasty (206 BCE–8 CE)—that is, almost five hundred years and fifteen generations back in time—Shen Yue traces their migration and vocations. In his flashback, the Shens were a southern family with a long tradition of farming, and later of officialdom as well, whose resilience was like the perennial flow of the Yellow River and the Ji River and far surpassed the Bans, one of the most celebrated historian families of the Han. (Shen Yue was himself a historian, having compiled the *Song shu*, the official history of the Liu Song dynasty.) In the next twenty lines, the poet leaps through the rest of the family history, leading up to himself, outlining the ups and downs but skipping past his father's execution in connection to the murder of a Liu Song emperor. His elegant lines are filled with a sense of pride as well as a sense of duty toward his family legacy, but most of all, they reveal the deep reflection of a man who was beginning to see the end.

Just more than halfway through the *fu*, the poet's reminiscences expand to larger histories. Here, letting his eyes roam outward from his house on the garden estate, he recalls various historical people and events. Looking south, he recognizes the "Square Mountain," where the first emperor of Qin (r. 246–210 BCE) claimed his sovereignty while making his way toward the ocean:

Merely shifting my feelings and letting my eyes roam,	聊遷情而徙睇
258　I recognize Square Mountain by the Homecoming Ford.	識方阜於歸津
There, circling the long shore of Cassia Isle,	帶脩汀於桂渚

260	The mighty Qin raised its first spade.	肇舉鍤於強秦
	Their route wound across Wu and reached toward Yue,	路縈吳而款越
262	Until it extended to the ocean, trespassing Min.	塗被海而通閩

[LS 13.239]

He also remembers the parties hosted by Cao Cao (155–220), the military strongman of the late Han period:

	In my make-believe, I mingled with the worthies of a bygone age,	謬參賢於昔代
270	And roamed by foot to this spot several times.	亟徒遊於茲所
	Attended by colorful banners, they coached side by side;	侍綵旄而齊轡
272	In the company of dragon boats, they spread out along the shore.	陪龍舟而遵渚
	Some, sitting on mat by ranks, were composing poetry;	或列席而賦詩
274	Others, passing the wine cup around, conversed in leisure.	或班觴而宴語
	The "gauzy curtain" faded away in one morning;	繐帷一朝冥漠
276	The Western Mausoleum—suddenly lush with undergrowth!	西陵忽其蔥楚

[LS 13.240]

The "Western Mausoleum" refers to the tomb of Cao Cao. Legend has it that Cao Cao's dying wish was to have his bed placed on the Bronze Sparrow Tower and covered by gauzy curtain, before which food was to be served daily and female performers were to dance on the fifteenth day of each month.

Shen Yue's historical reminiscing is ultimately concerned with death, loss, and destruction. As he continues to survey the view surrounding his estate, his reckoning of the inevitability of one's demise is brought closer to home. Gazing toward the Hall of Autumn Winds, where he and his fellow poets had celebrated the Double Ninth Festival twenty years before, he lets out these lines:

	All these, like frost or mist, have ceased to exist;	莫不共霜霧而歇滅
286	Along with wind and clouds, they have dispersed away.	與風雲而消散

[LS 13.240]

But it is the sight of what remains of the garden estate of the late Crown Prince Wenhui (458–493), whom the poet had served between 479 and 486, that most startles his heart:

	Catching sight of the eastern mountain, I let my gaze linger;	睇東巘以流目
300	Here my heart grieves and feels unsettled.	心悽愴而不怡
	It is the old garden of the former heir;	蓋昔儲之舊苑
302	Indeed, the ruins of the Panoramic Vista.	實博望之餘基
	Amongst tall woodlands were added cassia trees;	脩林則表以桂樹
304	Rows of grasses were topped by fragrant orchids.	列草則冠以芳芝
	Windblown balconies with layered flying eaves;	風臺累翼
306	Moonlit pavilions with tiered beams.	月榭重栭
	A thousand pillars rose up magnificently,	千櫨捷嶪

308	A hundred columns supporting them.	百栱相持
	Black carriage shafts drove through the woods;	皁轅林駕
310	Magnolia oars played on the rivers.	蘭枻水嬉
	After three years it was an affair of the past;	踰三齡而事往
312	Suddenly, two dozen years have passed, leading to today.	忽二紀以歷茲
	That all is destroyed, completely wiped out,	咸夷漫以蕩滌
314	It is no difference whether in the past or at present.	非古今之異時

[LS 13.240]

Crown Prince Wenhui is known for his obsession with ornate objects and elaborate construction, which Shen Yue clearly highlights in this depiction. According to one story, after the death of the crown prince, his father Emperor Wu (r. 483–493), in an outburst of anger at his extravagance, ordered all his "playthings" destroyed; another version of the story has it that the emperor eventually sold off the prince's garden estate. It should be noted that the prince's premature death was caused by poor health and was completely unrelated to his extravagance. But in Shen Yue's mind, the prince's posthumous loss of his garden estate is the same as all destructions in history.

The poet's reflections, whether on personal history or collective history, all lead to one question: How does one protect oneself from destruction? Throughout the entire *fu*, Shen Yue examines himself over and over again, and his answer always rests upon a reaffirmation of his Buddhist faith, such as in these lines:

	I respectfully behold:	敬惟
	The road to Emptiness is long and remote;	空路遼遠
376	The divine footprints far removed.	神蹤遐闊
	Thoughts in the mind amount to startling gusts,	念甚驚飆
378	While life is like an accumulation of bubbles.	生猶聚沫
	I turn homeward to the Wondrous Carriage in the Single Vehicle,	歸妙軫於一乘
380	And open the Mysterious Gate[4] through Triple Illumination.	啟玄扉於三達
	I wish to calm my mind, banishing all attachments,	欲息心以遣累
382	And I must shun human company, and then be free.	必違人而後豁

[LS 13.241]

The doctrine of "emptiness" (Sanskrit, *śūnyatā*; Chinese, *kong*) holds that all phenomena in the world, being reliant upon numerous external factors to exist, are unreal. The true grasp of this doctrine is tantamount to enlightenment itself. And the wisdom for grasping this ultimate truth includes "Triple Illumination," that is, "remembrance of past existence, divine insight into future existence, and knowledge that all pollution has ended in this present existence."[5] A mind that embodies Triple Illumination is free from burdens and unperturbed by worldly concerns. In the end, what the poet is proposing for himself is a path of detachment, the idea of which is behind his retreat to the Eastern Field.

In Shen Yue's own words, this is how he has come to reside in the suburbs:

	I am a person of narrow intent,	伊吾人之褊志
12	And have no great ambition for designing the world.	無經世之大方
	I long to reside in the forest, furling my wings;	思依林而羽戢
14	And I wish to flow with the water, hiding my scales.	願託水而鱗藏
	Indeed, I have no yearning for beautiful or magnificent buildings;	固無情於輪奐
16	Nor do I desire broad avenues or wide streets.	非有欲於康莊
	I combed through the vast emptiness of the eastern suburb,	披東郊之寥廓
18	And entered its boundless desertion covered in tangled underbrush.	入蓬藋之荒茫

[LS 13.236]

As it turns out, the "eastern suburb" is not a location in name only. As a symbol for his retirement from officialdom, it signifies not only his physical but also his mental departure from the capital city. It is in that sense that he seeks to "shun human company." Notice that Shen Yue's mental path of detachment is as Buddhist as it is Daoist, as he also intones these lines:

	Do not hanker after power in cities and towns;	不慕權於城市
130	Why solicit fame in the slaughterhouse and the marketplace?	豈邀名於屠肆
	I chant the "intangible-inaudible" as I seek out a house,	詠希微以考室
132	Feeling fortunate just to be sheltered from wind and frost.	幸風霜之可庇

[LS 13.238]

Here, he obviously has this expression from the *Laozi* in mind: "The great sound is inaudible, the great image is formless." As it was characteristic of his time and in contrast to the eremitic ideals of earlier times (see chapters 7 and 8), the poet's Buddhist faith existed side by side with his Daoist beliefs, seemingly without contradiction. An annotation to the *Laozi* says, "What is not heard when listened to is called 'inaudible'; what is not grasped when one reaches for it is called 'intangible.'"[6] Using these ideas and expressions to represent his private residence, Shen Yue gives light to the idea of a house "stripped down" to its bare function: protection from "wind and frost." However, the form of his new garden, as we shall see, is much more complex than that. In fact, his retreat to the suburbs is not a simple one either. In another part of the *fu*, again explaining his decision to move to the suburbs, he nonetheless contradicts his earlier statement:

	I rejected the sunbirds and picked the city;	排陽鳥而命邑
112	By its river and mountain built the foundations.	方河山而啟基
	I still guide the Crown Prince in Three Goodness;[7]	翼儲光於三善
114	And head the royal duties among the hundred officials.	長王職於百司

[LS 13.238]

His retirement is not a complete withdrawal after all. Here, he "rejects the sunbirds," the symbol of recluses, and even suggests that his choice for the suburb is based on its closeness to the capital city, Jiankang. This contradiction is only one among several more that are indicative of the poet's inner struggles.

GARDEN BEAUTY

We can only imagine the time, resources, and human labor that went into the construction of Shen Yue's Eastern Field garden estate, which was estimated at 430 acres. In his *fu*, he describes his effort to tame the wilderness: overgrowth is cut back, trees are planted, leaks and holes are patched, pathways are laid out, fences are built, windows are installed, and multistoried chambers are constructed. And he catalogs the plants and creatures that live there: an array of aquatic plants and land grasses, a variety of woodland birds and waterbirds, fish of various colors and sizes, and different specimens of southern bamboo. His intent, the poet claims, is not the same as that of those showy garden owners in history:

	Li Heng with his orange grove of a thousand trees,[8]	李衡則橘林千樹
172	And Shi Chong with his mixed fruits in ten thousand—	石崇則雜果萬株
	Both were the excessive display of unrestrained feelings—	並豪情之所侈
174	They are not that which will gratify my frugal aims.	非儉志之所娛

[LS 13.238]

His "frugal aims" result in a beauty that—even after being translated into poetic lines—is most alluring. Below are the most moving passages in his *fu*, where he presents his garden, changing ever so beautifully through the four seasons:

	The evening trees open their flowers;	晚樹開花
416	The early blossoms shed their spikes.	初英落蕊
	At times they are in different groves, separated into vermilion and green;	或異林而分丹青
418	Suddenly, as the wind comes, they are mixed together in red and violet.	乍因風而雜紅紫
	The purple lotus sprouts at night;	紫蓮夜發
420	The red water lily unfurls at dawn.	紅荷曉舒
	While a light breeze gently blows,	輕風微動
422	Their fragrance enfolds me.	芬芳襲余
	The wind rustles and patters through the garden trees;	風騷屑於園樹
424	The moon casts flickering shadows of the pool bamboos.	月籠連於池竹
	Long boughs spread out from the cassia by the eaves,	蔓長柯於簷桂
426	Yellow flowers come forth from the chrysanthemums in the courtyard.	發黃華於庭菊
	Ice hangs in the dips and encircles the isles;	冰懸塪而帶坻
428	Snow hovers over the pine trees and covers the wilds.	雪縈松而被野
	Ducks fly in flocks and do not disperse;	鴨屯飛而不散
430	Wild geese, soaring high, are ready to descend.	雁高翔而欲下

[LS 13.241–242]

From the Buddhist perspective, these seasonal things—no matter how beautiful they are in our eyes—are not real. But the garden owner, having built them all, cannot view them as unreal (figure 9.1). For him, "emptying out" the garden is a very personal and difficult struggle, in spite of the promise of the real "garden" in the Western Paradise of Amitābha Buddha, where blossoms shed

FIGURE 9.1 *Whiling Away the Summer* by Wu Li (1632–1718). Hand scroll, ink on paper. The garden and landscape culture reflected in Shen Yue's "*Fu* on Living in the Suburbs" finds resonance in Wu Li's painting, in which "birds, trees, bamboo, mist, and even rocks dance joyously around the hermit-scholar, who sits quietly reading in his idyllic domain."

by the bejeweled trees are said to accumulate four inches deep on the ground and, every few hours, are blown away by a heavenly wind. Near the close of his *fu*, Shen Yue faces his attachment to worldly beauty with complete honesty:

	All these are seasonal things to be cherished;	并時物之可懷
432	Though coming from outside, they are not unreal.	雖外來而非假
	Indeed, my feeling and nature are stored within them;	實情性之所留滯
434	I am the one who wills them, unable to let them go.	亦志之而不能捨也

[*LS* 13.242]

THE BUDDHIST MIND

Shen Yue concludes his *fu* with a confession, the last two lines of which completely reveal his feeling of guilt:

	Heaving a long sigh—what else is there to say?	長太息其何言
452	Still, I'm ashamed that my mind has not been singular.	羌愧心之非一

[*LS* 13.242]

Here, he certainly has his Buddhist faith, among other things, in mind. Even though he reproached himself for lacking "single-mindedness" in his Buddhist practice, Shen Yue produced one of the best analyses of *nian* ("thought-instant"), a core concept in the Buddhist theory of the mind. *Nian*, which often has the dual meaning of "concentrated thought" (Sanskrit *smṛti*) and "moment" (Sanskrit *kṣaṇa*) in Chinese usage, is the minute working of the mind. Understanding *nian* and being able to control it within one's own mind are signs of progress toward enlightenment. In an essay arguing for the Buddhist thesis "the spirit does not become extinct" (*shen bumie*), Shen Yue explains the confused state of the mind at the level of *nian*:

> If within a single thought-instant there are yet other thoughts [*yi nian er jian*], then there is no recourse for it to become complete. Since there is no means by which it can become complete together with others, chaos and entanglement invade the mind in alternation. One single thought-instant has not yet become complete [*yi nian wei cheng*] and other minor thoughts have already arisen along with one another. The minor thoughts that have arisen along with one another, like those before them, cannot become complete together with others.
>
> ["SHEN BUMIE YI," TAISHŌ 52:253C]

A mind saturated with competing *nian* was far from the "single mind" that he sought on his Buddhist path. Even though he did not spell it out, Shen Yue's analysis called forth the proposal of the Chengshi School of Buddhist scholasticism of his day: taking a gradual approach to enlightenment, the school emphasized the need to analyze the components of all perceptions, thereby "destructing" them. In other words, one needed to see what made up what was seen before she could realize that it was not real. Consequently, the program outlined by the Chengshi School trained the mind to analyze and differentiate all things in systematic and "minute" ways.

Although the influence of the Chengshi School would wane within a century, Shen Yue's analysis marked an important milestone not only in the Chinese perception of the mind but also in perception itself. Having realized the minute working of the mind—and the need to control it, thought-instance by thought-instance—how would one now see and hear the world? This brings us back to the story told at the start of this chapter.

REFINEMENT

According to Shen Yue, the difference between the "saint" who exists through eternity and the "ordinary person" who vanishes into extinction lies in "refinement" (*jing*). Here, he is referring to the refinement of the mind in the Buddhist sense: only the "saint" possesses such refinement as to be able to perceive with utmost subtlety. This is Shen Yue speaking as a Buddhist. As the proponent of a new poetics, he too called for refinement. In this case, he proposed "refined" sounds.

As should be clear, Shen Yue was a man of many talents. He happened to be a leader in a poetry movement that emphasized the use of tones to create "euphonic sounds" in poetry. To nonspeakers of Mandarin Chinese, the language can sound exceptionally "musical." As Shen Yue and his peers discovered, the musical quality of their language was due primarily to tones, which affected the shape, the pitch, and possibly the length of Chinese syllables. (Note that the Chinese of Shen Yue's time—often referred to as Middle Chinese—was very different from Mandarin Chinese; the tones of Middle Chinese, consequently, are not the same as those in Mandarin Chinese). Based on their observation, they concluded that there were four categories of tones (*sisheng*), which they named "level" (*ping*), "rising" (*shang*), "departing" (*qu*), and "entering" (*ru*). To Shen Yue's ear, the interaction among the four tones, when they were successfully crafted into a poem, sounded like this: high and then falling;

low and then rising. In a famous essay, he proposes that one should use syllables that have different tones—and not those with the same tone—within a line, or between the two lines, of a couplet. (Chinese words are predominantly monosyllabic and hence a syllable often also denotes a word.) This principle ensured that the sounds would "alternate," giving rise to a sense of constant changes as the lines unfold. Poetic sounds created as such, according to Shen Yue, were "refined" sounds.

Even though Chinese is widely known as a "tonal language" today, "tone" was a new concept in Shen Yue's time. Being able to differentiate the four tones and to consciously manipulate their combination in speech and poetry composition was challenging for many and helped to propel some individuals—such as Shen Yue—to the forefront of literary innovation and cultural novelty. Against this backdrop, we can now take a closer look at the "few lines" in Shen Yue's lengthy *fu* that had created much excitement for him and his young poet friend Wang Yun.

As discussed earlier, Shen Yue became ecstatic when Wang Yun pronounced the word for "rainbow" in the line "the joined arc of the Female Rainbow" as *ye* instead of *ni*. The meaning of the word is the same in either pronunciation. However, *ni* has "level" tone and *ye* has "entering" tone. If pronounced *ni*, the tone combination of the four words in the line will be level-level-level-rising; alternatively, pronounced as *ye*, the four words will yield level-entering-level-rising. Obviously, in the latter combination, the change or alternation in tones is more elevated, fulfilling Shen Yue's idea of using different tones in a line. For his ability to grasp the principle of tonal change and capture the "correct" tone in a single word, Wang Yun was deemed "one who truly knows sounds" by Shen Yue, the master of poetic sounds. Likewise, regarding the other two lines in question, Wang Yun's response—he "beat rhythmically and gave high praises"—showed that he fully understood and enjoyed their sonic beauty.

It would take another chapter to give a full depiction of the tone combinations and other unique sound patterns in Shen Yue's "*Fu* on Living in the Suburbs." Here, it suffices to point out that the entire piece was elegantly crafted, not only in imagery and diction but also in tones and rhymes. In proposing his principle for creating "refined" sounds, Shen Yue had attributed the ability to grasp and exercise the principle to "conscious thought" (*si*). In other words, the process of the mind was behind the refinement in sounds. That he insisted on the importance of differentiating a single tone among 452 lines starkly recalls his process of grasping thought-instance by thought-instance in his Buddhist essay. As far as perception—that is, the mind—was concerned, Shen Yue the Buddhist and Shen Yue the poet had overlapped.

Buddhism would go through many transformations after Shen Yue's time. The new poetics spearheaded by him and his fellow poets also would evolve, fundamentally influencing the course of Chinese poetry. In later history, Buddhism and poetry would continue to cross paths, lending ever more richness to the life and work of the Chinese literary class, as shown in chapter 13. In that sense, Shen Yue's story is only the tip of the iceberg, hinting at the emergence of a cultural milieu in which religion and poetry—as well as officialdom, scholarship, and other pursuits—were all intricately entwined. His struggle to remain "single-minded" is but a metaphor for the complexity of—and difficult negotiations in—the elite culture of medieval China.

MEOW HUI GOH

NOTES

1. *Fu* is a poetic genre that is sometimes described as a type of rhymed prose or prose poetry. It has several distinctive features, the most notable of which are its lengthiness, its use of a mix of long and short lines, its elevated diction, and its tendency to describe things and emotions in an exhaustive manner.
2. *Li jian* ("benefits from appointment") comes from the phrase *li jian hou* ("benefits from appointing aides") in the *Yijing* (*Book of Changes*), in the section for the third hexagram, "Zhun," which speaks about the difficulty of starting something and advises one to appoint helpers. Based on this reference, Shen Yue's line can mean his family had a difficult beginning in Haihun and decided not to establish themselves up there.
3. A *Shijing* (*Book of Poetry*) poem has these lines: "The mulberry and catalpa trees— / One must treat them with utmost respect." The trees here refer to those planted by one's ancestors to benefit future generations and have the extended meaning of ancestral residence.
4. The "Wondrous Carriage" (*miaozhen*) and the "Mysterious Gate" (*xuanfei*) are both metaphors for the Buddhist faith. The "Single Vehicle" is the doctrine that reaffirms that there is only one vehicle, that is, the Buddha himself.
5. Richard B. Mather, *The Poet Shen Yüeh (441–513): The Reticent Marquis* (Princeton, NJ: Princeton University Press, 1988), 208 n. 134.
6. Translation by Mather, *The Poet Shen Yüeh*, 187 n. 58.
7. The "Three Goodness" is to fulfill the duties to one's parents, to one's ruler, and to one's elders.
8. Li Heng (fl. ca. 258), having planted a thousand tangerine trees, told his son that he had a thousand "tree slaves" and hence did not need any food or clothing from him. Shi Chong (249–300), known for his wealth, had written boastfully about his garden.

PRIMARY SOURCES

LS   Yao Silian 姚思廉 (d. 637) et al. *Liang shu* 梁書 (Liang History). Beijing: Zhonghua shuju, 1997.

Taishō   Takakusu Junjirō 高楠順次郎 and Watanabe Kaikyoku 渡邊海旭, eds. *Taishō shinshū daizōkyō* 大正新修大藏經 (Taishō Revised Tripiṭaka). Tokyo, 1922–1936.

SUGGESTED READINGS

ENGLISH

Goh, Meow Hui. *Sound and Sight: Poetry and Courtier Culture in the Yongming Era (483–493)*. Stanford, CA: Stanford University Press, 2010. See especially 7–39 and 57–79.

Lin, Shuen-fu. "A Good Place Need Not Be a Nowhere: The Garden and Utopian Thought in the Six Dynasties." In *Chinese Aesthetics: The Ordering of Literature, the Arts, and the Universe in the Six Dynasties*, ed. Zong-qi Cai, 123–166. Honolulu: University of Hawai'i Press, 2004.

Mather, Richard B. *The Poet Shen Yüeh (441–513): The Reticent Marquis*. Princeton, NJ: Princeton University Press, 1988. See especially 175–223.

Tian, Xiaofei. *Beacon Fire and Shooting Star: The Literary Culture of the Liang (502–557)*. Cambridge, MA: Harvard University Asia Center, 2007. See especially 224–233.

CHINESE

Chen Qingyuan 陳慶元, ed. *Shen Yue ji jiaojian* 沈約集校箋 (A Collection of Shen Yue's Works, with Collation and Annotations). Hangzhou: Zhejiang guji, 1995.

Lin Jiali 林家驪. *Shen Yue yanjiu* 沈約研究 (A Study of Shen Yue). Hangzhou: Hangzhou daxue, 1999.

Xiao Zixian 蕭子顯 (489–537), *Nan Qi shu* 南齊書 (Southern Qi History). Beijing: Zhonghua shuju, 1997. See especially 52.898–900.

PART IV
THE TANG DYNASTY

❀ 10 ❀

KNIGHT-ERRANTRY

Tang Frontier Poems

Frontier poetry (*biansai shi*) is a major subgenre of *shi* (poetry) that emerges during the Tang dynasty, and, as the name suggests, is concerned with the poet's life and experience on the frontiers. But where were these frontiers depicted by Tang poets? If you've ever traveled through provinces such as Hebei, Shanxi, and the northern areas of Shaanxi, you've already retraced the route of the great Chinese frontier poets. If you move westward through Ningxia, Gansu, and Qinghai provinces, finally arriving in the Xinjiang region, you will have reenacted the epic journey undertaken by the great Tang poet Luo Binwang (ca. 627–after 684) roughly thirteen hundred years ago (figure 10.1).

But how could the frontiers have become so important as to give birth to a major topic in Tang poetry? Here we might consider the American Western, a nineteenth- and twentieth-century literary genre that achieved great popularity in twentieth-century film. Defining features include a harsh and desolate landscape, conquest of wilderness, confiscation of Native American territorial rights, war with indigenous peoples as well as civil war, the lure of adventure, loneliness and revenge, romanticized heroism, and self-made mavericks who become self-sacrificing heroes. This is a culture differently structured from the so-called civilized world. In the Western's social imaginary, institutional law no longer holds and traditional social order becomes skewed; here, personal honor and an individual sense of justice are recognized and celebrated.

In interesting and unexpected ways, the reasons for the popularity of frontier-knight poetry in the Tang might be said to parallel those for literature about the American West. Like the Western, Tang frontier poetry is concerned with war, adventure, heroism, patriotism, revenge, encounters with alien culture, and emotions associated with frontier life and landscape.

Frontiers imply conflict with foreign others. From the seventh to the ninth centuries, the Tang borders were populated by Turkic nomads, mainly Uyghur Turks (*Huihe*) and Eastern Turks (*Tujue*) in the north, Khitan (*Qidan*) in the northeast, and the Tibetan Empire in the southwest, called Tubo (*Tufan*) in dynastic China. These and many others already had a long history of military engagement with China by the time the aggressively expansionist Tang, annexing land and confiscating territorial rights, moved deep into Central Asia along the Gansu corridor.

But if Tang poets also ventured west, how did they—long described in classical and modern literature as effete, sentimental, even frail scholars—survive in an environment easily as hostile and rugged as the early US frontier? We know that images of the frontier portrayed in poetry of the Southern Dynasties (420–589) are purely fictive, created by poets who never visited the places they describe. By contrast, many of the frontier poets of the Tang ventured into and explored the frontier

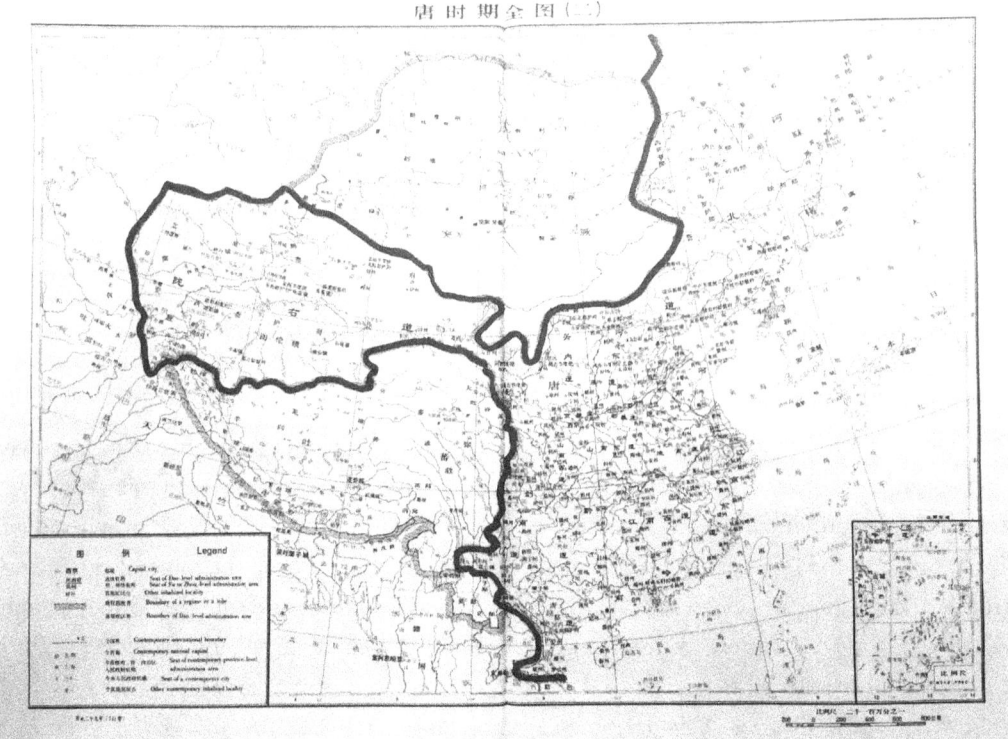

FIGURE 10.1 Tang dynasty map with the original names of the areas related to the stories of the knights described in this chapter. Reproduction from Tan Qixiang 譚其驤, ed., *Jianming Zhongguo lishi dituji* 簡明中國歷史地圖集 (Concise Historical Atlas of China) (Beijing: Zhongguo ditu chubanshe, 1996), 41–42.

or lived in border settlements on the margins of the frontier, while some even served in frontier armies.[1] What brought Tang poets to the frontiers?

Another important issue is why we find such a close association between knight-errantry and Tang frontier poetry. In early ancient China, the term "knight-errant" (*xia* or *youxia*) originally referred to feudal princes and those influential commoners who retained private swordsmen (*sijian*) for their own use as assassins or warriors. In the early Han, the distinction between *xia* and *sijian* began to merge as the Han court, seeking to confiscate political power from locals, incriminated or relocated local commoner-knights and their families. As a result, the early type of *youxia* went into decline and *sijian* began to identify themselves as *youxia*.[2]

The former *sijian* turned *youxia* found abundant employment in wealthy cities such as Chang'an, Luoyang, and Handan, places known for high-spirited youth who admired the knights.[3] The interaction of the knights with the youngbloods further shaped the tradition of so-called young urban knights as narcissistic, arrogant dandies and prodigals who nonetheless valued brotherly appreciation, friendship, and loyalty over life and money—even to the point of a willingness to die for those who recognize them. This young urban knight, a composite of two earlier traditions (the ancient *sijian* or assassin and the wealthy, unruly youth), makes a major contribution to the image of the young knight in Tang frontier poetry.

The knights, including the youngbloods, assassins, and professional swordsmen, typically fled to the frontiers or border towns after they had committed murder to avenge wrongs. Northwest frontiers, particularly the Yan, Zhao, You, and Bing areas, were rife with military conflict, and the local populations were known for their courage, belligerence, and skill in martial arts. The influx of roaming swordsmen, fugitive knights, and unruly youths significantly bolstered this reputation. These areas were therefore recognized as the birthplace of knight-errantry as well as the ideal of the military general in ancient China.[4]

In poetry, the tradition of the knight-errant first appeared during the third to sixth centuries, also a period of frequent military uprising. An early representative work, Cao Zhi's (192–232) "White Horse" ("Baima pian"), praises young knights from northwest border towns for their courage, fearlessness, excellence in martial arts, and strong patriotism. The poem established a major tradition of knight-errantry in Chinese poetry and had great impact on the works of the Tang.

But how and why did poets begin to cast themselves as the knights described in such poems? What are the other major topics, in addition to patriotism and heroism, celebrated in Tang frontier poetry of knight-errantry? And why did revenge, war weariness, and antiwar feelings become so prominent? These are the questions I kept in mind as I explored the relationship between military and knightly frontier heroism in these Tang poems.

KNIGHTS-ERRANT JOIN THE ARMY ON THE FRONTIERS

Tang poets were particularly interested in the topic of knights joining the army. In addition to the many precedents in earlier poems, this reflects the historical fact that the number of knights joining the army increased remarkably during the Tang, especially in the seventh and eighth centuries, when the Tang government was desperate to establish professional armies in order to better fight its wars in Central Asia. This desperation grew from both a surge in expansionist policies and the increased intensity of the wars. The existing "garrison militia" (*fubing*) recruiting system, organized by local peasants in the garrisoned areas, fell short, so a "mercenary recruiting" (*mubing*) system was enacted to recruit better-qualified soldiers.[5] The young knights who had mastered martial arts became the government's prime targets.

The knights described in Tang frontier poems might be ambitious and high-spirited young knights seeking opportunities to display their talents, urban youths hot for adventure, or fugitive knights looking for employment. Regardless of which type they were, once they became aware that the nation was in crisis, patriotism was the key sentiment that impelled them to join the army. Wang Wei's (701–761) "Song of the Unruly Youths" ("Shaonian xing") is a typical example:

SONG OF THE UNRULY YOUTHS 少年行

   Xinfeng is known for good wine worth ten thousand a gallon, 新豐美酒斗十千
2 Xianyang is famed for many young wandering knights. 咸陽遊俠多少年
   When their genuine congenial spirits meet, they drink to each other, 相逢意氣為君飲
4 Tethering their horses to the weeping willows by the tall tavern's side. 繫馬高樓垂柳邊

	They first became the Imperial Guards of the Han,	出身仕漢羽林郎
6	Then followed the General of Spirited Cavalry to battle in Yuyang.	出隨驃騎戰漁陽
	They knew the hardship on the frontier,	孰知不聞邊庭苦
8	Though dead, their chivalrous bones still smell sweet.	縱死猶聞俠骨香
	They can draw two carved bows at one time,	一身能擘兩雕弧
10	Hu cavalry thousands thick look like nothing to them.	虜騎千重只似無
	Sitting sideways on gold saddle while shooting white feathered arrows,	側坐金鞍調白羽
12	Five khans are shot to death one after another.	紛紛射殺五單于

[QTS 128.1305]

The above lines are actually three short poems taken from a series of four poems on young patriotic knights joining the army. I cite only the first three poems, which best represent knight-errantry. Each consists of four lines in a quatrain pattern. The first emphasizes their mutual admiration of wine. It's noteworthy that drinking is particularly highlighted in the poem to emphasize the knight's heroism. Although drinking was already a major poetic theme in pre-Tang literature, it was rarely associated with the knights-errant's life and habits, becoming a significant knightly feature only in the Tang.

This point is worth further elaboration in order to shed some light on the association of knight-errantry with wine drinking. From the *Shijing* (*Book of Poetry*) to the Six Dynasties period, imbibing alcohol had been used to describe friendship, a poet's temperament, and even a poet's life. But according to my research, before the Tang dynasty, and regardless of whether the genre was historical prose or poetry, the use of drinking to highlight a knight-errant's character—his bold, unrestrained temperament—was rarely seen. For example, a fondness for drink is never suggested among the four feudal princes of the Warring States period, men identified as noble knights and commoner knights, including Zhu Jia, Tian Zhong, Ju Meng, and Guo Jie, all found in the "Biography of the Wandering Knights" ("Youxia liezhuan") chapter of the *Shiji* (*Records of the Historian*). And in Guo Jie's case, his great dislike for alcohol is emphasized through a revealing story. The *Shiji* records that Guo Jie's nephew (his older sister's son) once tried to use the influence afforded him by his uncle's prestige to force his drinking companion to drink beyond his fill. Instead, this person became infuriated and fought and killed Guo Jie's nephew. Guo Jie laid the blame for this tragedy on his nephew, ignoring his sister's pressure to retaliate against her son's murderer, and in fact forgave the man. Guo Jie's impartiality and magnanimity in this case generated deep and widespread respect.

In addition, the "Biography of the Assassins" ("Cike liezhuan") chapter of the *Shiji* has accounts of the achievements of Cao Mo, Zhuan Zhu, Yu Rang, Nie Zheng, and Jing Ke, five men who used assassination to pay debts of gratitude. It is only when Jing Ke is described that his fondness for drinking is especially noted. Among the remaining four assassins, an enjoyment of alcohol is never used to describe their habits or character.

By the Wei-Jin and Northern and Southern dynasties periods, poems about knights-errant had begun to establish a link between knight-errantry and a penchant for drinking, using this predisposition to characterize the unique traits of knights-errant. However, it should be noted that these poems were rare; it is only with the Tang that we see a strong pattern of combining a fondness for drink with the bold, heroic spirit of knights-errant.[6] Parenthetically, this feature later exerts great influence on the depictions of martial arts and chivalry in late imperial China and modern times, especially in the fiction of Jin Yong (1924–).

Another prominent feature of this first quatrain is the importance of friendship. The young knights quickly and easily become friends through good wine and conversation, with an emphasis on their mutual appreciation. Once friends, they value loyalty and brotherhood over everything else, including their own lives. These two motifs also endure and are further celebrated in the chivalry novels (*wuxia xiaoshuo*) of late imperial China into modern times.

The second quatrain describes the knights' determination to join the Han army, regardless of danger, and how they become imperial guards, follow a general into battle, and experience great hardship on the frontiers—all in exchange for the glory of a chivalrous ideal. The first two quatrains describe the knight's heroic temperament, daily life, and patriotism. The third and final quatrains turn to focus on their heroic abilities and their exploits in hyperbolic displays of prowess and bravery, and relate how they master the martial arts and kill the tribal generals with ease and confidence.

We note that each line of the third quatrain demonstrates a particular knightly feature: in the first, a display of strength in archery that seems impossibly exaggerated as the knight draws two bows at once; then the nonchalant temerity in the face of vast enemy hordes; the elegant even aesthetic confidence of the virtuoso horseman and archer; and finally, the incomparable martial skill that can slay five enemy khans in quick succession. All of these features become defining traits of knight-errantry in later literary works about chivalry.

The fourth quatrain (not quoted above) serves as a series finale, telling how these heroic deeds and patriotic devotion win recognition from the imperial court, earning the knights eternal fame and honor. This merging of knight-errantry with military exploit—joining the army as a display of heroism and patriotism and to win honors and recognition—becomes a major motif in Tang frontier poems.

FRONTIER KNIGHTS PAY A DEBT OF GRATITUDE TO SOMEONE WHO APPRECIATES THEM

Another major theme of knight-errantry in Tang frontier poems is the knight-errant repaying a debt of gratitude, even with his life, to someone who appreciates him. Gao Shi (700–765), an important Tang frontier poet, exemplifies this quality in his "Ascending Mount Long" ("Denglong"). He traveled to the borders in his youth, wishing to join the army and contribute his talent to his nation. But his early official career was disappointing and his talent went unrecognized. Assigned to low-ranking posts in small county governments in the northern border areas, he was able to spend a great deal of time traveling the area, imaginatively retracing the paths of ancient knights. His "Ballad of the Youths from Handan" ("Handan shaonian xing") recounts that, on one such journey, he met a group of young knights and joined in their hunt, imbibing in the process the spirit of knight-errantry he so admired (*QTS* 213–214).

Though he was long dissatisfied with his career, Gao's talent was finally recognized by Geshu Han (d. 757), who appointed him to a high-ranking secretarial post in his military government. "Ascending Mount Long" relates Gao's acceptance of the post, and then his long, dangerous journey to the far western frontier to show his gratitude to Geshu:

ASCENDING MOUNT LONG 登隴

	On Mount Long's summit is a far-ranging traveler,	隴頭遠行客
2	On the mountain split currents of water.	隴上分流水
	The flowing waters of the rivers are endlessly running,	流水無盡期
4	The traveler's journey is not yet ended.	行人未云已
	I, of humble talent and shallow learning, deserve a low-ranking post,	淺才通一命
6	And carrying a lone sword with me, leave for a thousand miles.	孤劍適千里
	Should I not be longing for home?	豈不思故鄉
8	I am always grateful to the ones who appreciate my worth.	從來感知己

[*QTS* 212.2214]

There is a strong motif in classical Chinese poetry in which the poem opens with the poet climbing a peak to gaze longingly afar and homeward. The poet invokes that motif here, blending it with his journey to a remote frontier. Situating himself as a traveler on the mountain thus personally engages Gao intertextually with the poetic tradition while at the same time relating the historical and emotional circumstances of his particular journey.

The following two lines describe the seeming endlessness of the journey. Next, lines 5–6 show how he is determined to complete the journey in order to show his gratitude to Geshu Han. The final couplet places Geshu's recognition of the poet's worth above his personal homesickness. A sense of duty to the state and loyal recompense for favors create a high dramatic tension with the poet's private feelings and the poetic tradition on which he draws.

FRONTIER KNIGHTS AVENGE WRONGS

Revenge is another striking feature closely associated with knight-errantry in Chinese literature, in both poetry and fiction. The desire for vengeance can arise between individuals, families, or nations, and when victims find themselves unable to exact revenge, they will seek someone who can do it for them. Thus, knights highly skilled in martial arts become desirable as hired assassins. As to their willingness, we remember that an important feature of the knight is his ready gratitude to those who appreciate his talent. Entrusting such a task to a knight by offering payment is seen as a form of recognition of talent or worthiness, and even the assassination itself serves to pay the knight's debt of gratitude to his employer. In addition, a successful mission satisfies the knight's need for justice. Avenging wrongs for someone in distress, for a friend, or for the knight's own personal reasons thus became an important knightly virtue.

When the knights avenge wrongs for the state, it's considered patriotic, and Chinese knights are always patriotic and loyal. This unwavering loyalty of the knight finds expression in both traditional and modern Chinese chivalric literature and is especially common in Tang frontier poems, where knights may both avenge wrongs and serve in the army. Chen Zi'ang's (661–702) "Reflection on My Experiences ["Ganyu"] (No. 34)" is a good example of this:

REFLECTION ON MY EXPERIENCES (NO. 34) 感遇三八首之三四

	He said, "I am a sojourner from remote Yan,	自言幽燕客
6	Joining my friends for a long journey after binding my hair.7	結髮事遠遊
	If a red ball was drawn, then a civil officer would be killed,8	赤丸殺公吏
8	And when day came, I avenged a personal grudge.	白日報私讎
	To avoid being avenged, I fled to the seashore,	避仇至海上
10	Later I joined the army in this border area.	被役此邊州
	My homeland is three thousand miles away,	故鄉三千里
12	The river of the Liao is going far, far away.	遼水復悠悠
	I am always angry about the invasion of the Khitan troops,9	每憤胡兵入
14	But I am also ashamed of the Han state.	常為漢國羞
	How could I know that after winning seventy battles,	何知七十戰
16	This gray-haired old man would still not be enfeoffed as marquis?"	白首未封侯

[QTS 83.891]

This poem was written in 697, when the poet joined the army at the shores of the Bohai Sea and the Khitan were invading the northeastern borders. The first four lines of the poem (not quoted here) set the time, location, and scene of the poet's meeting with the knight-soldier. The poet then relates the knight-soldier's story, which forms the rest of the poem. Lines 5–10 relate how the young knight joins his knight friends for a long journey after coming of age, murders officials, avenges wrongs, and finally flees to the distant northeast border to avoid revenge. The following six lines tell of his nostalgia when he first resides in the frontier (lines 11–12), then describe the strong patriotic emotions that motivated his decision to leave family behind and join the army (lines 13–14), and finally relate that, although a seasoned veteran, he still serves at the frontier as a lowly soldier (lines 15–16). The poem conveys the poet's criticism of unjust rewards and promotions.

Lines 7–8, "If a red ball was drawn, then a civil officer would be killed, / And when day came, I avenged a personal grudge," are noteworthy as they provide a window through which we might imagine how the youngbloods try to make themselves look more like the real knights they wish to be. By day, they would have often wandered around seeking opportunities to redress injustice, such as defending people in distress from bullies, gangs, or corrupt officials. They might devote some time to collecting information on their targets, such as location of residences or offices. The night before the assassination, as the poem relates, they would draw lots to decide whether to kill a civil or a military officer the next morning. Perhaps they tossed and turned half the night, riddled with wrath, then woke in darkness to fetch their whetstones and sharpen their knives under the moon, striving to maintain their rhythm of vengeance to ready themselves for their mission. We can imagine them returning to the streets soon after sunrise, seeking out and perhaps ambushing their targets, and—with luck on their side—successfully complete their task.

POET-KNIGHTS ON THE FRONTIERS

Earlier frontier poets, such as those of the Southern Dynasties, generally based their poetic works about frontier life on legend and imagination rather than firsthand experience. But many Tang poets, in addition to poems describing frontier knights, wrote about their own lived experience on the borders.

The number of poets and literati joining the army increased significantly during the Tang. In addition to the need to earn a living (itself an important stimulus for poets to join), the Confucian ideal that made an official career a life goal for many Chinese poets was another important reason to join the army. The civil service examination, the main path for Tang poets' entry into the government, was a notoriously difficult examination that offered only a limited number of official posts each year.[10] But, as we have seen, the Tang court came to need higher-quality recruits to establish better professional armies as they expanded their operations in Central Asia. The number of poets joining the army, mostly as secretarial staff, therefore increased.

But again, outside of a few poets such as Li Bai (701–762), who was an excellent swordsman and knight, most Chinese poets have long been described as effete. With this nature or temperament, how could Chinese poets regard themselves as heroic knights? And why were they, whether they had joined the army or not, so inclined to identify themselves with the knight-errant?

James Liu and Yau-Woon Ma point out that knight-errantry was a mode of behavior rather than a profession; courage, a sense of chivalry and justice, patriotism, and utter devotion to friends or those who recognize their talent all qualify one as a knight.[11] In other words, it's the gallant temperament that matters more than martial arts skill and experience. Tang poets knew very well that the swordsmanship and archery of legend were both exaggerated and beyond their ability (just as we recognize as fiction the fantastic acrobatics in films such as Ang Lee's *Crouching Tiger, Hidden Dragon*). But in the army they could display chivalrous character in their patriotism, devotion, courage, and sense of justice (that is, in their opposition to enemy armies), as well as their willingness to share with comrades the joys and hardships of army life. Even poets who never joined the army, such as Du Fu (712–770), identified themselves with knights through chivalrous temperamental affinity; they could be further inspired by practicing knightly arts such as hunting and falconry. In sum, the knight-errant mind-set alone was believed to earn such poets the title of poet-knight.

Luo Binwang, an important frontier poet in the early Tang, showed his admiration for knight-errantry in his youth. His "Former Times" ("Chouxi pian") describes how he longed for ancient knights and spurned prominent political posts. Although he did not join the army until he was fifty-two, after years as a civil official, he gained a wealth of experience traveling to the far west and northwest, where he wrote many poetic works telling of his hardships there. His "Emotion Felt in a Frontier City" ("Biancheng youhuai") describes his personal reflections and the wild scenery around a deserted garrison located on the Hexi Corridor, while "Sunset in a Frontier City" ("Biancheng luori") describes what he saw and experienced on arrival in what is now the Turpan area.[12]

Among his poems on frontier knights, "Joining the Army" ("Congjun xing") is especially significant as it relates his service under Pei Xingjian (619–682) on a long and risky adventure to the far west, and it reflects his chivalric temperament, courage and determination to complete the mission, patriotic loyalty, and gratitude to Pei for recognizing his talents:

JOINING THE ARMY 從軍行

    For my whole life, only one glance is important,[13] 平生一顧重
2 My will and spirit are the highest among the troops. 意氣溢三軍
    When the army goes on an expedition, lances and spears shine in the sunlight, 野日分戈影
4 Stars in the sky unite with swords in patterns. 天星合劍文
    Our bowstrings embrace the Han moon, 弓弦抱漢月
6 Our horses' hooves trample the Hu earth. 馬足踐胡塵
    I do not seek only to survive on the frontier, 不求生入塞
8 But to devote my life to show gratitude to you. 唯當死報君

[QTS 78.840]

Du Fu, who is usually understood as a gentle, refined poet and highly unlikely to be associated with the image of the knight-errant, actually shows signs of the knight-errant temperament in his youth. Lines 41–48 of his well-known poem "Brave Wandering" ("Zhuangyou") describe his travel to the Shandong, Hebei, and Henan areas after he failed the civil service examination in 735, and relate how he enjoyed hunting, horseback riding, falconry, and all activities that made him feel like a knight. This suggests that, in Chinese history, knight-errantry has acted as an important inspiration for poets suffering from disappointment and frustration in their official careers. Many poets failed examinations, and some were even exiled to remote areas through political rivalries or scandals. Finding solace in knightly values helped ease their psychological pain:

BRAVE WANDERING 壯遊

    I traveled carefree in the areas of Qi and Zhao, 放盪齊趙間
42 Wearing soft fur horseback riding, I felt unrestrained. 裘馬頗清狂
    I sang standing on Congtai Terrace in spring, 春歌叢台上
44 I hunted traveling near Qingqiu in winter. 冬獵青丘旁
    I called my goshawk in the Zaoli forest, 呼鷹皂櫪林
46 I pursued game on the Yunxue ridge.[14] 逐獸雲雪岡
    I was ever shooting flying birds on unbridled horseback, 射飛曾縱鞚
48 And stretching my bow arm to fell the adjutant stork. 引臂落鶖鶬

[QTS 222.2363]

From these poems, we can infer a new, real pursuit of military heroism by the early and high Tang literati poets, and an important shift of literati ideals away from the exclusive practice of belles lettres prevalent during the Six Dynasties. In addition, the image of the poets conveyed in these poems debunks the popular negative image of Chinese literati as effete. The description of knight-errantry in the conventions and imagination of pre-Tang *yuefu* (Music Bureau) poets has given way to more realistic depictions of life and war on the frontiers.

WAR WEARINESS AND ANTIWAR OVERTONES

Many Tang frontier poems are concerned with knights who expect war to elicit courage and patriotism and then reward them with military position and honors. But many of the knights also convey a sense of war weariness or even antiwar overtones. As China endured a long period of military and political upheaval—from the third through the ninth centuries—common people, soldiers, knights, and poets alike became weary of the endless military combat. Poetic works of early times had already showed antiwar tendencies, but after centuries of war's hardships, Tang poets, especially in the late Tang, went so far as to actively encourage soldiers to desert, seek marriage alliances with enemy chieftains, or otherwise sue for peace through surrender, indemnity, or tribute arrangements.

One important frontier poet who clearly conveyed his disapproval of pro-war policies and long military campaigns was Li Qi (690–751). "An Old Ballad of Joining the Army" ("Gu congjun xing") suggests just such strong criticism. The first four lines describe the endless hardship of the soldier, laboring from dawn to dusk (watching for signal fires on mountaintops in the daytime, while watering horses by the river below at dusk), restless and sad every night (with nothing but sandstorms and the sad sound of the lute). The following four lines describe the harshness of the western border, which even the geese and locals find intolerable. The next couplet alludes to the story of Emperor Wu of the Han (r. 141–87 BCE) and to the closed Jade Gate pass[15] blocking the road home, so that even if soldiers could retire or desert, they would not get far. They have no choice but to continue fighting. The closing two lines satirize war, stating that the huge cost in casualties is for nothing but obtaining grapes for the imperial family.[16] This poem not only conveys a sense of war weariness but also expresses bitter antiwar sentiment:

AN OLD BALLAD OF JOINING THE ARMY 古從軍行

	In the daytime, climbing up the mountain to watch signal fires,	白日登山望烽火
2	At dusk, watering horses by the side of the Jiao River.[17]	黃昏飲馬傍交河
	Sandstorms blew in the dark, and the soldiers heard nothing but the sound of night watches,[18]	行人刁斗風沙暗
4	And the sad tones of the lute song of Princess Pipa.[19]	公主琵琶幽怨多
	We saw no towns, only wild clouds for ten thousand miles,	野雲萬里無城郭
6	And snow pell-mell covering the whole vast desert.	雨雪紛紛連大漠
	The Hu geese flew, honking in grief every night,	胡雁哀鳴夜夜飛
8	Even the Hu soldiers could not help crying.	胡兒眼淚雙雙落
	It was said that even Jade Gate pass was shut,	聞道玉門猶被遮
10	There was nothing the soldiers could do but follow the Qingche General.	應將性命逐輕車
	Soldiers' bones were buried in the wilds year after year,	年年戰骨埋荒外
12	For nothing but the grapes sent to the Han royal family.	空見蒲桃入漢家

[QTS 133.1348]

Li He (790–816), who lived a short but poetically significant life during the Tang, spent a couple of years (ca. 813–815) in the frontier towns of Shanxi and witnessed much suffering among the soldiers

FIGURE 10.2 Jianshui fortified pass, modern Jiuquan, Gansu province. This pass figures in the stories of the knights, including the poet-knights traveling with military missions to the West and the knight-soldiers guarding the border of the empire.

garrisoned there (figure 10.2). His "Life in Pingcheng" ("Pingcheng xia") describes a knight-soldier who can no longer bear his loneliness and homesickness. He therefore decides to die in flight or in the attempt to switch sides rather than to die in battle. An antiwar attitude permeates the poem:

LIFE IN PINGCHENG 平城下

	Hunger descends on Pingcheng,	饑寒平城下
2	A soldier watches the bright moon night after night.	夜夜守明月
	The sword given by his family when he parted loses its luster,	別劍無玉花
4	The wind from the great desert breaks his temple hairs.	海風斷鬢髮
	The great wall, long and extensive, seems to touch the gray sky,	塞長連白空
6	In the distance he sees the red banner of the Han.	遙見漢旗紅
	In the bluish tent, the short-flute plays,	青帳吹短笛
8	The smokelike fog of the night wets the dragon banner.	煙霧濕畫龍
	Wind blows the withered tumbleweeds up,	風吹枯蓬起
10	Inside the city, emaciated horses neigh.	城中嘶瘦馬
	"May I ask you, Officer of Fortifications,	借問築城吏
12	How many thousand miles away is the pass?"[20]	去關幾千里
	My only sorrow is my wrapped corpse sent home,	唯愁裹屍歸
14	I would not regret death by changing sides!	不惜倒戈死

[QTS 393.4439]

The poet offers a series of images—hunger, the moon, a sword given by the family as a parting gift, wind from an oceanic desert,[21] the wall stretching into the distance, a red military banner, nightly music from a flute, damp fog, and complaining horses—all of which the soldier saw, heard, and felt daily for years on the frontier. This bleak and unchanging landscape (like that in a cinema

Western) is made to express the soldier's increasing misery through endless campaigns, culminating in despair. The soldier's final sentiment condemns the purposelessness of war.

* * *

These poems show the many facets of knight-errant culture in Tang frontier poetry, from high-spirited youngbloods keen for justice to those seeking recognition and appreciation, avenger-knights, patriot or chivalrous poet-knights, and, finally, the soldier's war-weary disillusionment and indictment. Very different attitudes are developed and expressed toward foreign tribes and places, the military and war, and personal cultivation, particularly of the knightly virtues so intensely pursued. In addition, Tang frontier poems of knight-errantry also comprise much unprecedented subject matter, such as the bleak yet spectacular landscapes, and valuable details about alien cultures, including non-Chinese music and language. This variety of culture and subject matter greatly enriches the genre, earning the Tang a unique place in the tradition of Chinese poetry. In addition to their contribution to the Chinese poetic tradition, these Tang poems display a complex image of the knight-errant, distinct from that found in other literary forms. Reading and understanding the multiplicity of images and cultures embedded in this crucial motif of Tang poetry will lead us to a better appreciation of knight-errant culture in traditional Chinese literature.

TSUNG-CHENG LIN

NOTES

1. See Stephen Owen, ed. and trans., *An Anthology of Chinese Literature: Beginnings to 1911* (New York: Norton, 1996), 459–477, particularly 459–460.
2. Qian Mu, "Shi Xia" (Interpreting the Knights), in Qian Mu, *Zhongguo xueshu sixiang shi luncong disanji* (Treatise on the History of Chinese Academic Thought) (Taipei: Lianjing, 1997), 279–289; Chen Guanghong, "Guanyu Zhongguo zaoqi lishi shang youxia shenfen de chongxin jiantao" (Examination of the Status of Roaming Knights in Early Chinese History), *Fudan xuebao* (Social Sciences) 6 (2001): 119–126; and *Xia de renge yu shijie* (The Character and World of the Knight-Errant) (Shanghai: Fudan daxue chubanshe, 2005), 12–48.
3. Chang'an is modern Xi'an in Shaanxi province; Luoyang is in modern Henan province; and Handan is in the south of modern Hebei province.
4. The reference is to areas of northern China, especially around Beijing, Shanxi, Inner Mongolia, and Shandong. Specifically, Yan and Zhao mostly refer to the areas including Beijing, Tianjin, Shanxi, the northern part of Henan, and the southern part of the Inner Mongolia region. You refers to the northeastern part of Hebei and the western part of Liaoning, while Bing refers to the eastern and northern parts of Shandong. An important study of knight-errantry is Shi Nianhai, *Tangdai lishi dili yanjiu* (Studies in Tang History and Geography) (Beijing: Zhongguo shehui kexue chubanshe, 1998), 468–495.
5. See Charles O. Hucker, *A Dictionary of Official Titles in Imperial China* (Stanford, CA: Stanford University Press, 1985), 219 (entry 2093), and 337 (entry 4063).
6. For a discussion of the association between wine drinking and the poet's life in ancient China, see chapters 8 and 14.
7. Binding the hair by tying it on top of the head is a traditional Chinese coming-of-age ritual for boys of fifteen. At twenty, a capping (*ruoguan*) ritual initiates young men into adulthood.
8. This refers to a way to select whether to kill a civil or a military officer. Three colored balls were drawn from a cup, each of which charges the receiver to a different mission. A red ball requires the murder of a military officer, black

a civil officer. White means that the person will be responsible for the funeral of their comrades if they sacrifice their lives in the mission. See "Biography of Yin Shang" ("Yin Shang zhuan") in the *History of the Former Han* (*Hanshu*).
9. The Khitan (*Qidan*) were a nomadic people from the northeast of China. The line uses the word *hu*, a generic term for non-Chinese peoples of the north and west.
10. Even in the ninth century, two centuries after the inception of the civil service examination, only about thirty men each year successfully obtained the presented scholar (*jinshi*) degree, a title that qualified its recipients for government office. See Linda Rui Feng, "Chang'an and Narratives of Experience in Tang Tales," *Harvard Journal of Asiatic Studies* 71, no. 1 (June 2011): 35–68. For another useful study of Tang civil service examinations, please refer to chapter 11.
11. James Liu, *The Chinese Knight-Errant* (Chicago: University of Chicago Press, 1967), 1–13, 55–80; and Yau-Woon Ma, "The Knight-Errant in Hua-pen Stories," *T'oung Pao* 61, no. 4–5 (1975): 266–300.
12. The Hexi Corridor, also called the Gansu Corridor, refers to the important historical route through modern Gansu province that connects northern China to Central Asia. Turpan in the Turkestan region of central Asia, was called Xiyu in ancient China and is located in modern Xinjiang.
13. Behind the line is the implication that a mere sidelong glance of recognition from his superior makes his whole life of knightly virtue worthwhile.
14. Congtai may refer either to the terrace located in Handan of Hebei province or to the one in Shangshui of Henan province. Both were built during the Warring States period (ca. 476–221 BCE). Qingqiu, Zaoli forest, and Yunxue ridge are all located in modern Shandong province.
15. Yumen (Jade Gate) pass is located in the northwest part of Dunhuang in Gansu. It is an important pass to the Silk Road.
16. The grapes in the poem likely come from Turpan, which even now is well known for the fine quality of its grapes. Imperial Chinese families valued them highly.
17. Jiao River is located in the western part of the Turpan area and was an important military outpost in the Tang.
18. A *diaodou* is a wok made of copper, which is used both for cooking in the daytime and for ringing the watch of the night.
19. Princess Pipa originally refers to a daughter from a noble family, named Liu Xijun, during the reign of Emperor Wu of the Han. She was married to the Wusun tribal chief to ally the Han with the Wusun against the Xiongnu, the most powerful and threatening tribe on the northern frontier of the Han.
20. The pass here refers to Hangu Pass, located in the northeast of Lingbao city in Henan, which was an important pass in ancient China. This line suggests his plan of flight from the troops.
21. The desert is called the Hanhai in Chinese, referring to the Mongolian desert, also called the Gobi.

PRIMARY SOURCE

QTS   *Quan Tang shi* 全唐詩 (Complete *Shi* Poetry of the Tang). Beijing: Zhonghua shuju, 1999.

SUGGESTED READINGS

ENGLISH

Altenburger, Roland. *The Sword or the Needle: The Female Knight-Errant (*xia*) in Traditional Chinese Narrative*. Bern: Peter Lang, 2009.

Barr, Allan H. Review of *The Sword or the Needle: The Female Knight-Errant (*xia*) in Traditional Chinese Narrative*, by Roland Altenburger. *Harvard Journal of Asiatic Studies* 71, no. 1 (June 2011): 143–148.

Liu, James J. Y. *The Chinese Knight-Errant*. Chicago: University of Chicago Press, 1967. See especially 1–13, 55–80.

Ma, Yau-Woon. "The Knight-Errant in Hua-pen Stories." *T'oung Pao* 61, no. 4–5 (1975): 266–300.

Owen, Stephen, ed. and trans. *An Anthology of Chinese Literature: Beginnings to 1911*. New York: Norton, 1996, 371–517 (Tang poetry), 459–477 (frontier poetry).

CHINESE

Chen Guanghong 陳廣宏. *Xia de renge yu shijie* 俠的人格與世界 (The Character and World of the Knight-Errant). Shanghai: Fudan University Press, 2005, 12–48.

Chen Pingyuan 陳平原. *Qiangu wenren xiake meng* 千古文人俠客夢 (The Literati's Dream of the Knight-Errant Over a Thousand Years). Beijing: Beijing daxue chubanshe, 2010.

Lin Baochun 林保淳. "Cong youxia, shaoxia, jianxia, dao yixia: Zhongguo gudai xiayi guannian de yanbian" 從遊俠、少俠、劍俠、到義俠: 中國古代俠義觀念的演變 ("From the Wandering Knight, the Young Knight, and the Swordsman Knight to the Righteous Knight: The Transformation of the Ancient Chinese Concept of Knight-Errantry"). In *Xia yu Zhongguo wenhua* 俠與中國文化 (The Knight-Errant and Chinese Culture), edited by Danjiang daxue Zhongwenxi 淡江大學中文系 (Department of Chinese, Tamkang University), 91–130. Taipei: Taiwan xuesheng shuju, 1993.

Lin Xiangling 林香伶. "Tangdai youxia shige yanjiu" 唐代遊俠詩歌研究 ("Studies on Tang Poetry of the Knight-Errant"). Master's thesis. Taipei: Taiwan Zhengzhi University, 1994.

Yu Yingshi 余英時. "Xia yu Zhongguo wenhua" 俠與中國文化 ("The Knight-Errant and Chinese Culture"). In Yu Yingshi, *Wenhua pinglun yu Zhongguo qinghuai* 文化評論與中國情懷 (Cultural Critics and Chinese Sentiments), 257–310. Guilin: Guangxi shifan daxue, 2006.

❧ II ❧

TANG CIVIL SERVICE EXAMINATIONS

In 725, a man of letters named Zu Yong passed the presented scholar (*jinshi*) examination and earned his eligibility for office, mostly on account of the following poem:

LOOKING AFAR AT THE REMAINING SNOW ON
MOUNT ZHONGNAN   終南望餘雪

    The dark peaks of Mount Zhongnan were tall and beautiful;   終南陰嶺秀
2   The snow accumulated on top touched the verge of floating clouds.   積雪浮雲端
    The edges of forests brightened, with the skies clearing up;   林表明霽色
4   Inside the city, the chill of the dusk became stronger.   城中增暮寒

[QTS 131.1337]

If reciting and performing poems from the *Book of Poetry* were important cultural skills in the Eastern Zhou era, and explicating the allegorical meanings of those poems was critical in the Han, poetic composition also became an important medium of self-expression for educated men from the Han, as we have seen (chapters 1, 4, 7, 8, and 9). From the late seventh century onward, however, poetic composition became a critical component of Tang civil service examinations. An educated man, not necessarily from a family of wealth and power, could in theory rely on his poetic talent alone to earn his entry into officialdom. Poetry not only played an instrumental role in personal career advancement but also was a fundamental medium through which members of the examination community socialized and cemented ties with one another and interacted with broader social circles.

Poetic excellence was seen as an important criterion for selecting government officials, because of the traditional belief in the interconnections among the multivalent meanings of *wen*. The term referred to "patterns" of the cosmos, an intrinsically moral order from which "writing" had originated and on which human "culture" was predicated. While "literature" was a refined manifestation of writing and epitomized the literary aspect of human culture, "civil" governance embodied the political aspect, and Confucian classics manifested the normative ritual and ethical aspects. Because poetry was seen as the most prestigious form of literature, a poet, who had had a broad humanistic education and demonstrated his poetic excellence, came to be regarded as one who was culturally, morally, and politically qualified to serve in office, due to having understood and mastered the essence of *wen*, which pervades its different manifestations.

Though the principle of evaluating and recruiting talent is prescribed in Confucian canonical texts, the genesis of civil service examination system has been traced to the Han period. Disciples of national university specialists in five Confucian classics, such as the *Book of Poetry*, could be orally examined and granted government positions, though not regularly. From 132, local officials became responsible for assessing the moral character and learning of candidates from the area and then recommending them for office. Han emperors also frequently tested candidates orally with policy questions. Under the rule of the Sui dynasty (581–618), a system of annual degree examinations was established, and each prefecture was required to send three men every year to the capital.

Expanding on the Sui system, the Tang established three major types of examinations. The first was decree examinations, so called because the emperor would hold them on an irregular basis and preside over them within the palace. Candidates who were successful in these examinations received special appointments, bypassing the normal bureaucratic procedures. The second type was assessment examinations, which were held annually by the Ministry of Personnel to test candidates' qualifications for (re)appointments to positions of the sixth rank or lower. Because only a limited number of posts were available, eligible candidates were required to wait a certain number of years before applying for (re)appointments. The ministry also held special examinations, such as the selection of the preeminent in legal judgments (*shupan bacui*) and the erudite learning and grand composition (*boxue hongci*) examinations, in order to give fast-track promotions to the most outstanding members in the pool of candidates.

The third type was annual recruitment examinations, which were held at prefectures by local officials first and then at the court by the Ministry of Rites.[1] These examinations conferred degrees for specialized branches of expertise, such as law, mathematics, history, rituals, orthography, and Daoist scriptures. Among these, the presented scholar and the canonical expert (*mingjing*) were most attractive to aspirants, who numbered in the thousands during a regular year. Although the degree of canonical expert, which certified candidates' expertise in Confucian classics, was held in high regard at the beginning of the dynasty, the degree of presented scholar, with its low success rates (an average of 2 to 5 percent), surpassed it by the eighth century, becoming the most coveted title. Enthusiasts even compiled and circulated a registry of annual graduates.

The degree of presented scholar was prestigious because, being essentially a literary examination, the competition was an official avenue for recognizing the most talented men of letters in the empire. Although poetic composition could also be included in decree examinations or special selection examinations of the Ministry of Personnel, participants in these examinations were often presented scholar degree holders, who had already established themselves through the presented scholar examination and who wished to bypass the mandated waiting period (because the degree granted only an eligibility for office). In other words, to these men, triumph in extra examinations was icing on the cake, while the most critical hurdle lay in the presented scholar examination. Degree holders became celebrities within the elite, for the trajectories to upper echelons of Tang bureaucracy were now open to them. As a matter of fact, major cultural and political figures of the middle and late Tang often held degrees of presented scholar.

Poetic compositions became central components of the presented scholar examination after Emperor Gaozong (r. 649–683) stipulated, in a 681 edict, that the examination include belles lettres.

From 705 onward, the examination routinely included three parts: one on memorization of Confucian classics (*tiejing*), one on literary genres (*zawen*), and one on policy questions (*ce*). In the session on literary genres, candidates were usually asked to compose two poems: one rhapsody (*fu*) and one regulated verse (*lüshi*). While examiners set rhyming requirements, candidates were generally allowed to bring a rhyme book into the examination hall for reference. Some examiners are known to have allowed candidates to compose additional poems to make up for their poor performance in the memorization test of Confucian classics. They could also show flexibility toward the candidates' final submissions. Zu Yong's poem, cited at the beginning of this chapter, was actually only half the required length. He submitted this incomplete poem and explained that he had fully expressed the poetic meaning of the prescribed topic. He passed because his lines greatly impressed the examiner.

The emphasis on poetry in the presented scholar examination was not without controversy. In 763, Yang Wan (d. 777) submitted a famous memorial to criticize the trend of valuing superficial literary artifice rather than solid knowledge in the classics and histories; he even went so far as to recommend abolishing the presented scholar examination. His proposal was eventually abandoned because the court was worried about the consequences of disappointing the large number of enthusiastic participants who had striven hard for the degree year after year. Although a few other vocal critics later tried to reform the examination by getting rid of poetic compositions, popular support for the poetic mainstay continued, and its prestige only grew with time. The contemporary saying "Becoming a canonical expert at the age of thirty is considered too old, while obtaining a presented scholar degree at the age of fifty still young" indicates both the competitiveness of the presented scholar examination and the strong commitment of its candidates. In 901, for instance, of the five elderly people who passed, two were over seventy years old and the other three were more than sixty. As this example shows, many candidates were lifelong devotees of the presented scholar examination, and it was rare to pass on the first try.

Both the prefectural and the national competitions used similar poetic formats and criteria for selection. Poetic topics were chosen by examiners according to their personal preferences. The range was wide, from objects of the natural world—including the sun, the moon, stars, mountains, rivers, seas, flowers, trees, and animals—to contemporary political and cultural events or sentences taken from the written tradition. Examination rhapsodies tended to be shorter than their counterparts composed for other occasions, while the common regulated verse was in five-syllable lines with eight, twelve, or sixteen lines, which were the most popular types of regulated verse in the Tang (☞ *HTRCP* chap. 8). The famous poet Bai Juyi (772–846), for instance, exceled at the local examination in Xuanzhou (modern Anhui) in 799 with his "Rhapsody on Shooting and Hitting the Target" ("Shezhong zhenghu fu") and his verse "The Distant Peaks Stand Framed in My Window" ("Chuangzhong lie yuanxiu shi"). The following year, he passed the national competition, ranked fourth among the seventeen successful candidates, with his "Rhapsody on Whether People's Nature and Habits are Close to or Distant from Each Other" ("Xing xi xiang jin yuan fu") and his verse "Waters Containing Jades are Marked by Right-Angled Streams" ("Yushui ji fangliu shi"). Along with his policy discussion essays, these poetic compositions became samples well known to candidates after him because they aspired to his extraordinary success in passing all those highly competitive examinations on his first attempt.

Except for the poems of Zu Yong, Bai Juyi, and a few others, most examination poetry has traditionally been considered mediocre. Because candidates composed under pressure and in a limited amount of time, they might not be able to give their best performance. There was another important reason. Unlike later civil service examinations, the names of candidates on test sheets were not blocked and the examiner did not make decisions based solely on their impromptu performance under his watch. In fact, the main ground of competition for Tang candidates of the presented scholar degree was actually not in the examination hall but outside it. An aspirant's chance of success lay in the poetic reputation he had made for himself *before* taking the examination.

The most important way for a candidate to make a reputation was through the presentation of scrolls (*wenjuan* or *xingjuan*), or the submission of sample writings to an intended reader, such as an examiner or a potential patron. From the mid-eighth century, the examiner of the year routinely asked candidates to submit writing samples before the official examination so that he could evaluate more thoroughly the candidates' poetic talent. However, the sheer number of candidates made it impossible for the examiner to give equal attention to all the sample scrolls presented to him; instead, he relied heavily on the input of his colleagues, friends, and relatives to make final choices. These influential people became the main targets of scroll presentation as candidates tried to win their patronage.

Tang anecdotal literature is filled with dramatic vignettes of how candidates secured their examination success by courting powerful patrons. In a well-known story, the poet Wang Wei (701–761) is said to have enjoyed the favor of Prince Qi (d. 726) for his literary and musical talent. In the year when he tried to pass the prefectural examination for the capital district, the prince's powerful sister, Princess Yuzhen (ca. 693–ca. 762), had already decided to back another scholar to be the metropolitan district's best. Asking Wang to copy out ten of his best poems and to bring his lute, Prince Qi took him to the princess's house and introduced him as a musician. After the princess was greatly impressed by Wang's handsome looks and musical performance, Prince Qi revealed that Wang was also gifted in poetry and had him present his scroll to her. It turned out that the princess was already familiar with and admired those poems, which, as Wang's best works, had been in wide circulation. She then happily retracted her previous recommendation and sponsored Wang instead. Although the story does not mention whether she continued to support him at the next level of competition, candidates forwarded by the capital district usually had a much higher rate of success than their counterparts from other parts of the country. Whether or not the historical Wang Wei had indeed enjoyed powerful royal patronage, he became a successful presented scholar in 721 (☞ *HTRCP* C8.4, C10.4, C10.6–C10.7; *WBK* P24–P27; and chapter 13 of the present book).

Although the story of Wang Wei does not describe how the princess acted on his behalf, another on Du Mu (803–852) portrays in detail the behind-the-scenes maneuvers. According to this account, when the newly appointed examiner Cui Yan (768–836) left for Luoyang to preside over the presented scholar examination, his colleagues held a send-off banquet for him. Wu Wuling (d. 835), erudite at the national university at the time, arrived and told Cui that he had run into his students reading aloud Du Mu's "Rhapsody on Epang Palace" ("Epang gong fu"). Reciting the rhapsody from the beginning to the end for Cui, Wu demanded that Du Mu be passed as the top graduate. Cui declined, on the grounds that the top position had been filled by another. Wu then asked for fifth place, to which Cui agreed. Cui kept his promise, despite later revelations by others of Du Mu's personal shortcomings. The story is striking because it indicates that the list and ranking of those passing the examination could be negotiated and determined before the actual examination took place.

These stories do not depict the patrons' influence on the pass list as unfair, because recommendation was a central element of official appointment in Tang bureaucracy. An official bore responsibility for the person he recommended and could be punished if the person turned out to be unqualified. Moreover, as the stories emphasized, Wang Wei and Du Mu deserved their success because they had made their poetic reputations, although they still needed patrons to lobby on their behalf and to serve as referees/guarantors of their merits (for Du's poems, ☞ *HTRCP* C10.14–C10.16; *WBK* P22, P72).

In fact, public opinion played a very important role in Tang examination culture. When examiners passed men with wealth and family connections but without real talent, public outcries had more than once pressured the court to retest these candidates and fail some of them. Clearly, candidates from established families with good social connections, such as Wang Wei and Du Mu, would have easier time finding patronage and cultivating a favorable reputation. Du Mu himself reminisced that, when he participated in the presented scholar examination in 828, close to twenty officials had volunteered to be his patrons.

For candidates not as fortunate, the chance of success depended greatly on diligent and strategic presentations of scrolls. Although these scrolls of writing samples could cover a wide range of literary genres, such as memorials, stele inscriptions, eulogies, literary essays, philosophical discussions, and historical expositions, poetry (rhapsody and verse) took precedence. For example, in a cover letter to Supervising Secretary Chen Jing (presented scholar degree in 771) to introduce himself and ask for Chen's support, Bai Juyi explained that his scrolls had included one hundred verses and twenty pieces in other literary genres.

In preparing these scrolls, candidates had to decide carefully what to include, give their best calligraphic performance, and customize their presentations for different patrons. Tang etiquette required that one avoid the family taboos of the intended reader, that is, refrain from using characters used in the names of the person's parents or grandparents. In addition, presentation had to be timed so as not to be an inconvenience to the patron's busy schedule, and follow-up visits ought to be neither too frequent nor too sparse. A candidate also needed to take into consideration the taste of his intended reader. The late Tang poet Du Xunhe (846–904) is said to have selected simple poems to cater to the unsophisticated predilections of the powerful military general Zhu Wen (852–912), who ultimately brought the Tang to its end and established his own short-lived dynasty.

Scroll presentation was so central in the life of an examination candidate that it was also a major source of anxiety. Anecdotes from the Tang describe numerous tragicomic scenarios that must have struck a chord with regard to the emotional strains felt by members of the examination community. For instance, a man is said to have passed the presented scholar examination with scrolls that he stole from his cousin, a famous poet and hermit. To track down the thief, the poet left the mountains for the capital, eventually passing the examination himself. According to another story, a candidate bought a scroll at the Chang'an book market and circulated it as his own; unknowingly, he ended up presenting it to the original author. Another candidate is said to have accidentally switched the two scrolls prepared for different patrons; in doing so, he offended the first reader by evoking his family taboos. In contrast to the normal practice of selecting a handful of writing samples, another man deliberately presented forty scrolls to show off his voluminous production. Meanwhile, two candidates who called on the wrong door received a nice surprise: soon afterward, they learned that their unintended host had been appointed as the examiner of the year. The accidental friendship paid off, for the story ended with the host fulfilling his promise to let them pass.

Even when a candidate was able to win the support of his intended reader with his presented writing, he would still feel trepidation about his future. Zhu Qingyu (who passed in 826), for example, sent the following famous poem to his patron Zhang Ji (768–830) before the examination, in the hope of getting some reassurance:

PRESENTED TO ZHANG JI, DIRECTOR OF BUREAU OF WATERWAYS AND IRRIGATION, BEFORE THE [PRESENTED SCHOLAR] EXAMINATION 近試上張籍水部

    Last night red candles were laid out in the bridal chamber; 洞房昨夜停紅燭
2   Waiting for dawn, I was to pay tribute to my parents-in-law in front of the main hall. 待曉堂前拜舅姑
    After finishing my toilette, I asked my husband in a low voice: 粧罷低聲問夫壻
4   "Are my painted eyebrows in fashion or not?" 畫眉深淺入時無

[QTS 515.5892]

In the voice of a bride who is anxious to meet her parents-in-law for the first time and who asks her new husband whether her painted eyebrows are in fashion, Zhu Qingyu skillfully conveys his anxiety about the upcoming examination. By displacing the trio of candidate, patron, and examiner onto the standard set of family relations, the poem foregrounds the proper power relationship between them, in particular the strong, even intimate bonds between candidate and patron.

Zhang Ji is said to have answered with the following poem:

A REPLY TO ZHU QINGYU 酬朱慶餘

    The image of a girl from Yue with fresh makeup emerged at the center of the mirror; 越女新妝出鏡心
2   Knowing her own brightness and beauty, she nonetheless remained hesitant. 自知明豔更沈吟
    The silk from Qi is far from being the most valuable in the world of mortals; 齊紈未是人間貴
4   A single tune of her singing on picking water caltrop is worth ten thousand taels of gold. 一曲菱歌敵萬金

[QTS 386.4362]

In response to Zhu Qingyu's self-projection in a feminine persona, Zhang Ji, in the confident voice of an established man, lavishes praise on the girl/candidate to put her/his mind at ease. The external beauty and internal brightness of the girl become the metaphor for Zhu's talent, and the market value of her singing performance shows Zhang's valuation of Zhu, emphasizing his anticipation of Zhu's imminent success. In gendered performances, the poetic exchange between the patron and the protégé reiterates both their close relationship and their hierarchical status.

Poetry was not only an essential instrument for success before and during the presented scholar examination; it was also an important means of celebration and bonding in the post-examination phase. The poet Meng Jiao (751–814), for instance, succeeded in 796, after years of failure. He expressed his joy in the following poem:

AFTER PASSING THE PRESENTED SCHOLAR EXAMINATION　　登科後

	My failures of the past are not worth bringing up;	昔日齷齪不足誇
2	This morning I feel unrestrained, with endless streams of thoughts.	今朝放蕩思無涯
	Happily content with the spring breezes and on the back of a fast horse,	春風得意馬蹄疾
4	I finished seeing all the flowers of Chang'an within one single day.	一日看盡長安花

[*MDYSJ* 3.55]

In this poem, the contrast between the past and the present is overwhelming, as the poet enjoys his elevated status as a new star of the capital. Surveying the flowers of Chang'an on horseback, he himself also becomes the focal point of the public's envious gaze. The transformative power of success in the presented scholar examination for the life of an individual was emphasized time and again in celebratory poems, which often evoke the analogies of a mortal attaining the status of an immortal in heaven or a fish turning into a dragon by jumping over the Dragon Gate.

Successful candidates for the presented scholar examination were expected to perform a set of elaborate public rituals. Although details of these examination rituals varied over time, the central components included ceremonies of gratitude at court and public gatherings in different parts of the capital. After the pass list was issued, new graduates converged to thank their examiner for awarding them degrees. This more personal ritual, held at a private residence, formalized their emotional attachment (and political loyalty) to the examiner. Because of its potential for factionalism, however, this rite was banned in the Song (960–1279). From the mid-ninth century, new degree holders also conducted a procession through the central secretariat to declare their obligation to all the high officials who were present, sometimes including the emperor.

In addition to these rites of passage involving political authority, the cohort of new graduates also held a series of banquets and ceremonial gatherings. These served the dual purposes of bonding among themselves and public display. Each person had to contribute a certain amount of money to cover the cost of provisions and personnel, including musicians, courtesans, and caterers. The new graduates would gather to admire the spring flowers, sign their names at the Ci'en Monastery, and play games of hit-ball, among many other activities. The celebrations concluded with a grand feast, accompanied by parades and music, near the waters of the Qujiang resort. These occasions attracted a large audience and are said to have been an opportunity for eminent families to select sons-in-law from these new stars of officialdom.

Poetry was an integral part of all post-examination celebrations, for it was the fitting medium of commemoration for these people who were chosen for their poetic talent. Although group compositions were common at literati gatherings, they were particularly meaningful at the celebrations of new graduates. The poetic exchange between new degree holders helped to define their shared identity as the chosen few of the year, a marker and a bond that would endure throughout their lives. As the person who brought them together, the examiner enjoyed extensive, sincere compliments and looked forward to the bright futures of his protégés. This poetic bonding also extended to other people who were related to the examiner and the graduates in one way or another.

For instance, in 844, more than twenty years after his first appointment as an examiner, Wang Qi (760–847) assumed that role a third time and passed twenty-two candidates. Zhou Chi (793–851), his former graduate and now the prefect of Huazhou, sent a verse to congratulate him and his new graduates. In the poem, Zhou praised his former examiner for receiving the extraordinary honor of a third appointment as examiner and recalled his own success and their friendship in subsequent years. He also expressed his envy of the youthful new stars and, employing the rhetoric of regret that he could not be physically present because of his own duties, he called attention to his superiority as a high-ranking official. Wang and his new graduates each composed a poem in reply. For his part, Wang joyfully reaffirmed old and new bonds with his graduates. The new stars enthusiastically echoed Zhou in complimenting their examiner, while conveying their admiration of Zhou as a model of success.

Whereas poetry was critical for the cohort of new graduates, it was no less important for failed candidates. It was not unusual for these less fortunate people to vent their anger and frustration by composing and circulating anonymous poems criticizing their examiner. In one anecdote, an examiner passed Yan Biao as the top graduate because he mistook this candidate for a descendant of the loyalist martyr Yan Zhenqing (709–785). Understandably, he became the subject of public ridicule, as expressed in the lines of an anonymous doggerel: "The mind of the examiner is shallow and out of touch; / For he wrongly assumed Yan Biao as [an offspring of] Lord Yan." In another story, however, a candidate went against such cliché, sending to his examiner a poem of sorrow rather than resentment for not being selected; the examiner was so moved that he later let this candidate pass when he presided over the examination again.

Most failed candidates had to start another round of struggle, from scroll presentations to sitting for examinations. The post-examination period was often a time of travel, to go home for family visits and/or to seek patronage. If successful candidates were excited about the prospect of returning home and celebrating with their families, their unsuccessful counterparts were filled with disappointment and sorrow. Meng Jiao, for instance, composed the following emotional poem before his success in 796:

HAVING FAILED THE [PRESENTED SCHOLAR] EXAMINATION		落第
	It is hard for the moon of dawn to look bright;	曉月難爲光
2	It is hard for a sad man to have good moods.	愁人難爲腸
	Who said plants are flourishing in the spring?	誰言春物榮
4	Did he not see the frost on their leaves?	豈見葉上霜
	Eagles and fish hawks were distressed after falling into disgrace;	鵰鶚失勢病

6	Yet wrens are flying on borrowed wings.	鷦鷯假翼翔
	Having been rejected time and again,	棄置復棄置
8	I feel as if being cut by knives.	情如刀刃傷

[MDYSJ 3.50]

In addition, Meng Jiao also wrote other poems, entitled "Having Failed Once More" ("Zai luodi"), "A Farewell Poem to People Who Have Known Me in Chang'an, as I Go East for Home After Failing the Examination" ("Xiadi donggui liubie chang'an zhiji"), "To Censor Liu Fu in the East Censorate, as I Return to Wu Without Success" ("Shiyi gui Wu yin ji dongtai Liu Fu shiyu"), and "Traveling Southeast After Failing the Examination" ("Xiadi dongnan xing"). Similar poems can also be seen in the extant works of many educated men. Clearly, failure became a major poetic topos in its own right.

Friends of these distraught men usually tried to encourage and comfort them—again through poetry. Meng Jiao's good friend Han Yu (768–824), for example, wrote a poem entitled "To Scholar Meng" ("Meng sheng shi") to send him off after he failed the examination and decided to seek audience with Zhang Jianfeng, governor of Xuzhou. In this composition, Han expressed his high regard for Meng and his confidence that Meng would win the support of Zhang Jianfeng. Meng Jiao himself wrote similar sympathetic poems for other failed candidates, including "Farewell to Cui Yinliang, Who Failed the Examination" ("Songbie Cui Yinliang xiadi") and "Seeing off Wen Chu, Who Failed the Examination" ("Song Wen Chu xiadi"). While poetic exchanges facilitated extensive bonding between members of the examination community, as we see in the well-known friendship between Bai Juyi and Yuan Zhen (chapter 16), such poems from fellow men of letters, in particular, kept failed candidates going by offering sympathy, support, and hope.

Although candidates were preoccupied with their patrons and fellow examinees, their families also loomed large in their minds. Liu Deren (fl. 821–847), a middle Tang poet and son of a royal princess, wrote the following lines after decades of repeated failures: "Turning to look at my family, I should indeed feel ashamed; / Since I put on my hemp robe, my head has turned white [without success]." Unfortunately, he passed away before he could attain success, prompting extensive poetic tributes from his contemporaries. He became a symbol of the star-crossed candidate whose personal talent and lifelong persistence did nothing to ward off rejections.

Although most candidates' wives remain marginal or even invisible in the literary record, contemporary anecdotes reveal that some educated women also made their voices heard. The wife of Du Gao (presented scholar degree in 789), for instance, is said to have been so disappointed by her husband's failures that she sent him the following poem:

	You, my dear, indeed have extraordinary talent;	良人的的有奇才
2	How come you have been sent back year after year?	何事年年被放迴
	Now that I am embarrassed to face you again,	如今妾已羞君面
4	Please make sure to come at night when you arrive.	君到來時近夜來

[YQZ 10]

We are told that, upon seeing the poem, Du Gao immediately turned back to the capital and eventually passed. A later version of the story contains a sequel in which the wife wrote another poem to her husband after his success, this time congratulating him and expressing her anxiety that he would not come home and would make new romantic liaisons as a new celebrity in the capital.

Such anxieties were not unfounded, because members of the examination community were frequent visitors to the entertainment quarters. Courtesans were often trained in music, singing, dancing, and poetry. Xue Tao (768–831), a courtesan in southwest China, made a reputation for poetic talent and had extensive poetic exchanges with many important officials and writers. The intersections between courtesan culture and examination culture were particularly visible in contemporary poetry and narrative. Examination candidates often socialized with courtesans and other literati in the Pingkang Ward (also known as the Northern Ward), the red-light district of Chang'an. Poetry was an important medium in the development of personal bonds between candidates and courtesans, despite the underlying economic transaction in their relationship. Recalling his youthful experiences in the Northern Ward, Sun Qi (fl. 870–898) describes how a poem he wrote to compliment a girl, Wang Funiang, became her favorite, and she asked him to compose three more and to inscribe them on her wall. With her heart set on Sun, the girl later presented him with a poem, pleading with him to buy her freedom:

	Grieving day after day, I have no plan for my future;	日日悲傷未有圖
2	I do not bother to tell ordinary men what is on my mind.	懶將心事話凡夫
	I am not spilt water that cannot be gathered up again;	非同覆水應收得
4	I just want to ask if you, my immortal mate, are interested.	只問仙郎有意無

[BLZ 33]

Sun replied with a matching poem, using the same rhyming characters as her original:

	How did this delicate beauty come up with a plan for her future?	韶妙如何有遠圖
2	Yet unable to help her out, I am indeed not the right man for her.	未能相為信非夫
	Although a lotus is not tainted by the mud [from which it grows],	泥中蓮子雖無染
4	It is not proper [for me] to transplant it in [my] family garden.	移入家園未得無

[BLZ 34]

Politely, Sun Qi turned her down, explaining that her request was beyond his capacity. Sun and the heartbroken girl eventually went their separate ways, although she was clearly very much on his mind when he wrote his *Record of the Northern Ward* (*Beili zhi*).

In addition to romantic relationships, poems by courtesans and examination participants could also be personal in other ways, as they sympathized or bantered with each other. The courtesan world was also an unofficial sphere for poetic competitions among men, who vied with one another for women's attention and for recognition of their wit, taste, and personality.

Poetry was one of the most lasting legacies of the Tang examination culture. Gaining entry to the roll of officials through examinations was only one of many avenues in the Tang; despite the prestige and high visibility that presented scholar degree holders enjoyed, they represented only a small proportion of the total official intake. Nonetheless, the mechanism of tiered competitions and the cycles of examination participation and rituals foreshadowed the advent of an examination society in the

FIGURE 11.1 A Ming dynasty woodblock print illustration that portrays the top graduate of 1604 drunk in the examination cell, but fortunately awakened by a mysterious man in his dream just in time to complete his tests. Reproduction from Gu Zuxun 顧祖訓, ed., *Zhuangyuan tu kao* 狀元圖考 (Illustrated Survey of Top [Ming] Graduates) (Taipei: Mingwen shuju, 1991), 255.

Song and later (figure 11.1). Poetry continued to be a central part of the post-Tang examination curriculum, until the ascendancy of neo-Confucianism, which advocated classical learning and moral cultivation, led to its elimination in the late fourteenth century. It was, however, reinstated in the mid-eighteenth century and lasted through the late nineteenth century, shortly before the examination system was abolished in 1905. Despite the fluctuations in the status of poetic composition in the examination curriculum, poetry retained its critical role, for the next millennium, as a powerful medium of interpersonal communications that bound the examination community together.

MANLING LUO

NOTE

1. These examinations used to be held by a vice director of the Bureau of Evaluations in the Ministry of Personnel. After a dispute between a candidate and the presiding official erupted in 736, it became customary to have the director

of the Ministry of Rites serve as the examiner. The national-level tests were usually held in the capital Chang'an, but sometimes in the eastern capital Luoyang. Toward the end of the dynasty, when the court went into exile, the competitions were held where the court was stationed.

PRIMARY SOURCES

BLZ	Sun Qi 孫棨 (fl. 870–898). *Beili zhi* 北里誌 (Record of the Northern Ward). Shanghai: Gudian wenxue chubanshe, 1957.
MDYSJ	Meng Jiao 孟郊 (751–814). *Meng Dongye shiji* 孟東野詩集 (The Poetry Collection of Meng Dongye). Beijing: Renmin wenxue chubanshe, 1959.
QTS	Peng Dingqiu 彭定求 (1645–1719) et al., eds. *Quan Tang shi* 全唐詩 (Complete Tang *Shi* Poetry). 25 vols. Beijing: Zhonghua shuju, 1979.
YQZ	*Yuquanzi* 玉泉子 (Master Jade Spring). Beijing: Zhonghua shuju, 1958.

SUGGESTED READINGS

ENGLISH

Mair, Victor H. "Scroll Presentation in the T'ang Dynasty." *Harvard Journal of Asiatic Studies* 38, no. 1 (1978): 35–60.

Moore, Oliver. *Rituals of Recruitment in Tang China: Reading an Annual Programme in the* Collected Statements *by Wang Dingbao (870–940)*. Leiden: Brill, 2004.

Owen, Stephen, ed. *The Cambridge History of Chinese Literature*. Vol. 1. Cambridge: Cambridge University Press, 2010.

Rouzer, Paul F. *Articulated Ladies: Gender and the Male Community in Early Chinese Texts*. Cambridge: Harvard University Asia Center, 2001, 249–283.

Twitchett, Denis C. *The Birth of the Chinese Meritocracy: Bureaucrats and Examinations in T'ang China*. London: China Society, 1976.

CHINESE

Fan Shu 范攄 (fl. 875–888). *Yunxi youyi* 雲溪友議 (Master Cloud Creek's Discussions with Friends). Shanghai: Zhonghua shuju, 1959.

Fu Xuancong 傅璇琮. *Tangdai keju yu wenxue* 唐代科舉與文學 (Civil Service Examinations and Literature in the Tang). Xi'an: Shanxi renmin chubanshe, 1986.

Wang Dingbao 王定保 (870–940). *Tang zhi yan* 唐摭言 (Collected Accounts of the Tang). Shanghai: Shanghai guji chubanshe, 1978.

Xue Yongruo 薛用弱 (fl. 806–827). *Jiyi ji* 集異記 (Record of the Extraordinary). Beijing: Zhonghua shuju, 1980.

Zheng Xiaoxia 鄭曉霞. *Tangdai keju shi yanjiu* 唐代科舉詩研究 (Tang Examination Poetry). Shanghai: Fudan daxue chubanshe, 2006.

12

TANG WOMEN AT THE PUBLIC/PRIVATE DIVIDE

Writing, particularly of poetry, was a shared activity in Tang China. Many of the poems that have survived from the Tang and the surrounding dynasties were composed in response to other poems, as a part of correspondence, or in social gatherings that often included assigned topics, contests, and so forth. Writing was not, for the most part, accomplished in Virginia Woolf's "room of one's own" but rather in the rooms of others and with others. In this sense it was more a public than a private activity.

This presented a challenge for women's literary expression. Although women had not always been secluded in Chinese society, by the Tang seclusion had become the mark of respectable high-class society. By extension, a woman's writing was not for public consumption, for in the Chinese tradition, poetry was an expression of one's intent, and through it one made one's self known to others.[1] The writing woman, by exchanging or circulating her works, was in effect circulating her self—her emotions and thoughts, the interior self, the knowledge of which should be reserved for her husband and family. Women whose poems circulated widely were perhaps as morally suspect as women who allowed their beauty to be viewed widely. In this context, it should not be surprising that many women poets whose works survive from this period were courtesan-entertainers (*ji*), or Daoist nuns, who often functioned as de facto courtesans.

INNER/OUTER (*NEI/WAI*)

What I discuss here as the public/private divide is a way to familiarize the Western reader with one facet of the ritual distinction in traditional Chinese culture between inner (*nei*) and outer (*wai*). Respecting this distinction was a sign of the most basic level of civilization.[2] The women's quarters were known as the "inner" quarters, while the "outer" portions of a house or compound were the province of men. This distinction was enforced and reinforced through ritual prescriptions that governed the separation between inner and outer, female and male. One Song dynasty writer summarized the expectations as follows:

> In housing there should be a strict demarcation between the inner and outer parts, with a door separating them. The two parts should share neither a well, a washroom, nor a privy. The men are in charge of all affairs on the outside, the women manage the inside affairs. During the day, the men do not stay in their private rooms nor the women go beyond the inner door without good reason. A

woman who has to leave the inner quarters must cover her face.... The doorman and old servants serve to pass messages and objects between the inner and outer quarters of the house....

A girl ten or older does not go out, which means she remains permanently inside.³

These ritual expectations were originally laid out in the pre-Qin classic, the *Book of Rites* (*Liji*). During the Tang, there was a renewed interest in ritual propriety and the moral duties of women. The Han dynasty text *Admonitions for Women* (*Nü jie*) (ca. 106), by Ban Zhao (ca. 45–116), was largely ignored before the Tang, when it was reprinted along with three other texts as part of the *Classics for Women* (*Nü sishu*). One of these texts, the *Analects for Women* (*Nü lunyu*), clearly restates the ritual requirement for separation: "Inner and outer each have their place. Males and females gather separately. Women do not peek through the walls, nor step into the outer courtyard. If they go out, they must cover their faces. If they look out, they conceal their forms."⁴

So entrenched was this cultural boundary that it had long been exploited for poetic effect. One of the most common conventional female voices in the Chinese tradition is that of the "abandoned woman," a woman waiting for the return of a traveling or military man or lamenting her abandonment by an unfaithful husband or lover. In this tradition, known as the *guiyuan* (lament of the women's quarters), the inner/outer boundary is a ubiquitous trope, whether in the form of a doorway, a curtain, or an enclosed courtyard. The woman's grief is contained behind the curtain, but, correspondingly, the curtain suggests the bedchamber and the woman's empty bed, and the positioning of a female subject at the doorway—at the border of inner and outer—is also erotically charged. In this example from the Han dynasty "Nineteen Old Poems" (☞ *HTRCP* chap. 5; *WKB* P60), this connection is already apparent:

GREEN, GREEN, THE RIVERSIDE GRASSES　　青青河畔草

	Green, green, the riverside grasses,	青青河畔草
2	Thick and full, the willows in the yard.	鬱鬱園中柳
	Plump, plump, a woman in the tower	盈盈樓上女
4	Gleaming bright at the windowsill.	皎皎當窗牖
	Lovely, lovely her powder and rouge,	娥娥紅粉粧
6	Delicate, slender, a hand appears.	纖纖出素手
	Once a girl in a singing house,	昔為倡家女
8	Now the wife of a wanderer.	今為蕩子婦
	The wanderer doesn't return from his travels—	蕩子行不歸
10	It's hard to keep an empty bed alone.⁵	空牀難獨守

[*XQHWJNBCS* 329]

It is important to note that this distinction did not usually amount to a full purdah-type seclusion of women and that many women participated in commerce and exercised considerable authority in their households. Tang women attended public events, such as temple gatherings and even, as we will see, polo tournaments. However, the degree to which a family could demonstrate adherence to ritual practice was an important indicator of its status. As Patricia Ebrey puts it, "The upper class made its distinctiveness visible . . . by making its women invisible."[6] A talented woman who grew up in a family of lower social status was thus more likely to have the freedom (or the economic obligation) to cross this *nei/wai* boundary by entering the entertainment district or becoming a court entertainer (*gongji*). Conversely, a family whose fortunes went into decline might find itself obligated to place its educated daughters as entertainers or concubines. This was the case for Xue Tao (768–831), whose story will be related later.

Another avenue for women who needed to escape economic hardship, whether because of declining family fortunes or the loss of favor of a husband or patron, was to enter a Daoist or Buddhist monastery. By the Tang, Buddhism had a large and well-established monastic system, which influenced practitioners of popular Daoism to also create monasteries and convents. A woman who entered a Daoist nunnery might be known thereafter as a nun, whether she continued to live there or not; this was the case for Li Ye (d. 784) and Yu Xuanji (844?–868).

The lifestyle of nuns and courtesans by definition violates the barrier between public and private. Traditionally, Chinese women were defined by their relationship to their fathers, husbands, and sons. Nuns and courtesans, by leaving home and eschewing marriage and children, lived beyond the reach of these traditional relationships. This is not to say that these women enjoyed "freedom" in any modern sense of the world. The courtesan's movements and actions, in particular, were subject to the rules of her house, which functioned as a sort of stand-in for family, complete with a "mother." Her movements would have been limited to the entertainment districts of the large cities, beyond which she was not to venture. If she were lucky enough to secure a patron, she was at the mercy of his whims and could be sent away for any or no reason. However, her lifestyle did permit her to socialize extensively with men outside her immediate family and to be a part of their outer, public sphere.

Courtesans came in several varieties, which spanned the social ladder from common prostitutes to high-class and palace entertainers (*gongji*), whose primary duties were musical and literary. During the Tang, the government controlled official entertainment or brothel districts, in which courtesans were registered and classified by level and beyond which their movements were restricted.[7] The practice of frequenting these districts on the part of scholar-officials and elites was taken for granted and indeed expected (see chapter 11). The sexual aspect of the courtesan's life was secondary to her role as a social and literary partner or hostess. In this respect, she was similar to the Japanese geisha. Women of good families were sometimes educated so that they could cultivate their character through study and so that they could participate in poetic and literary exchanges within the family or within marriage. Women of lower rank, on the other hand, might have been sold at a young age and given their literary and musical training specifically for the purpose of serving as an entertainer.[8]

The courtesan was at once looked upon with suspicion, because she exercised her literary talents outside the confines of the family compound (where, even if sex was secondary, she enjoyed considerable freedom), and respected by her male literati clients and guests, functioning in many ways as their equal. Although literary nuns and courtesans were appreciated by their contemporaries for their poetry, music, and intelligent companionship, they would never escape the stigma of their chosen lifestyle, and neither path was considered an appropriate or desirable choice for one's daughter.

The association of literary talent with these questionable classes explains why, in at least one recorded case, a respectable Tang woman chooses to burn her collected poems upon her marriage, in order to devote herself to her domestic duties, as if the very existence of her writings is a threat to her ability to be faithful in her new role as wife:

> Lady Sun of Lechang was the wife of the student Meng Changqi. She was an expert in the composition of poems, but one day she burned her collected works because she felt that poetry was not the proper work of a married woman. From that day forward, she devoted herself solely to her wifely tasks.
>
> [TRYSHB 2215; TRANS. IDEMA AND GRANT, 165]

So strong was this association that it was difficult for people to separate literary talent from a morally questionable lifestyle. With regard to both Li Ye and Xue Tao, there exist anecdotes concerning their precocious poetic talent in childhood that assume this negative association:

> Li Jilan [Li Ye] was famed for her talents despite the fact that she was a woman. When she was five or six years old, her father carried her in his arms into the courtyard, where she composed a poem on roses, the last lines of which read:
>
> > If for a moment left unsupported by a trellis
> > They will tend to stray wildly in all directions.
>
> Her father said angrily: "This girl will later be blessed with literary style, but she is bound to end up as a fallen woman."
>
> [TRYSHB 841; TRANS. IDEMA AND GRANT, 180]

A similar anecdote exists concerning Xue Tao as a child:

> One day, her father pointed to the *wutong* tree in their courtyard, and recited:
>
> > In front of the courtyard steps an ancient *wutong* tree:
> > Its towering trunk rises up into the clouds.
>
> When he ordered Tao to continue the poem, she immediately responded with the following lines:
>
> > Its branches welcome birds from north and south,
> > Its leaves send off the winds that come and go.
>
> This left her father filled with sadness for a long time.
>
> [TRYSHB 1128; TRANS. IDEMA AND GRANT, 182]

Her father is sad because Xue Tao, in her ready completion of the quatrain, has employed a metaphor that suggests the life of a courtesan.

The historical accuracy of both of these anecdotes should be regarded with suspicion, as they are very likely the stuff of legends that grew up around these famous women poets. What they do show is, first, the way a young woman of good family might have been taught to write poetry in the context of her home; and second, the extent to which an extraordinary poetic talent would have been viewed as a harbinger of a disreputable fate. This was natural because, having no access to the well-bred man's path to civil service, a well-bred woman of literary talent during the Tang had no legitimate outlet for circulating her work in the broader society beyond the walls of her family compound.

The requirement to maintain the boundary between public and private extended all the way to the imperial court. In the case of the emperor, the pull of "private" affections was particularly feared because of the potential for the family of the emperor's lover (the "in-laws" [*waiqi*]) to exercise undue power and control over the emperor. (Yang Guifei is a prime example; see chapter 16.) In fact, this is exactly what happens in the case of Empress Wu, or Wu Zhao (better known as Wu Zetian, 627–705, r. 690–705), a palace woman whose power grows so great that she eventually becomes empress in her own right. Although her reign came to be viewed in the kind of negative light in which other female pretenders to power have been seen by posterity, Wu is also remembered as an able ruler. She is especially known for her expansion of the civil service examination system (see chapter 11). Her patronage of literary figures and her inclusion of poetry in the civil service examination would have lasting significance for the elevation of poetry during the Tang.

Wu Zetian also was an important patroness of Shangguan Wan'er (664–710), a remarkable palace woman who became an arbiter of poetic ability and a ghostwriter for both Empress Wu and her son and successor, Emperor Zhongzong. In this sense, Wu Zetian's reign marks a period of unprecedented female power in the public spheres of both the court and literary life.

THE STORY OF A TATTOOED WOMAN: SHANGGUAN WAN'ER

Wu Zetian entered the court as a consort to Emperor Taizong of the Tang in 640 at the age of thirteen. After Taizong's death, Wu became consort to his successor, Gaozong, and then Gaozong's "empress" in 655. By 665, she was performing imperial sacrifices—the only woman in history ever to have enacted this important ritual function reserved for the emperor himself. On the abdication of her son in 690, Empress Wu declared a new dynasty, the Zhou, with herself as its emperor—the only woman in Chinese history ever to take the title of Son of Heaven to herself. This dynasty would last until her death in 705, when power reverted to her son, the new Emperor Zhongzong.

During her years of influence, Wu Zetian was an important patroness of poets and of projects of Confucian and Buddhist scholarship. She is also remembered for her ruthlessness and great cruelty toward her rivals. When she replaced Empress Wang in the affections of Emperor Gaozong, she had that former empress, along with a former favorite imperial concubine, "flogged a hundred times, their arms and legs cut off, and their truncated bodies thrown into wine vats."[9] Nevertheless, she was posthumously given the title *Zetian*, meaning "models herself on Heaven" (figure 12.1).

Shangguan Wan'er was no stranger to Wu Zetian's ruthlessness. Along with other women of her household, she was raised as a slave in the court of Empress Wu, knowing that both her father and her grandfather had been executed for plotting against the empress. As she grew up, Shangguan quickly showed her talent and soon became indispensable to the empress. Following Empress Wu's

FIGURE 12.1 Woodblock print of Wu Zetian, from the *Li dai gu ren xiang zan* 歷代古人像贊 (Images and Eulogies of the People of Antiquity through the Dynasties). Ming dynasty (1498).

death in 705, she continued to serve at court through the reign of Emperor Zhongzong. Interestingly, female power continued to dominate the court under Zhongzong, in the person of Zhongzong's Empress Wei and her two daughters. It is thought that many of the works both of Empress Wu and of Zhongzong actually came from Shangguan's pen. Even after her execution, in 710, following the coup that placed Emperor Xuanzong (r. 712–756) on the throne, the new emperor commissioned the poet Zhang Yue (663–730) to assemble a collection of her works. She is known by the sobriquet Zhaorong, given to her by Emperor Zhongzong, and meaning "Shining Countenance." Zhang Yue writes glowingly of her literary powers:

> She was exceptional in virtue and the most talented member of her generation. Her perceptive insight and listening enabled her to probe the mysteries of the world and to reflect its underlying principles. When she opened a scroll, she absorbed everything in it like the ocean, as if she had heard it all before, and when she wrote, her brush moved like flying clouds, as if her reasoning had been organized in advance.[10]

In the same preface, Zhang Yue presents a very positive view of female influence over the emperor:

> To the high-ranking and powerful [the emperor] must listen with suspicion, while those who are low-ranking and cut off by protocol are kept apart from him. Frivolous advice from intimate attendants will tend to be discounted by him, while officials who are distant and of loyal minds will often seem refractory in what they say. He can listen only to voices of feminine charm and gentility, of nurturing

and benevolent hearts. These ladies are oblivious of self-gratification as they stand in the crossroads of the nine virtues, and they infuse their feelings into the garden of the six arts.[11]

The suggestion that women, because of their position outside the complex factions and loyalties of male court life, could exert a uniquely positive influence on the emperor is remarkable in the context of a tradition replete with warnings about undue feminine influence.

Shangguan is also remembered as a judge of poets. A story in Zhang Yue's preface concerns this unique role:

When the Lady of Pei [Shangguan's mother] was expecting, she dreamed of a giant who gave her a huge scale and said, "This will be used to weigh and measure the whole world." Subsequently, Zhaorong was born, and when she was one month old her mother said playfully to her, "Are you the one who is going to weigh and measure the whole world?" The child gurgled in response, "I am." That she should have had the power of speech even at birth shows that she was favored with divine intelligence. When Zhaorong was still in swaddling clothes, she was taken into the apartments of the palace women. Heaven itself was advancing her, so that her family was ruined but she was to support the nation. Her star was rising so that her inner power was perfected and she was entrusted with office.[12]

The "office" in question was presumably that of examiner, but anecdotes survive that tell of her serving also in a less formal capacity as a judge of poetic compositions:

On the last day of the First Month, Emperor Zhongzong visited the Kunming pond. When it came time to write verse, the officials composed more than a hundred poems on imperial command. A platform was set up in front of the imperial tent, and Shangguan Wan'er was ordered to select one of the poems to be the text for a melody the emperor had recently composed. The officials congregated in front of the platform.[13]

At some point during her service at court, Shangguan offended Empress Wu in some manner (no details about this survive). Rather than suffer her to be executed, the empress had her tattooed on the face—tattooing was a common means of branding someone a criminal for life. Nevertheless, she was returned to favor and became extremely influential in Empress Wu's court, so that from 696 to 709 "she composed all of the state documents in the name of the empress. Practically all important decisions regarding military and civil affairs as well as those concerning life and death were made by her alone."[14]

Perhaps in part because of the tattoo that marred her face, Shangguan Wan'er was able to enjoy unprecedented influence without suffering the suspicion and reproach usually reserved for so-called kingdom-toppling beauties (*qing guo*). The source of her power seems to have been primarily intellectual as opposed to sexual, so that even Empress Wu did not perceive her as a threat to her own power. Still, in her later years, as consort to Emperor Zhongzong, she would be known for her affairs and favoritism.

Among her best-regarded works is a series of twenty-five poems written in 710, not long before her execution, on her visit with Emperor Zhongzong to the residence of Princess Changning, his daughter by a concubine.

VISITING PRINCESS CHANGNING'S POOL, NO. 17

遊長寧公主流杯池二十五首之十七

  Cliffs and gorges to climb to heart's content,　嚴壑恣登臨
2 Delighting the eye while also rejoicing the heart.　瑩目復怡心
  The wind in bamboo is like a transverse flute;　風篁類長笛
4 Flowing waters stand in for the music of lutes.　流水當鳴琴

[QTS 5:63]

This series of poems presents Shangguan's solitary encounter with nature. In this example, we see the speaker's sensual and emotional response to an outing in rugged surroundings, where natural sounds stand in for the music of a social or court gathering. The poet finds a satisfaction and joy in nature that rivals or surpasses her enjoyment of the imperial court. During the middle Tang period that followed, poets would often attempt to portray in their poems the sense of being a recluse, despite the fact that in life their natural excursions were only limited. In this sense, Shangguan is at the cutting edge of a literary trend that would become the hallmark of the high Tang[15] (the designation given to the reign of Xuanzong [712–756], which is considered the golden age of Chinese poetry).

Shangguan Wan'er is one of the most influential women ever to have served at court, apart perhaps from Wu Zhao herself. Among the thousands of palace women, few exercised anywhere near this level of power and influence, whether in affairs of state or in cultural and literary life. Perhaps because she happened to live during an unusual period of feminine dominance at court, her influence was allowed to enter spheres traditionally reserved for men alone. The story of our next example, the poetess Li Ye (d. 784), was perhaps more typical of a literary woman at court.

THE STORY OF A TRAITOR: LI YE

Li Ye first proved her literary talents in her independent life as a Daoist nun, and then, later in life, was twice selected to serve the imperial court. In her case, induction into imperial service constituted a recognition of her already well-established talents. In the palace, the literary woman could pursue her very "public" art for the benefit of the most illustrious male patron, the emperor himself, while remaining properly "secluded" from the public eye by virtue of having been accepted into the imperial household. In this way, Li Ye's prestige and talent could be co-opted to benefit the emperor and his court while also being brought firmly under familial and imperial control.

Literary women in the palace had a history dating back at least to the Han, when Ban Zhao served as tutor to the Empress Deng. Ban canonized her instructions for younger women in her *Admonitions for Women*, a text detailing the morality and duties of a virtuous woman. Ban Zhao also made significant contributions to the *History of the Former Han* (*Han Shu*), which was initiated by her father and continued by her brother, the historian Ban Gu (32–92). She is best known, however, as a moralist. Ban Zhao's *Admonitions*, originally addressed to her own daughters, gained in popularity in the Tang and spawned imitations such as the *Book of Filial Piety for Women* (*Nü xiaojing*) and the *Analects for Women*, both of which imitated Ban Zhao's style, which itself emulated the Confucian classics.

By the Tang dynasty, the atmosphere of the court had changed. The Tang emperors were much more cosmopolitan than their Han predecessors, welcoming the performance of songs and dances from what was then known as the "West" (Central Asia), and generally participating in and encouraging the culture of poetic patronage and circulation that made the Tang the golden age of poetry. Emperor Xuanzong, in his enthusiasm for the popular new music that was entering China from Central Asia during the Tang, maintained a special official music conservatory, known as the *jiaofang*, or Entertainment Bureau, where some especially talented female entertainers served as instructors, as well as the *Liyuan* (Pear Garden), a kind of elite corps into which the best of the *jiaofang* entertainers were inducted to serve at official and imperial functions.

It was in this rich cultural atmosphere that Li Ye was invited to contribute her poetic talents. We do not know exactly what Li Ye's position at court was. We do know how it ended. In 783, during her second tenure at court under Emperor Dezong, the rebel Zhu Ci arose and briefly took control of the capital. During this period, Li Ye wrote a poem addressed to him that was so positive in tone it was considered treasonous when the young emperor returned and reestablished control of the capital. Li Ye was removed from the palace and beaten to death with a club. Her poem was read as evidence of her lack of loyalty to the throne. Unfortunately, we cannot examine the evidence, as the poem was considered too treasonous to be preserved by contemporary historians. Her death demonstrates the precarious nature of a court position; to have shown adequate loyalty to Emperor Dezong would certainly have meant placing her life in jeopardy under the rebel Zhu Ci.

One of Li Ye's best-regarded poems tells us something about the level of poetic skill she had attained, and also offers some glimpses into the cultural practice of poetry writing.

ATTENDING XIAO SHUZI WHILE LISTENING TO THE ZITHER;
THE TOPIC ASSIGNED TO ME WAS "SONG ON THE FLOWING
SPRINGS NEAR THE THREE GORGES"　從蕭叔子聽彈琴賦得三峽流泉歌

	My home once lay among the clouds of Mount Wu,	妾家本住巫山雲
2	I would often hear the Flowing Springs of that mountain.	巫山流泉常自聞
	The jade zither gradually reaches heights of desolation—	玉琴彈出轉寥夐
4	Just like what I used to hear in my dreams.	直是當時夢裡聽
	The Three Gorges are far off, several thousand miles,	三峽迢迢幾千里
6	Yet all at once they flow into these lonely inner chambers.	一時流入幽閨裡
	Huge rocks, tumbling cliffs, flow from these playing fingers,	巨石崩崖指下生
8	Flying rapids, running waves arise from the strings.	飛泉走浪弦中起
	At first it seems to be the angry sound of storm and thunder;	初疑憤怒含雷風
10	Then again, sobbing moans, as if unable to flow—	又似嗚咽流不通
	Swirling whirlpools, eddying rapids, as if expending their last—	迴湍曲瀨勢將盡
12	And now, again, dripping on smooth sand.	時復滴瀝平沙中
	I remember of old when Ruan Ji composed this tune,	憶昔阮公為此曲
14	Even Zhong Rong could not hear it enough.	能令仲容聽不足
	Play it once to the end, then play it again,	一彈既罷復一彈
16	I wish we could make these flowing springs go on forever!	願作流泉鎮相續

[*TNSR* 8]

The first thing we notice about this poem is how very specific and information-laden is its title, situating it carefully in terms of the social context in which it was composed.[16] This is a natural expression of the social character of the practice of writing a poem: it is a record of a specific moment and a specific occasion, complete with a cast of characters. In this case, the title tells us that Li Ye is in attendance on a man. Together, they are listening to a musical performance, and, at the same time, presumably all members of the party have been assigned topics on which they are to compose poems. Li Ye is assigned to compose a poem based on an earlier poem, written by the famous poet Ruan Ji (210–263) some five centuries earlier. (Zhong Rong, mentioned in line 14, is Ruan's nephew, Ruan Xian, a legendary musician.)

To answer the challenge of composing on this topic, Li Ye had to have a deep and wide-ranging literary education. Familiarity with the earlier poem would have been assumed. To be considered a really good poet, Li Ye should treat the topic with subtlety and use it to demonstrate her own originality and talent. Her poem captures the drama and energy of the zither playing as well as the power of the natural scene. At the same time, its references to Mount Wu seem to identify her with the goddess of Mount Wu, made famous in a long Han dynasty poem that details her sexual encounter with the King of Chu in a dream. As such, the poem demonstrates some degree of self-consciousness concerning Li Ye's position as a courtesan.

The very existence of poems like this shows the extent to which, during the Tang, literary women like Li Ye were participating as equals in literary gatherings with men, as the next story shows more dramatically:

Once [Li Ye] was among several gentlemen who had gathered at the Kaiyuan Temple of Wucheng. Liu Changqing of Hejian was suffering from a male ailment. Li Ye mocked him, saying, "The mountain air is finest at sunset." Liu answered her, "And all the birds are pleased to shelter there." All present laughed heartily, and the comments praised the both of them.

[*TNSR* 21]

Li Ye is quoting a poem by Tao Qian, which offers her the chance to create a pun on "mountain air" that refers to Liu's ailment (a hernia). In his response, Liu quotes another Tao Qian line but uses a word that rhymes with "bird" and refers to a phallus.[17] The story highlights the role of poetry in the clever, lighthearted banter on these occasions. Clearly, women of Li Ye's stature enjoyed great freedom in their interactions with the literati, even to the extent that they could engage with their male companions in this type of bawdy joking.

A contemporary critic, Gao Zhongwu (fl. ca. 787), associates Li's poetic talent with her "masculine" personality: "Since her expressions and air are masculine, her poetry is also unrestrained" (*TNSR* 21). To participate fully in the masculine world of poetry and to gain its accolades, she has on some level adopted a masculine posture toward the world, one that recognizes her poetic and erotic powers and is not content to hide them in characteristically feminine modesty. Gao Zhongwu goes on to describe one of Li Ye's five-character lines as among the finest in Chinese poetry, high praise indeed for a female poet.

THE STORY OF A COURTESAN: XUE TAO

Despite Li Ye's poetic reputation, the best-known woman poet of the Tang dynasty is the courtesan-poetess Xue Tao (768–831), in part because of her reputed friendship with several famous poets of the time, most notably Yuan Zhen (779–831) and Bai Juyi (772–846) (see chapter 16). Xue Tao is described as a "registered courtesan" (*yueji*) in the southwest city of Chengdu, and elsewhere as a "garrison courtesan" (*yingji*).

Xue Tao's life trajectory is a good example of how a woman might end up as a courtesan. The daughter of a low-ranking official, she started life as the child of a good family of the capital, Chang'an. Her father was posted to Chengdu, in the southwestern province of Shu (present-day Sichuan). After her father died, leaving her mother a widow, Xue Tao was invited by the governor of Shu, Wei Gao, to serve at his banquets and to compose poems. Since she was unmarried and without her father's income or protection, it is easy to see why Xue Tao would have accepted this offer. She served in this capacity for twenty years, during which time the governor actually put her name forward for an official post as collator, a kind of official librarian or editor. Though sources suggest that this request was denied, Xue Tao was so often referred to as *nüjiaoshu* ("female collator") that the term "collator" would later come to be used as a euphemism for a prostitute. After leaving her position in the governor's household, she lived independently in Chengdu, in her own home.

During her career, Xue Tao moved in common circles with many of the premier poets of the time, including Yuan Zhen. The story of her acquaintance with Yuan Zhen, which dates to 809, suggests that Xue Tao's fame extended beyond her hometown of Chengdu:

As soon as Minister Yuan . . . heard that among the registered courtesans of Sichuan there was a certain Xue Tao who was competent in poetry and extremely eloquent, he continuously longed for her in his heart. When he was appointed an investigation commissioner, he asked to be posted to Sichuan, but as he was judging cases in his capacity as censor, it was impossible for him to go to visit her. When he was later [relieved of his duties and] transferred to the position of commissioner, the prefect Yan Shou, knowing of Yuan Zhen's desires, again and again sent Xue Tao over to him. When Yuan Zhen was about to depart, he did not dare take her with him.

[TNSR 86–87; TRANS. IDEMA AND GRANT, 188]

Among Xue Tao's works is a series of "Ten Poems on Separation," which have traditionally been regarded as addressed to Yuan Zhen. The repetitive, programmatic form of the poem series also supports the view that they might have been composed as part of some sort of poetic exercise or game. This form should be apparent in the two examples provided here:

THE WRITING BRUSH SEPARATED FROM THE HAND (TEN POEMS ON SEPARATION) 筆離手（十離詩）

    With its shaft from Yue and hairs from Xuan, it used to suit him just right; 越管宣毫始稱情
2   It scattered petals and cast gems across crimson slips. 紅箋紙上撒花瓊

	All because after long use the tip has grown blunt,	都緣用久鋒頭盡
4	It no longer gets to be held in Xizhi's hand.	不得羲之手裡擎

[TNSR 74]

The best reeds for writing brushes were found in the region of Yue in southeastern China (toward Vietnam), while the best hair (wolf or rabbit) was fitted to writing brushes in the town of Xuancheng (in modern Anhui province). Xizhi, in line 4, refers to the famous calligrapher Wang Xizhi (321–379) of the Six Dynasties period, whose style Xue Tao was well known for emulating in her own highly regarded calligraphy. With both of these references, Xue Tao is tooting her own horn, even as she complains of having been set aside, perhaps because of her age. This is also true of her reference to "crimson slips," which brings to mind a special small, handmade stationery she created for the exchange of poems, which would later be known as "Xue Tao slips."

If this poem suggests that the pen has been set aside due to no fault of its own, other poems of the series suggest a major faux pas is the reason for the speaker's loss of favor, as in the following example:

THE FISH SEPARATED FROM THE POND
(TEN POEMS ON SEPARATION) 　　　　　魚離池（十離詩）

	Four or five autumns she frolicked and leapt in the lotus pond,	戲躍蓮池四五秋
2	Often flicking her crimson tail to tease the hook and line.	常搖朱尾弄綸鉤
	For no reason, it caught and broke the stem of a lotus bloom—	無端擺斷芙蓉朵
4	Now she can no longer swim in the clear waves.	不得清波更一遊

[TNSR 75]

This poem more clearly suggests the relationship of a lover, through its reference in line 1 to the lotus plant (*lian*), which is a close homonym to the word for "love" or "attachment."

It is also possible that Xue Tao wrote these poems to one of her patrons. Both Wei Gao and, later, another patron, Wu Yuanheng, at different times banished her to the border region. As mentioned, Xue Tao is sometimes referred to as a "garrison courtesan"; this is probably due to these periods of banishment, from which some of her poems survive. The suffering and homesickness associated with being posted to a border location were common and well-established themes in the poetry of the Tang, due to centuries of constant threat from "barbarians" along China's long northern and western borders and the need for officials to serve in those remote areas. As the title of the following poem suggests, Xue Tao was sent to serve a border garrison as a punishment. As such, her fate is not dissimilar to that of male officials, for whom a posting in a border region constituted a kind of exile.

EXILED TO THE BORDER, MY FEELINGS, SENT
TO SECRETARY WEI (FIRST OF TWO POEMS) 　　罰赴邊有懷上韋令公（其一）

	I had heard tell of the sufferings of the border,	聞道邊城苦
2	But only now that I'm here do I begin to understand.	而今到始知

	Ashamed, I take up a song from your courts	羞將門下曲
4	And sing it for these boys of the Pass.	唱與隴頭兒

[TNSR 30]

Xue Tao's punishment was temporary, and she ended up living out her days in her own home back in Chengdu, as an independent woman once again. Her offense must have been a mild one, considering the fates of Li Ye and of the final poet we will consider, Yu Xuanji, both of whom lost their lives.

THE STORY OF A MURDERESS: YU XUANJI

A few decades after Xue Tao's death, a Daoist nun by the name of Yu Xuanji hosted a gathering in her home. One of her male guests went to relieve himself in the courtyard behind her house. There, he noticed some flies gathering in a particular spot. When he examined it more closely, the area appeared to be stained with blood, and it gave off a smell of putrefaction. After he left, he told his servant about the smell. The servant confided in his brother, who was a member of the police, and who also happened to bear a grudge against Yu Xuanji. He gathered a group of officers with shovels and spades. Upon digging up that spot in Yu Xuanji's yard, the officers uncovered a corpse. Taken before the authorities, Yu Xuanji confessed to murdering her maid, Lüqiao, and burying her in the garden. Some months later, having reached only her midtwenties, she was executed.

This story might not have so captured the public imagination, had it not been for the fact that Yu Xuanji was a famous poetess and sometime companion of Wen Tingyun (813?–870), a well-known poet of the late Tang (on this poet, ☞ *HTRCP* C12.4–C12.5; *WKB* P46, P63–P64). As a young woman, Yu Xuanji had been the concubine of a high government official, the censor Li Yi. After Li Yi's wife became jealous of her, the relationship ended. This poem, alternately titled "To the Neighbor Girl" and "To Secretary Li Yi," expresses her complaint at her treatment:

	TO THE NEIGHBOR GIRL (OR, TO SECRETARY LI YI)	贈鄰女（寄李億員外）
	Shy of the sun, I block it with silken sleeve;	羞日遮羅袖
2	Spring worries, too lazy to rise for my toilet.	愁春懶起粧
	Priceless jewels are easily attained,	易求無價寶
4	But a man with a heart is hard to find.	難得有心郎
	Onto the pillow tears fall unseen;	枕上潛垂淚
6	Amidst flowers, a heart secretly breaks.	花間暗斷腸
	When I could watch Song Yu,	自能窺宋玉
8	What use to resent Wang Chang?[18]	何必恨王昌

[TNSR 96]

Song Yu is the romantic protagonist of a long pre-Qin poem attributed to him (on the *fu*, or rhapsody, ☞ *HTRCP* chap. 3). He successfully maintained his distance from a great beauty who watched him for three years from over a wall. Anyone who would inspire such dogged pursuit, by a great beauty at that, must be an extraordinary catch indeed. Wang Chang, likewise, is a commonplace for an attractive man. The implication is that one should not expend too many tears on an ordinary (if attractive) man when one has the potential to woo an extraordinary one. With these references, Yu Xuanji is deprecating her former lover and exhorting both herself and the unnamed "neighbor girl" not to waste time pining after someone who is not worth the trouble.

After being cast off by Li Yi, and while still only in her late teens, Yu Xuanji took up the life of a Daoist nun and went to live in a convent, one of the few avenues to an independent life available to women in Tang society. As a former concubine, her only other choices may have been to become a lower-level concubine in a large household or a courtesan. In fact, many Daoist nuns were treated as de facto courtesans, sought after by men for their intellectual and literary companionship and enjoying a level of social and sexual freedom that made them morally suspect in the eyes of many. Yu Xuanji's tenth-century biographer, Huangfu Mei, describes her lifestyle as follows:

> Her verses describing the delights of love were widely known among the literati. She herself was by nature as frail as the orchid and of a free disposition. She had numerous amorous attachments with the young gallants of the capital, who would compete with one another to win her favor. Some would visit her, bringing wine, and she would often sing verses to the accompaniment of the lute.[19]

We also know from one of her poems that this lifestyle included attending polo matches. The entry of polo into the culture is one example of Tang cosmopolitanism. Imported from Persia and Central Asia, the game was well established in China by the reign of Emperor Taizong (r. 626–649) and was a popular aristocratic pastime in the capital. Tang tomb figurines show women playing polo (figure 12.2), but this poem shows Yu Xuanji as a fan, not a player, of the sport.

ON PLAYING POLO 打毬作

The hard, round ball, clean and slippery, flies about like a shooting star, 堅圓淨滑一星流
2 Moon-shaped mallets vie and whack without end. 月杖爭敲未擬休
When unimpeded, the players pass back and forth; 無滯礙時從撥弄
4 When obstructed, they try to keep possession. 有遮攔處任鉤留
Turning and twisting, again and again, they follow after it— 不辭宛轉長隨手
6 It feels as if they'll go on and on and never reach the goal! 卻恐相將不到頭
In the end, the ball goes in, the end is in sight— 畢竟入門應始了
8 I hope you gain the prize for the first goal scored! 願君爭取最前籌

[*TNSR* 106]

We do not know to what extent more respectable women would have had access to events such as these during this period, but Yu Xuanji's poem clearly reflects a first-person experience of the game.

Knowing something of Yu Xuanji's lifestyle, let us return to the story of her infamy. The story began some months before her arrest, when Yu Xuanji left her home to attend a social gathering nearby. She instructed her maid Lüqiao to remain at home to tell any visitors where she was. It seems

FIGURE 12.2 Ceramic female polo player, northern China, Tang dynasty, first half of the eighth century. White slip and polychrome. Musee Guimet, Paris. Photo by Vassil.

she meant to instruct the maid to send her lover along to join her at the gathering. When Yu Xuanji returned home, Lüqiao told her that someone had stopped by but had then left upon hearing she was not in. Suspecting her maid of having invited him in for an assignation, Yu Xuanji relentlessly questioned her, stripped her, and proceeded to beat her to death. Before she died, according to Huangfu Mei's account, Lüqiao denounced Yu Xuanji and swore not to let her get away with her death:

> "You seek the way of the Dao and of immortality, yet you cannot forget the pleasures of the flesh. Instead you become suspicious and falsely accuse the chaste and the righteous. I will certainly die by your evil hands. If there is no Heaven, then I will have no recourse. If there is, who can suppress my fervent soul? I vow never to sink dully into the darkness and allow your lascivious ways to go on." Having thus spoken her mind, she expired on the floor. Frightened, Xuanji dug a pit in the backyard and buried her, assuring herself that no one would know of it.... Whenever anyone asked about Lüqiao, Xuanji would reply, "She ran away after the spring rains."[20]

When the corpse is eventually unearthed, the story goes, Lüqiao's appearance is almost untouched by death, as if in testament to the injustice of her fate.

Interestingly, there are several indications in the story that, despite her association with the murder, Yu Xuanji was still viewed with sympathy both by her contemporaries and by posterity. The suggestion that the person who initiated the investigation had a grudge against Yu Xuanji (for refusing to lend him money) casts the instruments of justice in the case in a negative light. Further, we are told, "in court circles there were many who spoke on her behalf. The city authorities reported the case to the emperor. . . . In the autumn, nevertheless, she was executed."²¹ The implication is either that the charges against her were trumped up or that, because of her talent and recognition, she might have been deserving of mercy or special treatment.

This sympathetic view of Yu Xuanji reflects the ambivalence with which the culture of the time regarded a woman of talent. She was at once to be admired and to be suspected. The association of literary talent with public availability made literary women prone to social censure even, as we see here, while enjoying widespread admiration. At the same time, her talent and abilities sometimes earned her special consideration. Yu Xuanji was not unconscious of the difficulty posed by being an intelligent, literary woman. In one of her most famous poems, she happens to pass the place where the names of those who have successfully passed the latest civil service examination are being written on the wall in calligraphy (the "silver hooks" of line 2). It is important to note that the successful candidates would likely have had to compose poems as part of their examination.

VISITING THE SOUTH TOWER OF CHONGZHEN
MONASTERY, I SEE THE NAMES OF SUCCESSFUL
EXAMINATION CANDIDATES BEING WRITTEN
ON THE WALL   遊崇真觀南樓睹新及第題名處

    Cloudy peaks fill my sight, a fine spring day—   雲峰滿目放春晴
2 Row by row the silver hooks appear from under their fingers.   歷歷銀鉤指下生
    I hate these silken garments that hide the lines of my verse,   自恨羅衣掩詩句
4 And look up with vain envy at the names on the list.   舉頭空羨榜中名

[*TNSR* 111]

Clearly, Yu Xuanji is aware of her abilities and recognizes that, were it not for her gender, she would have had no difficulty competing with her male contemporaries.

COURTESANS AND SONG LYRICS (*CI*)

One important window into the lifestyles of female entertainers and their male literati companions during the Tang is the large number of song lyrics that have come down to us. These were lyrics set to new, popular music from Central Asia that was making its entry into China. About two-thirds of the song titles listed in a record of songs being performed at court during the reign of Emperor Xuanzong of the Tang, the *Record of the Entertainment Bureau* (*Jiaofang ji*), also appear in the Dunhuang manuscripts, a trove of materials including largely popular and anonymous songs discovered in the early twentieth century.²² This suggests that entertainers both inside and outside the imperial court were performing songs set to this new music. As courtesans sang and wrote new lyrics for these songs, so did the literati who patronized them. These lyrics would become known as the *ci* (song lyric) genre of Chinese poetry (not to be confused with the lyric poem, or *shi*). In its early centuries largely confined to themes related to love and feminine beauty, the *ci* would eventually broaden its scope to include a wide range of thematic material (on this genre, ☞ HTRCP chap. 12 and 13).

The association of this new poetic genre with singing girls or courtesans was so strong that when the first literati anthology of *ci* poems was put together, the preface writer took pains to distance the genre from this association. Thematically, the *ci* would be dominated by feminine voice and concerns for the first couple of centuries of its existence, before taking on a broader sensibility in the Song dynasty.

In the following poem by the later poet Gu Xiong (fl. ca. 928, from the period of division following the Tang), written in the voice of a courtesan to her lover, we see reflected the practice of poetic exchange and composition of song lyrics:

TO THE TUNE "LOTUS-LEAF CUP" 荷葉杯

   When I call to mind your poem it's hardest— 我憶君詩最苦
2 Did you know? 知否
   Every last word full of care. 字字盡關心
4 I write my deep feelings, send them on crimson slips— 紅箋寫寄表深情
   Will you chant it? 吟麼吟
6 Will you chant it?[23] 吟麼吟

[QTWDC 720]

The speaker, here clearly marked as female by use of a masculine second-person pronoun in the first line, is remembering the man's lyric poem, or *shi*, a love poem that had been addressed to herself. In return, she composes this song lyric to send to him (on a crimson slip like Xue Tao's), hoping he will chant it or sing it. The title of the poem marks it as a song lyric; it is set to a fixed tune known as "Lotus Leaf Cup," one of hundreds of different tune titles, each of which would have dictated the number of characters per line as well as requirements for certain tones to fall in certain positions on the line, probably following the contours of the musical melody to which it was set.

Many songs depicting a feminine figure in the *ci* genre seem to have been inspired by courtesans. The typical subject is a woman in her bedchamber, often at her toilette or playing a musical instrument, or with the musical instrument significantly silent or set aside. The following anonymous poem from Dunhuang suggests the entertainment quarters are the context. (Another source attributes the poem to the literati poet, Ouyang Jiong [896–971].)

TO THE TUNE "BODHISATTVA BARBARIAN" 菩薩蠻

   A crimson brazier warms the chamber where the beauty sleeps; 紅爐暖閣佳人睡
2 Beyond the curtain, flying snow adds to the wintry chill. 隔簾飛雪添寒氣
   In the small court, the sound of pipes and singing, 小院奏笙歌
4 A fragrance wafts and settles on silken robes. 香氣簇綺羅
   Wine is poured, filling golden cups 酒傾金盞滿
6 Amid fragrant musk, a banquet is laid again, 蘭麝重開宴

	The gentleman is drunk as mud—	公子醉如泥
8	On the Avenue of Heaven, a horse is heard neighing.	天街聞馬嘶

[*QTWDC* 779]

The scene here is Luoyang, also known as the Eastern Capital, and the setting most likely a house of multiple courtesans, as one lies sleeping while the party continues in the courtyard. Clearly the "gentleman" in question has lingered there long, his horse becoming restless in the cold of the street. The poem paints a picture of aristocratic leisure and decadence but also points to the communal context of poetic and musical production and appreciation, in which female entertainers played an integral part.

* * *

Despite this central role in literary and social life, the stories of these women show how precarious and complex were the lives of talented women in the Tang. Women who succeeded in crossing the public/private divide and putting their talents to use were, on one hand, able to enjoy a degree of social freedom and influence that would have been unavailable to their more conventional, properly secluded sisters. Lower-class women placed into the entertainment industry could achieve a lifestyle and influence far beyond their birth. Courtesans were more than a merely decorative presence in the most prestigious male gatherings; they were active participants in the give-and-take of poetic production. On the other hand, a courtesan was always at the mercy of others; if she obtained a powerful patron, that patron could easily dismiss her (as often happened, for example, when the patron received an appointment in another city). And women's very ability to take part in public life made them a threat, potentially even to the well-being of the imperial court and the nation, and made them subject to suspicion, which too often ended in their deaths. Women like Shangguan Wan'er, and to a lesser extent Li Ye, could rise to positions of great influence, but they would never be masters of their own fates.

It is due to this level of freedom, however, that at least a few examples of women's writing have come down to us from this time period, providing us a window into the lives and aspirations of some very remarkable personalities. It would be some centuries before women of more respectable classes would begin to produce, circulate, and collect their writing without fear of being stigmatized, but when they did, they were standing on the shoulders of these women who, by way of their relationships and poetic exchanges with the most prolific literary figures of their time, had laid the foundation for the acceptance of women's intellectual and literary abilities on the part of the broader culture.

MAIJA BELL SAMEI

NOTES

1. *Shi yan zhi* (poetry gives voice to the intent) was the early pseudo-etymological definition of poetry from the *Book of Documents* (*Shujing*) that articulated an expressive view of the major poetic genre, the *shi*. See also the discussion of *yi yi ni zhi* in chapter 1.
2. Lisa Raphals, *Sharing the Light: Representations of Women and Virtue in Early China* (Albany: State University of New York Press, 1998), 195.

3. Patricia Ebrey's translation, from Ebrey, *The Inner Quarters: Marriage and the Lives of Chinese Women in the Sung Period* (Berkeley: University of California Press, 1993), 23–24. Ebrey is quoting the Congshu jicheng edition of *Sima shi shuyi* by Sima Guang (1019–1086).
4. Ebrey, *Inner Quarters*, 24.
5. This translation appears in Maija Bell Samei, *Gendered Persona and Poetic Voice: The Abandoned Woman in Early Chinese Song Lyrics* (Lanham, MD: Lexington Books, 204), 56–57.
6. Ebrey, *Inner Quarters*, 25.
7. Marsha Wagner, *The Lotus Boat* (New York: Columbia University Press, 1984), 83. See also Victor Xiong, "*Ji*-entertainers in Tang Ch'ang'an," in *Presence and Presentation: Women in the Chinese Literati Tradition*, ed. Sherry J. Mou (London: Macmillan, 1999), 149–169.
8. Wagner, *The Lotus Boat*, 84.
9. *Jiu Tang shu*, translated in Wilt Idema and Beata Grant, *The Red Brush: Writing Women of Imperial China* (Cambridge, MA: Harvard University Asia Center, 2004), 62.
10. Ronald Egan's translation of Zhang Yue's preface to the collected works of Shangguan Wan'er, *Tang Zhaorong Shangguan shi wenji xu, Shangguan Zhaorong wenji*, in *Women Writers of Traditional China*, ed. Kang-i Sun Chang and Haun Saussy (Stanford: Stanford University Press, 1999), 723. The text is taken from *Quan Tang wen* 225:17b–19a.
11. Chang and Saussy, *Women Writers*, 724.
12. Chang and Saussy, *Women Writers*, 724.
13. Ji Yougong, ed, *Tangshi jishi* (Beijing: Zhonghua shuju, 1965), 28. Translated in Idema and Grant, *Red Brush*, 65.
14. *Jinlong wenguan ji*, translated in Idema and Grant, *Red Brush*, 64.
15. See Stephen Owen, "The Formation of the Tang Estate Poem," *Harvard Journal of Asiatic Studies* 55, no. 1 (June 1995): 39–59.
16. On this, see Billy Collins's poem entitled "Reading an Anthology of Chinese Poems of the Sung Dynasty, I Pause to Admire the Length and Clarity of Their Titles," in *Sailing Alone Around the Room* (New York: Random House, 2001), 138–139.
17. See Timothy Wai Keung Chan, "Li Ye," in *Biographical Dictionary of Chinese Women: Tang Through Ming, 618–1644*, ed. Lily Xiao Hong Lee and Sue Wiles (Armonk, NY: M. E. Sharpe, 2014), 231.
18. This translation appears in Samei, *Gendered Persona*, 68–69.
19. Jeanne Kelly, trans., "The Story of Yu Xuanji," from *Sanshui xiaodu*, by Huangfu Mei (fl. 910), in *An Anthology of Classical Chinese Literature*, vol. 1, ed. John Minford and Joseph M. Lau (New York: Columbia University Press, 2000), 972. The story is found in TNSR 139–140.
20. Kelly, "The Story of Yu Xuanji," 973.
21. Kelly, "The Story of Yu Xuanji," 973.
22. Wagner, *The Lotus Boat*, 5. Wagner is drawing on the work of Jen Er-pei (Ren Erbei) and Chen Shih-chuan (Zhen Shizhuan).
23. A version of this translation appears in Samei, *Gendered Persona*, 133.

PRIMARY SOURCES

QTS   *Quan Tang shi* 全唐詩 (The Complete Tang Poems). 2nd ed. Taibei: Fuxing shuju, 1966.

QTWDC   Zhang Zhang 張璋 and Huang Yu 黃畬, eds. *Quan Tang Wudai ci* 全唐五代詞 (The Complete *Ci* Poems of the Tang and Five Dynasties). Shanghai: Shanghai guji, 1986.

TNSR	Chen Wenhua 陳文華, ed. *Tang nüshiren ji sanzhong* 唐女詩人集三種 (Three Collections of Tang Women Poets). Shanghai: Shanghai guji, 1984.
TRYSHB	Zhou Xunchu 周勛初, ed. *Tangren yishi huibian* 唐人軼事彙編 (A Collection of Anecdotes of Tang Personalities). Shanghai: Shanghai guji, 1995.
XQHWJNBCS	*Xianqin Han Weijin Nanbeichao shi* 先秦漢魏晉南北朝詩 (Complete Poems of the Pre-Qin, Han, Wei-Jin, and Northern and Southern Dynasties Periods). Beijing: Zhonghua shuju, 1983.

SUGGESTED READINGS

ENGLISH

Chang, Kang-i Sun, and Haun Saussy, eds. *Women Writers of Traditional China: An Anthology of Poetry and Criticism*. Stanford, CA: Stanford University Press, 2000.

Idema, Wilt, and Beata Grant. *The Red Brush: Writing Women of Imperial China*. Cambridge, MA: Harvard University Asia Center, 2004.

McMahon, Keith. *Women Shall Not Rule: Imperial Wives and Concubines in China from Han to Liao*. Lanham, MD: Rowman and Littlefield, 2013.

Mou, Sherry, ed. *Presence and Presentation: Women in the Chinese Literati Tradition*. London: Macmillan, 1999.

Wagner, Marsha. *The Lotus Boat: The Origins of Chinese Tz'u Poetry in T'ang Popular Culture*. New York: Columbia University Press, 1984.

CHINESE

Chen Zhongtao 陳忠濤. *Nan de youxin lang: Yu Xuanji de shi yu qing* 難得有心郎: 魚玄機的詩與情 ("A Man with a Heart is Hard to Find": Yu Xuanji's Poetry and Emotion). Beijing: Zhongguo yan shi chubanshe, 2014.

Chen Dongyuan 陳東原. *Zhongguo funü shenghuo shi* 中國婦女生活史 (A History of the Lives of Chinese Women). 1928. Reprint, Shanghai: Shanghai shudian, 1984.

Hu Wenkai 胡文楷. *Zhongguo lidai funü zhuzuo kao* 中國歷代婦女著作考 (Women's Literary Works in China through the Ages). Rev. ed. Shanghai: Shanghai guji, 1985.

Xie Tiankai 謝天開. *Da Tang Xue Tao* 大唐雪濤 (Xue Tao of the Tang). Beijing: Zhongguo wenshi chubanshe, 2015.

Xie Wuliang 謝無量, ed. *Zhongguo funü wenxue shi* 中國婦女文學史 (A History of Literature by Women in China). 1916. Reprint, Zhongzhou: Guji chubanshe, 1992.

13

POETRY AND BUDDHIST ENLIGHTENMENT

Wang Wei and Han Shan

Wang Wei (701–761) and Han Shan (fl. seventh, eighth, or ninth century), two authors famous for their connection to Buddhism, exemplify the profound influence of Chan Buddhism on the writing of poetry in the Tang dynasty (618–907). The imprint of Buddhism on both their lives is clearly evident from currently available sources, thus enabling modern readers to understand their poems in relation to the rise of Chan Buddhism in the Tang. These poems, in turn, offer us a unique glimpse of new Chan Buddhist ideals prominent in the high and middle Tang periods.

We start with Wang Wei. Known in Chinese literary history as the "Buddha poet" (*shifo*), Wang Wei's life and poetry together bear the distinctive imprint of Buddhism. The combination of his given name, Wei, with his courtesy name (*zi*), "Mojie," becomes "Wei Mojie"—the Chinese transliteration of Vimalakīrti, a venerated Indian Buddhist who chose to remain in the secular world, not quite abandoning secular comforts (figure 13.1). The following passage from the Vimalakīrti Sūtra describes Vimalakīrti's life:

> Though dressed in the white robes of a layman, he observed all the rules of pure conduct laid down for monks, and though he lived at home, he felt no attachment to the threefold world. One could see he had a wife and children, yet he was at all times chaste in action; obviously he had kin and household attendants, yet he always delighted in withdrawing from them. Although he wore jewels and finery, his real adornment were the auspicious marks; although he ate and drank like others, what he truly savored was the joy of meditation.
>
> [T 14:475.539A, LINES 19–22; TRANS. WATSON, 33]

Like Vimalakīrti, Wang Wei remained active in the world, serving as a government official, though in his later years especially, his extremely simple lifestyle emulated that of a lay Buddhist practitioner:

> He usually had vegetarian food instead of meat. In his later years, he became a strict vegetarian, and did not dress in a splendid fashion.... During his stay in the capital, he offered meals for more than ten famous Buddhist monks on a daily basis, and enjoyed discussions on profound philosophical issues with the monks. He had nothing in his reading room but a tea set, a mortar of Chinese medicine, a sūtra-reading desk, and a bed made of hemp rope. After returning home from the court, he devoted his time to sitting in meditation and chanting sūtras with burning incense.
>
> [JTS 5052]

FIGURE 13.1 Image of Vimalakīrti. Part of the eastern wall painting, cave 103 of Mogao Caves, Dunhuang (eighth century). Reprinted in He Shizhe 賀世哲, ed., *Dunhuang shiku quanji: Fahua jing huajuan* 敦煌石窟全集: 法華經畫卷 (A Complete Collection of Dunhuang Grottoes: A Volume of Paintings on the *Lotus Sūtra*) (Hong Kong: Shangwu yinshuguan, 1999), 214.

This description, from the Wang Wei biography in the *Old History of the Tang* (*Jiu Tang shu* [*JTS*]), probably offers a realistic depiction of his daily life—we see it echoed in Wang Wei's poem on his experience dining with monks:

A MEAL WITH THE MONKS FROM MOUNT FUFU	飯覆釜山僧
Of late I have learned the principles of clean and pure,	晚知清淨理
2　Daily I'm moving away from the crowds of men.	日與人羣疎
Awaiting monks from distant mountains,	將候遠山僧
4　I eagerly swept my humble thatched hut.	先期掃敝廬
And truly from cloudy peaks	果從雲峰裏
6　They came to my home of weeds.	顧我蓬蒿居
We dined on grass, eating pine nuts,	藉草飯松屑
8　burned incense, and read the books of the Way.	焚香看道書
We lit the lamp when daylight was almost gone,	然燈晝欲盡
10　and rang stone chimes at nightfall.	鳴磬夜方初

FIGURE 13.2 Wangchuan estate as painted in Guo Zhongshu's 郭忠恕 (fl. tenth century) copy, after Wang Wei's painting of the same subject. Collection of the National Palace Museum, Taipei, Taiwan. Courtesy of the National Palace Museum.

	We awoke to the joy of quietude;	已悟寂為樂
12	And this life was blessed with boundless restfulness	此生閒有餘
	Why think seriously of return?	思歸何必深
14	A lifetime is like the empty void.	身世猶空虛

[WYCJJZ 39; TRANS. YU, 141, WITH MODIFICATIONS]

Apparently, Wang Wei and the monks enjoyed the gathering. They sat on the grass, ate pine nuts, and studied sūtras together until the end of the day. What did the poet achieve from this experience? The last couplet provides a clue by pointing to the illusory nature of human life—one's life is just "like the empty void," so "why think seriously of return?"

Wang Wei's decision to convert to Buddhism is probably the result of his disappointment with his political career. As a very talented and ambitious young man who passed the civil service examination at age twenty, Wang Wei was once very successful in the royal court, with the backing of the prominent minister Zhang Jiuling (673–740). Zhang's dismissal in 737, however, marked a turning point in Tang politics as well as in Wang Wei's career. After this, Wang Wei retreated to his Wangchuan estate and led the life of a half-official, half-hermit (figure 13.2). His stay in the capital of Luoyang during the An Shi Rebellion (755–763) resulted in a compulsory official post working for the rebels.

Though he was, fortunately, forgiven for his perceived disloyalty, when the Tang government regained power, Wang Wei became extremely depressed. In one poem, he lamented his life and believed his sadness could only be diluted through conversion to Buddhism. From this point onward, Wang Wei sought solace in Buddhism by "sitting in meditation and chanting sūtras with burning incense" (*JTS* 5052). He piously abode by his Buddhist belief and sought to persuade his friends and relatives to convert to Buddhism: "Before his death, Wang Wei suddenly asked for a pen and wrote . . . several letters to his relatives and old friends. Most of these writings were attempts to persuade friends to follow the Buddhist tenets of self-cultivation. After finishing the letters, he put away the pen and passed away" (*JTS* 5053).

Having gone through ups and downs in his life, Wang Wei, in the end, identified himself as a Buddhist disciple. But we modern readers might still be curious; yes, Wang Wei suffered a lot in his life, but why choose Buddhism? To answer this question in a Buddhist manner: his conversion is due to his inborn tendency, or the "root of wisdom" (*huigen*; Sanskrit *prajñendriyam*), which predetermined his fate and this turn to Buddhism.

Taking a close look at Wang Wei's family background, we can see where the "root of wisdom" starts. Born to a mother who was a devout Buddhist, Wang Wei and his family maintained close friendships with several prestigious Chan masters. Wang Wei's mother, Lady Cui, as far as we know, sought a quiet and reclusive life by following Buddhist discipline. She preferred life in the mountains and forests, with simple clothes and a vegetable diet. For more than thirty years, she studied with the highly regarded Master Dazhao—the seventh patriarch in the Northern School of Chinese Chan Buddhism. Like their mother, Wang Wei's brother, Wang Jin (700–782) studied Buddhism with Master Dazhao and was well acquainted with Master Dazhao's disciple Guangde (fl. eighth century). From recently available materials, we know that Wang Wei, like his mother and brother, sometimes paid formal visits to Monk Xuan (fl. eighth century), another student of Master Dazhao, and corresponded frequently with Monk Xuan's disciple Yuanchong (713–777), who once visited his Wangchuan estate.

Almost all of the monks mentioned above belong to the Northern School of Chan Buddhism in the Tang dynasty. Chinese Chan Buddhism, established by Bodhidharma in the sixth century after his arrival from India, gradually took hold under the reign of Fifth Patriarch Hongren (601–674). However, after Hongren, various new schools developed and diverged. Among those schools, the most historically influential and significant are the Northern School, founded by Shenxiu (606–706), and the Southern School, founded by Huineng (638–713). The teacher of Wang Wei's mother and brother, Master Dazhao, also known as Puji (651–739), was a disciple of Shenxiu, founder of the Northern School. Meanwhile, Huineng revolutionized the traditional theory and practice of meditation and attracted a huge following in southern China during the seventh century, which led to the rise of the Southern School.

Although Wang Wei and his family were very familiar with several masters of the Northern School, Wang Wei also learned the Buddhist ideas of the Southern School in the 740s, after a meeting with Shenhui (684–758), a Chan master of the Southern School. Not known to researchers until the excavation of the Dunhuang materials in the early twentieth century, this meeting between Wang Wei and Shenhui undoubtedly marked a significant turn in the poet's beliefs. Before this event, Wang Wei was a follower of the Northern School, which valued self-cultivation, whereas after the meeting he accepted the ideas of the Southern School.

According to currently available sources, Wang Wei audited a debate between the Southern and the Northern schools at Lintuan Post in Nanyang, sometime in the 740s.[1] Leaders of both sides were prominent monks in the two schools at the time. The leader of the Southern School in this debate was Shenhui, one of Huineng's disciples, famous for his attempts to popularize Southern Chan Buddhism in eighth-century China. The leader of the other side was Huicheng (fl. eighth century), a renowned Chan master of the Northern School in the city of Nanyang.

In the middle of the debate, Wang Wei asked a question of Shenhui:

"How about freeing oneself through self-cultivation?"

Shenhui replied, "Everyone has a pure mind. [The mind that] you want to arouse your mind to cultivate it—that is actually a false mind that cannot be freed."

[SHHSCHL 85]

Upon hearing Shenhui's explanation, Wang Wei was, according to the same source, "extremely surprised as he had never heard this way of thinking from other prominent masters." He thought "this master's view is incredible!"

Interestingly, Wang Wei was not the only person who was impressed—Shenhui was impressed by Wang Wei's question as well. He thought, judging from this question, that Wang Wei already understood the Buddhist Way, and he thus invited Wang to write a biography in the form of a stele inscription for his teacher, Huineng, founder of the Southern School. The stele inscription written by Wang Wei—"Stele Inscription for the Sixth Patriarch, Master Neng" ("Liuzu neng chanshi beiming")—now constitutes the most important historical document for scholarly study of the early history of the Southern School. Though authored by Wang Wei, this essay seems to channel Shenhui's understanding of Chan Buddhism.

Why was Wang Wei so impressed by Shenhui's answer? Such a fresh interpretation of self-cultivation marks a major difference between the Northern and the Southern schools. Generally speaking, the difference between the two lies in their methods of attaining the ultimate Buddhist Way. Specifically, the Northern School focuses more on the use of meditation and other methods (*famen*; Sanskrit *dharma-paryāya*) to cultivate one's mind and nature, whereas the Southern School emphasizes the inborn purity of the practitioner's nature and asserts that the essential path to the Buddhist Way is "the purification of one's heart and the revelation of one's nature" (*mingxin jianxing*). It is easy to understand why Wang Wei, a man familiar with masters of the Northern School from his early years, was so surprised and impressed by Shenhui's understanding of self-cultivation.

The result is that Wang Wei's poems embody popular Chan Buddhist ideals upheld by both Northern and Southern schools. If we look through Wang Wei's entire oeuvre, we will discover views from both schools. The embodied Buddhist ideas from the Southern School are ubiquitous, while, at the same time, the influence of the Northern School on Wang Wei's poetry, often underestimated, is also noticeable.

Unlike that of Wang Wei, Han Shan's life is full of myths. If Wang Wei's case exemplifies the practices of writing poems and pursuing Chan Buddhist ideals by the literary elite, the current collection of poetry attributed to Han Shan (fl. seventh, eighth, or ninth century) exhibits a slice of popular Chan Buddhism in Tang society, independent of the divergence among schools.

It is interesting to note that Han Shan was ignored in China for many years, though he enjoyed great popularity in the United States. In the United States, during the 1950s, Gary Snyder (1930–) translated twenty-four Han Shan poems into "Cold Mountain poems" and read some of those translations in the famous Six Gallery reading, while his friend Jack Kerouac, after hearing the Cold Mountain poems, dedicated his popular novel *The Dharma Bums* to Han Shan—consequently making Han Shan a significant figure for the Beat generation. Snyder's approach to the Han Shan poems is derived from his personal interest in Chan Buddhism, and, in turn, the underlying Chan Buddhist aesthetics in the poems authored by Han Shan influenced the style of Snyder's poems. Through the Beat generation, Han Shan thus became a kind of spiritual guru for the hippie generation in the United States.

Nevertheless, unlike Wang Wei whose life path can be clearly constructed from current available materials, even the discussion of whether Han Shan was a real historical figure is controversial. Some scholars consider him to have been a real person, whereas others believe "Han Shan" is only a legendary figure who authored the so-called Han Shan poems (Han Shan *shi*), which could be translated as "poems by, of, or in Cold Mountain."

If we assume for now that a poet named Han Shan once lived, his life history presents a jigsaw puzzle of ambiguous and legendary pieces. First, the dates of his life are unclear. Traditional critics have asserted that Han Shan was active during the early Tang era, whereas modern scholars consider him a person active in later periods. The former group relies on Lüqiu Yin's (fl. seventh century) preface to the poetry collection attributed to Han Shan published during the Song dynasty (960–1279), which dates Han Shan as someone in the early Tang. In this preface, Lüqiu tells of his visit to Han Shan at Guoqing Temple in Tiantai while Lüqiu was serving as Prefect of Taizhou:

> No one knows just what sort of man Han Shan was. There are old people who knew him: they say he was a poor man, a crazy character. He lived alone, seventy *li* west of the Tangxing district of Tiantai at a place called Cold Mountain. He often went down to the Guoqing Temple. At the temple lived She De, who ran the dining hall. He sometimes saved leftovers for Han Shan, hiding them in a bamboo tube. Han Shan would come and carry it away. . . . He looked like a tramp. His body and face were old and beat. Yet in every word he breathed was a meaning in line with the subtle principles of things, if only you thought of it deeply. . . . His hat was made of birch bark, his clothes were ragged and worn out, and his shoes were wood. . . . I proceeded on my journey to my job at Taizhou. . . . and went to Guoqing. . . . I ordered Daoqiao and the other monks to . . . hunt up the poems written on bamboo, wood, stones, and cliffs—and also to collect those written on the walls of people's houses. There were more than three hundred. . . . It was all brought together and made into a book.
>
> [HSSZ 931–932; TRANS. SNYDER, 39–42][2]

Although this preface does not indicate a clear date for the visit, a local gazetteer indicates Lüqiu Yin held the post as prefect of Taizhou from 642 to 646, during the Zhenguan reign era (627–649)—clearly, the early Tang period.

However, judging from the same preface, it is also possible to assign these three hundred poems to a Han Shan in the ninth century. According to Lüqin Yin's preface, Han Shan was "a crazy character" whose "body and face were old and beat, his hat was made of birch bark, his clothes were ragged and worn out, and his shoes were wood," and "he looked like a tramp." Such a character corresponds to the figure who appears in the poems, and calls to mind the typical image of Chan masters during the middle Tang period, thus suggesting a later Han Shan, probably a Chan master in the ninth century.

Other, modern scholars, through careful textual research, have questioned the authenticity of the preface and have proposed that Han Shan was probably a person in the eighth century. They rely most heavily on Du Guangting's (850–933) *A Supplementary Biography of Immortals* (*Xianzhuan shiyi*), preserved in the *Extensive Records of the Taiping Era* (*Taiping guangji*) and compiled in the early tenth century. Du's account reads:

> People don't know who Han Shan was. Han Shan lived in reclusion on Mount Cuiping in Tiantai during the Dali reign period (766–779). That mountain is remote and snow-covered even in summer, and thus is named Cold Mountain. This is why he called himself Han Shan [Cold Mountain]. He was fond of writing poems. Once he composed a piece or a line, he would write it on the stones in the woods. Someone fond of his poems came along and collected them. There were more than three hundred poems. Most of them describe the emotional experiences of living in reclusion. Some satirize social customs and warn the public about societal ills. "The layman of Tongbai," Xu Lingfu [fl. 840], collected the poems, divided them into three volumes, wrote a preface, and got the poems published.
>
> [HSSZ 936]

Because this biography of Han Shan offers a very clear account of how the poems were written, circulated, collected, and published, as well as a summary of the two themes of the poems that correspond to the extant poetry collection attributed to Han Shan, it is deemed more reliable by many modern scholars. Thus, it becomes more reasonable to consider Han Shan as someone active in the middle Tang period, thereby placing him in roughly the same time period as Wang Wei (eighth century).

Nonetheless, assuming the poetry collection is authored by one person, scholars run into difficulties in their attempts to reconstruct the poet's life from the poems. There's a Han Shan nobleman in the capital of Chang'an who, after failing to obtain an official post through the civil service examination, left his family to roam the world freely. Another Han Shan seems to have joined the military and afterwards retreated to Tiantai in the chaos of the middle Tang An Shi Rebellion. We also see a Han Shan who rejected Confucianism for Daoism and led the life of a hermit, a lay Daoist adept seeking to become an immortal; ultimately, this Han Shan converted to Buddhism and lived roughly one hundred years. He wrote a continuous series of poems to record his personal reflections on his secular, Daoist, and Buddhist experiences. These are the "Han Shan poems" we read today.

Two different groups of poems have added another layer of mystery. The coexistence of two groups of poems has long baffled modern scholars, as they suggest two different levels of literacy. As Du Guangting notes, there are two topics in the collection—most of the poems "describe the emotional experiences of living in reclusion," though "some satirize social customs and warn the public about the societal ills" (*HSSZ* 936). Not only are the topics remarkably different but also the linguistic styles are divided. The first group, describing the life of reclusion, reveals a highly educated Han Shan, whereas poems in the second betray a rustic and colloquial style, suggesting a lower-class background for the poet. Although the latter group of poems rarely alludes to types of writing beyond the

Buddhist canon, poems of the former group often use allusions that refer not only to Buddhist classics but also to Confucian classics, the Daoist canon, and renowned literary works such as the *Book of Poetry* (*Shijing*), the *Zhuangzi*, *Strategies of the Warring States* (*Zhanguo ce*), "Nineteen Old Poems" ("Gushi shijiu shou"), *A New Account of the Tales of the World* (*Shishuo xinyu*), the *Liezi*, and poems authored by Tao Qian (365–427) and Xie Lingyun (385–433). Some poems even adapt the writing style of the *Songs of Chu* (*Chuci*)—for which the author gained exaggerated praise from later traditional critics, who thought that even the purported creators of such a style, Qu Yuan (ca. 340–278 BCE) and Song Yu (ca. 298–222 BCE), could not best Han Shan here.

Given the above contradictions in the poet's purported life paths and the poems' linguistic styles, would it be best to consider the author of the "Han Shan poems" a group of writers instead of an individual? If this is the case, it seems likely that one or more hermits in the Tiantai area and one or more Chan masters living among the commoners composed the poems currently attributed to Han Shan.

Although Wang Wei and Han Shan are different in terms of their life stories, there is no doubt that the influence of the Southern School remains pervasive in poems attributed to both. For Wang Wei, the tenets of the Southern School are exemplified in the attitude toward life conveyed through his poems. Since the Southern School holds that it is not necessary to cultivate one's mind, what is essential, instead, is to realize the pure character of one's mind and follow it in action. In real-life situations, for the followers of the Southern School, one's attitude toward life should be "letting oneself ride with the flux of causation and letting one's destiny take its own course" (*suiyuan renyun*; Sanskrit *pratyaya-pratītya anābhoga*). This is evident in Wang Wei's life and poetry.

In his middle years, Wang Wei often stayed at his Wangchuan estate, where he led a reclusive life as a hermit.[3] At this time, he seems to have held a view of life in accord with the Southern School. His famous poem "Zhongnan Retreat" ("Zhongnan bieye") embodies such an ideal, as noted by later commentators:

ZHONGNAN RETREAT 終南別業

In my middle years I have become rather fond of the Dao; 中歲頗好道
2 My latest home lies at the foot of Southern Mountain, 晚家南山陲
And each time I feel the urge, I go there alone. 興來每獨往
4 All fine things are empty, I know for sure. 勝事空自知
I walk to where the water ends, 行到水窮處
6 And sit and watch the clouds when they're rising. 坐看雲起時
Running into an old man of the forest, 偶然值林叟
8 I chat and laugh, forgetting when to return. 談笑無還期

[*WYCJJZ* 35; TRANS. YU, 171, WITH MODIFICATIONS]

"Becom[ing] fond of the Dao" in his first line, often annotated by later commentators as "learning the Buddhist Way," makes it possible to interpret this poem's most well-known couplet—"I walk to where the water ends, / And sit and watch the clouds when they're rising"—from a Buddhist perspective. By employing natural images such as water and clouds, this couplet speaks of Wang Wei's attitude of "letting oneself ride with the flux of causation and letting one's destiny take its own course." By holding to such a belief, Wang Wei was able to confront the ups and downs inevitable in the mundane world, the bad or good circumstances in his life, revealing that he had already grasped and internalized the essence of the Southern Chan principle in real-life situations.

In his later years, Wang Wei achieved a mental state that only "cares for tranquility alone," as described in another well-known poem, "In Response to Vice-Magistrate Zhang" ("Chou Zhang shaofu"):

IN RESPONSE TO VICE-MAGISTRATE ZHANG   酬张少府

  In my late years I have come to care for tranquility alone—   晚年惟好靜
2 The multitude of everyday affairs does not concern my heart.   萬事不關心
  A glance at myself: there are no greater plans.   自顧無長策
4 I only know to return to the old forest.   空知返舊林
  Pine winds blow, loosening my belt;   松風吹解帶
6 The mountain moon shines as I pluck my zither.   山月照彈琴
  You ask about reasons for success and failure: 君問窮通理
8 A fisherman's song enters the shore's deeps.   漁歌入浦深

[*WYCJJZ* 120; TRANS. YU, 197, WITH MODIFICATIONS]

Without any trace of artifice, this poem presents the author's mental state: "the multitude of everyday affairs does not concern [his] heart." He is now completely immersed in tranquility, which is echoed as well in the following lines, from "A Meal with the Monks from Mount Fufu" ("Fan Fufu shan seng"):

  Of late I have learned the principles of clean and pure,   晚知清淨理
2 Daily I'm moving away from the crowds of men.   日與人羣疎

As with the poems of Wang Wei, the Buddhist ideals embodied in the Han Shan poems belong to the Southern School, as many of these poems also portray purity of mind and nature and consider the pure mind the key for individuals in their approach to the Buddhist Way. Very often, in describing the purity of mind, Han Shan poems emphasize recognition of one's own nature rather than self-cultivation beyond oneself. One poem even highlights that the necessary requirement for becoming a Buddhist monk (*chujia* ["leave home"]) is to have a pure mind with no attachments. Once one is able to maintain the purity of one's nature and keep it from contamination, one can understand everything in the world. With a pure nature, and far away from all "afflictions" (*fannao*; Sanskrit *kleśa*), one can be unrestrained and truly know happiness and joy:

  Where Cold Mountain dwells in peace   寒山棲隱處
2 isn't on a traveled trail   絕得雜人過
  when he meets forest birds   時逢林內鳥
4 each sings their mountain song   相共唱山歌
  sacred plants line the streams   瑞草聯谿谷

6	old pines cling to crags	老松枕嵁岩
	there he is without a care	可觀無事客
8	resting on a perilous ledge	憩歇在巖阿

[HSSZ 676; TRANS. RED PINE, 47]

This piece by Han Shan resembles Wang Wei's poem in its literary style as well as in the ideals it embodies. When the poet here is unconcerned with mundane affairs, he sings with the mountain bird; when carefree and unhurried, he can rest gazing at the grass. This perfect attunement with nature, achieved through the shedding of all worldly attachments, undoubtedly bespeaks the Southern Chan Buddhist ideal of "letting oneself ride with the flux of causation and letting one's destiny take its own course" followed by Wang Wei.

Although the poems we've looked at indicate how Wang Wei and the Han Shan poet(s) embodied essential tenets of the Southern School in their lives and writings, other poems by Wang Wei indicate the influence of the Northern School. Wang Wei had befriended many Chan masters of the Northern School in his early years, and the expression of Buddhist ideals from this school is ubiquitous in his writings. The most frequently described Buddhist practice in his poems is perhaps Chan meditation in the traditional Northern School style. The following poem offers an example:

VISITING THE XIANGJI TEMPLE 過香積寺

	Where is the Xiangji Temple?	不知香積寺
2	Many a mile into a cloud-veiled peak.	數里入雲峰
	The old forest knows no path of man,	古木無人徑
4	But deep in the mountain, from where come the sounds of a bell?	深山何處鐘
	A babbling spring makes precipitous rocks sob,	泉聲咽危石
6	The feeble sunlight adds coldness to the green pine.	日色冷青松
	Evening approaching, by an empty pond's bend	薄暮空潭曲
8	I sit in meditation to subdue the venomous dragon.	安禪制毒龍

[WYCJJZ 131][4]

In this well-known poem, the last couplet, with its "meditation to subdue the venomous dragon," appears to allude to the practice of Chan meditation and Wang Wei's preference for the Northern School's commitment to it, given the crucial divergence between the Northern and Southern schools in the understanding of the relation between meditation and enlightenment.

For masters of the Northern School, meditation is a necessary component of Buddhist practice because Bodhidharma, the founder of Chinese Chan Buddhism, is believed to have practiced meditation. Daoxuan (596–667), a Chan master in the early Tang era, describes Bodhidharma's practice as "in a coagulated state, to abide in wall-examining" (*ningzhu biguan*) in his *Further Biographies of Eminent Monks* (*Xu gaoseng zhuan*). One possible interpretation of this phrase is to imagine that Bodhidharma "painted a circle on the wall with mud, sat and considered that picture as the object to watch."[5] This practice, according to modern scholar Lü Cheng (1896–1989), originated in southern India. Following the understanding of "wall examining," Fourth Patriarch Daoxin (580–651) instructed his students to "sit diligently, since sitting is a basic requirement" (*DHXBLZTJ* 166), and Fifth Patriarch Hongren, who could sit and meditate from the evening to the next morning without interruption, continued this practice. Shenxiu, the student of Hongren and the founder of the Northern School, followed Daoxin's and Hongren's ideas in proposing "fix your mind and meditate, stay your mind and be pure" (*ningxin ruding, zhuxin kanjing*), as summarized by Shenhui, attacker of the Northern School and a master of the Southern School. Later masters of the Northern School adhered to Shenxiu's idea and considered meditation an important method to achieve enlightenment.

However, since the Southern School focuses on the sudden awakening of one's pure nature, meditation is not necessary for the attainment of Buddhist enlightenment. For the Southern School, "meditation" (*ding*; Sanskrit *dhyāna*) equals "wisdom" (*hui*; Sanskrit *prajñā*), so meditation more than just sitting. The Platform Sūtra (*Tan jing*) records Huineng's explanations of meditation:

> What is it in this teaching that we call "sitting in meditation" (*zuochan*)? In this teaching "sitting" means without any obstruction anywhere, outwardly and under all circumstances, not to activate thoughts. "Meditation" is internally to see the original nature and not become confused.
>
> And what do we call Chan meditation (*chanding*)? Outwardly to exclude form is "chan"; inwardly to be unconfused is meditation (*ding*). Even though there is form on the outside, when internally the nature is not confused, then, from the outset, you are of yourself pure and of yourself in meditation. The very contact with circumstances itself causes confusion. Separation from form on the outside is "chan"; being untouched on the inside is meditation (*ding*). Being "chan" externally and meditation (*ding*) internally, it is known as Chan meditation (*chanding*).
>
> [*DHXBLZTJ* 19–20; TRANS. YAMPOLSKI, 140–141]

Different from that of the Northern School, Huineng's explanation is a quite new interpretation of the theory of meditation and consequently transforms earlier notions. For Huineng and other masters of the Southern School, meditation is not the practice of sitting there doing nothing; rather, it refers to a mental state "untouched on the inside" and free from active thoughts, which allows for the internal awakening of one's original nature: "internally to see the original nature and not become confused."

As a matter of fact, Wang Wei's poetic depiction of Chan meditation is no different from the many that appeared in Tang poems; it formed a pervasive theme primarily in their descriptions of tranquility. Since the practice of meditation requires the practitioner to block out external confusion and calm the mind through long, motionless sitting, many poems depict the ideal of Chan meditation in descriptions of the beauty of tranquility. The following poem by Wang Wei is an example:

AN AUTUMN NIGHT, SITTING ALONE	秋夜獨坐
Sitting alone I lament my graying temples,	獨坐悲雙鬢
2 In the empty hall, close to the second watch.	空堂欲二更
Mountain fruits are falling in the rain;	雨中山果落

4	Beneath the lamp insects chirp in the grass.	燈下草蟲鳴
	White hairs in the end are hard to alter,	白髮終難變
6	And yellow gold cannot be produced.	黃金不可成
	If you wish to know how to shed illness and aging	欲知除老病
8	The only way is to study those who were not born.	惟有學無生

[WYCJJZ 158; TRANS. YU, 148, WITH MODIFICATIONS]

When he is sitting alone here, Wang Wei's mind is not the "empty void" mentioned in "A Meal with the Monks from Mount Fufu." Instead, starting with a lament about aging, it shifts to an openness to both the quietness and the activity of the outside world. Wang Wei registers the chirping of insects beneath the lamp and the falling of fruits in the rain, showing the openness of his mind. Everything in his pure mind is woven into his poem in the form of artistic images. Through the depiction of natural images, Wang Wei's presentation of Chan Buddhist doctrines and practices is extremely effective. In this poem, he conveys his Buddhist understanding of the world by contrasting existence and nonexistence, motion and motionlessness—thus reaffirming the emptiness of everything.

This emptiness is perhaps the most widespread Buddhist theme in Wang Wei's poems. Although the whole collection contains various themes and styles, he is famous in Chinese literary history for his representation of the tranquil nature that, according to Buddhism, embodies the emptiness of everything. Wang Wei's use of a large variety of characters and words to indicate emptiness is also notable. For instance, the character "empty" (*kong*; Sanskrit *śūnya*) appears very frequently, as this character can refer to the Chan Buddhist principle or to empty natural scenery or to the emptiness of the poet's state of mind. Wang Wei sometimes uses this character to describe the emptiness and tranquility of the surrounding scene; at other times he uses it to express the Buddhist doctrine in a very direct manner. He sometimes even combines *kong* with *ji* (quiet), for both are characters descriptive of the scenery and convey the poet's subjective feelings, inspired by external scenes. "Empty" and "quiet" are thus closely connected to the Chan Buddhist mind in Wang Wei's poetry collection. So, in "Visiting the Xiangji Temple," discussed earlier, the "empty pond" in the last couplet not only is a simple description of the scene before the poet but also is closely related to the tranquility of Wang Wei's Chan-like mind.

The tranquility that embodies the emptiness of everything is not a state of complete silence. Since Chan Buddhist thought sees everything in the world as connected through a gathering of chains of "causation" (*yuan*; Sanskrit *nidāna*) that does not have a self-nature, according to the perspective of the Middle Way in Mahāyāna Buddhism, emptiness is neither a simple "not having" (*wu*; Sanskrit *abhāva*) nor the opposite of "having" (*you*; Sanskrit *bhāva*) but a "false having" (*jia you*; Sanskrit *prajñapti-sat*) gathered by causations without any self-nature. So it is absolutely wrong for one to cling to having, while it is faulty to cling to emptiness. If one clings to emptiness, Buddhism considers this phenomenon "false emptiness" (*wan kong*; Sanskrit *jaḍa*), which is also a mistake. Therefore, emptiness is no impediment to the temporal existence of the physical phenomena, and one's nature of quietude is not a complete silence either.

Thus, Wang Wei's depicting of sound and color to express quietness and emptiness accords with fundamental Chan Buddhist ideals. Also famous for his painting, Wang has a keen eye for changes of color and light in nature, and likewise his poems often describe the transience and emptiness of "forms" (*xiang*; Sanskrit *lakṣaṇa*) in the world. The following poem, "The Deer Fence" ("Lu zhai"), is perhaps the best example of how he captures the transience, variation, and transformation of natural scenes that at once are and are not a "having":

THE DEER FENCE 鹿柴

   On the empty mountain, no one is seen   空山不見人
2 But the sound of voices is heard   但聞人語響
   Returning: light enters the deep forest   返景入深林
4 Again: it shines on the green moss   復照青苔上

[WYCJJZ 243][6]

On the empty mountain, we hear human voices yet see no man; we see light but only as it is reflected back. This impresses readers with an ambiguous sense of being between tangibility and intangibility, or, according to the Buddhist reading offered by Charles Egan, this poem suggests an impossible separation between the other shore and this shore, as "empty mountain" here "is the mountain as it *really* is from the perspective of an enlightened person" while "enlightenment is not transcending one reality to reach another but is the discovery of the law body within *this* reality." Images like the light and moss thus became "important symbols for . . . the enlightenment . . . and a symbol of absolute truth."[7]

The ambiguous sense between tangibility and intangibility in the previous poem changes to an impression of transience in the second poem of the same series:

MAGNOLIA ENCLOSURE 木蘭柴

   Autumn mountains embrace the lingering light.   秋山斂餘照
2 Flying birds follow companions ahead.   飛鳥逐前侶
   Brilliant blue-green—at times distinct and clear;   彩翠時分明
4 Evening mists without a place to be.   夕嵐無處所

[WYCJJZ 244; TRANS. YU, 202]

In "Magnolia Enclosure" ("Mulan zhai"), as dusk falls and flying birds follow their companions, returning home, the color of the mountains gradually blurs, their shadows becomes misty, while the actual evening mists are invisible—everything once tangible is intangible now and returns to emptiness. Just like the previous piece, this poem can be considered a perfect illustration of the nature of Chan Buddhist enlightenment.

As a matter of fact, in many poems from Wang Wei's late period, the natural objects described are not necessarily scenes drawn from reality. These scenes are neither portrayals of a specific time or space nor images that require an understanding or appreciation of a specific event. An overview of these natural objects reveals their intangibility: they are not concrete but seem, rather, to arise from his mind. In other words, all the images are distilled through the poet's subjectivity and hence are the poet's "inscape." The natural tranquility seen in Wang Wei's poems is thus a representation of both nature and his mind. Images are selective, abstract, and consistent with the poet's mental state. Conversely, through those natural images, the poet expresses his inner serenity so it is keenly felt. There is no trace of an "I" in the poems, but it is also difficult to assert the existence of a completely objective nature. It seems best to consider natural objects as a medium for conveying the poet's Chan-like mind, even though the poem contains no "I" (nonexistence of "I"; *wu wo*) on the textual surface. Indeed, in the best of his landscape poems, the poet unfailingly demonstrates his view of the universe while hiding the self.

Just as with the writings of Wang Wei, many of the Han Shan poems describe in great detail the natural scenery surrounding a recluse. Since the poet inscribed his words on the forest stones—according to Du's account—it's only natural that we'd find pervasive literary representation of natural images related to mountains and woods in the Han Shan collection.

Here and there, we come across depictions of Cold Mountain as an isolated, inaccessible place:

	People ask the way to Cold Mountain	人問寒山道
2	but roads don't reach Cold Mountain	寒山路不通
	in summer the ice doesn't melt	夏天冰未釋
4	and the morning fog is too dense	日出霧朦朧
	how did someone like me arrive	似我何由屆
6	our minds are not the same	與君心不同
	if they were the same	君心若似我
8	you would be here	還得到其中

[HSSZ 40; TRANS. RED PINE, 47]

In such a place, the scenery looks mysterious:

	The place where I've retired;	以我棲遲處
2	the mysteries are hard to explain	幽深難可論
	without any wind the vines all sway	無風蘿自動
4	despite no fog the bamboo stays dark	不霧竹長昏
	why do the mountain streams cry	澗水緣誰咽
6	or clouds suddenly gather on the ridge	山雲忽自屯
	why am I in my hut at noon	午時庵內坐
8	when I first feel the sun's heat	始覺日頭暾

[HSSZ 467; TRANS. RED PINE, 157]

As we see here, many Han Shan poems on reclusion describe mountains, stones, streams, flowers, grass, pinewood, a fresh breeze, white clouds, and moonlight. These images reflect more than a particular reclusive lifestyle and its natural setting; they also embody Buddhist ideals. Both Wang Wei and Han Shan combine Chan Buddhism with the realities of a recluse's life to create an artistic representation of Chan Buddhist ideals.

So, for instance, in writing of the purity of one's mind or nature, Han Shan poems often compare the pure mind with natural images such as clouds, moon, or sky—the same metaphors frequently used by Chan masters of the Southern School. Huineng, founder of the Southern School, said:

> Your own natures are always pure. The sun and the moon are always bright, yet if they are covered by clouds, although above they are bright, below they are darkened, and the sun, moon, stars, and planets cannot be seen clearly. But if suddenly the wind of wisdom should blow and roll away the clouds and mists, all forms in the universe appear at once. The purity of the nature of man in this world is like the blue sky; wisdom is like the sun, knowledge like the moon.
>
> [DHXBLZTJ 21–22; TRANS. YAMPOLSKI, 141–142]

Huineng had selected the sun, the moon, and the blue sky as symbols for wisdom, knowledge, and man's pure nature. The same use of natural images appears frequently in Han Shan poems:

	Today I sat before the cliffs	今日巖前坐
2	I sat until the mist drew off	坐久煙雲收
	a single crystal stream	一道清谿冷
4	a towering ridge of jade	千尋碧嶂頭
	a white cloud's dawn shadow not yet moving	白雲朝影靜
6	the bright moon's night light still adrift	明月夜光浮
	a body free of dust	身上無塵垢
8	a mind without a care	心中那更憂

[HSSZ 744; TRANS. RED PINE, 237, WITH MODIFICATIONS]

The recluse sits before a cliff under the moon, free from "dust" and enjoying the serenity of a mind without attachments. Images such as "crystal stream," "white cloud," and "bright moon" in the first six lines suggest a Buddhist reading of the last couplet, which not only depicts a recluse with a pure mind but also points to the Southern Chan Buddhist idea of enlightenment: a state when the body is "free of dust" and the mind is "without a care." The whole poem presents the reclusive lifestyle as well as the hermit's Chan Buddhist state of mind.

In contrast to such poetry on reclusion, the other group of Han Shan poems, attributable to one or more Chan master poets, reveals the authors' fervent exhortations to popular Buddhist doctrines or lifestyles in a very direct manner. Colloquial and sometimes even vulgar, these poems urge people to keep a vegetarian diet, or expound on the bitterness of reincarnation or the brevity of life. An example of the last group:

	Inside Jade Hall is a curtain of pearls	玉堂掛珠簾
2	behind it lives a graceful girl	中有嬋娟子
	her beauty transcends the immortals	其貌勝神仙
4	her skin is like that of a peach	容華若桃李
	spring mists rise in the east	東家春霧合

6	autumn winds stir in the west	西舍秋風起
	thirty years from now	更過三十年
8	she'll look like chewed sugarcane	還成苷蔗滓

[*HSSZ* 45; TRANS. RED PINE, 49]

After describing the girl's beauty as it "transcends the immortals / her skin is like that of a peach," the poem suddenly presents the opposite physical state: decay and ugliness. In only thirty years, a beautiful woman will become a worn out, white-haired old woman—"chewed sugarcane."

The metaphor is in fact borrowed from a Buddhist text. "Chewed sugarcane" is likened to an ugly and old person in the Mahāyāna Mahāparinirvāṇa Sūtra, a Mahāyāna Buddhist canon: "The same is the case with sugarcane. When it is pressed, what remains behind has no taste. The same regarding the prime of life and youthful colors. When old-age presses down on one, nothing remains of the three tastes" (*T* 12:374.436b, lines 27–29; trans. Yamamoto, 168). The Han Shan corpus contains an abundance of new, Buddhism-inspired expressions, like "chewed sugarcane." Many of them are vulgar yet thought-provoking, strange yet penetrating—in any case, clearly expressive of Buddhist ideas.

Thus, in spite of the ambiguity of the authorship and the variety of linguistic styles of Han Shan poems, they undeniably reflect the profound influence of Buddhism on the writing of poetry. The poems on reclusion allow us a glimpse into the new Southern Chan ideals in the high and middle Tang periods, including, for instance, an emphasis on the purity of mind/nature and the advocacy of the revelation of one's own nature without any practice. By contrast, the other group of poems embodies a more general ideal and common practice of Chan Buddhism, focused on the rewards of a vegetarian diet and the revelation of life and beauty's brevity.

* * *

Poems authored by Wang Wei and Han Shan are different yet share commonalities, for they both illustrate how Chan Buddhism imbued the writing of poetry with new expressions, themes, topics, and styles in the high Tang and middle Tang periods (for more of Wang Wei's poems, ☞ *HTRCP* C8.4, C10.4, C10.7; *WKB* P15, P26–P27, P39, P55–P56). Comparatively speaking, Wang Wei's poems reveal how an upper-class literary elite practiced Chan Buddhism and prescribed its ideals through writings, whereas the poetry collection authored by Han Shan displays a variety of writing styles under the influence of popular Chan Buddhism. Both collections of poems authored by Wang Wei and Han Shan thus embody Chan ideals, depict the reclusive lifestyle of Buddhist practitioners, and reveal the popular perception of Buddhist enlightenment in the Tang society. Ultimately, the two stand out in the history of Chinese literature for introducing a new model that instills a Chan Buddhist mind into Tang poetry.

CHEN YINCHI AND JING CHEN

NOTES

1. As to the exact year of the meeting, scholars hold different ideas: some maintain that Wang Mei met Shenhui by the end of the Kaiyuan era, in 740, while some date the meeting to the beginning of the Tianbao era, in 745.
2. With the change of romanization style to pinyin; the same is true for the rest of this chapter.
3. Zhongnan retreat and Wangchuan estate are two place names frequently mentioned in Wang Wei's poems. Some scholars consider Zhongnan retreat and Wangchuan estate to be two separate locations, whereas others disagree and propose that both names refer to Wang Wei's Wangchuan estate in the Zhongnan region. The latter is probably true, as Zhongnan refers to a large area where his Wangchuan estate was located.
4. English translation here is cited from Jie Cui and Zong-qi Cai, *How to Read Chinese Poetry Workbook* (New York: Columbia University Press, 2012), 53.
5. Lü Cheng, *Zhongguo foxue yuanliu lüejiang* (Beijing: Zhonghua shuju, 1979), 308.
6. Translated by Charles Egan, in Zong-qi Cai, ed., *How to Read Chinese Poetry: A Guided Anthology* (New York: Columbia University Press, 2008), 207.
7. See Charles Egan's interpretation of this poem, in Zong-qi Cai, ed., *How to Read Chinese Poetry*, 207–209.

PRIMARY SOURCES

HSSZ	Xiang Chu 項楚 (1940–), ed. *Hanshan shizhu* 寒山詩註 (The Poetry of Han Shan, with Commentaries). Beijing: Zhonghua shuju, 2000.
JTS	Liu Xu 劉昫 (887–946) et al. eds. *Jiu Tang shu* 舊唐書 (Old History of the Tang). Beijing: Zhonghua shuju, 1975.
SHHSCHL	Yang Zengwen 楊曾文 (1939–), ed. *Shenhui heshang chanhualu* 神會和尚禪話錄 (Record of the Chan Buddhist Talks of Master Shenhui). Beijing: Zhonghua shuju, 1996.
DHXBLZTJ	Yang Zengwen 楊曾文 (1939–), ed. *Dunhuang xinben liuzu tanjing* 敦煌新本六祖壇經 (The New Dunhuang Version of the Sixth Patriarch's Platform Sūtra). Shanghai: Shanghai guji chubanshe, 1993.
T	Takakusu Junjirō 高楠順次郎 (1866–1945), Watanabe Kaikyoku 渡辺海旭 (1872–1933) et al. eds. *Taishō shinshū daizōkyō* 大正新脩大藏經 (The Taishō Tripiṭaka). 100 vols. Tokyo: Taishō Issaikyō Kankōkai, 1924–1932.
WYCJJZ	Zhao Diancheng 趙殿成 (1683–1743), ed. *Wang youcheng ji jianzhu* 王右丞集箋注 (The Poetry of Wang Wei, with Commentaries and Annotations). Shanghai: Shanghai guji chubanshe, 1984.

SUGGESTED READINGS

ENGLISH

Chung, Ling. "Han Shan, Dharma Bums, and Charles Frazier's *Cold Mountain*." *Comparative Literature Studies* 48, no. 4 (2011): 541–565.

Red Pine (Bill Porter), trans. *The Collected Songs of Cold Mountain*. 2nd ed. Port Townsend, WA: Copper Canyon Press, 2000.

Snyder, Gary. "The Cold Mountain Poems of Han-shan." *Evergreen Review* 2, no. 6 (Autumn 1958): 68–80. Reprinted in *Riprap and Cold Mountain Poems*. San Francisco: Four Seasons Foundation, 1965, 33–64.

Watson, Burton, trans. *The Vimalakīrti Sūtra*. New York: Columbia University Press, 1997.

Yamamoto, Kōshō, trans. *The Mahāyāna Mahāparinirvāṇa Sūtra*. Revised by Tony Page. London: Nirvana, 2007. http://www.shabkar.org/download/pdf/Mahaparinirvana_Sutra_Yamamoto_Page_2007.pdf.

Yampolski, Philip B., trans. *The Platform Sūtra of the Sixth Patriarch: The Text of the Tun-huang Manuscript with Translation, Introduction, and Notes*. New York: Columbia University Press, 1967.

Yu, Pauline, trans. *The Poetry of Wang Wei: New Translations and Commentary*. Bloomington, IN: Indiana University Press, 1980.

CHINESE

Chen Tianmin 陳鐵民. *Wang Wei xintan* 王維新探 (New Investigation of Wang Wei). Beijing: Beijing shifan xueyuan chubanshe, 1990.

Chen Yunji 陳允吉. *Fojiao yu zhongguo wenxue lungao* 佛教與中國文學論稿 (Papers on Buddhism and Chinese Literature). Shanghai: Shanghai guji chubanshe, 2010.

Lü Cheng 呂澂. *Zhongguo foxue yuanliu lüejiang* 中國佛學源流略講 (A Brief Discussion on the History of Chinese Buddhism). Beijing: Zhonghua shuju, 1979.

❋ 14 ❋

DRINKING ALONE BENEATH THE MOON

Li Bai and the Poetics of Wine

SONG FOR THE EIGHT IMMORTALS OF THE CUPS   飲中八仙

> That's Li Bai: one dipper of wine, one hundred poems—   李白一斗詩百篇
> 2   Asleep in some bar in Chang'an.   長安市上酒家眠
> Even the emperor's summons did not bring him on board,   天子呼來不上船
> 4   He himself proclaimed, "Your servant is an Immortal-in-his-Cups!"   自稱臣是酒中仙

[LBJJZ 1834]

This image of Li Bai (701–762) as a wine-loving poet,[1] carelessly giving himself over to the liberating (and soporific) effects of his favorite brew, sprawled unconscious in the capital after spending himself in a wild frenzy of impossibly excellent poetry writing, is as indelible as it is polarizing. To readers over the centuries, the seemingly infinite number of anecdotes and casual remarks asserting Li's passion for drink provoke everything from outright admiration to wry bemusement—and even, in not a few cases, to angry defenses and denials.[2]

The occasional misguided moralistic objection aside, the significance of wine and intoxication in both the substance of Li Bai's works and the construction of this poet's persona is not to be passed over lightly. Wine and drunkenness serve as complex, sometimes contradictory, poetic signs that, properly understood, provide us with a window into the ideals of social behavior, self-expression, and aesthetic propensities of the times. Li Bai embraced those signs unequivocally and deployed them with flair and subtlety, both capitalizing on and departing from the constellation of connotations that came with them.

Poetic references to wine drinking hardly originated with Li Bai; they date back to perhaps the tenth century BCE, when the earliest strata of the *Shijing* (*Book of Poetry*) are thought to have been composed. As Michael Fishlen explains, in the *Book of Poetry* "wine is frequently used to formalize bonds of brotherhood, political alliance, and more broadly, community relations," but it can also "reflect a sense of well-being and can be a social lubricant which, if taken to excess, leads to moral decay."[3] This observation relies on the *Book of Poetry* as the most dependable documentation of social practice and, perhaps reasonably, refrains from speculating about any possible divergence between its documentary and its literary value. In any case, the use of wine as an evocative lyrical trope does not become demonstrably widespread until considerably later, at the dawn of the period known as the Six Dynasties (220–581).

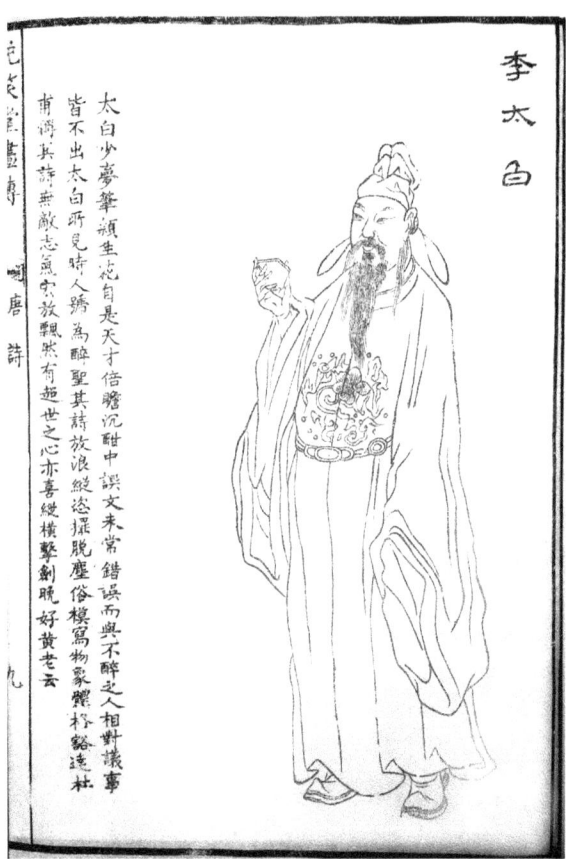

FIGURE 14.1 Li Taibai (aka Li Bai), by Shangguan Zhou 上官周 (1665–1752?). Qing dynasty woodblock print (1743), reprinted by the *Shanghai Journal* Office 申報館 (*Shenbao* guan) as *Zhu Zhuang's Portraits from the Hall of Late Blossoming* 晚笑堂竹莊畫傳 (Wanxiao tang zhuzhuang hua zhuan) (1921).

This age of dazzling cultural effervescence, which extended from just before the fall of the Han dynasty, in 220, to the reunification that took place with the founding of the Sui, in 581, saw the dissolution of the empire into a number of independent, competing kingdoms. These kingdoms succeeded each other, and sometimes overlapped, as different rulers and their clans strove for dominance. During this same period, another kind of striving occupied the literati: the quest for alternatives to the Confucian orthodoxy that had dominated the Han court. Daoism, the newly imported doctrines of Buddhism, and the non-Han cultures thriving around the periphery began to attract more serious attention, and the practice of the esoteric, philosophical debates known as "pure talk" (*qingtan*) was on the rise (see chapter 7).

There are many angles from which to consider the emergence of wine drinking in the literature of this period, ranging from sheer rebelliousness and escapism to rising interest in a Daoist-inspired freedom from prescribed social and moral constraints. As an increasing sense of helplessness in the face of wrenching political and social upheaval took hold, poetry grew as a medium through which individuals could express feelings of frustration, loss, and impotence. In one of the earliest and especially enduring threads of poetry emerging around the time of the fall of the Han, admonitions to "seize the day"—to grab pleasure while one still can—became more common, and that bittersweet pleasure often took the form of drinking, often in the context of banquets (☞ *HTRCP* chap. 5).

Though this would prove to be an important theme—and, as we shall see, one that was to be embraced by Li Bai, hundreds of years down the line—another, much less obvious wine-related trend emerging around the fall of the Han dynasty was the growing interest among the literati, especially in the Wei-Jin period (220–440), in the art and practice of character appraisal. True, men had long been discussing the central importance and frustrating elusiveness of the accurate appraisal of character. As far back as the sixth century BCE, Confucius (551–479 BCE) worried about it; two hundred years later, Mencius (372–289 BCE) boasted of his own talent for "understanding language" (and, thus, the people using that language); and the great poet Qu Yuan's (ca. 340–278 BCE) attributed poem *Encountering Misery* (*Li Sao*) bitterly laments the tragedy of being misunderstood. The smooth functioning of government and the welfare of those who lived under it were thought to depend on the ruler's ability to discern the true nature of people, while its absence all but guaranteed imperial failure. But the Wei-Jin perspective on the significance of character appraisal was different. If the ancients were more inclined to see the correct discernment of human nature as a matter of utmost political importance, thinkers during the Wei-Jin era saw it as a matter of spiritual, psychological, and—in the largest sense—aesthetic integrity.

Inspired, at least in part, by the question of how to discern and define the range of attributes and idiosyncrasies encompassed by human character, the Liu-Song prince Liu Yiqing (403–444) and his anonymous assistants compiled a collection of anecdotes known as *A New Account of Tales of the World* (*Shishuo xinyu*). The myriad characters—in both senses of the word—preserved therein, however, are not merely behavioral templates to aid in seeing through social veneers; nor should the snippets of behavior depicted in this book be read as strictly biographical. Rather, these anecdotes are perhaps best seen as performative, both depicting and, in the process, enacting exemplary moments of what one scholar has described as fully realized attempts at "self-fashioning."[4] As such, they make clear precisely which traits the elite of the Wei-Jin period saw as especially desirable: behavior and speech that are genuine, forthright, and consistent with one's nature.

No wonder, then, that so many of these portrayals of the most admired men of the age involve the practice of imbibing. In a not always subtle (but most persuasive) way, the liberating effects of wine, related in many anecdotes, are linked not with the loss of control but with a character's self-realization. The men portrayed as most authentic are often described as being under the influence; closely attuned to the urgings of their spirit, they are depicted as being better able to choose whether and to what extent to give in to those urgings—and to what extent to give themselves over to social standards and rules.

The *Shishuo* chapter titled "Free and Unrestrained" contains a pithy verbal portrait of just such a state of controlled (and controlling) chaos. Liu Ling (d. after 265), one of the Seven Worthies of the Bamboo Grove (*Zhulin qixian*), most commonly associated with drinking, is depicted in a state of inebriation that inspires a moment of self-revelation of the purest (and most provocative) sort:

On many occasions Liu Ling, under the influence of wine, would be completely free and uninhibited, sometimes taking off his clothes and sitting naked in his room. Once, when some people saw him and chided him for it, Ling retorted, "I take heaven and earth as my pillars and roof, and the rooms of my house as my pants and coat. What are you gentlemen doing in my pants?"

[*SSXYJS* 3:858; TRANS. SLIGHTLY MODIFIED FROM MATHER, 402]

Even today, it is hard to read this and other episodes in "Free and Unrestrained" without a smile, a twinge of envy and, perhaps, not a little embarrassment. This response is no doubt the very key to their meaning. The chapter containing this story brings together examples of behavior so unrestrained and eccentric, so extreme in its departure from social conventions, that it can only be thought of as stemming from one's unpolished inner nature. Fully three-fifths of the anecdotes included in this chapter attribute such admirably unfiltered words and actions to drinking. In its more explicit passages the chapter is studded with direct assertions attributing to wine the power to bring one into a state of transcendence or to protect and maintain the requisite intimate, authentic connection between one's body and one's spirit.[5]

The path leading from the ideal of the perfect correspondence between body and spirit, between actions and urges, to the poetic ideal of a seamless correlation between words and feelings is fairly direct. Even if we were to put aside the ancient tradition espousing the unmediated passage from inner stirrings to literary expression, we still would conclude that the ideal of authenticity dominant in this period implies perfect integrity in all things—linguistic expression included. And so, when we shift our gaze from the world of eccentric, self-conscious intellectuals to the contemporaneous world of poetry, it is the figure of Tao Yuanming (ca. 365–427) who appears before our mind's eye. Although his poetry was not appreciated until centuries after his death, he now stands as the earliest poet to be idealized as a truly authentic man. Not coincidentally, he is also the one whose name is most intimately associated with wine (☞ *HTRCP* chap. 6; chapter 8 of the present volume).

The "Tao Yuanming" that emerges from the accumulated evidence bequeathed to us by biographical entries in the official histories, his own writings, and unofficial sources is that of a man who, oppressed by the constraints and demands of his workaday life as a petty official, leaves it all behind to "return to farm and field," where he is free to heed the urgings of his inner nature. Eking out but a poor livelihood on the farm for himself and his family, he immerses himself in a life of reading the classics, writing poems of pure, unmediated expression, and, whenever possible, indulging in the drinking of wine with (or without) his rustic friends.

Among the testimonies to the virtues of such a life is the famous "Biography of Master Five Willows" ("Wuliu xiansheng zhuan"):

It is not known where the master lived, nor are we certain of his real name. Beside his cottage were five willow trees, so he took his name from them. He lived in calm and contentment, a man of few words, with no desire for glory or gain. He liked to read but didn't try too hard to understand. Yet whenever there was something that caught his fancy, he would be so happy he would forget to eat. He had a wine-loving nature, but his household was so poor he couldn't always get hold of wine. His friends, knowing how he was, would invite him to drink. And whenever he drank, he would drink his fill. He intended to get drunk, and once he did, he would withdraw, not really caring whether his friends begged him to stay or allowed him to leave. His dwelling was a shambles, providing no protection against wind or sun. His coarse clothes were full of holes and patches; his plate and pitcher most often empty. And thus, he was at peace. He often composed literary works for his own amusement, giving a rather good account of his own inclinations. He forgot to care about gain or loss, and in this way lived out his life.

[*TYMJJZ* 502–506; TRANS. MODIFIED FROM OWEN, 314]

Reading this oft-quoted "biography," we can see how wine and drinking are integral to its vivid rendering of the fictive Master Five Willows, a man who is able to hear and follow, exclusively, the urgings of his own heart. Indeed, no excuses need be made, for what he loves he loves completely, and—as his friends well know—his is simply a "wine-loving nature." Heeding that nature by getting drunk simply allows him to heed his nature that much more—shall we say—inattentively. A lesser, comic version of Zhuangzi's iconic perfected man,[6] Master Five Willows feels, yet remains untouched by, physical discomfort or societal expectations.

Five Willows's seemingly unassuming, natural indifference to the hoary values of ancestral and political honor is easy to accept at face value, and his willingness to pay the price of physical discomfort only makes that stance appear all the more admirable. But complications arise once we are told (as we are by the four separate historical biographies of the poet) that "Master Five Willows" is a highly literary rendering of the erudite poet Tao Yuanming—by none other than Tao Yuanming himself.

It is an intriguing thing: a baldly fictional autobiography, a self-portrayal that demands the recognition of an audience even as it blocks the audience's comprehension. As another eloquent example of performative self-fashioning (in the spirit of the Seven Worthies), this piece enables Tao to point to himself while seeming to point elsewhere; or, put another way, it allows him to point to himself while dismissing the value of such pointing. No one is fooled, of course, and probably no one was meant to be; everyone familiar with his writings will immediately recognize him here.[7]

Read against the Wei-Jin world that gave rise to the *Shishuo*, this and other examples of Tao's unabashed self-fashioning cohere in interesting ways with the value of honest revelation associated with character appraisal. His ale-tinged writings project frankness and simplicity but, in stark contrast with the avatars of the Bamboo Grove, the character he fashions for himself escapes taxonomy. His is, for want of a better term, a lyric self and, as such, one that resides tucked away in the interstices of even seemingly simple language and gestures. In like manner, wine drinking in his poetry represents a shift from the symbolic register of the *Book of Poetry* and the *Shishuo* to a lyrical one: from a clearly delineated, ritual, communal sign (whether of sociability or its opposite) to the more nuanced poetic figuration of the movements of one person's feelings (*qing*)—that is, one person's mutable responses to a world in flux.

More than three hundred years later, at the height of the Tang dynasty, the poet Li Bai seems to have also enjoyed wine drinking, at least enough to provoke the propagation of a cluster of anecdotes that, over time, have conspired to depict a man as ostentatious and flamboyant as his poetic use of wine is subtle and multivalent. The "free and unrestrained" poetic persona that emerges from these anecdotes hails untarnished from the Bamboo Grove denizens captured in the *Shishuo*. One need only consider one particularly famous vignette, preserved in two slightly different versions in the official histories handed down to us, the *Old Tang History* and the *New Tang History* (*LBJJZ* 1784–1786). According to this story, Li Bai shows up drunk one day when summoned to the imperial court, sits down, and, raising his feet, commands the high minister Gao Lishi (684–762) to remove his shoes for him. This is outrageous enough, but because the *Old Tang* and *New Tang* histories belong to a narrative genre that prizes the pedagogical value of causality over that of self-contained tidbits of character typology, they tie this behavior to its apparent consequences: in this case, Li Bai's banishment from the court and his subsequent unfettered—and so, not necessarily unhappy—wanderings "over lakes and seas."

As one might expect, as time goes on and portraits of the poet proliferate, the fateful significance of this action becomes amplified. Soon, writers tell the story, complete with dialogue, of how Gao Lishi, in his extreme humiliation, convinced the emperor's favorite and powerful concubine, Yang Guifei (719–756), that Li Bai's "Qingping Melodies" ("Qingping diao"), which she loved and took to be implicit praise of her beauty, were actually criticizing her undue influence over the emperor. To add insult to Gao's injury, some versions depict Li Bai as having written the "Melodies" on imperial command, while drunk. Although he did nothing more than splash some water on his face in preparation, goes the story, the poems were perfect; he did not go back and revise them, and they did not seem to require the change of even the merest word.

The marvelous constellation of meanings that can be gleaned from this story explains its persistent attraction. We have Li the untrammeled spirit, publicly besting the arrogant minister in a way that the latter most richly deserved, only to be unjustly slandered—and ultimately sent into exile—for having (perhaps) spontaneously spoken truth to power. Alternatively, we have Li the inebriated artist, foolishly but irresistibly humiliating the powerful minister, only to be predictably and perhaps deservedly sent out into the wilderness on the strength of unsubstantiated charges, where he was probably more comfortable anyway. Either way, the portrait that emerges well fits the uncomplicated image of one who is "free and unrestrained" temporarily dwelling at the heart of the most highly regulated place imaginable: the imperial court at Chang'an.

One might well ask what drunkenness had to do with any of it, or even what lesson readers were expected to draw from the invocation of drunkenness here and throughout the official and unofficial accounts of the poet's life. In particular, we might wonder whether we are meant to believe that his drinking aided his ability to write poetry or, to the contrary, that his talent was such that even in a state of extreme drunkenness his poetry writing was unimpeded. Perhaps the best answer is the simplest: that, in contrast with the rather black-and-white portrayal of the anecdotal man, the wine-drinking facet of Li Bai's self-portrait functions primarily as a symbol, connoting the same kind of authenticity—that same perfect correspondence between words and feeling, urges and actions—that we saw in its evocations in Wei-Jin culture. In this, it is consonant with other tales that swirl around his persona, including his swordsmanship, his stint as a Daoist adept (which, like drinking, is "explained" by some as a reaction to his rejection by the court), and his willful obfuscation of his place of birth.

Things get more interesting, and more complicated, when we turn to Li Bai's poetic writing. Take, for example, his wonderfully exuberant poem "Bring in the Wine" ("Jiang jin jiu"), which has stood the test of time as an exemplary carpe diem (seize the day) work in the *yuefu* (Music Bureau) style.[8]

BRING IN THE WINE[9] 將進酒

	Can't you see:	君不見
2	The waters of the Yellow River coming down from heaven,	黃河之水天上來
	swiftly rushing to the sea, never to return?	奔流到海不復回
4	Can't you see:	君不見
	In the bright mirrors of lofty halls, grief over graying hair:	高堂明鏡悲白髮
6	blue-black silk in the morning, turned to snow by nightfall?	朝如青絲暮成雪
	For satisfaction in this life, we must go to the limits of pleasure,	人生得意須盡歡

8	Never face the moon, your golden goblet empty!	莫使金樽空對月
	The talents that Heaven instilled in me must be put to use—	天生我材必有用
10	Squander a thousand pieces of gold, they will yet be returned.	千金散盡還復來
	So, boil a sheep, butcher an ox, make merry for a while,	烹羊宰牛且為樂
12	and when the time is right for drinking, down three hundred cups.	會須一飲三百杯
	Hey, Master Cen!	岑夫子
14	Ho, Danqiu!	丹邱生
	Bring in the wine!	將近酒
16	Keep the cups coming!	杯莫停
	And while I sing you a song,	與君歌一曲
18	I ask that you listen:	請君傾耳聽
	Bells and drums and scrumptious morsels are not what should be prized;	鐘鼓饌玉不足貴
20	I only want to be forever drunk and never sober up.	但願長醉不復醒
	The sages and worthies of ancient times all lie silent and ignored,	古來聖賢皆寂寞
22	Only great drinkers have a fame that lingers on.	惟有飲者留其名。
	In olden days, the Prince of Chen held a banquet in Ping-le Hall:	陳王昔時宴平樂
24	Ten thousand cash for a gallon of wine? They surrendered to pleasure and laughs!	斗酒十千恣歡謔
	And so, my host, what do you mean, saying you are short on cash?	主人何為言少錢
26	Directly now, go! Buy some wine, and I'll pour some for you!	徑須沽取對君酌
	My fine dappled horse,	五花馬
28	My extravagant furs,	千金裘
	Call the boy to take them out, and trade them for some wonderful wine,	呼兒將出換美酒
30	so together we might wash away the sorrows of all time.	與爾同銷萬古愁

[LBJJZ 1:225–229]

At first blush, this poem seems quite straightforward. Reading it today, even in translation, you still seem to hear Li Bai's full-throated singing in your ears and to see him gesticulating wildly before your eyes. This vivid invitation to join the party, to throw our cares to the wind, is more than what it seems, however. For Li Bai to adopt the ancient *yuefu* style is to trade in a particular kind of lyrical currency, one that engages the practice of poetic role playing. Early *yuefu*, more often than other forms of traditional Chinese poetry, contain stories populated by dramatis personae who are familiar to their readers.

In this particular poem, the hyperbolic language, the tone and extended rhythm of unrestraint, clearly suggest "authentic" self-presentation. The speaker's direct address to the reader supports this effect, and the invocation of wine as both the subject of and the impetus for this wild mode of expression only intensifies this feeling that what we are reading and imagining is the true, unvarnished Li Bai. But this is a *yuefu*, and a latter-day one at that, and that choice of genre raises the specter of impersonation—in this case, self-impersonation. A sensitive reader may well find himself or herself picturing Li Bai wearing a mask that replicates his own face, and may even reasonably conclude that this is not a mere joke but a statement about what it means to be authentic in a time when any poetic act involves some form of implicit imitation of past poetic acts. Is this a proclamation of in vino veritas (in wine [there is] truth)? Or is it an invitation to reconsider the "truth" of old assumptions such as these? As a man of his times, Li Bai understood better than most the connotative value of the rich array of motifs, conventions, and signs that the poets of his day had inherited, and wine was no exception. Indeed, one of the hallmarks of Li's poetry is his ability not only to deploy the elements of this rich inheritance in a skillful manner but also to draw attention to his role as a poet deploying that inheritance—and thus to redefine the notion of authentic self-expression for his times.

And so, when he appropriates the power that wine had by now accrued as a sign of lyrical authenticity, that same standard of authenticity seems to spur him to acknowledge that he recognizes wine as precisely that. In the poem "On the Ninth" ("Jiu ri"), we see Li Bai engaging, in his way, in the celebration of the Double Ninth Festival.

	ON THE NINTH	九日
	Today, the sky is fine,	今日雲景好
2	The water green and autumn's mountains gleaming.	水綠秋水明
	I take the gourd and pour some "rose-cloud nectar,"	攜壺酌流霞
4	Pluck a chrysanthemum and float cold petals on it.	搴菊泛寒榮
	The land extends far, pine and stone are ancient,	地遠松石古
6	The wind carries aloft the clarity of string and reed.	風揚絃管清
	A peek in the goblet reflects a joyful face,	窺觴照歡顏
8	Alone I smile and drink myself.	獨笑還自傾
	A fallen hat, drunk beneath mountain moon,	落帽醉山月
10	In vain I sing of missing my friend.	空歌懷友生

[*LBJJZ* 2:1206–1207]

As one is expected to do on this occasion, Li Bai writes this poem from the perspective of one who ascends to a high place, drinks wine with chrysanthemum petals floating on top, looks at the moon, and thinks of distant loved ones. The simple diction of the opening two couplets, and their depiction of the poet's nearly seamless conformity to the demands of the holiday, convey an unassuming freshness that revivifies the timeless comforts of ritual with the specific experience of the poet in a specific moment in time.

There is one phrase in this opening, however, where Li Bai subtly but decisively draws attention to his exceptional perspective: his reference in line 3 to the wine as "rose-cloud nectar," a liquor enjoyed by the immortals, sometimes referred to as being able to dispel feelings of hunger for several months at a time. Read in the context of Li Bai's body of work, this is more than a pretty conceit; it is a reminder of his status as "banished immortal" (*zhexian*)[10] and is consonant with his many poetic descriptions of cavorting in the celestial realms with transcendents. Read in the context of the Double Ninth Festival, it transforms the shared communal wine of ritual remembrance into the individual nectar of self-exceptionality.

The lyrical but conventional ensuing third couplet picks up on both of these implications, confirming that the poet is indeed in a high place, while making it equally clear that he is separated from the festivities being enjoyed by others. It is this solitude, as much as the holiday itself, that spurs him to compose the next couplet:

	A peek in the goblet reflects a joyful face,	窺觴照歡顔
8	Alone I smile and *drink myself*.	獨笑還自傾

Beneath this playful, cheerful gesture in the face of solitude is an invocation of that earlier wine-drinking poet renowned for his poems on the Double Ninth Festival, Tao Yuanming, who wrote these lines in his poem "Drinking Wine, No. 7" ("Yinjiu qi qi") (☞ *HTRCP* C6.3):

	With but one goblet, I toast alone;	一觴聊獨進
6	My cup emptied, *I myself pour* from the gourd.	杯盡壺自傾

[*TYMJJZ* 252 (EMPHASIS ADDED)]

To say that Li Bai is here alluding to Tao in order to align himself with that earlier poet's expressive authenticity is not only simplistic but also misses the point. By playing somewhat outrageously with Tao's phrase "I myself pour" (*zi qing*; literally "self-pour") and making it readable as "I drink myself," he creates ambiguity where there was none. In the process, he pointedly turns Tao Yuanming from a forebear into a trope and transforms Tao's stoic and frequently wineless solitude into a foil for his own *truly* unfettered (and therefore more patently authentic) merrymaking.

Spying—and then imbibing—his own reflection, Li Bai's gesture recalls a similar one he makes in the most famous of his poems, "Drinking Alone Beneath the Moon" ("Yuexia du zhuo"). In that poem, wine enables him to multiply himself into a company of three (himself, the moon, and his shadow), only to eliminate his "companions" when he has drunk to the limit. The poem is worth a little detour before returning to the conclusion of "On the Ninth."

"DRINKING ALONE BENEATH THE MOON" 月下獨酌

	A jug of wine among the flowers,	花間一壺酒
2	drinking alone with no one close.	獨酌無相親
	I raise my cup, invite the bright moon,	舉杯邀明月
4	I face my shadow, and we become three.	對影成三人
	But the moon does not know how to drink,	月既不解飲
6	And my shadow merely follows my body.	影徒隨我身
	Still, for the moment, I'll take moon and shadow as companions—	暫伴月將影
8	our revelry must last until spring.	行樂須及春
	I sing—the moon swings and sways,	我歌月徘徊
10	I dance—my shadow breaks and shimmers.	我舞影零亂
	As long as I'm awake, we can share this pleasure,	醒時同交歡
12	but once I'm in a drunken sleep, each will go his way.	醉後個分散
	Forever let us be joined in this journey without cares,	永結無情遊
14	and promise to meet on a distant bank of clouds.	相期邈雲漢

[*LBJJZ* 2:1331]

In this poem, Li Bai fluidly pushes the wine-induced feeling of "freedom and lack of restraint" past the limit of its own conventions. In the guise of the drunken poet, Li Bai surprises with this bittersweet meditation on the ironic impossibility of truly holding on to the knowledge of the brevity of human life. Our understanding of our own ephemerality is itself an ephemeral thing, he seems to say, and readers who know what he means—who recognize the tone of forced lightheartedness—will have to join him in what amounts to a judgment of the whole carpe diem tradition of which this poem is ostensibly a part. He implicitly reframes the venerable call to seize the day as the innocent and earnest poeticizing of another time, just as, in his poem "On the Ninth," he reframes Tao Yuanming's "drinking himself" as a quaint attempt to simply heed his own desires.

When "On the Ninth" closes, the banished immortal has shifted his lofty gaze from Tao, a fellow poet, to Shan Jian (253–312), who was no poet at all:

A fallen hat, drunk beneath mountain moon,	落帽醉山月
10 In vain I sing of missing my friend.	空歌懷友生

The fallen hat will remind readers of Shan Jian, a two-dimensional figure of inebriated uninhibitedness who was immortalized in the *Shishuo*. According to the *Shishuo* (23.19), when Shan Jian drank, he would head off for Gaoyang Pond and return so drunk that he was unaware that his hat was on upside down, thereby provoking the townspeople to make up a song about him. "Immortal" that he is, Li Bai, having just made light of a serious poet, now turns around and takes just a little bit seriously a comic figure, making him into a foil for his own melancholy. As Li Bai would have us understand, whereas Shan Jian recovered his hat, askew though it was on his head, Li Bai's hat remains fallen; whereas Shan's acquaintances witnessed his folly and good-naturedly turned it into a song, Li Bai has no friendly witnesses. He is left not to be sung to but to sing—in vain—alone, missing his unnamed friends, who are, simply, elsewhere.

In a certain way, one might read Li Bai's pointedly masterful and contrary invocations of fellow wine enthusiasts Tao Yuanming and Shan Jian as a warning, or perhaps as a plea, to his future would-be biographers: tempting though it may be, wine is not what makes me "free and uninhibited." Rather, he seems to say, please see these many wine-soaked allusions and tales as an invitation to deeper understanding. However, even this interpretation ultimately does not satisfy. The problem is that, in other instances, Li Bai rescinds this invitation even as he extends it, signaling to his readers that any attempt to penetrate his presented persona will be in vain. One striking example of this does not even mention wine, perhaps because it's not necessary; it simply calls to mind Tao Yuanming:

DIALOGUE IN THE MOUNTAINS	山中問答
You ask me why I perch here in green mountains,	問余何意棲碧山
2 I smile and don't answer, my heart at its ease.	笑而不答心自閑
Peach blossoms on flowing water darkly depart,	桃花流水窅然去
4 There is a world apart, not among men.	別有天地非人間

[*LBJJZ* 2:1095]

In this poem, Li Bai invokes Tao Yuanming's story "Account of Peach Blossom Spring" ("Taohua yuan ji"), which depicts a lost world out of time (see chapter 8). True, he is not recalling his wine-drinking predecessor so much as his writing, but in a literary world where writing is the primary path to understanding the writer, and in light of Tao's already established association with purity and authenticity, the reference to "Peach Blossom Spring" cannot but bring its author to mind. In this poem, then, it is not that wine is used as a sign of authenticity; rather, authenticity—that perfect, wordless correspondence between one's heart and one's behavior—obliquely suggests the ethos of wine. Or, perhaps more precisely, this poem conveys a state in which wine, like language—like Zhuangzi's fish trap[11]—no longer needs to be used, neither as a catalyst nor even as a lyrical sign. In this way, as paradoxical as it may seem, the poet is asking us to understand that he no longer has a need to be understood. One thing we do understand is that, without the centuries of wine-soaked writings that preceded him and without his (and our) knowledge of those writings, wine's omission would not speak to us quite as eloquently as it does.

PAULA VARSANO

NOTES

1. Throughout this chapter, I adhere to the convention that refers to *jiu* as "wine." However, as has been discussed in numerous contexts, grape wine was a relative rarity even in the Tang dynasty; rice- and millet-based ale was by far the norm. See David Knechtges, "Gradually Entering the Realm of Delight: Food and Drink in Early Medieval China," *Journal of the American Oriental Society* 117, no. 2 (1997): 237–239.
2. Li Bai's uncle, Li Yangbing, for example, asserts in his preface to the earliest anthology of Li Bai's poetry that the poet only turned to drinking after having been slandered at court and sent away. A later writer, Shen Guang, in his "Notes on the Li Bai Wine Pavilion" goes further, lamenting that, far from being a creative catalyst, wine only dulled Li Bai's senses and addled his mind (*LBJJZ* 1910).
3. Michael Fishlen, "Wine, Poetry, and History: Du Mu's 'Pouring Alone in the Prefectural Residence,'" *T'oung-pao* 80, no. 4–5 (1994): 262–263.
4. Nanxiu Qian, *Spirit and Self in Medieval China: The Shih-shuo hsin-yü and its Legacy* (Honolulu: University of Hawai'i Press, 2001), 37.
5. Qian, *Spirit and Self*, 135–136.
6. In chapter 2 of the *Zhuangzi*, "Discourse on Making Things Equal" ("Qiwu lun"), the perfected man, or as Victor Mair translates it, "ultimate man" (*zhiren*), is described as one who understands nothing of gain or loss, benefit or harm, and who is unfazed by extremes of heat and cold. Mair, *Wandering on the Way: Early Taoist Tales and Parables of Chuang Tzu* (New York: Bantam Books, 1994), 21; *ZZJS* 45–46.
7. It is important to note, however, that the issue before us does not concern the truth value of this self-portrait. Not only has it by now become cliché to point out the paradox inherent in such explicit expressions of spontaneous authenticity, but also one scholar has already laid out the perils of taking a strong stance either for or against its biographical veracity. See Robert Ashmore, *The Transport of Reading: Text and Understanding in the World of Tao Qian (365–427)* (Cambridge, MA: Harvard University Press, 2010), esp. 11–16.
8. The term *yuefu* originally meant "music bureau," an office probably founded during the Qin Dynasty (221–206 BCE) and expanded under Emperor Wu of the Han to provide music for court ceremonies and state sacrifices and, perhaps, to collect folk songs. By extension, the term came to refer to early folk ballads that were either collected by the court or composed by court literati in a folk-ballad style (☞ *HTRCP* chap. 4). By Li Bai's time, the term "*yuefu*" was applied to poems that drew on the titles and story lines of the earlier ballads.

9. See Stephen Owen's translation and discussion in *The Great Age of Chinese Poetry: The High Tang* (New Haven, CT: Yale University Press, 1981), 125–126.
10. This sobriquet was supposedly first bestowed on Li Bai by the director of the imperial library, He Zhizhang (659–744), upon his reading of one of Li Bai's poems. Suggesting the poet's ability to write freely, with disregard for the rules that more "mortal" poets had to observe, the nickname stuck.
11. In chapter 26 of the *Zhuangzi*, "External Things" ("Waiwu pian"), we find the famous line "The fish-trap is for catching fish; once you've caught the fish, you can forget about the trap" (*ZZJS* 406). As translated by Mair, *Wandering on the Way*, 276.

PRIMARY SOURCES

LBJJZ	Ju Tuiyuan 瞿蛻園 and Zhu Jincheng 朱金城, eds. *Li Bai ji jiaozhu* 李白集校注 (*A Critical Edition of Li Bai's Collected Works with Commentaries*). 2 vols. Shanghai: Shanghai guji chubanshe, 1980.
SSXYJS	Liu Yiqing 劉義慶. *Shishuo xinyu jianshu* 世說新語箋疏 (*A New Account of Tales of the World with Notes and Commentary*). Notes and commentary by Yu Jiaxi 余嘉錫. 3 vols. Beijing: Zhonghua shuju, 2007.
TYMJJZ	Yuan Xingpei 袁行霈, ed. *Tao Yuanming ji jianzhu* 陶淵明集箋注 (*The Collected Works of Tao Yuanming with Notes and Commentary*). Beijing: Zhonghua shuju, 2003.
ZZJS	Guo Qingfan 郭慶藩, ed. *Zhuangzi jishi* 莊子集釋 (*Collected Explanations of the Zhuangzi*). In *Zhuzi jicheng* 諸子集成 (*Collected Works of the Masters*). 8 vols. Beijing: Zhonghua shuju, 1954. Vol. 3 reprint, 1993.

SUGGESTED READINGS

ENGLISH

Fishlen, Michael. "Wine, Poetry, and History: Du Mu's 'Pouring Alone in the Prefectural Residence.'" *T'oung-pao* 80, no. 4–5 (1994): 260–297.

Knechtges, David. "Gradually Entering the Realm of Delight: Food and Drink in Early Medieval China." *Journal of the American Oriental Society* 117, no. 2 (1997): 229–239.

Liu I-ch'ing. *A New Account of Tales of the World*. 2nd ed. Trans. Richard B. Mather. Ann Arbor: University of Michigan Center for Chinese Studies, 2002.

Owen, Stephen, ed. and trans. *An Anthology of Chinese Literature: Beginnings to 1911*. New York: Norton, 1996.

———. "Death and the Feast." In *The Making of Early Chinese Classical Poetry*, 178–213. Cambridge, MA: Harvard University Asia Center, 2006.

———. "Li Po: A New Concept of Genius." In *The Great Age of Chinese Poetry: The High T'ang*, 109–143. New Haven, CT: Yale University Press, 1981.

Qian, Nanxiu. *Spirit and Self in Medieval China: The Shih-shuo hsin-yü and its Legacy*. Honolulu: University of Hawai'i Press, 2001.

Varsano, Paula. *Tracking the Banished Immortal: The Poetry of Li Bo and its Critical Reception*. Honolulu: University of Hawai'i Press, 2003.

CHINESE

Ge Jingchun 葛景春. "Li Bai yu Tangdai jiu wenhua" 李白與唐代酒文化 (Li Bai and Wine Culture in the Tang Dynasty). *Hebei daxue xuebao* 河北大學學報 (Journal of Hebei University, Social Sciences) 3 (1994): 50–58.

Huang Yongjian 黃永健, "Cong Li Bai de shangyong kan Tangdai de jiu wenhua" 從李白的觴詠看唐代酒文化 (Li Bai's Drinking and Poetry Writing and Wine Culture in the Tang Dynasty). *Zhongguo wenhua yanjiu* 中國文化研究 (Studies on Chinese Culture) 2 (2002): 25–33.

Ke Guiwen 柯貴文, "Maodun chengjiu de shipian" 矛盾成就的詩篇 (A Poem Composed in Contradictions). *Wenshi zhishi* 文史知識 (Learning of Literature and History) 12 (2003): 77–83.

15

DU FU

The Poet as Historian

The Tang dynasty (618–907) was notable for its great political, economic, and cultural achievements, which rivaled the heights of the Han dynasty (206 BCE–220 CE) and provided a model for later dynasties to emulate. At the same time, the historical memory of the dynasty was inextricable from the An Shi Rebellion, which spanned the years 755 to 763, brought about the death of possibly millions of people, and almost ended the dynasty. For traditional historians, the key actors at the heart of this event were the Emperor Tang Xuanzong (r. 712–756); the beautiful Yang Yuhuan (719–756), often referred to as "Prized Consort" (*Guifei*); the Turko-Sogdian general An Lushan (ca. 703–757) and his childhood friend Shi Siming (703–761); and the reviled prime minister Yang Guozhong (d. 756). The blind infatuation of Xuanzong for Yang, the Prized Consort, and the bitter enmity between An Lushan and Yang Guozhong, would result in a historical trauma that marked the political decline of the Tang over the next century and a half.

Although the events of the rebellion were commemorated in a host of literary and historical writings, no single writer has been as closely identified with this moment in Chinese history as the famed Tang poet Du Fu (figure 15.1). Du Fu (712–770) was born to a distinguished official family in the capital region of Chang'an. He was unsuccessful in his early attempts to pass the civil service examinations and only secured an official appointment by submitting three rhapsodies to the emperor. However, before he could take up his new position, the An Shi Rebellion broke out, causing Xuanzong to flee to Sichuan and Du Fu to embark upon a lifetime defined by sometime employment and much wandering.

He wrote many poems over the course of his life, and while many of them celebrate the private aspects of family life or address personal moments of happiness, the critical reception of Du Fu has often emphasized his role as a witness to the age, cementing his image as "poet-historian" (*shishi*). This is noted as early as the second part of the Tang dynasty, by the anecdotist Meng Qi (fl. 841–886), who wrote, "Du Fu met with the An Lushan disaster and wandered in exile through Longyou and Shu. He set it all forth in his poems, and by parsing the lines, one can understand his underlying intent. There was perhaps nothing that he omitted, and thus his contemporaries referred to him as the 'Poet-Historian'" (*LDSHXB* 15). The sobriquet Poet-Historian would be repeated in Du Fu's biographical entry in the *New History of the Tang Dynasty* (*Xin Tang shu*) (*XTS* 201.5738) as well as by numerous later scholars in the following centuries.

Yet it should be noted that Du Fu's acts of witnessing were never simply reportage but were born of a combination of historical reference, personal experience, and literary invention. The sense of historical realism that later readers have noted in Du Fu's testimony was more than just a reflection

FIGURE 15.1 Du Gongbu, (aka Du Fu), by Shangguan Zhou 上官周 (1665–1752?). Qing dynasty woodblock print (1743), reprinted by the *Shanghai Journal* Office 申報館 (*Shenbao* guan) as *Zhu Zhuang's Portraits from the Hall of Late Blossoming* 晚笑堂竹莊畫傳 (Wanxiao tang zhuzhuang hua zhuan) (1921).

of the hermeneutical expectations of traditional Chinese literary culture; it was also the product of Du Fu's extraordinary poetic imagination, of his compelling powers of vivid description. Du Fu reimagined his wartime experiences through poetry, and the fidelity of his representations was not to historical facticity as much as to the truth that could paradoxically be accessed through the fictive strategies of literary form.

This productive tension between historical experience and literary representation informs the poems that are now collectively known as "The 'Three Officers' and 'Three Partings' Poems" ("Sanli sanbie shi") (*DSXZ* 7.523–539; *QTS* 217.2282–2285). Each of these poems takes the form of a vignette—a brief, evocative, anecdotal narrative. In this way, Du Fu is able to represent the broader sweep of the An Shi Rebellion, which was complex and not easily reduced to linear narrative, within the more manageable scale of exemplary individual experience. Du Fu's poetic vignettes provide compelling specificity, the sense of personal drama, and the human stakes, locating the vast consequences of the event within accounts of a telling moment or encounter.

THE "THREE OFFICERS" POEMS

We begin with the "Three Officers" poems. The first poem of this set, "The Officer at Xin'an" ("Xin'an li"), has a short preface attached to it: "Composed after retaking the capital. Though the two capitals have been retaken, the rebels still flood the lands." Traditional and modern scholars have latched on to this detail, along with other historical references made in the poems, to identify a date of 759 for composition of the set. The retaking of the capitals in that year was without question a significant turning point in the rebellion, though the war was far from over.

Some historical context is useful to understand the background to the poems. The emperor was by that point Tang Suzong (r. 756–762), who had claimed the throne in 756, shortly after his father, Xuanzong, had decamped to Sichuan. An Lushan had died in 757, assassinated by his own son, An Qingxu (d. 759), who carved open his bedridden father's belly, spilling his guts on the floor. By the end of 757, the Tang forces had succeeded in retaking both Chang'an and Luoyang, and were increasing pressure on the rebels, who had split into two main factions, one led by An Qingxu and the other by Shi Siming. In 759, An Qingxu was in danger of being captured by Tang forces, when Shi Siming came to An Qingxu's rescue, defeating a vastly larger imperial army commanded by Guo Ziyi (697–781) at Yecheng. Shi Siming then executed An Qingxu, ostensibly for the crime of patricide.

Nevertheless, what immediately concerns Du Fu is not so much the grand theater of imperial disaster but the small-scale hardships that take place in the lives of the ordinary people. After all, the sufferings of the commoners would continue, no matter who was victorious on the dynastic level. The ongoing troubles of the rebellion therefore become the backdrop to Du Fu's real focus: how the wartime circumstances were experienced within the domain of the ordinary, at the level of the human.

I will begin somewhat out of order with "The Officer at Tong Pass" ("Tongguan li"), the second poem of the "Three Officers" poems, which differs significantly from the other two in theme and in terms of historical context. Here, Du Fu encounters an officer in charge of rebuilding the defensive structures at Tong Pass, the fortification that the Tang general Geshu Han (d. 757) had commanded. Although Geshu Han counseled patience and caution, believing that the best strategy would be to outwait An Lushan and allow dissension to arise among the rebel troops, the prime minister, Yang Guozhong, insisted that the general lead the troops out of his strategic position and engage with the rebels on open ground. Having no other choice, Geshu Han went to meet the rebels in battle, and the resulting battle was a disaster for the Tang army. The rebels not only seized Tong Pass but also captured Geshu Han (who was handed over by his own soldiers).

In the poem, Du Fu begins by describing the bustling scene of construction and the impressive height of the fort's walls. He then asks the officer whether the defenses will ward off barbarian invaders. The officer replies:

	"Reaching the clouds, the ramparts form a line,	連雲列戰格
10	Even flying birds cannot cross them.	飛鳥不能踰
	If the Turks come, just guard it from here,	胡來但自守
12	How again would cares come to the Western Capital?	豈復憂西都
	Sir, just you look at these strategic points,	丈人視要處
14	So narrow they'll admit but a single chariot.	窄狹容單車
	When trouble comes just grab a long pike,	艱難奮長戟
16	For all eternity you'd just need a single man."	萬古用一夫

The officer's confidence is born of the technological intelligence built into the fortifications. The soldiers who man the fort are almost an afterthought; all that is needed is one man with a long pike. Yet, as Du Fu points out in his response:

	"But how sad, the battle at Apricot Grove,	哀哉桃林戰[1]
18	A million soldiers were turned into fish.	百萬化為魚
	Please instruct the commander guarding this pass,	請囑防關將
20	Be careful not to imitate the example of Geshu Han."	慎勿學哥舒

[DSXZ 526–528; QTS 217.2283]

The main problem, as Du Fu notes, is that even the most cunningly designed fortification may be undone by unwise commanders. His rejoinder to the officer shifts between rumination and direct address, ending with a reminder that Geshu Han, too, once thought his position safe. Du Fu is a humanist, and thus it is the man who matters most of all to him, more than any cunning strategy or technical savvy. Baldly didactic in ways that the other two "Officers" poems are not, "The Officer at Tong Pass" reads more like a parabolic scene of instruction.

The thematic and tonal difference is not immediately evident in the opening lines of the first poem of the set, "The Officer at Xin'an," which begins with Du Fu meeting an officer in charge of the conscription of troops:

	I was traveling on the road to Xin'an,	客行新安道[2]
2	I heard shouting and noise as they conscripted troops.	喧呼聞點兵
	So I went and asked the officer of Xin'an,	借問新安吏
4	"The district's small, yet how can it lack grown men?"	縣小更無丁
	"A memo from headquarters came down last night,	府帖昨夜下
6	Next we are to select the younger lads to go."	次選中男行

The poet's initial question conveys his surprise that the officer is conscripting mere youths, and in reply, the officer dully repeats the orders that he is carrying out. Du Fu's next question is addressed to the officer and yet it also provides an apostrophic transition from the scene of the encounter to the ruminative lines that follow:

	"But the younger lads are far too young,	中男絕短小
8	How can they guard the king's city?"	何以守王城
	The plump boys have mothers to see them off,	肥男有母送
10	The thin boys are all alone, without anyone.	瘦男獨伶俜
	The white waters at dusk flowed to the east,	白水暮東流
12	In green mountains there were still sounds of tears.	青山猶哭聲

Even though the conscription is community-wide, Du Fu perceives an inequality that exists between the relatively privileged and the impoverished: the "plump boys" still have their mothers, while the "thin boys" have no one left to them at all. Missing for all of the youths, of course, are the fathers, who have already gone to war, never to return. From this scene, the poet's eyes follows the waters' flow, out toward the east, and yet he still cannot escape the misery of separation, the sounds of crying following him even as he turns away. Drawn back into the scene, Du Fu now addresses all of the wailing mothers and sons, as a community that is united in its grief:

	"Don't you allow the eyes to be wept dry,	莫自使眼枯
14	Hold back your tears that flow freely.	收汝淚縱橫
	When eyes weep dry, then you see the bone,	眼枯即見骨
16	Heaven and Earth in the end lack all feeling."	天地終無情

There is no comfort that he can give the conscripts and their mothers; for Du Fu, the purpose of poetry is not to assuage their grief but simply to bear witness to their suffering. In any case, what can he say that would make a difference? The universe itself is uncaring, without feeling, and the poetic imagination can do nothing to change this.

Du Fu turns away again, this time to comment on the historical situation that has impelled this conscription. He writes:

	Our army has taken Xiangzhou,	我軍取相州
18	Day and night I look to their pacification.	日夕望其平
	Who expected the rebels to be so hard to outwit?	豈意賊難料
20	The returning army has been scattered from the camps.	歸軍星散營。[3]

Here we find reference to the battle at Yecheng (referred to by the name of Xiangzhou). Although Guo Ziyi may have "taken" Yecheng, laying siege to An Qingxu, he would not succeed in its pacification. Du Fu softens the description of the Tang armies' defeat, referring to them as the "returning army," though it is clear that the rebels have "scattered" them "from the camps." Thinking on this recent setback, Du Fu attempts to provide a small measure of comfort to the conscripts, telling them that life in the army will not be that bad. He writes:

	We get supplies, being nearby the old fortifications,	就糧近故壘
22	When training soldiers we stay near the former capital.	練卒依舊京[4]
	In digging moats, don't go down to the water,	掘壕不到水
24	In pasturing horses, the labor is also light.	牧馬役亦輕
	What's more, then, the king's army is disciplined,	況乃王師順
26	His care and nurture is utterly manifest.	撫養甚分明
	Seeing the sojourners off, do not weep tears of blood,	送行勿泣血
28	The vice director is just like a father or elder brother.	僕射如父兄[5]

[DSXZ 523–526; QTS 217.2282–2283]

It is not clear whether Du Fu truly means what he says, or whether he believes it. Perhaps, in the face of wailing women and boys, he finds that he must speak a comforting falsehood to give some hope to those who would otherwise "weep tears of blood" in their despair. Whereas he earlier had proclaimed the heartlessness of heaven and earth, here he attempts to convince his audience that the emperor truly cares, that Vice Director Guo Ziyi is like a father or an elder brother. The bitter truth, of course, is that the emperor does not know the sufferings of these mothers and boys and that the conscripts' true fathers and elder brothers are likely dead, killed in the rout that was the battle at Yecheng. Though Guo Ziyi might yet lead the troops to victory, he is but a poor substitute for their loss.

The poem "The Officer at Shihao" ("Shihao li"), the third of the "Officers" poems, shares with the first poem the common theme of conscription. In this last poem, Du Fu describes officers coming into the village of Shihao to round up any able-bodied person still available.[6] He sees an old man escape by leaping over a wall and then witnesses the old man's wife pleading with the angry officer. This monologue takes up most of the poem:

	I listened as the wife presented these words to him,	聽婦前致詞
8	"My three sons were garrisoned at Yecheng.	三男鄴城戍
	One son sent a letter, which just came,	一男附書至
10	The other two sons were recently killed in battle.	二男新戰死
	The surviving one is just living on borrowed time,	存者且偷生
12	The dead ones will be forever departed.	死者長已矣
	In the house now there are no other persons,	室中更無人
14	There is only a suckling grandchild.	惟有乳下孫
	With this grandchild, the mother has not yet left,	有孫母未去
16	Though she comes and goes, lacking full clothes.	出入無完裙
	This old crone's strength may be fading,	老嫗力雖衰
18	I request to go back with the officer tonight.	請從吏夜歸
	I can quickly respond to duties at Heyang,	急應河陽役[7]
20	Also I can prepare the morning meals."	猶得備晨炊

To this plea, there is no response, though the officer seems to grant the old woman her request. The poem ends with a bleak scene:

	As night drew long, the sound of speech ended,	夜久語聲絕
22	I seemed to hear weeping and whimpering.	如聞泣幽咽
	At daybreak I climbed the road before me,	天明登前途
24	Alone I took my leave of the old man.	獨與老翁別

[DSXZ 528–530; QTS 217.2283]

It would appear that the old woman has left with the officer, saving her husband from certain death, though he now has no one left in the village to care for him, or to care for. The poet offers no words of comfort now, nor has he any advice to give to the old man who remains by himself in the desolate village. When the exigencies of war impel the government to take both the young and the old to fight its wars, there is no restitution that poetry can provide. All the poet can do is to bear witness to the old couple's powerlessness, as well as his own impotence in the face of such suffering.

THE "THREE PARTINGS" POEMS

In contrast to the "Three Officers" poems, in which Du Fu speaks as himself, the "Three Partings" poems are presented through the voices of typological figures: a newlywed woman whose husband has been conscripted, an old man leaving home to join the army, and a conscript who has returned to find his village gone. The shift of perspective is significant: the poet no longer speaks as witness to the sufferings of others but instead presents testimony as if directly from another person's perspective. The interpretive basis of the poems is thereby also shifted, from an assumption of autobiographical truth to a more overtly dramatic mode. Even so, though these poems may not claim to possess lyric nonfictionality, there is nonetheless a historical expectation for the poems, connected as they are to the An Shi Rebellion.

The first poem of the "Three Partings" poems, "Parting When Newly Wed" ("Xinhun bie"), begins with a stock metaphorical image: "The dodder vine attaches itself to thistle and hemp, / But if you pull away its tendrils, it will not grow." The dodder vine here is usually understood as the wife, who depends upon the husband for support, though, in this case, the husband has been conscripted for war. The woman then goes on to lament:

	If a woman is married to a campaign-bound soldier,	結髮為妻子
4	She might as well be tossed away by the side of the road.	不如棄路傍
	My hair was still in knots when I became your wife,	結髮為妻子
6	But I never warmed the mat upon your bed.	席不煖君床
	At dusk we married, but at dawn you took your leave,	暮婚晨告別
8	Was not that perhaps too rushed, too hasty?	無乃太匆忙

[*DSXZ* 530–534; *QTS* 217.2284]

Although the two are married, they have never known the pleasures of wedded life. She married him as a young girl, and he immediately went off to war, without fulfilling his conjugal duties.

However, the irony of the situation is expressed in the next couplet: "You are traveling, although not too far, / Guarding the frontiers, you have gone to Heyang." Heyang refers to the city that controlled the River Bridge, to the northwest of Luoyang, the Eastern Capital. This bridge was cut by the general Feng Changqing (d. 756) in late 755, in the vain hope of stopping An Lushan from crossing the Yellow River to seize Luoyang. The bitter truth of the wife's abandonment is that her husband is not being stationed at some unknowably distant land, as an earlier Tang frontier poem might have had it, but is in the vicinity of the Eastern Capital—which is now the new Tang frontier.

The rest of the poem elaborates the wife's stalwart resignation in the face of the rebellion's reality. Yet life is now uncertain: "As for my person, my position is not yet clear, / In what way should I pay respects to my in-laws?" Not having had a chance to be bedded by her new husband, she cannot offer hope of children to her in-laws; she thus occupies an insecure position within her new household. She states how she would accompany him on military campaign if she could, though she realizes that if wives were allowed to follow the army, this would weaken the soldiers' resolve. In the end, she bravely reiterates her intention to be faithful, putting away her fancy clothes and eschewing makeup, and to wait for his return, even if she knows better than to hope.

At the other end of the span of marriage is the speaker of "Parting as Old Age Nears" ("Chuilao bie"), an old man who prepares to leave his aged wife behind in order to join the campaign. However, unlike the first "Parting" poem, here the opening is much more direct: "The surrounding lands are not yet settled and calm, / Those nearing old age can find no safety." This couplet recalls the preface to "The Officer at Xin'an," which also emphasized how there was not yet peace in the lands, though the impact of the chaos is much more personal for the old man, who goes on to state: "Sons and grandsons have all died within the ranks, / So what need is there for me to survive alone?" Having no one left to carry on his family line, he embraces the chance to serve in the army, unlike the old man in "The Officer at Shihao," who ran from the conscription officer and allowed his wife to take his place. Still, he knows that this parting from his wife will certainly be the last one; neither his age nor the circumstances of the age make it likely that the two will meet again.

From this, the poem then shifts into a description of the war and its consequences, and in doing so, lodges the otherwise conventional narrative within a defined historical and geographic space:

	At Earthgate Pass, the walls are unyielding,	土門壁甚堅[8]
18	At Apricot Garden, the crossing is also hard.	杏園度亦難[9]
	The circumstances differ from those beneath Ye's walls,	勢異鄴城下[10]
20	And though I may die, that time is still far off.	縱死時猶寬
	In a lifetime there are partings and reunions,	人生有離合
22	So why blame it on the onset of old age?	豈擇衰老端
	I recall the past, days when I was young and strong,	憶昔少壯日
24	I tarry and look back, and in the end, heave a long sigh.	遲回竟長歎
	All the lands everywhere have been garrisoned,	萬國盡征戍
26	Beacon fires are spread over the mountain ridges.	烽火被岡巒
	Piled up corpses stink among the grasses and trees,	積屍草木腥
28	Flowing blood reddens the streams and springs.	流血川原丹
	What country can be called a "happy land"?	何鄉為樂土[11]
30	How can I dare to keep hesitating here?	安敢尚盤桓

[DSXZ 534–537; QTS 217.2284]

Earthgate Pass was a major fortification that had been seized by An Lushan's forces in 755, during his march south toward the capital region. In the following year, it was retaken by the Tang governor and famed calligrapher Yan Zhenqing (709–785). The Apricot Garden ford was where, in 758, Guo Ziyi crossed the Yellow River to inflict a massive defeat upon the forces led by An Qingxu. Yet, despite these victories, the Tang would still face major setbacks, such as the blow dealt by Shi Siming at Yecheng. The descriptions of the militarized and bloodied landscape underscore the point that there is, as yet, no end to the fighting, that the suffering of the common people is far from over. While the old man seeks to comfort his wife, telling her that death is still some time away and that life is full of partings and reunions, he knows that there is no "happy land," no place that is free from the chaos of the rebellion. The poem ends with the old man taking his leave from his humble dwelling, a figure of utter impotence and abjection: "Spirits collapsing, my insides are all crumbled, broken."

The last of the poems, "Parting Without a Home" ("Wujia bie"), provides an ending of sorts to the narrative arc of the "Three Partings." Here the speaker is a conscripted soldier who returns home to find himself now a stranger in his home village, with nothing left of the life that he once knew. He begins by invoking the historical context: "How desolate, the aftermath of the Tianbao reign, / In the gardens and cottages, only weeds are left." He then surveys the consequences of war, which are never confined to the gory battlefields but will continue to be felt for generations in the decimated villages that once supplied the soldiers:

	In my village there were over a hundred families,	我里百餘家
4	But in the age's chaos, each went a different way.	世亂各東西
	From those who survive, no news comes,	存者無消息
6	And those who have died are now dirt and mud.	死者為塵泥
	This poor fellow, because his ranks were broken,	賤子因陣敗
8	Has returned home to seek out familiar paths.	歸來尋舊蹊
	Having traveled long, I see the vacant lane,	久行見空巷
10	The sunlight is emaciated, the weather dreary.	日瘦氣慘悽
	All I meet with are foxes and raccoon dogs,	但對狐與狸
12	With stiff fur, they angrily bark at me.	豎毛怒我啼
	Of all my neighbors, who was still there?	四鄰何所有
14	Just one or two aged widows.	一二老寡妻

This is a scene familiar to readers of early classical verse, in which the returning traveler finds that the home he had abandoned has not survived in his absence. Nature has reclaimed the homestead, with wild animals now making their dens in the structures that once housed his family and neighbors. Only one or two widows remain, women who were once newlyweds like the speaker of the first "Parting" poem.

Despite all of this, the soldier must eat, and so he returns to the work of farming, which will ensure at least his own survival. This attempt to rebuild his life, however, is short-lived, since the war is not yet over:

	When the district officers knew I had arrived,	縣吏知我至
20	They summoned me to practice with war drums.	召令習鼓鞞
	Although I am with conscripts in my own province,	雖從本州役
22	Within my home, there was no one to say farewell.	內顧無所攜
	Traveling nearby, it was only this single person,	近行止一身
24	Going to far lands, in the end I am even more lost.	遠去終轉迷
	My hometown has already been swept away,	家鄉既盪盡
26	Far or near, the situation was all the same.	遠近理亦齊

In a sense, it does not matter that he is once again forced to serve in the army, since there was nothing to which he could return home and no one left to take leave of. No matter where he ends up, it will all be the same set of dire circumstances, since devastation has visited all of the lands equally. Yet there is one loss in particular that haunts him:

	Forever will I feel pain for my long ailing mother,	永痛長病母
28	Who, five years ago, I abandoned by a valley ditch.	五年委溝谿
	She gave birth to me but got none of my support,	生我不得力
30	All our lives, the two of us bitterly sighing.	終身兩酸嘶
	In a person's lifetime, parting without a home,	人生無家別
32	How could I still count as one of the common folk?	何以為烝黎

[*DSXZ* 537–539; *QTS* 217.2284–2285]

The reference to "five years" helps buttress the interpretation of the poem as composed in 759, which would have been the fifth year of the rebellion. More to the point, however, it is with this scene that the "Three Officers and Three Partings" poems come full circle. If the "The Officer at Xin'an" bore witness to the separation of youths and their mothers, the poem "Parting Without a Home" expresses the guilt of the now grown soldier who left his mother to go to war. What marks the speaker, more than any other loss, is the fact that he left his mother behind and that, without her, there is no sense of home.

Du Fu's literary sobriquet, the Poet-Historian, alludes to the way in which he bore witness to the An Shi Rebellion through his poetry (for his other poems, ☞ *HTRCP* C8.1–C8.2, C9.1–C9.3, C10.14; *WKB* P20, P44, P52, P80–P81, P85, P91–P94). Nevertheless, as we have seen here, Du Fu was not simply interested in recounting the events of the rebellion as a totalizing narrative but rather sought to represent the war years through his own personal experiences and to give voice to those whose experiences would not otherwise be commemorated. The vignettes that he constructs, both of himself and of others, are "microhistories," which is to say, microscale narrations of the ordinary that have interpretive implications for the macrohistorical contexts in which they are embedded. And yet, because these stories do not already exist, because no historian of the time would have thought to write a historical narrative that dealt with commoners and not with emperors and officials, these vignettes would have to be inventions of poetry.

There are, of course, elements of the fictive in all traditional historiography, which sustains narrative interest through the use of anecdotes, reconstructed dialogue or speeches, and other episodic devices. For the historian, the purpose of anecdotes and the like is to provide a sense of vivid realism for the otherwise fact-based grand narratives, and in the interest of that sense of realism, any detour into fictive construction can be pardoned or ignored. Poetry, however, is not based on the historian's notion of factuality—even granting traditional assumptions of lyric nonfictionality—but on something closer to what might be called the aptness of its representation. Du Fu may never have met any of the officers or figures that he brings to life in the "Three Officers and Three Partings" poems—these may be utterly fictional constructs—yet the skill with which he represents them trumps their possibly historical nonfactuality. This is not the concern of poetry, or at least is not Du Fu's concern in the writing of poetry. For him, these vignettes are true in a more important sense, as they capture experiences from the An Shi Rebellion that could not exist in any other form. What the poet bears witness to is a sense of history more sympathetic and more generous than any historiographic work from this time.

JACK W. CHEN

NOTES

1. "Apricot Grove" refers to the region where Tong Pass was located.
2. Xin'an was located to the west of Luoyang, in the northwest of modern-day Henan.
3. This is understood as a reference to Guo Ziyi's defeat at Yecheng.
4. This refers to Luoyang.
5. "Vice director" refers to Guo Ziyi, who was demoted to this position following an earlier military defeat, in 757.
6. The location of Shihao is debated by traditional critics.
7. Guo Ziyi, after his defeat at Yecheng, retreated to Heyang.
8. Earthgate Pass was the fifth of the eight major passes along the Taihang mountain range, located to the west of modern Shijiazhuang in Hubei province.
9. Apricot Garden is a ford located in modern Ji prefecture in Henan province.
10. This is a reference to Guo Ziyi's 759 defeat at Yecheng.
11. "Happy land" is a reference to the *Shijing* (*Book of Poetry*) poem "Shuo shu" ("Big Rat"; Mao no. 113) (☞ *HTRCP* chap. 1; *WKB* P01; chapter 4 of the present volume).

PRIMARY SOURCES

DSXZ	Qiu Zhao'ao 仇兆鰲, ed. *Du shi xiangzhu* 杜詩詳注 (Du Fu's Poetry with Detailed Annotations). 5 vols. Beijing: Zhonghua shuju, 1979.
LDSHXB	Meng Qi 孟棨, comp. *Benshi shi* 本事詩 (Poems with Source Anecdotes). In Ding Fubao 丁福保, ed. *Lidai shihua xubian* 歷代詩話續編 (Sequel to *Remarks on Poetry Through the Ages*). Beijing: Zhonghua shuju, 1981.
QTS	*Quan Tang shi* 全唐詩 (Complete Poems of the Tang). 25 vols. Beijing: Zhonghua shuju, 1960.
XTS	Ouyang Xiu 歐陽修 and Song Qi 宋祁, eds. *Xin Tang shu* 新唐書 (New History of the Tang Dynasty). 20 vols. Beijing: Zhonghua shuju, 1975.

SUGGESTED READINGS

ENGLISH

Chou, Eva Shan. *Reconsidering Tu Fu: Literary Greatness and Cultural Context*. Cambridge: Cambridge University Press, 1995.
Davis, A. R. *Tu Fu*. New York: Twayne, 1971.
Hawkes, David. *A Little Primer of Tu Fu*. Oxford: Clarendon, 1967.
Hung, William. *Tu Fu: China's Greatest Poet*. 2 vols. Cambridge, MA: Harvard University Press, 1952.
McCraw, David. *Du Fu's Laments from the South*. Honolulu: University of Hawai'i Press, 1992.
Owen, Stephen. *The Great Age of Chinese Poetry: The High T'ang*. New Haven, CT: Yale University Press, 1981.
Owen, Stephen, trans. and ed. *The Poetry of Du Fu*. 6 vols. Berlin: De Gruyter, 2016.
Twitchett, Denis. "Hsüan-tsung (Reign 712–56)." In *Cambridge History of China*. Vol. 3, part 1, *Sui and T'ang China, 589–906*, 333–463. Cambridge: Cambridge University Press, 1979.

CHINESE

Chen Yixin 陳貽焮. *Du Fu pingzhuan* 杜甫評傳 (Critical Biography of Du Fu). 2nd ed. 3 vols. Beijing: Beijing daxue chubanshe, 2011.

Fu Gengsheng 傅庚生. *Du Fu shilun* 杜甫詩論 (Essays on Du Fu's Poetry). Shanghai: Shanghai guji chubanshe, 1985.

Gu Pengnian 顧澎年. *Du Fu shili de feizhan sixiang* 杜甫詩裏的非戰思想 (Antiwar Thought Within Du Fu's Poetry). Shanghai: Shangwu yinshuguan, 1928.

Wang Huibin 王輝斌. *Du Fu yanjiu xintan* 杜甫研究新探 (New Investigations Into Du Fu Studies). Hefei: Huangshan shushe, 2011.

Xiao Difei 蕭滌非. *Xiao Difei Du Fu yanjiu quanji* 蕭滌非杜甫研究全集 (Complete Collection of Xiao Difei's Studies on Du Fu). 3 vols. Harbin: Heilongjiang jiaoyu chubanshe, 2006.

16

POETRY AND LITERATI FRIENDSHIP

Bai Juyi and Yuan Zhen

The unusually intelligent and incisive Yuan Zhen became famous for his talents in his early years, and befriended Bai Juyi from Taiyuan. As a poet, Yuan was highly accomplished in describing scenery and objects. Contemporary commentators of poetry called the pair "Yuan-Bai." Both well-dressed elites and low-class commoners read and circulated their poems as written in the "Yuanhe style."[1]

For twenty years, his [Bai Juyi's] poems have been copied on the walls of imperial palaces, temples, and post houses, and read aloud by aristocrats and concubines, herders and stablemen. Everywhere they are copied and duplicated, flaunted and sold, and used to barter for wine or tea. In Yangzhou and Yuezhou, my and Letian's poems are often copied into books and sold in the markets. In some egregious cases, there are people who go so far as to steal our names and outrageously sell their own poems mixed together with ours. Nothing can stop it. Once I went to Pingshui Market, and found that the village school children there vied with each other to learn poetry. I gathered them together to ask them what they learned. They all responded, "The teacher taught me poems by Letian and Weizhi."[2] They certainly didn't know that I myself was Weizhi. There was also a merchant from Kyerim who eagerly tried to buy poems, saying that the prime minister of the kingdom often paid a gold coin per poem and could always tell the forgeries from the authentic. Since the birth of literary writings, such wide circulation has never been seen before.[3]

In the early ninth century, the inseparable companion poets Bai Juyi (772–846) and Yuan Zhen (779–831) dominated the Tang literary world (figures 16.1 and 16.2). The two poets' works attained a vast and penetrating popularity, not only occupying the center of the culture but also reaching beyond the boundaries of the Tang Empire, helping to shape the overall character of Asian literature as a whole. Their literary writings, running a gamut of developments, were broad in subject matter, diverse in forms and genres, and inclusive of social classes of varying degrees of literacy. In order to shape the reception of their poems, they engaged in a wide array of literary activities and performances that gratified the reading public; their anecdotes and legends enjoyed wide currency, and they succeeded in becoming cultural celebrities.

Bai Juyi and Yuan Zhen met around 802 in the capital Chang'an as promising young men actively advancing their careers and interacting with social elites. The two poets soon became close friends, sharing both literary interests and the political ambition to reform the weakening empire in the grave and long-standing aftermath of the An Shi Rebellion (*An Shi zhi luan*) (755–763). They gladly accepted

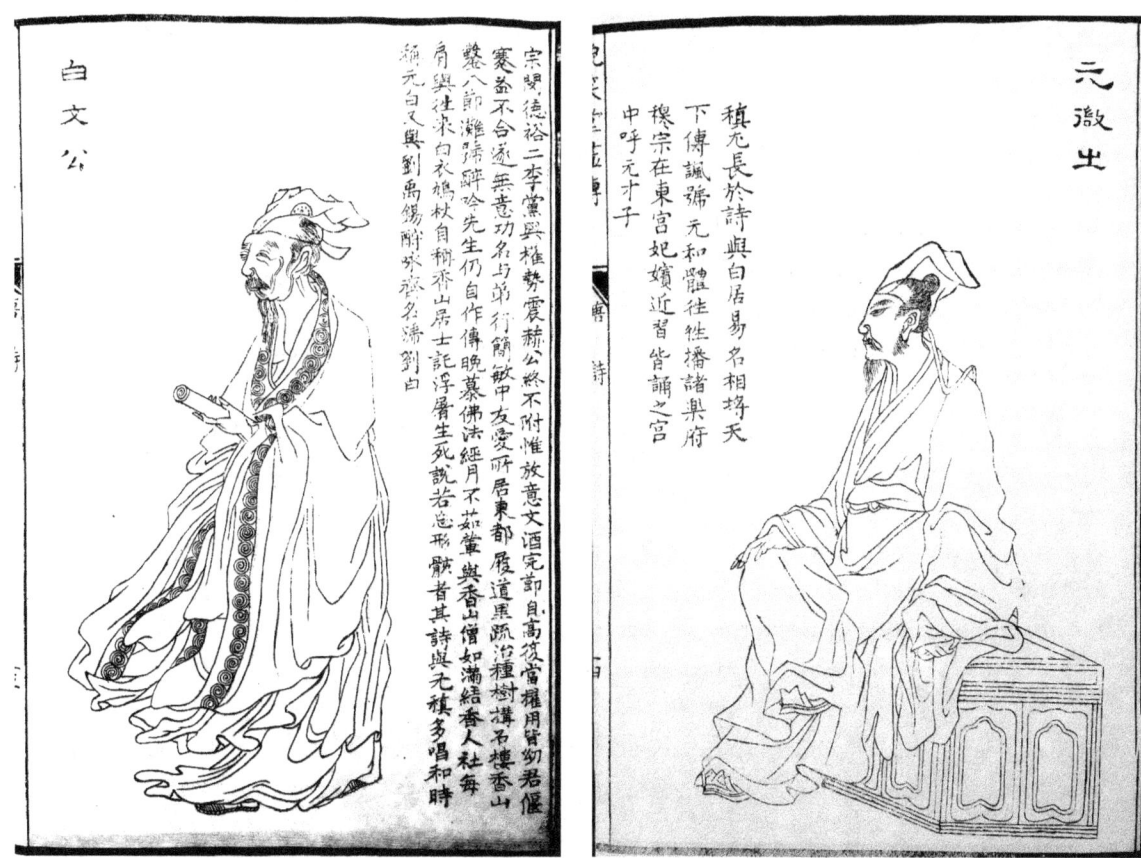

FIGURE 16.1 AND 16.2 Bai Wengong (aka Bai Juyi), left, and Yuan Weizhi (aka Yuan Zhen), right, by Shangguan Zhou 上官周 (1665–1752?). Qing dynasty woodblock print (1743), reprinted by the *Shanghai Journal* Office 申報館 (*Shenbao guan*) as *Zhu Zhuang's Portraits from the Hall of Late Blossoming* 晚笑堂竹莊畫傳 (Wanxiao tang zhuzhuang hua zhuan) (1921).

"Yuan-Bai" as a collective denomination representing a kind of poetic duet, a new literary trademark, and a mutual admiration society designed to encourage the appreciation of others. The amalgamation of Yuan-Bai, as it spanned more than three decades and spawned several hundred poems, amounted to an ideal friendship that informed many of their poetic innovations, from their early narrative poems aimed at direct social protest, to their later experiments in long, regulated verse that displayed great virtuosity.

Because the two poets' most important literary experiments were formed on the basis of a deeply intertwined and extended poetic dialogue, their achievements would be undervalued were they to be considered only separately. Indeed, for their contemporaries, Yuan Zhen and Bai Juyi's mutuality was inevitable, as they both reinforced it over the course of many years and used their collaboration as a powerful mechanism to multiply the influence of their poetic enterprise, in part by creating anecdotes and legends about themselves.

One early example of this is Yuan Zhen's tale of dream telepathy in the year 809. The basic plot was recorded by the Song dynasty scholar Ji Yougong in his *Records of Tang Poetry* (*Tangshi jishi*).[4] The text epitomizes Yuan and Bai's intentional romanticizing of their friendship and their incorporation of it in their corresponding pieces:

Yuan Zhen was appointed Imperial Censor in the fourth year of the Yuanhe reign [in 809] and went to Zitong to supervise law cases there. Bai Juyi and his brother Bai Xingjian bade him farewell at the west gate of the city. After ten days, the Bai brothers went roaming by the Qujiang Lake and went to the Ci'en Temple with Li Jian. Drunk on wine, Bai Juyi wrote a poem:

When flowers bloom, we all get drunk to soothe the melancholy of spring.	花時同醉破春愁
Tipsy, I break some flowering boughs to count the wine cups with,	醉折花枝作酒籌
And suddenly recall my old friend traveling afar,	忽憶故人天際去
And count the days he has been gone, supposing that today he reached Liangzhou.	計程今日到梁州

Ten days later, Bai Juyi received Yuan Zhen's letter, from which he learned that Yuan Zhen had arrived in Liangzhou ten days earlier. There is also a poem in Yuan Zhen's letter:

In my dream, you brothers were on the headstream of the Qujiang,	夢君兄弟曲江頭
And went on to visit the Maternal Kindness Temple.	也到慈恩寺院遊
The manager of the post house ordered the servants to lead the horses.	驛吏喚人排馬去
When I awoke I was surprised to find myself in the old Liangzhou.	忽驚身在古梁州

Yuan Zhen and Bai Juyi had a spiritual communion that surpassed the distance of a thousand *li*. "Gan Meng Ji" ("The Story of the Dream Telepathy") is an account of this story.

[TSJS 563]

The story showcases the unique ways in which the two poets tried to invoke wonder from their readers by multiplying real and imaginary spaces in their interactive writings. Dream provides a dramatic framework in which a long tradition of dream interpretation can come into play. From the ancient text *Rites of Zhou* (*Zhouli*) to Tang poems, dreams had been seen as both revealing the dreamer's thoughts and foretelling future events. This story both draws on and modifies this tradition.

Yuan Zhen's dream enfolds the area of Qujiang, one of the most famous scenic spots in Chang'an, where a party of his peers gathers. At the time, he was in fact staying in a faraway post house, as revealed by Bai Juyi's poem composed at the same time. Yuan Zhen's dream is a result of his longing for reunion with Bai, but this reason is absent in the story for the purposes of a more dramatic surprise. His dream does not foretell the future but is verified by what happens simultaneously. In this way, dreams, places and people, poetry, narrative, and letters all come into play to engender an enhanced connectivity and a dramatic synchronization, giving the expanding geographic distance a new meaning as the tangible measure of a poetic friendship. As Yuan Zhen went farther on his trip, he continued to send poems back to Chang'an, and Bai Juyi responded with his own array of poems. As a result, both poets established poetic sequences that corresponded in thematic and formal concerns.

As we can see in this story and in many of Yuan and Bai's poems, the post house often held a special meaning as a cultural space for traveling poet-officials. The Tang post houses not only served as a postal system that configured routes of information and contact but also provided accommodation and transportation services to traveling government officials. Writing, exchanging, and collecting poetry along the routes threaded by the post houses created new literary rhythms and a unique poetic sensibility in travel literature of the time.

Before Yuan Zhen's experience of dream telepathy, he stopped at a post house, where he saw on its eastern wall the names of politicians Li Fengji (758–835) and Cui Shao (fl. ninth century), written on their way to Yunnan. On the northern wall were Bai Juyi's poems, and also poems that Bai's Daoist friend Wang Zhifu (fl. 806), whom Yuan did not know, had written in response. Traveling alone, Yuan read the poems as if talking with friends new and old, and he recorded this experience on the wall in the form of poems titled "Two Poems on the Wall of Luokou Post" ("Luokou Yi er shou"). The first poem reads:

Those lines on the walls of the hall of the post house	郵亭壁上數行字
2　are the names of Cui and Li, and poems by Wang and Bai.	崔李題名王白詩
For a long time no one has spoken to me.	盡日無人共言語
4　I did not leave these walls until I set out.	不離牆下至行時

[YZJBNJZSGJ 141]

The words inscribed on the walls established carefully demarcated domains that nevertheless allowed others to enter. Though people passed by the place at different times, they could join in a dialogue that expanded the mode of exchange poems and added more improvisatory elements.

Yuan Zhen's poem seems plain on the surface, but with a handful of quick brushstrokes it succinctly captured the moment in which he felt compelled to write in order to reunite with Bai Juyi. The poem also continued the conversation between Bai and Wang and linked it with the two names on the other wall, bringing together different routes and suggesting a sense of overlapping time and space created through the channel of official missions. This merging of the two groups is disrupted by the second poem, which reimagines them in the present time and place:

Beyond the border two stars deal with the southern barbarians.	二星徼外通蠻服
2　Overnight a Hanlin scholar drafts an imperial edict by lamplight.	五夜燈前草御文
On my road to Dongchuan, I am exactly halfway between them.	我到東川恰相半
4　In my sight the moon is in the south, the clouds in the north.	向南看月北看雲

[YZJBNJZSGJ 142]

Here time and space are reconfigured according to the officials' positions in the political system of the empire. The "two stars" stand for the two emissaries, Li Fengji (758–835) and Cui Shao (fl. ninth century), who were sent to the empire's southern boundary. At the same time, Yuan Zhen imagines Bai Juyi, at the time a scholar at the imperial Hanlin Academy (*Hanlin yuan*), drafting an edict for the emperor. Yuan Zhen then reflects on his own presence during his mission to Sichuan and realizes that he is between Chang'an and the southern border area. Looking to the south, he imagines that the moon is shining above the two emissaries, and to the north the clouds loom above Bai Juyi, while he is in between, writing this impromptu poem. Thus, Yuan Zhen uses this poem as a way to navigate the intricate political world and reconnect with his peers in a symbolic way.

On a larger social scale, the stories and poems occasioned by post houses also reflect the attitudes and values of a rising social and intellectual meritocracy based on the civil service examination system (*keju*). *Keju* was first established during the Sui dynasty, and it continued on to flourish during the Tang as an important mechanism to promote highly educated people for government recruitment.

Literary accomplishment was an important criterion for the exam, as candidates were required to compose regulated verse consisting of twelve lines in a strictly regulated form.

While preparing for the examination in the capital, candidates from nonaristocratic families used the opportunity to advance their careers, interact with social elites, and form friendships that would evolve into intertwined literary schools and political factions. Major poets of the middle Tang, such as Han Yu (768–824), Liu Zongyuan (773–819), Liu Yuxi (772–842), Yuan Zhen, and Bai Juyi were all members of this community. Though varying in their specific political and literary orientations, they shared a similar desire to rectify the social injustices of the time and to restore power to the empire, even as it was gradually disintegrating.

At the turn of the ninth century, both Yuan Zhen and Bai Juyi were young candidates who prepared for and excelled in several subcategories of the civil examination. While Yuan Zhen took an expedited path to pass the canonical expert (*mingjing*) examination at the age of fourteen, Bai Juyi was awarded the more prominent presented scholar (*jinshi*) title after many years of hard work. The two like-minded young poets then joined forces and studied together for the decree writing exam (*zhiju*), writing and debating intensely on issues of social and political improvement. In what leisure time they had, they immersed themselves in the cultural life of the Qujiang area, which was dotted with imperial gardens, public parks, and temples.

In contrast to their high Tang (712–756) predecessors such as Li Bai and Du Fu, whose political careers were largely unimportant, Yuan Zhen and Bai Juyi became veteran politicians engaged in many important political struggles and in factional infighting that sometimes escalated to a life-threatening level. Both poets spent years in exile and suffered the pain and humiliations of demotion, libels and conspiracies, serious diseases, impediments to communication, temporary unemployment, separations and bereavements of family members, and so on.

While in exile, dramatizing contingency and coincidence again became the two poets' stock-in-trade way to call and respond to their respective alter egos. The following poem tells how Yuan discovered Bai's poetry in an unlikely situation, and how it restored hope to him at a difficult time:

ON SEEING LETIAN'S POEM 見樂天詩

Arriving at Tongzhou as the sun was sinking to the west, 通州到日日平西
2 the house by the river was abandoned, a tiger's tracks in the mud. 江館無人虎印泥
Suddenly across the ruined eaves and fractures 忽向破簷殘漏處
4 I saw your poem inscribed on the center of a pillar. 見君詩在柱心題

[YZJBNJZSGJ 639]

In June 815, the demoted Yuan Zhen arrived at his temporary housing in Tongzhou (now in Sichuan province), where he would stay before taking up his new post as an adjutant, a position without much power. He had spent three months on the road in poor health, making the difficult journey from the capital Chang'an toward an unpredictable future, often wondering whether he would return alive. When he arrived at the desolate house at dusk, he found suspicious traces of an animal and was seized by the idea that they had been made by a tiger. Not knowing whether the creature was still lying in wait, he surveyed the house, and suddenly, as if by magic, there appeared on a pillar a poem by Bai Juyi, composed some fifteen years earlier to celebrate the life of polished urbanity and sensual enjoyment in the capital.

Using swift transitions, Yuan Zhen's concise quatrain connects itself with Bai Juyi's poem, thereby providing an account of the significance of reading, writing, and spreading poetry in the empire's dangerous periphery. Both poets had powerful enemies in the court, who were responsible for their exile, as well as political allies avidly longing for their return. Although Bai Juyi's lines copied on the column do not address Yuan Zhen's misadventure, they function within Yuan's poem as a counter-force both to the grave political reality in the capital and to the intimidating new environment he was obliged to face.

By this time, the two poets had already begun to make the searching out and reading of each other's poetry a common topic in their exchange poems. In the same year, Bai Juyi was demoted. On the road to Jiangzhou (now in Jiangxi province), he addressed Yuan Zhen as follows: "Each time I arrive at a post house I first dismount, / Following the walls and circling the pillars for your poetry" (*BJYSJJZ* 1212).

In this couplet, Bai Juyi assumes that it is likely he will find Yuan Zhen's poems in every post house, either written by Yuan himself or copied out by his admirers. Both poets had often seen their work presented and circulated in public spaces, and their mutual promotion helped further expand their sphere of influence among readers.

During that same year, Yuan Zhen wrote a quatrain commemorating the experience of copying Bai Juyi's poems onto the wall of a Buddhist temple:

COPYING LETIAN'S POEMS ON THE WALLS OF THE KAIYUAN TEMPLE IN LANGZHOU 閬州開元寺壁題樂天詩

  I missed you so much that I copied out your poems. 憶君無計寫君詩
2 I finished a thousand lines, but whom could I tell? 寫盡千行說向誰
  They are written on the walls of Langzhou's East Temple. 題在閬州東寺壁
4 Who can say when I shall see you again? 幾時知是見君時

[*YZJBNJZSGJ* 744]

Bai Juyi then copied Yuan Zhen's poems onto a folding screen and wrote a poem in response:

IN RESPONSE TO WEIZHI 答微之

  You wrote my poems across the temple walls, 君寫我詩盈寺壁
2 I filled a folding screen with your lines. 我題君句滿屏風
  I do not know where we shall meet again, 與君相遇知何處
4 two weeds floating in the sea. 兩葉浮萍大海中

[*BJYSJJZ* 1375]

The poem's central figure is the floating weeds, with its Buddhist implications of life's transience and fortuity. As the first couplet shows, the poets anticipate an imaginary reunion by collecting each other's poems and presenting them in their own calligraphic hand, creating substituted images of themselves as the ideal reader of their alter ego. The action of copying each other's poems in both public and private became a symbolic synchronization of their separated lives. In this vein, the two poets can imagine a spiritual reunion without breaking from their own life trajectories.

Another method of poetic call and response was to echo their past exchange poems while addressing their current situations. In 804, Bai Juyi wrote a poem addressing Yuan Zhen:

BY THE QUJIANG; THINKING OF YUAN THE NINTH 曲江憶元九

Without a companion, since Spring I have seldom gone out, 春來無伴閒遊少
2 every pleasure without you is two-thirds less. 行樂三分減二分
Today in the Apricot Garden, 何況今朝杏園裏
4 without you, I feel nothing for the many I meet. 閒人逢盡不逢君

[BJYSJJZ 1014]

Yuan Zhen must have been greatly impressed by this quatrain, admiring the subtle voice expressing longing for his companionship in the crowded environs of the Apricot Garden. Thirteen years later, Yuan Zhen replied to these lines in an exchange poem, in response to this poem sent to him by Bai Juyi:

DREAMING OF WEIZHI 夢微之

I rose this morning disconsolate, 晨起臨風一惆悵
2 you are in Tongzhou, the Pen River a barrier between us. 通川溢水斷相聞
What made you miss me so much? 不知憶我因何事
4 Last night I dreamt of you. 昨夜三更夢見君

[BJYSJJZ 1357]

When Yuan Zhen received Bai's poem, he was seriously ill with malaria, which enhanced his desire for consolation from his old friend. His poem both responds to Bai's present poem and echoes the old one with a sure hand:

IN RESPONSE TO LETIAN, WHO FREQUENTLY DREAMT OF ME 酬樂天頻夢微之

Myriad mountains and rivers obstruct our letters. 山水萬重書斷絕
2 Since you dream of me I know you miss me. 念君憐我夢相聞
Now I am so sick that my soul tumbles in torment, 我今因病魂顛倒
4 I dream of useless others and not of you. 惟夢閒人不夢君

[YZJBNJZSGJ 750]

Demonstrating the intensity of Yuan Zhen's anxiety, the poem is unexpectedly powerful in acting out his pathos in answer to Bai Juyi's longing for community. It responds to Bai Juyi's dreaming of him by not reciprocating and thus creates a more powerful affirmation of his emotions toward his friend by veering off, in a dramatic diversion, to his disturbed mental state. Again, in this short poem Yuan Zhen engages in an extended colloquy that transcends time and space. By alluding to and answering Bai Juyi's previous poem, the former colloquy is reactivated while the present one finds a direction toward the past; they enter each other as indissolubly as two streams of memories and feelings, both dwelling in time and transcending time.

The poetic dialogue between Yuan Zhen and Bai Juyi continued after Yuan's death in 831, though only in Bai's imagination:

DREAMING OF WEIZHI 夢微之

    You were buried under the yellow spring, your bones eroded by mud. 君埋泉下泥銷骨
2 For a time I will stay in the human world with snowy hair. 我寄人間雪滿頭
    On the vast indistinct night platform, 阿衛韓郎相次去
4 do you know that A Wei and Han Lang died one after another? 夜台茫昧得知不

[BJYSJJZ 2668]

In the final couplet, Bai Juyi is referring to Yuan Zhen's daughter, A Wei, and his daughter-in-law, Han Lang, both of whom had passed away. He questions the existence of the human soul after death, tingeing his own image with a sense of self-mourning. In a paradoxical way, he even claims that the loss of Yuan Zhen could mean the end of his poetic career:

WAILING FOR WEIZHI 哭微之

    How can we meet again in this life? 今生豈有相逢日
2 The one who is not dead will not forget this pain for an instant. 未死應無暫忘時
    After these three poems I will wipe away my tears 從此三篇收淚後
4 And never chant another poem for the rest of my life. 終身無複更吟詩

[BJYSJJZ 2874]

Bai Juyi continued to write poetry for another decade, but he always regarded Yuan Zhen's companionship as being central to his poetic enterprise and professed that Yuan's death tragically weakened his own poetic power.

Yuan Zhen's reputation declined soon after he died, whereas Bai Juyi remains one of the most celebrated Chinese poets, and his legacy remains vibrant in East Asian cultures. Yuan Zhen is now primarily known as a sidekick who complemented Bai Juyi's much greater achievements. Had Bai Juyi foreseen this, he would have been the first to defend the greatness of his friend, and, as it turns out, this disregard for Yuan Zhen has also meant a loss to Bai, since some of their most valuable and intricate interactions have consequently been consigned to oblivion.

To attest that Yuan Zhen's poetic power both equals and differs from Bai Juyi's, we may choose an example, by way of comparison, in which both poets deal with the same subject matter: the tragic love story between Yang Yuhuan (719–756) and Emperor Xuanzong (r. 712–756). Bai Juyi's poem is the long ballad "Song of Lasting Pain" ("Chang hen ge"), comprising 120 lines in heptasyllabic structure; Yuan Zhen's is the quatrain "The Temporary Palace" ("Xinggong").

Bai Juyi wrote "Song of Lasting Pain" in 806, half a century after the An Shi Rebellion, while he was away from Chang'an. When he returned to Chang'an, a month after composing the poem, he quickly heard a story about its popularity, which he later retold in a letter to Yuan Zhen: "I also heard that General Gao Xiayu [?–826] wanted to hire a singing girl. The singing girl boasted, 'I can recite scholar Bai's "Song of Lasting Pain." How can I be treated as other singing girls?' Her price was raised accordingly."[5] As a poet who carefully studied his readers' responses, Bai Juyi suggested that the general, who was famous for his rudeness and vulgar language, and the singing girl had reached a consensus that his poem was distinguished and valuable. The poem in fact became Bai's most celebrated piece, in his own time as well as in literary history.

The long ballad assumes the voice of a storyteller and starts with Emperor Xuanzong's search for the most beautiful girl in his empire, introducing the reader to a world where beauty is the highest value and where love transcends death and the mundane world. As Bai Juyi describes her, the heroine Yang Yuhuan has matchless beauty:

	When she turned around with smiling glance she exuded every charm;	回眸一笑百媚生
8	in the harem all who wore powder and paint of beauty then seemed barren.	六宫粉黛無顔色

Bai Juyi carefully avoids exposing the real story of Yang's first encounter with Emperor Xuanzong and the well-known fact that Yang was originally the emperor's own daughter-in-law, meaning that their union was a case of incestuous adultery, an example of the underlying dark side of the Tang royal family. The speaker of the poem feels indifferent to his apparent distortion of history, but, subtly modulated by Bai's rhetoric, his voice never sounds pretentious, and he succeeds in gradually distancing the love story from history. The lovers' first encounter is presented in an erotic scene that invites the reader to share the emperor's gaze upon Yang's gorgeous body:

	In springtime's chill he let her bathe in Hua-qing Palace's pools	春寒賜浴華清池
10	whose warm springs' glistening waters washed flecks of dried lotions away.	溫泉水滑洗凝脂
	Those in attendance helped her rise, in helplessness so charming—	侍兒扶起嬌無力
12	this was the moment when first she enjoyed the flood of royal favor.	始是新承恩澤時

The most sensual moment in the poem, this scene has been adopted by many later fictions, dramas, and paintings about Yang. Stripped, washed, and helped to stand, her body is exhibited as a radiant center. Although there is no depiction of sexual intercourse, these four lines touch the quintessence of erotic literature, in that the eroticism is essentially visual and invites voyeuristic imagination.

In addition to the direct exposure of the erotic, the poem also makes profound use of the description of music to map the popular imagination about the secret life of the inner palace:

	The high places of Mount Li's palace rose up into blue clouds,	驪宮高處入青雲
28	where the music of gods was whirled in winds and everywhere was heard.	仙樂飄飄處處聞

Here the palace is presented as a special space: elevated into the sky yet grounded by the ubiquitous presence of music and sensual pleasure. Not long after, the An Shi Rebellion suddenly interrupted Yang's famous performances of music and dance and simultaneously brought the destruction of the romantic world supported by Emperor Xuanzong's authority:

	The kettledrums from Yu-yang came, making the whole earth tremble	漁陽鼙鼓動地来
32	and shook apart those melodies "Coats of Feathers, Rainbow Skirts."	驚破霓裳羽衣曲

Only these two lines directly address the historical turning point of the An Shi Rebellion, the fall of the Tang capital. Yet, in Bai Juyi's ballad, the rebellion is presented by a simple synecdoche, "the kettledrums from Yu-yang," designed to emphasize its musical quality, which both alludes to and conflicts with the music of Yang. Although "making the whole earth tremble," the kettledrums lack the gravity that matches the nightmarish magnitude of the rebellion, as is presented, for example, in the high Tang poet Du Fu's great poems. Rather, Bai Juyi has the rebellion come swiftly and musically, as if it is merely the bridge in a long story, a pause in a change of scenes. Bai also wisely avoids any digressions on the rumor about the incestuous adultery between the rebellious general An Lushan and Yang. In the poem, Yang belongs entirely to the emperor, faithful even after her death.

The rest of the poem tells how much Emperor Xuanzong missed Yang after her execution during the rebellion. As we can see in the poem, curiously enough, the emperor thinks about Yang day and night but never dreams about her, which symbolically indicates he cannot reunite with Yang by means of his own imagination:

	On forever, living and dead, were parted through the years,	悠悠生死別經年
74	and never once did her wondering soul find way into his dreams.	魂魄不曾来入夢

In the poem, a Daoist magician comes to the emperor's aid and finds Yang on an immortal island. The poem eventually reaches its dramatic peak when Yang gives the Daoist magician several ornaments as a token of her love for the emperor. The poem flashes back to the past, and at the moment Yang tells the Daoist magician about her private commitment to the emperor, her identity is proven:

	On the seventh day of the seventh month, in the Palace of Lasting Life,	七月七日長生殿
116	it was midnight, no one else was there, as they whispered privately:	夜半無人私語時
	if in Heaven, may we become those birds that fly on shared wings;	在天願作比翼鳥
118	or on Earth, then may we become branches that twine together.	在地願為連理枝

In the end, the poem unifies past and present, the private and the supernatural, and elevates the love of Emperor Xuanzong and Yang to an immortal status:

	Heaven lasts, the Earth endures, yet a time will come when they're gone,	天長地久有時盡
120	yet this pain of ours will continue and never finally end.	此恨綿綿無絕期

[BJYSJJZ 943–944; TRANS. OWEN, 442–447]

This long ballad is one of Bai Juyi's most accomplished poems, for its artistic merits and its enthusiastic reception. It continues to be praised to this day. It certainly inspired Yuan Zhen to write his own long ballad, "The Ballad of the Lianchang Palace" ("Lianchang gong ci"), which traces the rise and fall of the high Tang and features both Emperor Xuanzong and Yang. Although a strong poem in its own right, it does not achieve the sublimity of Bai Juyi's ballad.

Yet Yuan Zhen's quatrain "The Temporary Palace" stands out as a poem that can vie with "Song of Lasting Pain." As the Ming writer and critic Qu You (1347–1427) observes, "Bai Juyi's 'Song of Lasting Pain' has one hundred and twenty lines, but we do not mind that it is so long. 'The Temporary Palace' only has four lines, but we tend to forget that it is so short."

	In the old palace that has crumbled,	寥落古行宮
2	the garden blossoms redden in the silence.	宮花寂寞紅
	A white-haired palace maiden remains,	白頭宮女在
4	at her leisure, still speaking of Emperor Xuanzong.	閑坐說玄宗

[YZJBNJZSGJ 194]

In the first couplet, the poem delicately describes a helpless situation, and then it quietly gathers strength as it imagines an old palace maiden as a witness and storyteller of the history of the high Tang. She is alone and at ease, as if after several decades she has become accustomed to repeating the same story, and even appears indifferent to it. This gives rise to an even deeper sense of the pain of having lost a golden time and evokes the reader's sympathy for an unconscious victim of history.

But what story does she tell? The poem ends here, and the reader is left wondering. The white-haired maiden is not as articulate and passionate a rhetorician as the narrator in Bai's "Song of Lasting Pain," and the poem gives no more than the emperor's name. In "The Temporary Palace," the voice of the lonely storyteller is muffled, as her telling of the story fades into the background, creating a powerful, lingering overtone that slows the reader down into a trance that manages to encompass the whole range of Bai Juyi's ballad.

This comparison between Bai's ballad and Yuan's quatrain provides only a glimpse into how the two poets influenced and competed with each other during their long poetic careers (for more poems of Bai, ☞ *HTRCP* C11.4; *WKB* P07). As this chapter reveals, Bai Juyi was by no means a grand literary figure who rose as sui generis and stood in a class of his own. He instead belonged to a literary milieu of great fertility and fraternity, in which he received constant support as well as competitive poetic incentive. Without Yuan Zhen and the long-standing collective of "Yuan-Bai," Bai Juyi would have become a different and perhaps less celebrated poet. For his part, Yuan Zhen used Bai's poetic genius to inspire his own work, creating poetry that strongly resonated with both personal and historical meaning.

From the metropolis of Chang'an to various far-flung post houses, from an overseas island to a temporary palace, Yuan Zhen's and Bai Juyi's poems fit into a broader cultural context and came quickly to represent the ascending middle Tang *jinshi* community within which the two poets played a pivotal role. These works also served to further an enterprise by two distinct poetic voices: to embrace the empire within the compass of strong political and literary forces that were as paralleled, counterpointed, and intertwined as the two poets' lives. Although Yuan Zhen has often been underrepresented in literary history, the collective Yuan-Bai has left a permanent mark on Chinese literature.

AO WANG

NOTES

1. From Liu Xu et al., "The Biography of Yuan Zhen" ("Yuan Zhen zhuan"), in *Old History of the Tang* (*Jiu Tang shu*) (Beijing: Zhonghua shuju, 1975), 4332.
2. Bai's courtesy name is Letian; Yuan's is Weizhi.
3. From Yuan Zhen's "Preface to *Bai Juyi's Collected Works Compiled During the Changqing Reign*" ("Baishi Changqing ji xu"), which he helped to edit in 824. See Yang Jun, ed., *Yuan Zhen ji biannian jianzhu, sanwen juan* (Xi'an: Sanqin chubanshe, 2008), 932.
4. The story also appeared in "The Record of Three Dreams" ("Sanmeng ji"), attributed to Bai Xingjian (776–826), as well as in the late Tang author Meng Qi's (fl. 841–886) *Poems in Their Original Occasions* (*Benshi shi*). I choose Ji's version because the poems quoted in Bai Xingjian's story are slightly different from those in Yuan and Bai's standard collected poems, and Meng's version is much simplified.
5. See Bai Juyi, "Yu Yuanjiu shu" (A Letter to Yuan the Ninth), in *Bai Juyi wenji jiaozhu* (The Collated and Annotated Prose Works of Bai Juyi), edited by Xie Siwei (Beijing: Zhonghua shuju, 2011), 325.

PRIMARY SOURCES

BJYSJJZ	Xie Siwei 謝思煒, ed. *Bai Juyi shiji jiaozhu* 白居易詩集校註 (The Collated and Annotated Poetic Works of Bai Juyi). Beijing: Zhonghua shuju, 2006.
TSJS	Ji Yonggong 計有功. *Tangshi jishi* 唐詩紀事 (Records of Tang Poetry). Shanghai: Shanghai guji chubanshe, 1987.
YZJBNJZSGJ	Yang Jun 楊軍, ed. *Yuan Zhen ji biannian jianzhu, shige juan* 元稹集編年箋註詩歌卷 (Yuan Zhen's Collected Works, Chronicled with Notes and Commentaries: Poetry). Xi'an: Sanqin chubanshe, 2008.

SUGGESTED READINGS

ENGLISH

Owen, Stephen, ed. and trans. *An Anthology of Chinese Literature: Beginnings to 1911*. New York: Norton, 1996.
Shields, Anna M. "Remembering When: The Uses of Nostalgia in the Poetry of Bai Juyi and Yuan Zhen." *Harvard Journal of Asiatic Studies* 66, no. 2 (2006): 321–361.

Wu, Shuling. "The Development of Poetry Helped by Ancient Postal Service in the Tang Dynasty." *Frontiers of Literary Studies in China* 4, no. 4 (2010): 553–577.

CHINESE

Bai Juyi 白居易. "Yu Yuanjiu shu" 與元九書 (A Letter to Yuan the Ninth). In *Bai Juyi wenji jiaozhu* 白居易文集校註 (The Collated and Annotated Prose Works of Bai Juyi), ed. Xie Siwei 謝思煒. Beijing: Zhonghua shuju, 2011.

Ji Yonggong 計有功. *Tangshi jishi* 唐詩紀事 (Records of Tang Poetry). Shanghai: Shanghai guji chubanshe, 1987.

Liu Xu 劉昫 et al. *Jiu Tang shu* 舊唐書 (Old History of the Tang). Beijing: Zhonghua shuju, 1975.

Yuan Zhen 元稹. "Baishi Changqing ji xu" 白氏長慶集序 (Preface to *Bai Juyi's Collected Works Compiled During the Changqing Reign*). In *Yuan Zhen ji biannian jianzhu, sanwen juan* 元稹集編年箋註散文卷 (Yuan Zhen's Collected Works, Chronicled with Notes and Commentaries: Prose), ed. Yang Jun 楊軍. Xi'an: Sanqin chubanshe, 2008.

❋ 17 ❋

LI HE

Poetry as Obsession

A STRANGE SOUND IN THE NIGHT

In the middle of the night one night in the tenth month of year five of the Taihe era [831] an urgent cry was heard outside my rooms, announcing the delivery of a sealed letter. I said to myself, "There is surely something strange afoot."[1]

With their air of mystery, these opening lines would fit seamlessly into a collection of ghost stories. What lay behind this particular nighttime disturbance, however, was not the return of a restless soul but the reappearance of a misplaced packet of poems. This is the preface to the first compilation of the poetry of Li He (courtesy name Changji [790–816]) (figure 17.1), written fifteen years after Li He's death by Du Mu (803–852), himself a major late Tang poet. Still, this preface does reveal much that is "strange," and even ghostly, about those poems and their author:

> I quickly brought a light, and when I opened the letter, my expectation was confirmed: it was from Master Shen [Shushi; fl. early ninth century], academician of the Academy of Assembled Worthies, and it read, "My late friend Li He and I were devoted friends during the Yuanhe era [806–820], inseparable day and night, sharing all our food and drink together. When Li He was about to die, he handed me the songs he had composed over the course of his life, divided into four bundles, totaling 233 poems. These past several years I've roamed north, south, east, and west, and I thought I'd misplaced them somewhere. Tonight, when my head cleared after a bout of drinking, I was unable to get back to sleep, so I browsed through my books and papers—and suddenly I came across those poems Li He gave me. One by one I called to mind those past events, all our conversations and happy excursions—and each place, each natural scene, each day and night, each cup of wine, each meal, all were clearly present before me, with nothing left out. I found myself weeping. And Li He left no family or kinfolk behind whom I could offer support or visit in his memory, so I'm always regretting how I must muse on my friend, and chant and savor his words, and nothing more. You, sir, then, do me a kindness, and compose a preface to Li He's collection for me, giving a full account of how this came about—this would bring some comfort to my feelings."[2]

In Chinese tradition, ghosts are souls of the dead who, lacking living descendants to provide them the pacifying sustenance of remembrance, tears, and sacrificial offerings, are often forced to solicit

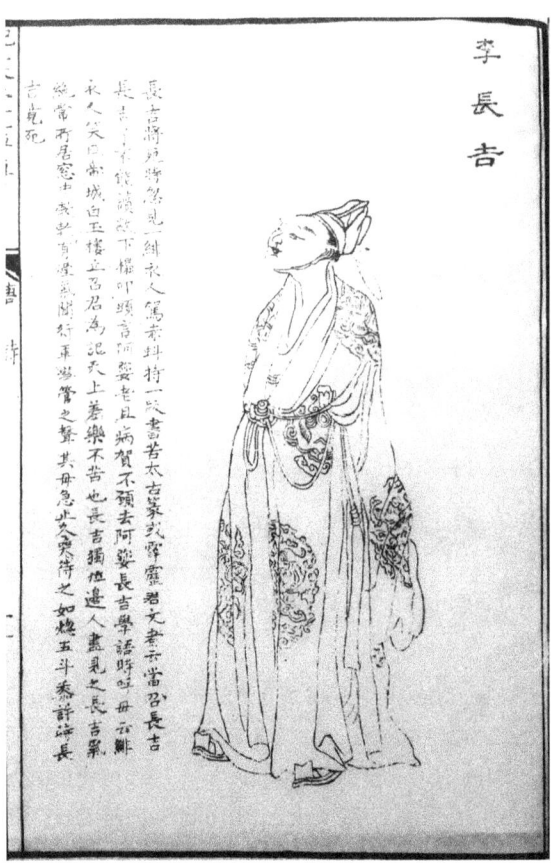

FIGURE 17.1 Li Changji (aka Li He), by Shangguan Zhou 上官周 (1665–1752?). Qing dynasty woodblock print (1743), reprinted by the *Shanghai Journal* Office 申報館 (*Shenbao guan*) as *Zhu Zhuang's Portraits from the Hall of Late Blossoming* 晚笑堂竹莊畫傳 (Wanxiao tang zhuzhuang hua zhuan) (1921).

the sympathy and assistance of strangers. Thus, although Li He does not appear here as a ghost in the literal sense, his fate—a young man dead at twenty-six, with few surviving relatives, nearly forgotten by even his closest friends—casts him in a ghostlike role. The moment recounted above, when the unexpected reappearance of an old bundle of papers brings memories of Li He flooding back to the mind of a sleepless and distracted Shen Shushi, could be recast as a ghost story proper, with minimal alteration.

Li He became the emblematic "cursed poet." Just as his text escaped oblivion only due to the fortuitous events outlined in Du Mu's preface,[3] his poetry itself is haunted to an extreme degree by a sense of the incompleteness and fragility of his own contact with the literary and cultural legacy of the past, and by a keen awareness that many powerful and beautiful things from long ago, which ought to deeply matter, were lost forever. His poems are often disorienting records of intensely personal visions, challenging the possibility of being shared among contemporaries, let alone posterity. The general tone of pessimism about the permanence of memory in Li He often extends to include a sense of doom about his own survival, whether as person or as text. The fact of his untimely death compounded this sense of doom for later readers, who saw in Li He's works the fragments and preliminary sketches of a poetic talent that never achieved its final form.

A CAREER BLIGHTED

As he was fond of mentioning, Li He had a distant claim of kinship with the Tang imperial house. His father, Li Jinsu, had held at least two official posts, albeit relatively minor and not at court.[4] The primary vocation for a young man of Li He's background and upbringing would naturally have been to succeed in the examination system and rise to prominence in the service of the Tang Empire, and this was indeed the path he set out on. Apart from his family background, the most significant factor shaping Li He's short and undistinguished career appears to have been his connection with members of the circle of Han Yu (768–824), a renowned and distinctive literary stylist and a key cultural and political power broker of the era.

The *Selected Accounts from the Tang* (*Tang zhi yan*), a collection of anecdotes about the Tang's successes and failures in identifying and promoting talented scholars to prominence in public service, includes a story about Li He as a child prodigy: When Li He was seven years old, his name was trumpeted about the capital for his lyrics in long and short lines. At that time, Han Yu and Huangfu Shi (777–835) looked over what he had written and found it remarkable, yet they did not recognize the author. They said to each other, "If this is an ancient, it is one we do not know; if it is someone of the present age, then how can we not know him?"

Just then, someone mentioned the current doings of Li Jinsu, and the two masters rode together to his home and asked to see his son. After a short while Li He came out, with his hair done in the pigtails of a child, weighed down by a robe too large for him. The two masters didn't believe he could be the author of the works they'd read, so Li He gave a demonstration on the spot, cheerfully accepting their command. He grasped a brush and dipped it in ink, as calmly as if no one were watching. He titled the piece "A Lofty Carriage Calls" ("Gao xuan guo"):

	Splendid tunics embroidered with kingfisher, green as scallion;	華裾織翠青如蔥
2	Bridles heavy with golden rings, swaying and jangling.	金環壓轡搖玲瓏
	Horse hooves pound the ears with thunderous boom;	馬蹄隱耳聲隆隆
4	They enter the gate and dismount amid auras of rainbow.	入門下馬氣如虹
	It's said they're: Talents of the Eastern Capital,	云是東京才子
6	Grand masters of writing;	文章鉅公
	The twenty-eight astral lodges arrayed in their breasts,	二十八宿羅心胸
8	Primal essence effulgent, piercing through the midst.	元精耿耿貫當中
	Composing *fu* before the palace, their voices touch the sky;	殿前作賦聲摩空
10	Pens that patch creation's work, leave nature with no claim.	筆補造化天無功
	This wide-browed bookish wanderer, saddened by autumn tumbleweed:	龐眉書客感秋蓬
12	Who knows if this dead grass might flower again in reviving breeze?	誰知死草生華風
	I am now a wild goose, drooping wings amidst ocean's vastness;	我今垂翅附冥鴻
14	Another day unabashed I'll be the snake that turns to dragon.	他日不羞蛇作龍

[*LCJ* 1:1.87]

Han Yu and Huangfu Shi, the story goes, were duly awestruck by this performance and departed with their new protégé in tow (*TWD* 2:1669).

For better or worse, this particular tale of literary marvels happens to be conclusively refutable: it cannot have happened in this way. Although Li He's connection with Han Yu, and with Huangfu Shi and other members of Han Yu's circle, is a crucial fact of his biography, their meeting can only have happened much later.[5] Still, such fantasies reflect how Li He's early readers imagined him and may offer insights into his work.

The poem itself is genuine, but it is almost uncomfortably direct in its flattery and its plea for patronage. The poet's own appearance in line 11 as a "wide-browed bookish wanderer" is striking, and comports with Li Shangyin's (ca. 813–858) account in his "Short Biography of Li He" ("Li He xiao zhuan") that Li He was "thin and frail, with joined eyebrows and long nails" and that "he could compose with painstaking craft and write fast" (*QTW* 8:780.17A [8149]). But what makes the poem memorable is the single line "Pens that patch creation's work, leave nature with no claim." The idea of writer as demiurge is one that attracted Han Yu himself, and by capturing this ideal so vividly, Li He seems to suggest that he partakes of this power as well. By reimagining the scene of Li He's discovery by Han Yu, through this anecdote, early readers confirmed a sense of his gifts as something strange, beyond the normal course of nature, and hinted at forebodings about what retribution they might incur.[6]

A second episode, better substantiated, casts Li He as a young man unlucky in his birth. Having gained literary renown at the capital, and preparing to take the *jinshi* (presented scholar) examination—the single most important and prestigious gateway to career success for a man of letters—he fell victim to a whisper campaign instigated by jealous rivals, which suggested that he should be deemed ineligible for that exam because of the similarity in sound between the name of the examination and that of Li He's father, Li Jinsu. Han Yu, as Li He's patron, wrote an essay in defense of Li He, asking rhetorically, "If the father's name is Ren, shall the son be forbidden to be a human being (*ren*)?"[7] The details of the controversy and its aftermath remain cloudy, but it appears that Li He did take the *jinshi* exam, but failed. Whatever role the taboo controversy may have played, he felt slighted and resentful about this setback, which, given the shortness of his life, was to be for practical purposes definitive.

Li He did eventually secure a legacy appointment, based on his father's former rank, as "vice director for ceremonial" (*feng li lang*), a post near the bottom rung of officialdom and the only office he was ever to occupy. This vice director served as something like a properties and stage manager for court ceremonies, charged with inventorying ritual implements and supplies and with directing participants where to stand, when to bow, when to say their lines, and so forth. In a poem addressed to Chen Shang (presented scholar degree 814), another aspiring writer aligned with Han Yu, Li He was blunt about his sense that his talent was being wasted:

	In wind and frost I attend at the sacred altar,	風霜直齋壇
30	Where black bands loop through bronze seals of office.	墨組貫銅綬
	With a menial's ingratiating postures,	臣妾氣態間
32	My only wish is to wield dustpan and broom.	唯欲承箕帚
	When will heaven's eyes open for once,	天眼何時開
34	So that this ancient sword may let out one roar?	古劍庸一吼

[*LCJ* 1:2.232–233]

In his poetry, Li He was deeply fascinated with sacrificial rites and with spectacles of imperial power. It was thus no doubt bitterly ironic to Li He that the one post he held involved him in court ceremonial, but in a role so lowly he found it demeaning. The final image of the roaring sword in these lines draws on a Southern Dynasties (420–589) anomaly account concerning a sword left behind in a tomb whose occupant has become immortal. When grave robbers broke into the tomb to plunder it, the sword howled, filling the robbers with terror, and then slowly ascended into the sky.[8] An ancient artifact, a remnant of ancient power, buried and neglected and yet capable of bursting into mysterious action—such images abound in Li He's poetry and often, as here, serve as figures for the poet and his craft.

LOST MUSIC

The anecdote about Li He's childhood promise appears in the *Selected Accounts from the Tang* alongside stories of other star-crossed talents of the previous century, whom Wei Zhuang (836–910) listed in a memorial submitted to the Tang throne in 900. He requested the posthumous bestowal of *jinshi* degrees and official ranks on these men, as a gesture of setting right the wrong their fates had done them.[9] There is no record of Wei Zhuang's proposal being carried through, but Li He did receive an unofficial but enduring posthumous promotion of a sort, in the way many readers came to remember him. A persistent later tradition held that Li He's poems had been adopted into the repertoire of the imperial academy musicians and that, as a result, he was appointed to the vacant post of "harmonizer of the pitch pipes" (*xie lü lang*), a court post for music experts, more than a full grade higher than his actual rank of vice director of court ceremonial. In fact, during the Song and later, he was as likely to be referred to as Li Xielü (Li, Harmonizer of the Pitch Pipes) as Li Fengli (Li, Vice Director of Ceremonial), and there is even an edition of his poetry referring to him by his fictitious title.

Though factually baseless, this posthumous "promotion" sheds light both on Li He's image as it took shape among early readers and on the view of his poetry and its function. That first compilation that Shen Shushi rediscovered fifteen years after Li He's death was given the title *Li Changji geshi ji* (*Collected Song-Poems of Li Changji*). The distinctive designation "song-poem" (*geshi*) highlights an aspect of Li He's work that early readers often singled out in describing his poetry: his boldly innovative approach to composing new lyrics to ancient "Music Bureau" (*yuefu*) tune titles from the Han (206 BCE–220 CE) to Southern Dynasties period.

The tradition that Li He served as harmonizer of the pitch pipes is demonstrably fictitious. When it comes to the oft-repeated claim that his lyrics were set to music and performed, the situation is more complex, but there is no evidence that this was ever done with his most characteristic phantasmagoric works, composed as song-poems of one type or another. A close friend of Li He's, writing after Li He's death, lamented precisely that Li He's ancient-style *yuefu* could *not* be set to music.[10] What seems to have attracted Li He to the ancient titles was not the prospect of having them sung by performers but the idea of a poem as a vehicle for reimagining lost ancient music. How this fascination was linked to his conception of his own poetic craft is suggested in the following odd work:

TEASING PRELUDE ON THE BITTER BAMBOO 苦篁調笑引

    Let me tell of events from when Xuanyuan was on earth: 請說軒轅在時事
2 Ling Lun gathered bamboo, twenty-four stalks. 伶倫採竹二十四
    Ling Lun gathered them from the Kunlun mountains; 伶倫採之自崑邱
4 Xuanyuan decreed he should divide them so as to make twelves. 軒轅詔遣中分作一二
    Ling Lun used them to set right the tones and scales; 伶倫以之正音律
6 Xuanyuan used them to attune primal breath. 軒轅以之調元氣
    At that time when the Yellow Emperor ascended to heaven, 當時黃帝上天時
8 Twenty-three of the pipes he took along with him, 二十三管咸相隨
    Leaving only one pipe to be blown in the human world. 唯留一管人間吹
10 Those lacking virtue cannot obtain this pipe; 無德不能得此管
    This pipe lies buried at the shrine of Shun. 此管沉埋虞舜祠

[LCJ 1:3.327]

The legend of the Yellow Emperor (Huang Di), a sage ruler of high antiquity (here also referred to by his alternate title, Xuanyuan) and his assistant, the music master Ling Lun, would seem to belong firmly in the realm of fantasy, but actual sets of pitch pipes, maintained as a ceremonial emblem of the harmonization of cosmic and human forces, played a real role in the symbolic and ritual language of imperial legitimacy in later ages. Li He gives a characteristic twist to the tradition, suggesting that Ling Lun's authentic pitch pipes have returned to heaven, where they more properly belong, and that worldly music can only approximate that ancient sagely music via the single fragmentary pipe left behind. The image of this pipe, the buried remnant of a lost cosmic music, is one of pathos and hidden power.

Li He's use of the titles of lost songs of antiquity is informed by an impulse to stretch the limits of ear and imagination to hear lost sounds from the ancient past. Some such impulse underlies the following work, a song-poem composed not to a traditional *yuefu* title but instead on a topic gleaned from an early medieval tale of the uncanny:

SONG OF THE BRONZE IMMORTAL TAKING LEAVE OF THE HAN 金銅仙人辭漢歌

In the eighth month of year five of the Qinglong era of Emperor Ming of the Wei [237], an imperial decree was issued, commanding the palace officers to drive wagons west to take the basin-bearing immortals of Emperor Wu of the Han, with the intention of erecting them before the palace. When the palace officers had detached the basins, an immortal, on the point of being loaded into the wagons, shed copious tears. Thereupon Li He, descendant of Tang imperial princes, composed the "Song of the Bronze Immortal Taking Leave of the Han."

魏明帝青龍五年八月詔宮官牽車西取漢孝武捧露盤仙人、欲立置前殿。宮官既拆盤、仙人臨載乃潛然淚下。唐諸王孫李長吉遂作金銅仙人辭漢歌。

	Master Liu of Maoling, the "Autumn Wind" wayfarer:	茂陵劉郎秋風客
2	At night one hears horses' neighing, at dawn no tracks remain.	夜聞馬嘶曉無跡
	Osmanthus trees by painted balustrades still suspend their autumn scent,	畫欄桂樹懸秋香
4	But his thirty-six palaces are emerald with lichen rot.	三十六宮土花碧
	The Wei officers drive their wagons across a thousand *li*,	魏官牽車指千里
6	From the eastern passes a sour wind shoots the pupils.	東關酸風射眸子
	In vain bearing the Han moon out the palace gates;	空將漢月出宮門
8	Recalling his lord, he sheds pure tears like liquid lead.	憶君清淚如鉛水
	Blasted orchids send off this traveler on the Xianyang road;	衰蘭送客咸陽道
10	If heaven had feeling, heaven too would grow old.	天若有情天亦老
	Carrying his basin he goes out in desolate moonlight;	攜盤獨出月荒涼
12	The town by the Wei already far, the sound of waves grows faint.	渭城已遠波聲小

[*LCJ* 1:2.159–160]

There are echoes here of the traditional literary meditation on the past, where contrasts between the evanescence of human life and achievement and the impassive permanence of the natural world are a staple. In lines 3 and 4, for example, the osmanthus blossoms still send their fragrance through the air, while the ruins of the old Han palace complex sink in gaudy decay. But the usual binary of past versus present that underpins such works is complicated here: the recollection of Han dynasty imperial splendor is not framed in the poet's present but rather within an anomaly tale dated to the third century. Li He's interest here lies not in drawing moral lessons but rather in the vertiginous imaginative leap involved in projecting oneself into the perspective of the tale's protagonist—an ancient bronze statue, forlorn remnant of a powerful emperor-poet's doomed efforts to escape mortality.

This poem's tenth line is so striking that it took on a life of its own as an aphorism. Read in isolation, it is a vividly counterfactual expression of a somewhat conventional sentiment: unfeeling (*wu qing*) nature is immune to the transience and decline that feeling (*you qing*) humans cannot avoid. The line's real strangeness, and Li He's parting of ways with the commonplace, only emerges clearly within its setting in this poem, which centers on the bronze immortal's uncanny crossing of the boundary between *you qing* and *wu qing*. The receding sound of water with which the poem ends would fit naturally at the close of an excursion or parting poem, but what would there be lovely but conventional becomes here hauntingly uncanny because we must imagine the river's fading sound from the bronze immortal's perspective.

Ancient musical discourse was strongly centered on the musical tastes and habits of rulers, both because these had the greatest implications for the common good and therefore needed to be properly directed and controlled, and because it was rulers who naturally had the means to enjoy music to the utmost. Another of Li He's renowned song-poems explores this latter dimension with breathtaking abandon:

THE KING OF QIN DRINKS 秦王飲酒

	Astride a tiger, the King of Qin roams the universe's eight bounds;	秦王騎虎遊八極
2	His swordgleam flashes in the void: the sky turns turquoise.	劍光照空天自碧
	Xihe goads on the sun, which gives a glassy clang;	羲和敲日玻璃聲
4	Ash of kalpa fires blown utterly away, all eras are made level.	劫灰飛盡古今平
	From dragon-head pours wine: invite the wine-star to drink!	龍頭瀉酒邀酒星
6	The gold-nutted *pipa* twangs in the night;	金槽琵琶夜棖棖
	Rain-sheets off Dongting Lake come to blow the panpipes.	洞庭雨腳來吹笙
8	Wanton with wine, he rebukes the moon, makes it reverse its course;	酒酣喝月使倒行
	Beneath silver clouds in serried ranks, the jasper hall grows light;	銀雲櫛櫛瑤殿明
10	The majordomo of the palace gate announces the first watch.	宮門掌事報一更
	In the flowery loft the jade phoenix's voice is coyly ferocious;	花樓玉鳳聲嬌獰
12	Pink patterning of mermaid gauze sends fragrance, mild and pure;	海綃紅文香淺清
	Yellow-robed beauties dance stumblingly, offering a thousand-year wine horn.	黃鵝跌舞千年觥
14	From the immortals' candelabra, the wax-smoke faint;	仙人燭樹蠟煙輕
	The goddess Greenlute's eyes, bleary with flooding tears.	青琴醉眼淚泓泓

[LCJ 1:3.311–312]

The sound image in the poem's third line is justly renowned, both as a striking instance of Li He's inimitable style and as an example of his method of developing poetic figures. We might contrast Li He's use of the myth of the sun-charioteer Xihe with Du Fu's, in these closing lines of a poem on the cliffs of the Yangzi River's Qutang gorge:

	When Xihe's winter course draws near,	羲和冬馭近
8	She fears lest her sun carriage topple.	愁畏日車翻[11]

Xihe's flight is figured as a ride in a literal carriage that might be tipped over by obstacles on the celestial "ground" on which she travels. But this figure, while fantastic, is grounded in Du Fu's perspective, gazing at the cliffs, and becomes readable as a hyperbolic expression of their dizzying height. Li He's Xihe image, by contrast, serves not as an ornament to a description but instead as a tool for a process of defamiliarization that leaves behind stable frames of reference. Xihe as sun-charioteer suggests whipping the sun; the sun as an object one could strike suggests an orb of glass. In the sun's glassy clang we encounter a distinctive product of Li He's work: a hauntingly vivid impression that resists attempts to ground it in a recognizably human perspective. Li He's song-poems evoke a sort of music, but it is not music of this world.

THE BROCADE BAG

In his preface to Li He's collection, Du Mu observes that, in many of Li He's best-known poems, "in seeking to capture how things are and what they're like, he goes off leaving the common pathways of composition far behind—and it's most difficult to grasp what he's doing" (*QTW* 8:753.10B [7807]). This idea of wandering far from "common pathways" finds a quite literal echo in Li Shangyin's "Short Biography":

> He'd frequently wander off on a mule led by a little servant boy, with an ancient tattered brocade bag on his back. Whenever some poetic idea came to him he'd write it down and throw it in the bag. When he returned in the evening, his mother would have a servant girl take the bag and pull out the contents, and whenever she saw that he'd written a lot, she'd say, "This child will only rest when he's vomited out his heart." Then she'd lay out a lamp and give him dinner, and he'd take the new writing from the servant girl and, rubbing fresh ink and stacking up papers, he'd complete the new poems, which he then threw in another bag. Except when he was very drunk, or on days when he had to pay mourning calls, this was his habitual practice.
>
> [*QTW* 8:780.17A–17B (8149)]

We picture Tao Qian beside his chrysanthemums or Li Bai with his wine cup; it is revealing that when later readers imagined Li He, they would most likely imagine him as he appears here, wandering aimlessly on his mule, followed by a servant, compulsively composing lines of poetry. Many of his poems, composed on the road or in rented or borrowed lodgings in Chang'an or Luoyang, do reflect a wandering life, and the most frequented pathways reflected in his poems are those between his home county, Changgu, and Luoyang, the Tang's eastern capital. His poem entitled simply "Poem of Changgu" ("Changgu shi"), at more than a hundred lines, is too long to allow for more than a sampling here, but examining one section from the poem's first half (lines 11–56) may provide some insights into Li He's wanderings as well as his compositional methods:

	Through layered enclosures gleams a twisting passage;	層圍爛洞曲
12	By the fragrant path, aging pinks are drunk.	芳徑老紅醉
	Massed insects carve an ancient willow;	攢蟲鏤古柳
14	A cicada cries from its lofty hiding place.	蟬子鳴高邃
	A broad sash, the yellow creeper trails;	大帶委黃葛
16	Purple reeds by narrow creek banks cross.	紫蒲交狹涘
	Stone coins: lichen blooms, overlapping and piled;	石錢差復藉
18	Thick leaves all in unctuous coils.	厚葉皆蟠膩
	Washed sands delight in level whiteness;	汰沙好平白
20	A standing horse imprints green characters.	立馬印青字
	Evening fins disport themselves at leisure;	晚鱗自遨遊
22	A gaunt crane stands alone at nightfall.	瘦鵠暝單峙
	Droning, the chirr of the damp mole crickets;	嘹嘹溼蛄聲
24	A choking spring, startled, bubbles up.	咽源驚濺起

Critics have pointed to similarities in compositional form between this poem and the long linked verse (*lian ju*) poems of Han Yu and Meng Jiao.[12] In linked verse, two or more participants, beginning from a single opening line, take turns composing an even-numbered (rhyming) line followed by an odd-numbered (nonrhyming) first line for the following couplet, which it then falls to the next participant to complete. Linked verse is thus a form both of composition and of social interaction, in which friends compete to outdo preceding lines in ingenuity and audacity.

The "Short Biography" describes Li He as spurning poetry competitions or poems on set topics, and his "Poem of Changgu" is not a real linked verse produced collaboratively but a similar barrage of arresting lines produced as a solitary pastime. Its composition is less like a large-scale landscape painting than an extended but narrow hand scroll, dazzling us with a lengthy series of mesmerizing, small-scale scenes while withholding any comprehensive vista. Whether or not its most striking lines were actually composed on those legendary long walks with the brocade bag, the "Poem of Changgu" inevitably calls to mind that iconic description of Li He at work. (For more poems of Li He, ☞ *HTRCP* C9.4; *WKB* P21, P95.)

Larger shapes do emerge in this chain of striking images and poetic conceits, as in the sections centered on two ritual and historical sites, one a temple dedicated to the goddess Orchid Scent (*Lanxiang shennü*), said to have ascended into immortality from a hill thereafter known as "Goddess's Table," another the ruin of the Empress Wu Zetian's Fuchang palace. Though passages of the poem fall under the influence of these sites, however, there is remarkably little clear signaling of large-scale orientation. In prose accounts of encounters with gods or goddesses, the sense of awe surrounding a divinity's appearance is often enhanced by its unexpectedness: signs of an imminent epiphany are often easy to miss, or are discernible only in hindsight. The passage in "Poem of Changgu" describing the vicinity of Goddess's Table builds to a culmination that is all the more uncanny for the way it seems to unfold without the conscious design of the poet:

	Gently winding, the road of the Jade Perfected;	紆緩玉真路
26	The divine lovely one within the orchid blossoms.	神娥蕙花裏
	Threads of algae tangle amid creek-bed stones;	苔絮縈潤礫
28	Mountain fruits bend down, ochre and purple.	山實垂赬紫
	Small cypress trees the image of layered fans;	小柏儼重扇
30	From fat pine trunks oozes marrow of cinnabar.	肥松突丹髓
	A singing stream rushes with resounding echo,	鳴流走響韻
32	Autumn on hillocks brings forth shining tassels.	墾秋拖光穗
	An oriole warbles: Min maiden's song.	鶯唱閩女歌
34	A waterfall hangs: Chu silk canopy.	瀑懸楚練帔
	Wind and dew are filled with smiling eyes.	風露滿笑眼
36	Linked crags, alternately stretched or toppled.	駢岩雜舒墜
	Tangled bamboo bursts out from stony outcrops,	亂條迸石嶺
38	Thin throats raucous amid island eddies.	細頸喧島滮
	A sunbeam sweeps away obscuring darkness,	日腳掃昏翳
40	New clouds reveal their flowery recesses.	新雲啟華閟
	Calm mildness weary of summer's light;	謐謐厭夏光
42	An autumn breeze conveys pure air.	商風道清氣
	In high slumber the countenance of her who took jade;	高眠服玉容
44	Burning cassia offered up at the celestial table.	燒桂祀天几
	Robes of fog trail and flutter in the night,	霧衣夜披拂
46	A sleeper by the altar witnesses her true form in dream.	眠壇夢真粹

Temples and ruins offered Li He the chance to explore effects of simulacra and virtual presence. A phrase like "robes of fog" (*wu yi*) in line 45 might elsewhere read as a straightforward metaphor, but in the precinct of a goddess, the boundary between figural and real is uncertain. Similarly, in the passage on the Fuchang palace ruins, the past is both lost and hauntingly present:

	Awaiting the carriage, perched simurghs have grown old;	待駕棲鸞老
48	Former palace's pepper-scented walls, collapsed.	故宮椒壁圮
	Several echoes from those jingling bells	鴻瓏數鈴響
50	Set loose a wandering minister's chilly musings.	羈臣發涼思
	Dark vines clasp shut the bolted crimson gate,	陰藤束朱鍵
52	The dragon canopy now infested with hill sprites.	龍帳著魈魅
	Emerald brocade, with appliqué of flowering tamarisk:	碧錦帖花檉
54	A fragrant quilt to serve the remnants of majesty.	香衾事殘貴
	Dust once stirred by song on rotten timbers remains;	歌塵蠹木在
56	Ribbons trailed in dance: long clouds are their likeness.	舞綵長雲似

[*LCJ* 2:4.474–475]

The product of Li He's efforts to "capture how things are and what they're like" as he wanders raptly through the landscape is no descriptive verisimilitude. In the figure of the "wandering minister" here it is impossible to draw the line between Li He himself and some displaced courtier who once attended Empress Wu's court in all its splendor as it rested at the Fuchang "transit palace." Here, poetry serves not as a vehicle for moral reflection on the transience of glory or for critique of excesses of pride but rather as the space in which that glory, though fragmented and diffused, is made to seem uncannily present once more.

THE SUMMONS

This chapter began by considering Du Mu's strange and vivid account of the night when a fortuitous chain of circumstances allowed the survival of the relatively few poems of Li He that we have. Li Shangyin's "Short Biography of Li He" gives us an even stranger and more vivid account of Li He's own tragically premature death. An elder sister of Li He's had married into the Wang family, Li Shangyin's in-laws. This is the account of Li He's death, as told by this sister:

When Changji was about to die, he suddenly saw, in broad daylight, a person in crimson robes, driving a carriage pulled by red dragons, and bearing a tablet: the writing on it was like the seal-script of high antiquity, or thunder-script on stone inscriptions, announcing a summons of Changji. Changji couldn't read a word of it, and quickly climbed down from his bed and kowtowed, saying, "Mommy is old and sick; I don't want to leave her." The crimson-robed person laughed, "The Emperor of Heaven has completed construction of White Jade Loft and summons you instantly to compose the dedicatory inscription. Besides, tasks in heaven are pleasant, not tiresome...." Changji remained there alone, weeping—all those present saw it. After a while, Changji's breathing stopped. By the window where he'd always sat there appeared a pulsating vapor. They heard the sound of carriages moving and the music of pipes and flutes. His mother hurriedly ordered everyone to stop crying. After a time, about as long as it takes to cook five pints of millet, Changji finally died. His elder sister married into the Wang family is not the sort of person who could fabricate accounts about Changji—this really was what she saw.

[QTW 8:780.17B–18A (8149)]

The stories surrounding Li He's career mirror and illuminate key questions set in motion in the poems themselves. That the account of Li He's death passed on by his sister ends with Li He's departure to the service of a celestial empire, and with the tones of an uncanny and otherworldly music fading into the distance, is indeed strange. Whether the story of the summons originated from a final creative act by the poet, from the imaginative empathy of those close to him—or indeed from an incursion of the uncanny—it marks the point where biography and poetic power merge.

ROBERT ASHMORE

NOTES

1. Du Mu, "Preface to the Song-Poems of Li Changji, Vice Director of Ceremonial of the Taichang Bureau" ("Taichang si Fengli lang Li Changji geshi xu"), in *QTW* 8:753.9B–11A [7806–7807].
2. Du Mu, "Preface to the Song-Poems of Li Changji."
3. In another story (of dubious credibility), a jealous cousin borrowed an earlier, more complete manuscript of Li He's poems and threw it down a latrine. See Zhang Gu, *Youxian guchui*, in *TWD* 2:1450.
4. Specifically, his family traced its origins through Li Liang, an uncle of the Tang founder, Emperor Gaozu (r. 618–626). See *TCZ* 2:5.283–295. Li Jinsu was also a distant relative and friend of Du Fu. See *DSXZ* 5:22.1934.
5. A more plausible version of the story of Han Yu's discovery of Li He's talent involves Li He sending a packet of poems to Han Yu to solicit his patronage; this would have been around 808, when Li He was nineteen. See Zhang Gu, *Youxian guchui*.
6. On nature's retribution against Li He and other poets, see Lu Guimeng, "Postface to the 'Short Biography of Li He'" ("Shu 'Li He xiao zhuan' hou"), in *QTW* 9:801.20A–21A [8418].
7. "A Disputation on Taboo Words" ("Hui bian"), in *QTW* 6:558.1A–2A [5644].
8. See the discussion in Wu Qiming, *Tang yin zhiyi lu* (Shanghai: Shanghai guji chubanshe, 1986), along with *LCJ*, 1:2.238, note 19.
9. "Submission requesting posthumous bestowal of first-grade 'presented scholar' titles on Li He, Huangfu Song et al." ("Qi zhui ci Li He Huangfu Song deng jinshi ji di zou"), in QTW 9:889.3B–4A [9287–9188].
10. See Shen Yazhi's "Preface Bestowed on Parting for Licentiate Li Jiao" ("Song Li Jiao xiucai xu"), in *QTW* 8:735.13B–14B [7593–7594].
11. Du Fu, "Qutang liang ya" ("The Two Banks of Qutang Gorge"), in *DSXZ* 4:18.1557.
12. See, for example, the Qing critic Wu Rulun, ed., *Li Changji geshi pingzhu* (*Annotations and Commentaries on the Poetry of Li Changji [Li He]*) (Taibei: Yiwen shuju, 1922), 3.15A); and, more recently, the extensive discussion in Stephen Owen, *The End of the Chinese "Middle Ages": Essays in Mid-Tang Literary Culture* (Stanford, CA: Stanford University Press, 1996), 34–47. The Japanese scholar Harada Kenyū pushed this idea still further, positing that Li He imagined this poem and the long erotic verse "Tormented" ("Nao gong"; *LCJ* 1:3.341–342) as dialogues between two characters. See *RGKS*, 2:9–73 and 2:290–378.

PRIMARY SOURCES

LCJ   Wu Qiming 吳企明, ed. *Li Changji geshi biannian jianzhu* 李長吉歌詩編年箋注 (Explanatory and Lexical Notes to the "Song-Poems" of Li Changji, Chronologically Arranged). 2 vols. Beijing: Zhonghua shuju, 2012.

DSXZ   Qiu Zhao'ao 仇兆鰲 (1638–1713), ed. *Du shi xiangzhu* 杜詩詳注 (Du Fu's Poetry with Detailed Annotations). 5 vols. Beijing: Zhonghua shuju, 1979.

QTS   *Quan Tang shi* 全唐詩 (Complete Poems of the Tang). 25 vols. Beijing: Zhonghua shuju, 1960.

QTW   Dong Gao 董誥 et al., eds. *Quan Tang wen* 全唐文 (Complete Tang Prose). 11 vols. Beijing: Zhonghua shuju, 1983.

RGKS   Harada Kenyū 原田憲雄, ed. *Ri Ga kashihen* 李賀歌詩編 ("Song-Poems" of Li He). 3 vols. In Tōyō bunko 東洋文庫 (Oriental Library), no. 645, 649, 657. Tokyo: Heibonsha, 1998.

TCZ   Fu Xuancong 傅璇琮 et al., eds. *Tang caizi zhuan jiaojian* 唐才子傳校箋 (Annotations on the Biographies of Tang Talented Scholars). 5 vols. Beijing: Zhonghua shuju, 1989.

TWD   Ding Ruming 丁如明 et al., eds. *Tang wudai biji xiaoshuo da guan* 唐五代筆記小說大觀 (Compendium of "Notation-Book" Anecdote Collections of the Tang and Five Dynasties). 2 vols. Shanghai guji chubanshe, 2000.

SUGGESTED READINGS

ENGLISH

Frodsham, J. D., trans. *Goddesses, Ghosts, and Demons: The Collected Poems of Li He (Li Chang-ji, 790–816)*. Revised ed. San Francisco: North Point Press, 1984.

Owen, Stephen. *The End of the Chinese "Middle Ages": Essays in Mid-Tang Literary Culture*. Stanford, CA: Stanford University Press, 1996.

Schafer, Edward. *The Divine Woman: Dragon Ladies and Rain Maidens in T'ang Literature*. Berkeley: University of California Press, 1973.

CHINESE

Wu Qiming 吳企明. *Tangyin zhiyi lu* 唐音質疑錄 (Record of Queries on Tang Poetry). Shanghai: Shanghai guji chubanshe, 1986.

Wu Qiming and Shen Huile 沈惠樂, eds. *Li He ji qi zuopin xuan: Li He, Li He shiwen xuanzhu* 李賀及其作品選: 李賀, 李賀詩文選注 (Li He and His Selected Works: *Li He* and *Selected Prose and Poetry of Li He*). Shanghai: Shanghai guji chubanshe, 1999.

Wu Rulun 吳汝倫 (1840–1903), ed. *Li Changji geshi pingzhu* 李長吉歌詩評注 (Annotations and Commentaries on the Poetry of Li Changji [Li He]). Taibei: Yiwen shuju, 1922.

ACKNOWLEDGMENTS

This book began with the conference "Stories of Chinese Poetic Culture: From Earliest Times Through the Tang," held at the University of Illinois, Urbana-Champaign, on October 19–20, 2012. The conference was generously funded by the Chiang Ching-kuo Foundation. A grant of graduate assistantship was later awarded by the College of Liberal Arts and Sciences, the University of Illinois, to aid in the manuscript preparation. In 2016, the Research Grants Council of Hong Kong, SAR, awarded me a Humanities and Social Sciences Prestigious Fellowship, giving me precious time to prepare the final manuscript for publication.

In addition to acknowledging the financial support of these institutions, I wish to express my gratitude to my friends as well as my colleagues, students, and staff at the University of Illinois. In particular, I wish to thank David Der-wei Wang, director of the North American Center of the Chiang Ching-kuo Foundation, for his valuable guidance and support. My special thanks also go to Leon Chai and Cara Ryan for their illuminating comments on some parts of the manuscript, to Zhang Xiaohui for his meticulous and comprehensive editorial assistance, including the compilation of "Chronology of Historical Events" and "Thematic Contents," and to Wang Mei for her help in securing permissions for graphic material.

The contributors to this volume wish to thank the two anonymous readers for their insightful comments and suggestions. We are deeply indebted to Jennifer Crewe, associate provost and director of Columbia University Press, for her enthusiastic support and professional guidance. We are also very grateful to Christine Dunbar and Leslie Kriesel for overseeing the production process and to Todd Manza for his meticulous copyediting.

CONTRIBUTORS

Robert Ashmore is associate professor of classical Chinese literature at the University of California, Berkeley. He received his MA from Beijing University in 1992 and his PhD from Harvard University in 1997. His research interests include lyric poetry and poetic theory, song and musical performance, and traditional concepts of identity and personality in Chinese literature of the third through eleventh centuries. He is the author of *The Transport of Reading: Text and Understanding in the World of Tao Qian (365–427)* (Harvard 2010). He is currently working on a book manuscript on the literary culture of the early ninth century.

Alan Berkowitz (1950–2015) was Susan W. Lippincott professor of modern and classical languages and professor of Chinese at Swarthmore College. He received his BA from the University of Vermont in 1975 and his MA (1980) and his PhD (1989) from the University of Washington, in classical Chinese language and literature. He served as president of the Early Medieval China Group, as book review editor for *Early Medieval China*, and as a board member of the T'ang Studies Society. His primary research interests encompassed the poetry and culture of the Six Dynasties and Tang period. He is the author of *Patterns of Disengagement: The Practice and Portrayal of Reclusion in Early Medieval China* (Stanford 2000) and coeditor of *Handbook of Early Medieval Texts* (Berkeley 2015). He explored the intersection of literature, culture, and intellectual history and wrote on the literature of reclusion, biography, medieval poetry, ritual eulogies, Daoism, Buddhism, the cultural role of the *qin* zither, and tea. He also was working on the correspondence between G. W. Leibniz and Joachim Bouvet, a Jesuit scientist at the Kangxi emperor's court (see http://www.leibniz-bouvet.org).

Zong-qi Cai is professor of Chinese and comparative literature at the University of Illinois at Urbana-Champaign, and the Lee Wing Tat Chair Professor of Chinese Literature, Lingnan University, Hong Kong. Among his books in English are *The Matrix of Lyric Transformation: Poetic Modes and Self-Presentation in Early Chinese Pentasyllabic Poetry* (Michigan, 1996), *Configurations of Comparative Poetics: Three Perspectives on Western and Chinese Literary Criticism* (Hawai'i 2002) and the *How to Read Chinese Poetry Workbook* (with Jie Cui, Columbia 2012). In addition, he has edited *A Chinese Literary Mind: Culture, Creativity, and Rhetoric in* Wenxin diaolong (Stanford 2001); *Chinese Aesthetics: The Ordering of Literature, the Arts, and the Universe in the Six Dynasties* (Hawai'i 2004); *How to Read Chinese Poetry: A Guided Anthology* (Columbia 2008); and *Sound and Sense of Chinese Poetry* (Duke 2015). He is also the cofounding editor in chief of the *Journal of Chinese Literature and Culture* and editor in chief of *Lingnan Journal of Chinese Studies* 嶺南學報.

Jack W. Chen is associate professor of Chinese literature at the University of Virginia. He received his PhD from the Department of Comparative Literature at Harvard University, his MA in comparative literature from the University of Michigan, Ann Arbor, and his BA in literature from Yale University. He has broad interests in the literature of the medieval period, with a particular focus on poetry, literary thought, and anecdotal writings. He is the author of *The Poetics of Sovereignty: On Emperor Taizong of the Tang Dynasty* (Harvard 2010) and is coeditor, with David Schaberg, of *Idle Talk: Gossip and Anecdote in Traditional China* (GAIA 2013). He has also published articles on imperial poetry, gossip and historiography, early medieval reading practices, donkey braying, coinage, and the use of data visualization techniques for literary analysis. His current research is divided between a book-length study of the *Shishuo xinyu* and a study of what reading ghost poetry can tell us about literary history.

Jing Chen is a PhD candidate in the Department of East Asian Languages and Cultures at the University of Illinois, Urbana-Champaign. Her research interests include classical Chinese poetry, Ming-Qing literature, and literary criticism. She is currently completing a dissertation on the publication and reception of poetry anthologies in late imperial China.

Chen Yinchi is professor of Chinese literature at Fudan University. A specialist in classical Chinese literature and poetics with a focus on Buddhist and Taoist literature, he is the author of *A Study of Zhuangzi's Thought on Art and Literature* 莊學文藝觀研究 (1994), *Buddhism and Literature in Sui and Tang China* 隋唐佛學與中國文學 (2002), *An Introduction to Chinese Buddhist Literature* 佛教文學 (2003), *Literary Tradition, Taoism, and Buddhism in Medieval China* 文學傳統與中古道家佛教 (2015), and *Non-Action and Happiness: Six Studies on the* Zhuangzi 無為與逍遙: 莊子六章 (2016).

Yu-yu Cheng is chair professor of Chinese literature at National Taiwan University. Her research interests include discourses of space, body, and the lyrical tradition in Chinese literature. She is devoted to developing pioneering and interdisciplinary interpretations of classical Chinese literature by combining Eastern and Western humanistic thought. Cheng has published numerous books, including *"Literary Ch'i" in Six Dynasties Literary Theory* 六朝文氣論探究 (1988), *The Situation Aesthetics in Six Dynasties* 六朝情境美學綜論 (1996), *Gender and Nation: Discourses of* Encountering Misery *in Han and Jin Rhapsodies* 性別與家國: 漢晉辭賦的楚騷論述 (2000), *The Poet in Text and Landscape: Mutual Definition of Self and Landscape* 文本風景: 自我與空間的相互定義 (2005), *Metaphor: Crossing Categorical Boundaries in Ancient Chinese Literature* 引譬連類: 文學研究的關鍵詞 (2012), and others. Additionally, she has published dozens of papers on related topics in academic journals.

Meow Hui Goh is associate professor of Chinese literature at the Ohio State University. A specialist in medieval Chinese literature and culture, she is the author of *Sound and Sight: Poetry and Courtier Culture in the Yongming Era (483–493)* (Stanford 2010). Her current book project examines the memory of chaos in early medieval China through different forms of writing that depict the collapse of the Han dynasty and its aftermath.

Wai-yee Li is professor of Chinese literature at Harvard University. She earned her BA from the University of Hong Kong and her PhD (1987) from Princeton University. Her research spans topics ranging from early Chinese thought and narrative to late imperial Chinese literature and culture. Her recent publications include *The Readability of the Past in Early Chinese Historiography* (Harvard 2007) and *Women and National Trauma in Late Imperial Chinese Literature* (Harvard

2014). She is also coeditor of *The Columbia Anthology of Yuan Drama* (Columbia 2014) and coauthor of *The Letter to Ren An and Sima Qian's Legacy* (University of Washington 2016). Her annotated translation of *Zuozhuan*, in collaboration with Stephen Durrant and David Schaberg, was published in 2016 by the University of Washington Press. She is currently coediting *The Oxford Handbook of Classical Chinese Literature* with Wiebke Denecke and Tian Xiaofei.

Xinda Lian is professor of Chinese language and literature at Denison University. He received his MA and PhD from the University of Michigan. His research interests include Song dynasty poetry, Song dynasty literati culture, and the stylistic analysis of the *Zhuangzi* text. He is the author of *The Wild and Arrogant: Expression of Self in Xin Qiji's Song Lyrics* (Lang 1999) as well as a variety of book chapters and articles on Song dynasty literature and the study of the *Zhuangzi*.

Tsung-Cheng Lin is associate professor of Chinese studies at the University of Victoria, Canada. He received a BA from Fu-Jen Catholic University in Taiwan, followed by an MA in linguistics at Indiana University, Bloomington. He received his PhD from the University of British Columbia, Canada, and spent a year doing postdoctoral research at Kyoto University in Japan. His primary research interests are concerned with the narrative tradition in classical Chinese verse, the poetry of late imperial China, the tradition of the knight-errant in premodern Chinese poetry, and the poetic transition from eighteenth-century to early republican China. His forthcoming book publications include *From Tradition to Modernity: Historical and Critical Perspectives on Poetic Transition from Eighteenth-Century to Early Republican China* 從傳統過渡到現代的詩歌演變：十八世紀至民初 and *A Collection of Essays on Classical Chinese Literature in Honor of Professor Kawai Kozo* 川合康三教授榮休紀念中國古典文學研究論文集.

Olga Lomova is professor of Chinese literature at Charles University in Prague. Her research interests include medieval Chinese poetry, the history of Chinese literature, and the intellectual transformation of China under Western influence in the early twentieth century. She is author and coauthor of several research monographs published in the Czech language, including a monograph on the style of Wang Wei's nature poetry, a book about funerary genres in the early medieval period, and an extensive translation from the *Shiji*, with explanatory reading notes.

Manling Luo is associate professor of Chinese literature at Indiana University, Bloomington. She received her BA and MA from Peking University and her PhD from Washington University in Saint Louis. Her research interests include premodern Chinese narratives, Chinese literati culture, traditional Chinese literature, and gender and culture studies. She is the author of *Literati Storytelling in Late Medieval China* (University of Washington, 2015).

Stephen Owen is James Bryant Conant University Professor at Harvard University. He earned a BA (1968) and a PhD (1972) in Chinese language from Yale University, and his research interests include premodern Chinese literature, lyric poetry, and comparative poetics. Much of his work has focused on the middle period of Chinese literature (200–1200); however, he also has written on literature of the early period and the Qing. Among his numerous books and articles are *An Anthology of Chinese Literature: Beginnings to 1911* (Norton 1996), *The Making of Early Chinese Classical Poetry* (Harvard Asia Center 2006), and *The Late Tang: Chinese Poetry of the Mid-Ninth Century (827–860)* (Harvard Asia Center 2006). His translation of the complete poetry of Du Fu is published under the title *The Poetry of Du Fu* as the inaugural volume of the Library of Chinese Humanities series (De Gruyter 2015).

Gregory Patterson is assistant professor of Chinese at the University of South Carolina. He received his PhD (2013) from Columbia University. His main areas of interest are medieval Chinese poetry (third to tenth centuries), traditional Chinese theories of literature, poetry and imperial institutions in medieval China, and modern interpretations of classical Chinese poetry. He is currently writing a book about place and memory in the late work of the Tang poet Du Fu.

Nanxiu Qian is professor of Chinese literature at Rice University. She received her MA (1982) from Nanjing University, China, and her PhD (1994) from Yale. Her research interests include classical Chinese literature, women and gender studies, and studies on the Sinosphere. She is the author of *Politics, Poetics, and Gender in Late Qing China: Xue Shaohui (1866–1911) and the Era of Reform* (Stanford 2015) and *Spirit and Self in Medieval China: The* Shih-shuo hsin-yu *and Its Legacy* (Hawai'i 2001). She has also edited and coedited several academic volumes, such as the *Different Worlds of Discourse: Transformations of Gender and Genre in Late Qing and Early Republican China*, with Grace Fong and Richard J. Smith (Brill 2008).

Maija Bell Samei is an independent scholar who has taught part time at the University of North Carolina at Chapel Hill. She received her PhD in Chinese literature from the University of Michigan and is the author of *Gendered Persona and Poetic Voice: The Abandoned Woman in Early Chinese Song Lyrics* (Lexington Books 2004). She is also the English translator of Li Zezhou's *Huaxia meixue* 華夏美學 (The Chinese Aesthetic Tradition) (Hawai'i 2010).

Paula Varsano is associate professor of Chinese literature at the University of California, Berkeley. She earned her BA from Yale and her PhD (1988) from Princeton. Her research focuses on classical poetry and poetics from the third through the eleventh centuries, with a particular interest in literature and subjectivity, the evolution of spatial representation in poetry, the history and poetics of traditional literary criticism, and the theory and practice of translation. She is the author of *Tracking the Banished Immortal: The Poetry of Li Bo and Its Critical Reception* (Hawai'i 2003) and editor of *The Rhetoric of Hiddenness in Traditional Chinese Culture* (SUNY 2016). She is currently at work on a book titled *Coming to Our Senses: Locating the Subject in Traditional Chinese Literary Writing*.

Ao Wang is assistant professor of Asian languages and literatures at Wesleyan University. He received his BA from Peking University, his MA from Washington University in Saint Louis, and his PhD from Yale University. His main academic interest is classical Chinese poetry. He has also published five books of his own poetry and has been the recipient of prizes such as the Anne Kao Poetry Prize and, most recently, the New Poet Prize from *People's Literature*.

GLOSSARY-INDEX

This index does not contain thematic entries, as they are already provided in the thematic table of contents beginning on page vii

"After Passing the Presented Scholar Examination" 登科後 ("Dengke hou"), 179
"Ai Ying" 哀郢 ("Lament for Ying"), 40
"An Autumn Night, Sitting Alone" 秋夜獨坐 ("Qiu ye du zuo"), 215–216
An Lushan 安祿山 (ca. 703–757), 10, 236–238, 242–243, 257
An Qingxu 安慶緒 (d. 759), 238, 240, 243
An Shi zhi luan 安史之亂 (An Shi Rebellion), 207, 211, 236–237, 242, 245, 258, 256–257
"A Reply to Zhu Qingyu" 酬朱慶餘 ("Chou Zhu Qingyu"), 178
"Attending Xiao Shuzi While Listening to the Zither; the Topic Assigned to Me Was 'Song on the Flowing Springs Near the Three Gorges'") 從蕭叔子聽彈琴賦得三峽流泉歌 ("Cong Xiao Shuzi ting tanqin fude sanxia liuquan ge"), 194

ba 霸 (overlord), 19
Bai Juyi 白居易 (courtesy name Letian 樂天 [772–846]), 5, 9, 130, 175, 177, 181, 195, 248–260
"Baima pian" 白馬篇 ("White Horse"), 110, 161
"Baishi Changqing ji xu" 白氏長慶集序 ("Preface to *Bai Juyi's Collected Works Compiled During the Changqing Reign*"), 259–260
Bai Xingjian 白行簡 (776–826), 250, 259
Ban Gu 班固 (32–92), 15, 26, 45–47
Ban Jieyu 班婕妤 (48 BCE–2 CE), 9
Ban Zhao 班昭 (ca. 45–116), 90, 186, 192
Bao Si 褒姒 (consort of King You of Zhou), 21
Beili zhi 北里誌 (*Record of the Northern Ward*), 184
Benshi shi 本事詩 (*Poems in Their Original Occasions*), 246
"Ben wei" 本味 ("Original Flavor"), 53
bi 比 (analogues), 73
"Biancheng luori" 邊城落日 ("Sunset in a Frontier City"), 166
"Biancheng youhuai" 邊城有懷 ("Emotion Felt in a Frontier City"), 166
biansai shi 邊塞詩 (frontier poetry), 159
bing xuan kan er dai chi 冰懸埳而帶坻 (ice hangs in the dips and encircles the isles), 146
bixing 比興 (analogical-affective images), 75
bo shi 博士 (erudites), 2, 68
bo xue 博學 (broad learning), 52
boxue hongci 博學宏詞 (erudite learning and grand composition), 174

Boyi 伯夷 (ca. eleventh century BCE), 6
bulei 不類 (inappropriate for the occasion or for the speaker's status and situation), 15
"By the Qujiang; Thinking of Yuan the Ninth" 曲江憶元九 ("Qujiang yi Yuan Jiu"), 254

"Cai fan" 采蘩 ("Picking Artemisia"), 23
cainü 才女 (talented woman), 127
Cao Biao 曹彪 (see Prince Baima), 113
Cao Cao 曹操 (155–220), 5, 7, 99–105, 116, 148
Cao Chong 曹沖 (196–208), 107
Cao Mo 曹沫 (fl. seventh century BCE), 162
Cao Pi 曹丕 (Emperor Wen of Wei [187–226, r. 220–226]), 62, 99, 106–112
Cao Ren 曹仁 (168–223), 112
Cao Song 曹嵩 (d. 193), 100
Cao Teng 曹騰 (fl. 120–late 150s), 100
Cao Zhi 曹植 (192–232), 5, 107, 109–110, 112
ce 策 (policy questions), 174
Chan 禪 (Meditation School of Buddhism), 7
chanding 禪定 (Chan meditation), 215
"Chang hen ge" 長恨歌 ("Song of Lasting Sorrow"), 256
"Changgu shi" 昌谷詩 ("Poem of Changgu"), 269–270
"Changwu" 常武 ("Abiding Martial Power"), 19
Chengshi 成實 (*Satyasiddhi* School of Buddhism), 8, 153
Cheng Xuanying 成玄英 (fl. 631–643), 116
Chen Jing 陳京 (presented scholar degree in 771), 177
Chen Shang 陳商 (presented scholar degree in 814), 264
Chen Zi'ang 陳子昂 (661–702), 164
Chong'er 重耳 (see Lord Wen of Jin), 17–20, 22
"Chouxi pian" 疇昔篇 ("Former Times"), 166
"Chou Zhang shaofu" 酬張少府 ("In Response to Vice-Magistrate Zhang"), 213
"Chuangzhong lie yuanxiu shi" 窗中列遠岫詩 ("The Distant Peaks Stand Framed in My Window"), 175
Chuci 楚辭 (*Songs of Chu*), 4, 30, 40, 44–47, 52, 55, 212
"Chuilao bie" 垂老別 ("Parting as Old Age Nears"), 243
chujia 出家 (leave home; to become a monk), 213
"Chuju" 出車 ("Send Out the Chariot"), 19
Chunqiu 春秋 (*Spring and Autumn Annals*), 2, 13, 57, 68
ci 詞 (song lyric), 200–203
"Cike liezhuan" 刺客列傳 ("Biography of the Assassins"), 162
ciye lianjuan 雌霓連蜷 (the joined arc of the Female Rainbow), 146
cizong 辭宗 (the supreme master of literature), 146
Confucius 孔子 (551–479 BCE), 6, 13, 15, 18, 26, 30
cong jun suo yu 從君所欲 (following the ruler's desires), 166
"Congjun xing" 從軍行 ("Joining the Army"), 59
"Copying Letian's Poems on the Walls of the Kaiyuan Temple in Langzhou" 閬州開元寺壁題樂天詩 ("Langzhou Kaiyuan Si bi ti Letian shi"), 194
cui wei 崔嵬 (tall and towering), 55
Cui Shao 崔韶 (fl. ninth century), 251
Cui Yan 崔郾 (768–836), 176

"Da er Guo shi san shou" 答二郭詩三首 ("In Reply to the Two Guos, Three Poems"), 120

da fu 大賦 (great rhapsody), 51–53

da jia 大家 (great family), 90

Dali 大曆 (766–779), 211

"Daming" 大明 ("Great Brightness"), 20

Dao, the 道 (the Way), 141–142

Daoxin 道信 (580–651), 215

Daoxuan 道宣 (596–667), 214

"Da Pang canjun" 答龐參軍 ("In Reply to Aide Pang"), 134

daren 大人 (Great Person), 116

"Daren xiansheng zhuan" 大人先生傳 ("Biography of the Great Person"), 123

"Dasheng" 達生 ("Mastering Life"), 123

da yitong 大一統 (Great Unity), 56–57

Dazhao 大照 (aka Puji 普寂 [651–739]), 208

"Denglong" 登隴 ("Ascending Mount Long"), 163

Di 狄 (a barbarian group), 19

"Dialogue in the Mountains" 山中問答 ("Shanzhong wenda"), 232

"Diao Qu Yuan fu" 吊屈原賦 ("Lament for Qu Yuan"), 31

ding 定 (meditation; Sanskrit *dhyāna*), 215

ding zhong zhi bian 鼎中之變 (transformation within the cauldron), 54

Donghuang Taiyi 東皇太一 (Emperor of the East; the Supreme One), 42

"Dong shan" 東山 ("Eastern Hills"), 103

Dongtian 東田 (Eastern Field), 147

Dong Zhongshu 董仲舒 (179–104 BCE), 56

Dong Zhuo 董卓 (d. 192), 100

"Dreaming of Weizhi" 夢微之 ("Meng Weizhi"), 255

duanzhang 斷章 (cutting the section), 15

duanzhang quyi 斷章取義 (to cut off a *Shijing* section to derive a desired meaning), 3, 70

Du Fu 杜甫 (712–770), 4, 7, 74–75, 130, 233–245

Du Gao 杜羔 (presented scholar degree in 789), 181

Du Guangting 杜光庭 (850–933), 211

Duke Zhou 周公 (Zhou Gong [fl. 1100 BCE]), 67, 103–104

Duke Zhuang (of Zheng) (鄭) 莊公 (Zheng Zhuang Gong [757–701 BCE]), 71

Du Mu 杜牧 (803–852), 177, 268, 271

"Du *Shanhai jing*" 讀山海經 ("On Reading the *Classic of Mountains and Seas*"), 134

Du Xunhe 杜荀鶴 (846–904), 117

Du Yu 杜預 (222–285), 18

Emperor Cheng (of the Han) 漢成帝 (Han Chengdi [r. 33–7 BCE]), 9

Emperor Dezong (of the Tang) 德宗 (Tang Dezong 唐德宗 [r. 779–805]), 193

Emperor Gaozong (of the Tang) 唐高宗 (Tang Gao Zong [r. 649–683]), 3, 174, 189

Emperor Gaozu (of the Tang) 唐高祖 (Tang Gao Zu [r. 618–626]), 270

Emperor Taizong (of the Tang) 唐太宗 (Tang Taizong [r. 626–649]), 189, 198

Emperor Wen (of the Han) 漢文帝 (Han Wendi [r. 180–157 BCE]), 270

Emperor Wu (of the Han) 漢武帝 (Han Wudi [r. 141–87 BCE]), 2, 9, 31, 42, 45–46, 51, 56–59, 61–63, 68

Emperor Wu (of the Southern Qi) 南齊武帝 (Nan Qi Wudi [r. 483–493]), 270

Emperor Xian (of the Han) 漢獻帝 (Han Xiandi [181–234, r. 189–220]), 101, 106

Emperor Xuanzong (of the Tang) 唐玄宗 (Tang Xuanzong [r. 712–756]), 190, 192–193, 236, 256–258
Emperor Zhongzong (of the Tang) 唐忠宗 (Tang Zhongzong [r. 684, 705–710]), 9, 189–191
Empress Wu 武后 (see Wu Zetian)
"Epang gong fu" 阿房宮賦 ("Rhapsody on Epang Palace"), 176
"Exiled to the Border, My Feelings, Sent to Secretary Wei (First of Two Poems)" 罰赴邊有懷上韋令公（其一）("Fa fubian youhuai shang Weiling Gong, qiyi"), 196

famen 法門 (method; Sanskrit *dharma-paryāya*), 209
"Famous Capital" 名都篇 ("Ming du pian"), 111
"Fan Fufu shan seng" 飯覆釜山僧 ("A Meal with the Monks from Mount Fufu"), 206, 213
Fan Li Sao 反離騷 (*Anti-Li Sao*), 46
fannao 煩惱 (afflictions; Sanskrit *kleśa*), 213
Fan Xuanzi 范宣子 (?–548 BCE), 15, 17
feng 風 (airs or folk songs), 67
Feng Changqing 封常清 (d. 756), 243
fenggu 風骨 (air and bone), 114
feng li lang 奉禮郎 (vice director for ceremonial), 264
fu 賦 (rhapsody), 112, 132, 143, 146, 149, 151–152, 154–155, 175–177
fubing 府兵 (garrison militia), 151
fuli 府吏 (petty clerk in a district or prefecture), 92
fushi 賦詩 (presenting a *Shijing* poem), 1–3; (to recite, chant, or sing a *Shijing* poem), 13–15, 17, 19–22, 25–26

"Gan meng ji" 感夢記 ("The Story of the Dream Telepathy"), 250
"Gan shi bu yu fu" 感士不遇賦 ("Moved by the Scholar Not Meeting His Time"), 143
"Ganyu" 感遇 ("Reflection on My Experiences"), 164
Gao Lishi 高力士 (684–762), 227
gao shi 高士 (high-minded men), 132
Gao Shi 高適 (700–765), 163
Gao Xiayu 高霞寓 (?–826), 256
"Gao xuan guo" 高軒過 ("A Lofty Carriage Calls"), 263
Gao Zhongwu 高仲武 (fl. ca. 787), 194
geng 更 (night watch), 94
geshi 歌詩 (song-poem), 265, 272–273
Geshu Han 哥舒翰 (d. 757), 163–164, 238–289
gongji 宮妓 (court entertainer), 187
Gongzi Wei 公子圍 (Prince Wei of Chu, later King Ling of Chu; see King Ling of Chu), 20–22
"Graveyard Song" 蒿里行 ("Hao li xing"), 101
"Guan ju" 關雎 ("Ospreys"), 65
Guangde 廣德 (fl. eighth century), 208
"Guangling san" 廣陵散 ("Melody of Guangling"), 118
"Gu congjun xing" 古從軍行 ("An Old Ballad of Joining the Army"), 166
guifei 貴妃 (Prized Consort), 236
"Guimao sui shichun huaigu tianshe" 癸卯歲始春懷古田舍 ("Remembering the Ancients on My Farm in Early Spring in the Year *Guimao*"), 134
"Guiqulai xi ci" 歸去來兮辭 ("Leaving for Home!"), 131
guiyuan 閨怨 (lament of the women's quarters), 186
"Gui yuan tian ju" 歸園田居 ("Returning to Dwell in My Gardens and Fields"), 133

Gujin tushu jicheng 古今圖書集成 (*Complete Collection of Illustrations and Writings from Past and Present*), 63
Guo Maoqian 郭茂倩 (1041–1099), 92
Guo Xiang 郭象 (252–312), 6
Guoyu 國語 (*Discourses of the States*), 18, 20, 27n16, 28, 52
Guo Ziyi 郭子儀 (697–781), 238, 240–242, 243
gushi 古詩 (ancient-style poems), 108–109, 113
"Gushi shijiu shou" 古詩十九首 ("Nineteen Old Poems"), 104, 212
"Gushi wei Jiao Zhongqing qi zuo" 古詩為焦仲卿妻作 ("Old Poem Composed for the Wife of Jiao Zhongqing"), 78
Gu Xiong 顧敻 (fl. ca. 928), 201
"Handan shaonian xing" 邯鄲少年行 ("Ballad of the Youths from Handan"), 163

Han fu 漢賦 (Han rhapsody), 61
Hanlin yuan 翰林院 (Hanlin Academy), 251
Han ren 漢人 (Han Chinese), 51
Han Shan 寒山 (fl. seventh, eighth, or ninth centuries), 7, 218, 220
Han Shan *shi* 寒山詩 (Han Shan poems, or poems by, of, or on Cold Mountain), 219
Hanshu 漢書 (*History of the Former Han*), 15, 171
Han Text 韓 (one of the four major texts of the *Book of Poetry* in Han times), 68
Han Yu 韓愈 (768–824), 181, 263–264
Hanyu 漢語 (Chinese language), 51
Han Yuefu 漢樂府 (Han Music Bureau), 108–109, 113
"Having Failed the [Presented Scholar] Examination" 落第 ("Luodi"), 181
he 何 (what), 119
He suo wen er lai, he suo jian er qu 何所聞而來、何所見而去 (What had you heard that made you come, and what have you seen that makes you leave?), 119
"He Shui" 河水 ("The Yellow River"), 18
He Zhizhang 賀知章 (659–744), 234
Hongren 弘忍 (601–674), 205, 215
Hou Fei 后妃 (presumably Tai Si, the main wife of King Wen; see King Wen), 69–70, 74
Hou Han shu 後漢書 (*History of the Later Han*), 114
"Huaisha" 懷沙 ("Embracing the Sand"), 40
Huang Di 黃帝 (Yellow Emperor; see Xuanyuan), 266
Huangfu Mei 皇甫枚 (fl. 910), 198–199, 203
Huangfu Shi 皇甫湜 (777–835), 263, 272
Huang lan 皇覽 (*The Imperial Reader*), 62
hui 慧 (wisdom; Sanskrit *prajñā*), 215
Huicheng 惠澄 (fl. eighth century), 209
huigen 慧根 (root of wisdom; Sanskrit *prajñendriyam*), 208
Huihe 回紇 (Uyghur Turks), 159
Huineng 慧能 (638–713), 208–209, 215, 219
Huiyuan 慧遠 (334–416), 141
Huo Qubing 霍去病 (140–117 BCE), 56
Hu Yan 狐偃 (fl. seventh century BCE), 17
"Hu ye" 瓠葉 ("Gourd Leaves"), 22

"In Response to Letian, Who Frequently Dreamt of Me" 酬樂天頻夢微之 ("Chou Letian pin meng Weizhi"), 254
"In Response to Weizhi" 答微之 ("Da Weizhi"), 253

ji 妓 (courtesan-entertainer), 185
ji 寂 (quiet), 216
jian 見 (to see), 119
Jian'an qizi 建安七子 (Seven Talents of the Jian'an era), 104
"Jiang jin jiu" 將進酒 ("Bring in the Wine"), 228
Jiang Yan 江淹 (444–505), 144
"Jiang Zhong Zi" 將仲子 ("I Beg of You, Zhong Zi"), 70
jiaofang 教坊 (Entertainment Bureau), 193
Jiaofang Ji 教坊集 (*Record of the Entertainment Bureau*), 200
"Jiaoju fu" 郊居賦 ("*Fu* on Living in the Suburbs"), 146
Jiao Te Sheng 郊特牲 (chapter in the *Liji*; see *Liji*), 94
Jia Yi 賈誼 (200–168 BCE), 4, 30–32, 41, 45
jia you 假有 (false having; Sanskrit *prajñapti-sat*), 216
Jie 桀 (aka King Jie [1728–1675 BCE], the last ruler of the Xia dynasty), 127
Ji Kang 嵇康 (223–262), 6, 116–128
jing 精 (refinement), 153
Jingjie xiansheng 靖節先生 (A Man of Tranquility and Integrity), 131
"Jingjie zhengshi lei" 靖節徵士誄 ("Elegy for the Summoned Scholar Known Posthumously as the Man of Tranquility and Integrity"), 141
Jing Ke 荊軻 (?–227 BCE), 162
jinshi 進士 (presented scholar), 171, 173, 252, 259, 264, 265, 272
Jin shu 晉書 (*History of Jin*), 139
Jin Yong 金庸 (1924–), 163
jiu 酒 (wine, ale), 233
"Jiude song" 酒德頌 ("Eulogy to the Virtue of Wine"), 125
Jiuge 九歌 (*Nine Songs*), 42
"Jiu ri" 九日 ("On the Ninth"), 230
Jiu Tang shu 舊唐書 (*Old History of the Tang*), 221, 259
Jiu zhang 九章 (*Nine Stanzas*), 41
Ji Yougong 計有功 (fl. twelfth century), 203, 249
jueju 絕句 (quatrain), 5
ju li 巨麗 (huge and gorgeous), 59
jun chen zhi yi 君臣之義 (the righteousness of the ruler-subject relation), 59
junxian zhi 郡縣制 (county-commandery system), 51
junzi 君子 (superior man), 123
Juzhi 駒支 (fl. 559 BCE), 15–17

keju 科舉 (civil service examination system), 251
King Huai (of Chu) 楚懷王 (Chu Huai Wang [?–296 BCE]), 32–33
King Ling (of Chu) 楚靈王 (Chu Ling Wang [r. 540–529 BCE]), 21
King Qingxiang 頃襄王 (Qingxiamg Wang [r. 298–263 BCE]), 33
King Shao 召公 (Shao Gong [1046–995 BCE]), 67
King Tai (of Zhou) 周太王 (Zhou Tai Wang, a legendary figure during the Shang dynasty), 60
King Wen (of Zhou) 周文王 (Zhou Wen Wang [r. 1099–1050 BCE]), 20, 67–69, 72
King Wu (of Zhou) 周武王 (Zhou Wu Wang [d. 1043 BCE]), 101
King Xuan (of Zhou) 周宣王 (Zhou Xuan Wang [r. 827–782 BCE]), 18
King You (of Zhou) 周幽王 (Zhou You Wang [r. 781–771 BCE]), 21
King Zhou (of Shang) 商紂王 (Shang Zhou Wang [d. 1046 BCE]), 101

kong 空 (empty; Sanskrit *śūnya*), 216
kong (xing) 空（性）(emptiness, Sanskrit *śūnyatā*), 149
"Kongque dong nan fei" 孔雀東南飛 ("Southeast Flies the Peacock"), 78, 94n2
Kong Yingda 孔穎達 (574–648), 17, 75
"Kongzi shi lun" 孔子詩論 ("Confucius's Discourse on Poetry"), 18

Lady Zhen 甄后 (Zhen hou [183–221]), 110
Lanxiang shennü 蘭香神女 (goddess Orchid Scent), 270
Laozi 老子 (ca. 571–ca. 471 BCE), 8, 76
lei 類 (kinds), 54
leishu 類書 (encyclopedia), 62
li 麗 (beautiful), 109
"Lianchang gong ci" 連昌宮詞 ("The Ballad of the Lianchang Palace"), 256
lian ju 聯句 (linked verse), 269
lianlei 連類 (connecting kinds), 54
lianmian ci 連綿詞 (reduplicative binomes), 55
"Lian yu du yin" 連雨獨飲 ("Drinking Alone in Incessant Rains"), 135
Li Bai 李白 (701–762), 4, 7, 130, 166, 223–236, 252, 269
Li Changji geshi ji 李長吉歌詩集 (*Collected Song-Poems of Li Changji*), 265
Lienü zhuan 列女傳 (*Collected Life Stories of Exemplary Women*), 90
Li Fengji 李逢吉 (758–835), 251
Li Guang 李廣 (d. 119 BCE), 56
Li He 李賀 (courtesy name Changji 長吉 [790–816]), 6, 168, 261–272
"Li He xiao zhuan" 李賀小傳 ("Short Biography of Li He"), 264
Liji 禮記 (*Book of Rites*), 2, 68, 90, 94, 123, 188
li jian 利建 (benefits from appointment), 155
Li Jian 李建 (?–823), 250
li jian hou 利建侯 (benefits from appointing aides), 155
Li Jinsu 李晉肅 (fl. second half of eighth century), 263
Lin Xiangru 藺相如 (329–259 BCE), 52
Linxia fengqi 林下風氣 (Bamboo Grove aura), 127
Li Qi 李頎 (690–751), 168
Li Sao 離騷 (*Encountering Misery*), 4, 6, 31–33, 37–46, 225
Li Shangyin 李商隱 (ca. 813–858), 264, 269, 271
Liu An 劉安 (prince of Huainan [179–122 BCE]), 31
Liu Bei 劉備 (161–223), 106
Liu Deren 劉得仁 (fl. 821–847), 181
Liu Jun 劉峻 (courtesy name Xiaobiao 孝標 [462–521]), 116
Liu Ling 劉伶 (d. after 265), 116–119, 125–127
Liu Xiang 劉向 (77–6 BCE), 40, 90
Liu Xijun 劉細君 (aka Princess Pipa [Pipa Gongzhu 琵琶公主; ca. 121–101 BCE]), 171n19
Liu Yiqing 劉義慶 (403–444), 116, 128, 225
Liu Yu 劉裕 (aka Emperor Wu of the Liu Song [363–422; r. 420–422]), 130
"Liuyue" 六月 ("The Sixth Month"), 18
Liu Yuxi 劉禹錫 (772–842), 252
Liu Zongyuan 柳宗元 (773–819), 252
"Liuzu neng chanshi beiming" 六祖能禪師碑銘 ("Stele Inscription for the Sixth Patriarch, Master Neng"), 209
Li Ye 李冶 (aka Li Jilan 李季蘭 [d. 784]), 9, 187–189, 192–195, 197, 202, 203

li yi 禮儀 (etiquette and propriety), 91
Li Yuan 李淵 (see Emperor Gaozu of the Tang)
Liyuan 梨園 (Pear Garden), 193
"Looking Afar at the Remaining Snow on Mount Zhongnan" 終南望餘雪 ("Zhongnan wang yuxue"), 173
Lord Hui (of Jin) 晉惠公 (Jin Huigong [r. 651–637 BCE]), 15–16
Lord Mu (of Qin) 秦穆公 (Qin Mugong [r. 659–621 BCE]), 17, 19, 21
Lord Wen (of Jin) 晉文公 (Jin Wengong [r. 636–628 BCE]), 17–20
Lord Xiang (of Lu) 魯襄公 (Lu Xianggong [r. 572–542 BCE]), 14
Lord Zhao (of Lu) 魯昭公 (Lu Zhaogong [r. 541–510 BCE]), 14
Lü An 呂安 (?–262), 121
luan 亂 (coda), 122
Lü Cheng 呂澂 (1896–1989), 214, 221
"Lu ming" 鹿鳴 ("Deer"), 103
"Lun wen" 論文 ("On Literature"), 107
Luo Binwang 駱賓王 (ca. 627–after 684), 159, 166
"Luokou Yi er shou" 駱口驛二首 ("Two Poems on the Wall of Luokou Post"), 251
Lüqiu Yin 閭丘胤 (fl. seventh century), 210
lüshi 律詩 (regulated verse), 175
Lüshi chunqiu 呂氏春秋 (*The Annals of Lü Buwei*), 53
Lu Text 魯 (one of the four major texts of the *Book of Poetry* in Han times), 68
Lu Xiujing 陸修靜 (406–477), 141
Lü Xun 呂巽 (fl. 262), 121
"Lu zhai" 鹿柴 ("The Deer Fence"), 217
"Lüyi" 綠衣 ("Green Coat"), 27

Mao Chang 毛萇 (fl. the Former Han), 66
Mao Heng 毛亨 (fl. the Former Han), 66, 68
Mao shi 毛詩 (Mao Text of the *Book of Poetry*), 66
Mao shi zheng yi 毛詩正義 (*Correct Meanings of the Mao Text of the* Book of Poetry), 75
Mao shi zhuan 毛詩傳 (Mao Tradition of the *Poetry*), 27
"Mao xu" 毛序 ("Mao Prefaces"), 66
"Mao zhuan" 毛傳 ("Mao Commentaries"), 68
meiren xiangcao 美人香草 (the Fair One [especially a beautiful woman] and aromatic plants), 47
Mei Sheng 枚乘 (d. ca. 140 BCE), 53
mei wei 美味 (lovely flavor), 54
Meng Jiao 孟郊 (751–814), 179–181, 269
Meng Qi 孟棨 (fl. 841–886), 236, 259
"Meng sheng shi" 孟生詩 ("To Scholar Meng"), 181
mengzhu 盟主 (leader of the covenant), 17
"Mian Shui" 沔水 ("River Mian"), 18
Ming emperor, Yongle 永樂帝 (Yongle di [r. 1402–1424]), 63
mingjing 明經 (canonical expert), 174, 252
mingxin jianxing 明心見性 (the purification of one's heart and the revelation of one's nature), 209
minjian 民間 (folk), 93
mo 貘 (giant panda), 61
Monk Xuan 璿上人 (fl. eighth century), 208
"Moshang sang" 陌上桑 ("Mulberry Along the Lane"), 92
mubing 募兵 (mercenary recruiting), 181
"Mulan zhai" 木蘭柴 ("Magnolia Enclosure"), 217

Nan Zhong 南仲 (see Zhang Zhong)

nei 內 (inner), 155

nian 念 (thought-instant; minute working of the mind), 122

Nie Zheng 聶政 (?–397 BCE), 132

"Nineteen Old Poems" 古詩十九首 (see "Gushi shijiu shou")

ningxin ruding, zhuxin kanjing 凝心入定、住心看净 (fix your mind and meditate, stay your mind and be pure), 195

ningzhu biguan 凝住壁觀 (in a coagulated state, to abide in wall-examining), 194

"Ni wange ci" 擬輓歌辭 ("In Imitation of the Lyrics of the 'Song of the Coffin Bearers'"), 107

nüjiaoshu 女校書 (female collator), 165

Nü jie 女誡 (*Admonitions for Women*), 60, 156

Nü lunyu 女論語 (*Analects for Women*), 156

Nü sishu 女四書 (*Classics for Women*), 156

Nü xiaojing 女孝經 (*Book of Filial Piety for Women*), 162

"On Playing Polo" 打毬作 ("Daqiu zuo"), 198

"On Seeing Letian's Poem" 見樂天詩 ("Jian Letian shi"), 262

Ouyang Jiong 歐陽炯 (896–971), 201

Ouyang Xiu 歐陽修 (1007–1072), 6

paihuai 徘徊 (to walk back and forth, to hesitate), 99

Pei Songzhi 裴松之 (372–451), 115

Pei Xingjian 裴行儉 (619–682), 166

ping 平 (level tone), 163

"Pingcheng xia" 平城下 ("Life in Pingcheng"), 169

ping yin da yi 憑音達意 (to rely on sound to convey meaning), 55

pin wei 品味 (taste), 54

"Presented to Zhang Ji, Director of Bureau of Waterways and Irrigation, Before the [Presented Scholar] Examination" 近試上張籍水部 ("Jin shi shang Zhang Ji shuibu"), 98

Prince Baima 白馬王 (Baima Wang, aka Cao Biao [195–251]), 93

Prince Qi 岐王 (Qi Wang [d. 726]), 178

Prince Rencheng 任城王 (Rencheng Wang, aka Cao Zhang [ca. 189–223]), 93

Prince Xiao of Liang 梁孝王 (Liang Xiao Wang [168–143 BCE]), 52

Princess Yuzhen 玉眞公主 (Yuzhen Gongzhu [ca. 693–ca. 762]), 146

Puji 普寂 (651–739; see Dazhao), 208

qi 氣 (life force, vital energy), 107, 116

Qidan 契丹 (Khitan), 159, 171

qie 妾 (concubine or female servant, modest self-address of "I"), 91

"Qi fa" 七發 ("Seven Stimuli"), 53

Qi Ji 綺季 (a famous hermit during the early Han dynasty), 122

qilin 麒麟 (mythical unicorn), 61

qin 琴 (zither), 118

"Qinfu" 琴賦 ("Rhyme-Prose on the Zither"), 122

qing 情 (feelings), 237

qing guo 傾國 (kingdom-toppling beauties), 191

"Qingping diao" 清平調 ("Qingping Melodies"), 228

qingtan 清談 (pure talk), 224

"Qingying" 青蠅 ("Blue Flies"), 15

Qi Text 齊 (one of the four major texts of the *Book of Poetry* in Han times), 68

"Qiwu lun" 齊物論 ("Discourse on Making Things Equal"), 233
qu 去 (departing tone), 153
quan 全 (intact), 123
Quanzi 犬子 (Puppy), 52
"Que chao" 鵲巢 ("Magpie's Nest"), 23
que chao jiu zhan 鵲巢鳩占 (the cuckoo taking over the magpie's nest), 23
Qu Ping 屈平 (see Qu Yuan)
"Qutang liang ya" 瞿塘兩崖 ("The Two Banks of Qutang Gorge"), 268
Qu You 瞿佑 (1347–1427), 258
Qu Yuan 屈原 (ca. 340–278 BCE), 4, 26, 30–47, 52, 212

ren 人 (person), 116; (human being), 264
rendan 任誕 (uninhabited and eccentric), 124
renlun jianshi 人倫鑑識 (character appraisal), 127
"Rhapsody on Wine" 酒賦 ("Jiu fu"), 94
Rong 戎 (a barbarian group), 15–17
Rong Qi 榮期 (aka Rong Qiqi 榮啓期, a famous hermit during the Spring and Autumn period), 122
ru 入 (entering tone), 154
Ruan Ji 阮籍 (210–263), 6, 116, 118, 123–127, 193–194
Ruan Xian 阮咸 (234–305), 116–117
ruoguan 弱冠 (a capping ritual initiating young men into adulthood), 170

San Cao 三曹 (Three Caos), 99
san cong 三從 (triple subordination), 90
Sanguo yanyi 三國演義 (*Romance of the Three Kingdoms*), 99
Sanguo zhi 三國志 (*Records of the Three Kingdoms*), 115
"Sanli sanbie shi" 三吏三別詩 (the "Three Officers" and "Three Partings" poems), 237
"Sanmeng ji" 三夢記 ("The Record of Three Dreams"), 259n4
shang 上 (rising tone), 183
Shang bo chujian san pian jiaodu ji 上博楚簡三篇校讀記 (*Essays on Collating and Annotating Three Texts from the Shanghai Museum Chu Bamboo Strips*), 27n11
shangdi 上帝 (God on High), 56
Shangguan Wan'er 上官婉兒 (sobriquet Zhao Rong [664?–710]), 9, 159–172, 173n10
Shang shu 尚書 (*Book of Documents*), 2, 56, 68, 91, 103, 202n1
"Shan gui" 山鬼 ("Mountain Spirit"), 42
Shan Jian 山簡 (253–312), 232
Shan Tao 山濤 (205–283), 119
"Shao nan" 召南 ("Shao South"), 67
"Shaonian xing" 少年行 ("Songs of the Unruly Youths"), 161
shen 神 (spirit), 123
shen bumie 神不滅 (the spirit does not become extinct), 153
shengren 聖人 (Sage), 116
Shenhui 神會 (684–758), 208–209
shenren 神人 (Spiritual Person), 116
"Shen shi" 神釋 ("Spirit Resolves"), 138
Shen Shushi 沈述師 (fl. early ninth century), 261–262
Shenxiu 神秀 (606–706), 208, 213
Shen Yue 沈約 (441–513), 7–8, 147–154

"Shezhong zhenghu fu" 射中正鵠賦 ("Rhapsody on Shooting and Hitting the Target"), 176
shi 詩 (poetry), 169
shifo 詩佛 (Buddha poet, aka Wang Wei), 4, 205
shigui 詩鬼 (ghost poet, aka Li He), 4
"Shihao li" 石壕吏 ("The Officer at Shihao"), 211
Shiji 史記 (*Records of the Historian*), 1, 9, 19, 162
Shijing 詩經 (*Book of Poetry*), 1–2, 9, 13, 33, 55, 65–70, 74–78, 102–104, 162, 212, 223
Shi keyi xing 詩可以興 (the *Book of Poetry* is capable of inspiring), 69
Shi pin 詩品 (*Grading of Poets*), 131
Shi qiong er hou gong 詩窮而後工 (Only when one is in dire straits does one's poetry become refined), 6
shisheng 詩聖 (sage poet, aka Du Fu), 4
shishi 詩史 (poet-historian), 236
Shishuo xinyu 世說新語 (*A New Account of Tales of the World*), 116, 124, 212, 225, 227, 232
Shi Siming 史思明 (703–761), 236, 238, 243
shixian 詩仙 (immortal poet, aka Li Bai), 4
shi yan zhi 詩言志 (poetry gives voice to the intent), 202n1
"Shiyi gui Wu yin ji dongtai Liu Fu shiyu" 失意歸吳因寄東台劉復侍御 ("To Censor Liu Fu in the East Censorate, as I Return to Wu Without Success"), 181
shi yu 嗜欲 (sensual desire), 181
"Short Song" 短歌行 ("Duan ge xing"), 103
Shuduan of Gong 共叔段 (Gong Shuduan [754 BCE–?], younger brother of Duke Zhuang of Zheng), 70–71
Shujing 書經 (aka *Shang shu*; see *Shang shu*), 103
"Shu jiu" 述酒 ("An Account of Wine"), 135
Shun 舜 (ancient sage-king), 16, 34, 37
"Shuo shu" 碩鼠 ("Big Rat"), 246n11
shupan bacui 書判拔萃 (selection of the preeminent in legal judgments), 174
Shuqi 叔齊 (ca. eleventh century BCE), 6
shusi 攄思 (to release one's thoughts), 122
Shusun Bao 叔孫豹 (?–538 BCE), 22–24, 27
si 思 (conscious thought), 122
sijian 私劍 (private swordsmen), 160
"Sijiu fu" 思舊賦 ("Recalling Old Friends"), 126
Sima Qian 司馬遷 (145–86? BCE), 4, 19, 30–33, 40–41, 46
Sima Xiangru 司馬相如 (179–127 BCE), 2, 46, 51–63
Sima Zhao 司馬昭 (posthumously titled Emperor Wen of the Jin, 211–265), 119, 121–126
sisheng 四聲 (four categories of tones), 154
"Songbie Cui Yinliang xiadi" 送別崔寅亮下第 ("Farewell to Cui Yinliang, Who Failed the Examination"), 181
"Song of the Bronze Immortal Taking Leave of the Han" 金銅仙人辭漢歌 ("Jin tong xianren ci Han ge"), 267
"Song of Yan" 燕歌行 ("Yan ge xing"), 107
"Song on Enduring the Cold" 苦寒行 ("Ku han xing"), 102
Song shu 宋書 (*History of the Liu Song Dynasty*), 117, 131
"Song Wen Chu xiadi" 送溫初下第 ("Seeing off Wen Chu, Who Failed the Examination"), 181
Song Yu 宋玉 (ca. 298–222 BCE), 30, 40, 52, 197, 212
Su Che 蘇轍 (1039–1112), 134
Su Dongpo 蘇東坡 (aka Su Shi 蘇軾 [1037–1101]), 7, 130, 133–134
suiyuan renyun 隨緣任運 (letting oneself ride with the flux of causation and letting one's destiny take its own course; Sanskrit *pratyaya-pratītya anābhoga*), 212
Sun Qi 孫棨 (fl. 870–898), 182

Sun Quan 孫權 (182–252), 106
Sunzi 孫子 (well-known Chinese military strategist [ca. 544–496 BCE]), 100
Sunzi bingfa 孫子兵法 (*Art of War*), 100
Su Qin 蘇秦 (d. 317 BCE), 52
Su Shi 蘇軾 (see Su Dongpo)

Taiping guangji 太平廣記 (*Extensive Records of the Taiping Era*), 211
Taiping yulan 太平御覽 (*An Imperial Reader of the Taiping Era*), 62
Tai Si 太姒 (the main wife of King Wen; see Hou Fei), 68
Tang 湯 (Shang king, aka King Tang of Shang [r. ca. 1617–1588 BCE]), 53–54
"Tang di" 棠棣 ("Plum Tree"), 25
Tangshi jishi 唐詩紀事 (*Records of Tang Poetry*), 249
Tang Suzong 唐肅宗 (Emperor Suzong of the Tang [r. 756-762]), 238
Tang Xuanzong 唐玄宗 (see Emperor Xuanzong of the Tang)
Tang zhi yan 唐摭言 (*Selected Accounts from the Tang*), 263
Tan jing 壇經 (the Platform Sūtra), 215
"Taohua yuan ji" 桃花源記 ("Account of Peach Blossom Spring"), 140, 233
"Taohua yuan shi" 桃花源詩 ("Peach Blossom Fountainhead"), 140
Tao Qian 陶潛 (aka Tao Yuanming 陶淵明 [365-427]), 4, 7, 130–144, 194, 212, 269
Tao Yuanming 陶淵明 (see Tao Qian)
"*Tao Yuanming wenji* xu" 陶淵明文集序 ("Preface to *Tao Yuanming's Collected Works*"), 143
Tao zhengjun 陶徵君 (Summoned Scholar Tao, aka Tao Qian), 131
"Teasing Prelude on the Bitter Bamboo" 苦篁調笑引 ("Ku huang diao xiao yin"), 266
"The Fish Separated from the Pond (Ten Poems on Separation)" 魚離池（十離詩）("Yu li chi [Shi li shi]"), 196
"The King of Qin Drinks" 秦王飲酒 ("Qin Wang yinjiu"), 268
"The Writing Brush Separated from the Hand (Ten Poems on Separation)" 筆離手（十離詩）("Bi li shou [Shi li shi]"), 195
"Though Tortoise Lives Long" 龜雖壽 ("Gui sui shou"), 106
Tian wen 天問 (*Heaven Questions*), 40
tianxia 天下 (all under heaven), 51–52, 56–63
tianzi 天子 (Son of Heaven), 56
"Tian Zifang" 田子方 (a chapter in the *Zhuangzi*), 118
tiejing 帖經 (memorization of Confucian classics), 175
"Tongguan li" 潼關吏 ("The Officer at Tong Pass"), 238
"To the Neighbor Girl (or, To Secretary Li Yi)" 贈鄰女（寄李億員外）("Zeng Linnü [Ji Li Yi Yuanwai]"), 197
"To the Tune 'Bodhisattva Barbarian'" 菩薩蠻 ("Pusa man"), 201
"To the Tune, 'Lotus-Leaf Cup'" 荷葉杯 ("Heye bei"), 201
Tufan 吐蕃 (Tubo), 159
Tujue 突厥 (Eastern Turks), 159

"Untitled Verse, No. 2 of 2" 雜詩（二之二）("Za shi, er zhi er"), 108

"Viewing the Ocean" 觀滄海 ("Guan cang hai"), 105
"Visiting Princess Changning's Pool, No. 17" 遊長寧公主流杯池二十五首之十七 ("You Changning Gongzhu liubei chi ershiwu shou zhi shiqi"), 192
"Visiting the South Tower of Chongzhen Monastery, I See the Names of Successful Examination Candidates Being Written on the Wall" 遊崇真觀南樓睹新及第題名處 ("You chongzhen guan nanlou du xin jidi timing chu"), 200
"Visiting the Xiangji Temple" 過香積寺 ("Guo Xiangji si"), 214, 216

wai 外 (outer), 185
"Wailing for Weizhi" 哭微之 ("Ku Weizhi"), 255
waiqi 外戚 (in-laws), 189
"Waiwu pian" 外物篇 ("External Things"), 234n11
Wang Changling 王昌齡 (698–757), 5
Wang Han 王翰 (fl. 710), 5
Wang Jin 王縉 (700–782), 208
Wang Qi 王起 (760–847), 120
Wang Rong 王戎 (234–305), 117
Wang Wei 王維 (701–761), 4, 161, 176–177
Wang Xizhi 王羲之 (321–379), 196
Wang Yi 王逸 (fl. 114–119), 4, 30, 40–47
Wang Yun 王筠 (481–549), 146
wang zhi 王治 (kingly governance), 54
wan kong 頑空 (false emptiness; Sanskrit *jaḍa*), 149
wan wu 萬物 (ten thousand things), 54
Wei Gao 韋皋 (745–805), 195–196
Wei Hong 衛宏 (fl. 25–57), 66
Wei Mojie 維摩詰 (Chinese transliteration of Vimalakīrti), 205
Wei Qing 衛青 (d. 106 BCE), 56
weiyan 微言 (subtle words), 15
weiyan dayi 微言大義 (indirect though pointedly conveyed moral intent), 15
Wei Zhao 韋昭 (204–273), 18
Wei Zhuang 韋莊 (836–910), 265
wen 文 (cultivation), 17, 25; (pattern, writing, culture, literature, civil [governance]), 25, 173–174
wen 聞 (to hear), 119
Wenhui 文惠 (Crown Prince Wenhui [458–493]), 176
wenjuan 溫卷 (presentation of scrolls; see also *xingjuan*), 176
Wen suo wen er lai, jian suo jian er qu 聞所聞而來，見所見而去 (I heard what I heard so I came, and I saw what I have seen so I am leaving), 119
Wen Tingyun 溫庭筠 (813?–870), 197
Wenxuan 文選 (*Anthology of Refined Literature*), 58
wenxue 文學 (literature), 52
"White Horse" 白馬篇 ("Baima pian"), 161
wo 我 (first-person pronoun "I"), 102
wu 物 (things), 61
wu 無 (not having; Sanskrit *abhāva*), 216
Wuhuan 烏桓 (a northern nomadic people), 134
"Wujia bie" 無家別 ("Parting Without a Home"), 244
Wuli 吾離 (grandfather of Juzhi; see Juzhi), 15
"Wuliu xiansheng zhuan" 五柳先生傳 ("Biography of Master Five Willows"), 130
wu qing 無情 (unfeeling), 267
wushi san 五石散 (five-mineral powder), 124
wutong 梧桐 (Chinese parasol tree), 87, 188
wu wo 無我 (containing no "I"; nonexistence of "I"), 218
Wu Wuling 吳武陵 (d. 835), 176
wuxia xiaoshuo 武俠小說 (chivalry novels), 163

wu yi 霧衣 (robes of fog), 271

Wu Yuanheng 武元衡 (758–815), 196

Wu Zetian 武則天 (also known as Wu Zhao, Empress Wu, Empress of Zhou Dynasty or Tang Zhou Wudi 唐周武帝 [r. 690–705]), 9, 189, 270

Wu Zhao 武曌 (see Wu Zetian)

xia 俠 (knight-errant; see also *youxia*), 5, 160

"Xiadi donggui liubie chang'an zhiji" 下第東歸留別長安知己 ("A Farewell Poem to People Who Have Known Me in Chang'an, as I Go East for Home After Failing the Examination"), 181

"Xiadi dongnan xing" 下第東南行 ("Traveling Southeast After Failing the Examination"), 181

xiang 相 (forms; Sanskrit *lakṣaṇa*), 217

Xiang Xiu 向秀 (ca. 221–ca. 300), 6, 116–118, 126–127

xianyuan 賢媛 (worthy ladies), 127

Xianyun 獫狁 (identified as barbarians), 18

Xianzhuan shiyi 仙傳拾遺 (*A Supplementary Biography of Immortals*), 211

xiao 孝 (filial piety), 89

Xiaobiao 孝標 (Liu Jun's courtesy name; see Liu Jun), 116

"Xiaomin" 小旻 ("Lesser Heaven"), 21

"Xiaoming" 小明 ("Lesser Brightness"), 21

"Xiaopan" 小弁 ("Lesser Joy"), 21

Xiao Tong 蕭統 (501–531), 130

Xiaoya 小雅 (lesser odes), 21

"Xiaoyao lun" 逍遙論 ("On Free Roaming"), 127

"Xiaoyao you" 逍遙游 ("Free Roaming"), 116

"Xiaoyuan" 小宛 ("Lesser"), 20

Xie Lingyun 謝靈運 (385–433), 7, 114, 212

xie lü lang 協律郎 (harmonizer of the pitch pipes), 265

Xihe 羲和 (sun-charioteer), 268

"Xin'an li" 新安吏 ("The Officer at Xin'an"), 237

"Xinchou sui qiyue fujia huan Jiangling yexing Tukou" 辛醜歲七月赴假還江陵夜行塗口 ("Written in the Seventh Month of the Year *Xinchou* in Tukou While Traveling at Night Returning to Jiangling After Leave"), 133

xing 興 (affective image), 17, 69, 75–76, 78

"Xinggong" 行宮 ("The Temporary Palace"), 256

xingjuan 行卷 (scrolls presentation; see also *wenjuan*), 176

"Xing xi xiang jin yuan fu" 性習相近遠賦 ("Rhapsody on Whether People's Nature and Habits are Close to or Distant from Each Other"), 175

"Xing ying shen" 形影神 ("Body, Shadow, Spirit"), 138

"Xing zeng ying" 形贈影 ("Body Presents to Shadow"), 138

"Xinhun bie" 新婚別 ("Parting When Newly Wed"), 242

Xin Tang shu 新唐書 (*New History of the Tang Dynasty*), 236

Xiongnu 匈奴 (a nomadic people), 99, 111

"Xiong Xiucai gong rujun zengshi" 兄秀才公入軍贈詩 ("To My Elder Brother the Lord Xiucai on His Joining the Army"), 118

Xuanxue 玄學 (Abstruse Learning, also known as Dark Learning or Mysterious Learning), 116, 118–119, 126–127

Xuanyuan 軒轅 (Yellow Emperor [Huang Di 黄帝]), 266

Xue Tao 薛濤 (768–831), 9, 182, 187–188, 195–197, 201

Xu gaoseng zhuan 續高僧傳 (*Further Biographies of Eminent Monks*), 214

Xu Lingfu 徐靈府 (fl. 840), 211

Xun Qing 荀卿 (aka Xunzi or "Master Xun" [312–230 BCE]), 26
Xunzi 荀子 (see Xun Qing)
Xu Shao 許劭 (150–195), 100
Xu You 許由 (an ancient sage), 122, 127

Yang Guifei 楊貴妃 (aka Yang Yuhuan [719–756]), 189, 228
Yang Guozhong 楊國忠 (d. 756), 236, 238
Yang Wan 楊綰 (d. 777), 175
Yang Xiong 揚雄 (53 BCE–18 CE), 46
Yang Yuhuan 楊玉環 (see Yang Guifei)
yan wai zhi yi 言外之意 (meaning beyond words), 76
Yan Yanzhi 顏延之 (384–456), 130, 136, 141, 143–144
Yan Ying 晏嬰 (d. 500 BCE), 54
Yan Zhenqing 顏真卿 (709–785), 180, 243
yanzhi 言志 (articulating intent), 27n3
Yan Zhitui 顏之推 (531–ca. 595), 91
Yao 堯 (ancient sage-king), 16, 34, 122, 126
yaqin 雅琴 (elegant zither), 122
"Ye you sijun" 野有死麕 ("There Is a Dead Doe in the Wilds"), 24
Yijing 易經 (*Book of Changes*), 2, 68, 116, 155n2
yin 隱 (reclusion), 132
"Ying da xing" 影答形 ("Shadow Replies to Body"), 138
yingji 營妓 (garrison courtesan), 195
yi nian er jian 一念而兼 (if within a single thought-instant there are yet other thoughts), 153
yi nian wei cheng 一念未成 (one single-thought instant has not yet become complete), 153
Yin Jifu 尹吉甫 (852–775 BCE), 18
"Yin jiu" 飲酒 ("Drinking Wine"), 135
"Yinjiu qi qi" 飲酒 其七 ("Drinking Wine, No. 7"), 231
"Yin Shang zhuan" 尹賞傳 ("Biography of Yin Shang"), 171n8
yishi 遺詩 (lost poems), 14
Yiwen leiju 藝文類聚 (*Collection of Literature Arranged by Kind*), 62
Yi Yin 伊尹 (?–?), 53
yi yi ni zhi 以意逆志 (use [the interpreter's] mind to meet the intent [of the author]), 13
yong bing 用兵 (warfare), 52
"Yonghuai shi" 詠懷詩 ("Poems Singing of My Innermost Thoughts"), 124
Yongle dadian 永樂大典 (*Yongle Encyclopedia*), 62–63
"Yong pinshi" 詠貧士 ("In Praise of Impoverished Gentlemen"), 141
Yongzheng emperor (of the Qing) 雍正帝 (Yongzheng di [r. 1722–1735]), 63
you 有 (having; Sanskrit *bhāva*), 216
you qing 有情 (feeling), 267
you shui 遊說 (traveling persuaders), 52
"Youfen shi" 幽憤詩 ("On Sorrow"), 121
youxia 遊俠 (knight-errant; see also *xia*), 160
"Youxia liezhuan" 遊俠列傳 ("Biography of the Wandering Knights"), 163
youzi 遊子 (wanderer), 10
yuan 緣 (causation; Sanskrit *nidāna*), 216
Yuanchong 元崇 (713–777), 208
Yuanhe reign 元和 (806–820), 250

"Yuan you" 遠游 ("Far Roaming"), 43
Yuan Zhen 元稹 (courtesy name Weizhi 微之 [779–831]), 259n1
"Yuan Zhen zhuan" 元稹傳 ("The Biography of Yuan Zhen"), 249–259
Yuefu 樂府 (Music Bureau; see also Han Yuefu), 108, 168, 228
yuefu 樂府 (Music Bureau poetry), 5, 78, 92–93, 229, 265–266
Yuefu shi ji 樂府詩集 (*Collection of Yuefu Poems*), 92
yueji 樂妓 (registered courtesan), 195
"Yuexia du zhuo" 月下獨酌 ("Drinking Alone Beneath the Moon"), 231
"Yufu" 漁父 ("The Fisherman"), 40
Yu Jiaxi 余嘉錫 (1884–1955), 126
Yu Rang 豫讓 (?–453 BCE), 162
"Yushui ji fangliu shi" 玉水記方流詩 ("Waters Containing Jades are Marked by Right-Angled Streams"), 175
Yu tai xin yong 玉台新詠 (*New Songs from a Jade Terrace*), 78
Yu Xuanji 魚玄機 (844?–868), 9, 187, 197–200, 203n19, 20, 21
"Yu Yuanjiu shu" 與元九書 ("A Letter to Yuan the Ninth"), 259n5

"Zai chi" 載馳 ("I Gallop"), 27n2
"Zai luodi" 再落第 ("Having Failed Once More"), 181
zawen 雜文 (literary genres), 175
"Zeng Baimawang Biao" 贈白馬王彪 ("To Cao Biao, the Prince of Baima"), 113
Zhai Zhong 祭仲 (prime minister of Zheng [?–682 BCE]), 70, 72
Zhang Ji 張籍 (768–830), 178
Zhang Jiuling 張九齡 (673–740), 207
Zhang Qian 張騫 (200–114 BCE), 56, 61, 63
Zhanguo ce 戰國策 (*Strategies of the Warring States*), 212
Zhang Yi 張儀 (?–310 BCE), 32, 52
Zhang Yue 張說 (663–730), 190
Zhang Yugu 張玉穀 (1721–1780), 118
Zhang Zhong 張仲 (fl. early ninth to late eight century BCE), 19
Zhao Cui 趙衰 (?–622 BCE), 22
Zhao Hun 招魂 (*Summoning the Soul*), 40
Zhaorong 昭容 (see Shangguan Wan'er)
Zhao Wu 趙武 (?–541 BCE), 26
zhen 真 (genuineness), 123
zheng 正 (the right course), 117
"Zheng jian" 鄭箋 ("Zheng Annotations"), 68
Zheng Xuan 鄭玄 (127–200), 17, 68–69, 70, 72–76
Zhenguan 貞觀 (627–649), 210
"Zhengyue" 正月 ("First Month"), 21
zhexian 謫仙 (banished immortal), 230
Zhi Dun 支遁 (314–366), 126
zhi guo 治國 (administration), 52
"Zhi jiu" 止酒 ("Stopping Wine"), 136
zhiju 制舉 (decree writing exam), 252
zhiren 至人 (Perfected Person), 116, 118–120, 122–123, 126–127; (perfected man, ultimate man), 6, 227, 233n6
zhi wei 至味 (perfect flavor), 54
zhizu 至足 (perfect contentment), 127
zhong he 中和 (balanced harmony), 59

Zhong Hui 鍾會 (225–264), 119–123
"Zhongnan bieye" 終南別業 ("Zhongnan Retreat"), 212
Zhong Rong 鍾嶸 (468–518), 131
"Zhongyong" 中庸 ("Doctrine of the Mean"), 123
Zhou 紂 (aka Shang Zhou Wang, King Zhou of Shang [d. 1046 BCE]), 73
Zhou Chi 周墀 (793–851), 180
Zhouli 周禮 (*Rites of Zhou*), 52, 250
"Zhou nan" 周南 ("Zhou South"), 67
zhuandui 專對 (to respond independently), 13
Zhuang Ji 莊忌 (?–?), 53
"Zhuangyou" 壯遊 ("Brave Wandering"), 167
Zhuangzi 莊子 (ca. 369–ca. 286 BCE), 6, 76, 116, 118, 126–128
Zhuangzi, the 莊子 (book), 116–123, 125–127
Zhuan Zhu 專諸 (?–515 BCE), 162
Zhu Ci 朱泚 (743–784), 193
zhu hou zhi li 諸侯之禮 (the proper ritual etiquette of the feudal lords), 59
zhuishi duixing 墜石堆星 (The fallen rocks are piled up to the stars), 146
Zhulin qixian 竹林七賢 (Seven Worthies of the Bamboo Grove), 116, 225
"Zhun" 屯 (a section in the *Yijing*), 155n2
Zhu Qingyu 朱慶餘 (presented scholar degree in 826), 178
Zhu Wen 朱溫 (852–912), 177
zhu wen jue jian 主文譎諫 (to employ indirect expressions to make subtle remonstrance), 75
Zhu Xi 朱熹 (1130–1200), 17, 21
zi 字 (courtesy name), 205
Zichan 子產 (ca. 580–522 BCE), 52
zifu zijie 自賦自解 (to recite a poem and supply one's own interpretation), 24
"Zijin" 子衿 ("Blue Are Your Gown's Folds"), 104
"Zi ji wen" 自祭文 ("Sacrificial Offering to Myself"), 136
zi qing 自傾 (self-pour), 231
ziran 自然 (one's natural inclinations), 120; (naturalness), 138
Zixia 子夏 (507 BCE–?), 66
"Zixu/Shanglin fu" 子虛/上林賦 ("Sir Vacuous/Imperial Park Rhapsody"), 52
zizu 自足 (self-contentment), 126
zongzi 粽子 (sweet rice cake wrapped in leaves), 4
Zou Yang 鄒陽 (?–?), 53
zuochan 坐禪 (sitting in meditation), 215
Zuozhuan 左傳 (*Zuo Tradition*), 22, 27n2, 52
zuo yong tianxia 坐擁天下 (to embrace "all under heaven" from where you sit), 63
Zu Yong 祖詠 (presented scholar degree in 725), 173

GPSR Authorized Representative: Easy Access System Europe, Mustamäe tee
50, 10621 Tallinn, Estonia, gpsr.requests@easproject.com